D1609869

EU pharmaceutical regulation

MANCHESTER
1824
Manchester University Press

European Policy Research Unit Series

Series Editors: *Simon Bulmer, Peter Humphreys* and *Mick Moran*

The European Policy Research Unit Series aims to provide advanced text-books and thematic studies of key public policy issues in Europe. They concentrate, in particular, on comparing patterns of national policy content, but pay due attention to the European Union dimension. The thematic studies are guided by the character of the policy issue under examination.

 The European Policy Research Unit (EPRU) was set up in 1989 within the University of Manchester's Department of Government to promote research on European politics and public policy. The series is part of EPRU's effort to facilitate intellectual exchange and substantive debate on the key policy issues confronting the European states and the European Union.

Titles in the series also include:

Globalisation and policy-making in the European Union   Ian Bartle

Transatlantic economic relations   Michelle P. Egan (ed.)

The politics of health in Europe   Richard Freeman

Immigration and European integration   Andrew Geddes

Agricultural policy in Europe   Alan Greer

The European Union and the regulation of media markets   Alison Harcourt

Mass media and media policy in Western Europe   Peter Humphreys

The politics of fisheries in the European Union   Christian Lequesne

Sports law and policy in the European Union   Richard Parrish

The rules of integration   Gerald Schneider and Mark Aspinwall

Fifteen into one?   Wolfgang Wessels, Andreas Maurer and Jürgen Mittag (eds)

Extending European cooperation   Alasdair R. Young

Regulatory politics in the enlarging European Union   Alasdair Young and Helen Wallace

EU pharmaceutical regulation

The politics of policy-making

Govin Permanand

Manchester University Press
Manchester and New York
distributed exclusively in the USA by Palgrave

Copyright © Govin Permanand 2006

The right of Govin Permanand to be identified as the author of this work has been asserted by him in accordance with the Copyright, Designs and Patents Act 1988.

Published by Manchester University Press
Oxford Road, Manchester M13 9NR, UK
and Room 400, 175 Fifth Avenue, New York, NY 10010, USA
www.manchesteruniversitypress.co.uk

Distributed exclusively in the USA by
Palgrave, 175 Fifth Avenue, New York,
NY 10010, USA

Distributed exclusively in Canada by
UBC Press, University of British Columbia, 2029 West Mall
Vancouver, BC, Canada V6T 1Z2

British Library Cataloguing-in-Publication Data
A catalogue record for this book is available from the British Library

Library of Congress Cataloging-in-Publication Data applied for

ISBN   0 7190 7272 7 *hardback*
EAN   978 0 7190 7272 7

First published 2006

15 14 13 12 11 10 09 08 07 06   10 9 8 7 6 5 4 3 2 1

Edited and typeset by
Frances Hackeson Freelance Publishing Services, Brinscall, Lancs
Printed in Great Britain
by Biddles Ltd, King's Lynn

Contents

Preface   *page* vi
List of abbreviations   vii
List of tables and figures   x
Acknowledgements   xii

1 EU pharmaceutical policy: towards an understanding   1
   of the issues
2 Regulating the European medicines sector   19
3 Theorising the development of Community competence   47
   in pharmaceuticals
4 Networks and the 'politics of policy'   69
5 'Client politics': the Supplementary Protection Certificate   92
6 'Entrepreneurial politics': the European Medicines Agency   117
7 'Majoritarian politics': the pricing and reimbursement of   151
   medicines in the EU
8 Conclusions   180

   Appendices   205
   References   217
   Index   239

Preface

This book is concerned with European Union pharmaceutical policy – its content, how it is made, the regulatory framework it represents – and is premised on such policy having to serve, in parallel, public health, healthcare and industrial policy needs at supranational and national levels. How these often conflicting needs are or are not reconciled in EU policy outcomes, and what role the sector's main stakeholders play in pushing their own agendas within this context, is the focus.

At the time of writing, a three-year 'review of Community pharmaceutical legislation' has just been completed, and the outcome is a package of four legislative instruments governing medicines in the EU. Although this new package falls outside the current study, which mainly covers developments to early 2003 when the review was still under way (under the Prodi Commission), references are made to the new legislation and different stages in its development where appropriate. These are invoked in order to show, primarily, the direction of policy proposals for the sector and the thinking behind them. Noteworthy is that the new legislation does not effect any changes which alter or compromise the conclusions offered here on the nature and dynamics of EU policy-making in the sector, the relationships between the stakeholders, nor the orientation and mechanisms of the regulatory framework. The underlying arguments and findings retain their currency, and could be brought to bear in any follow-up examination or cognate research *vis-à-vis* the new legislation.

Abbreviations

ABPI	Association of British Pharmaceutical Industry
AESGP	*Association Européenne des Spécialités Pharmaceutiques Grand Public* (Association of the European Self-Medication Industry)
AgV	*Arbeitschaft der Verbraucherverbände e.V.* (German consumer association, see VZBV)
AIM	*L'Association Internationale de la Mutualité* (International Association of Mutual Benefit Societies)
BÄK	*Bundesausschuss der Ärzte und Krankenkassen* (German Federal Standing Committee of Physicians and Sickness Funds)
BEUC	*Bureau Européen des Unions de Consommateurs* (European Consumers' Organisation)
CAP	Common Agricultural Policy
CCC	Consumer's Consultative Committee
CDER	(FDA) Center for Drug Evaluation and Research
CEC	Commission of the European Communities
CECG	Consumers in the European Community Group
CHMP	Committee for Medicinal Products for Human Use (formerly Committee for Proprietary Medicinal Products)
CMS	Concerned Member State
CP	*Comité Permanent des Médecins Européens* (Standing Committee of European Doctors)
CPMP	Committee for Proprietary Medicinal Products (EMEA – see CHMP)
CSD	Committee on Safety of Drugs
DG	Directorate-General
DG1A	Former trade directorate of original DG1 for external affairs
DGIII	(ex) Industrial Affairs DG

DGIII/E/F	(ex) Unit for Pharmaceuticals and Cosmetics of DGIII
DGIV	(ex) Competition DG
DGV	(ex) Employment, Industrial Relations and Social Affairs DG
DGV/F	(ex) Public Health Unit of DGV
DGXXIV	(ex) Consumer Policy and Consumer Health Protection DG
DG Sanco	Health and Consumer Protection Directorate-General
DoH	Department of Health
DTC	Direct-to-Consumer Advertising
EAEPC	European Association of Euro-Pharmaceutical Companies
EC	European Community(ies)
ECJ	European Court of Justice
EEA	European Economic Area
EEC	European Economic Community
EFPIA	European Federation of Pharmaceutical Industries and Associations
EFTA	European Free Trade Area
EGA	European Generic medicines Association
EMEA	European Medicines Agency (formerly, European Agency for the Evaluation of Medicinal Products)
EP	European Parliament
EPAR	European Public Assessment Report
EPC	European Patent Convention
ESC	Economic & Social Committee
EU	European Union
Euratom	European Atomic Energy Community
FDA	Food & Drug Administration
G10	High Level Group on Innovation and the Provision of Medicines
GATT	General Agreement on Tariffs and Trade
GDP	Gross Domestic Product
GIRP	*Groupement International de la Répartition Pharmaceutique Européenne* (European Association of Pharmaceutical Full-line Wholesalers)
HAI	Health Action International
ICA	Intergroup on Consumer Affairs (European Parliament)
ICH	International Conference on Harmonisation
IGC	Intergovernmental Conference
INN	International Non-proprietary Name
ISDB	International Society of Drug Bulletins
MCA	Medicines Control Agency
MEP(s)	Member(s) of the European Parliament
MHRA	Medicines and Healthcare Products Regulatory Agency
NAFTA	North American Free Trade Agreement
NCE	New Chemical Entity

NDA	New Drug Application
NHS	National Health Service
OTA	(US) Office for Technology Assessment
OTC	Over-the-Counter (medicines)
PDUFA	Prescription Drug User Fee Act
PhRMA	Pharmaceutical Research and Manufacturers of America
PIC	Pharmaceuticals Inspections Convention
PIRC	Public Interest Research Centre
PPBH	Pharmaceutical Partners for Better Healthcare
PPRS	(UK) Pharmaceutical Price Regulation Scheme
R&D	Research & Development
RMOs	*Références Médicales Opposables* (French compulsory guide-lines for pharmaceutical reimbursement)
RMS	Reference Member State
SEA	Single European Act
SEM	Single European Market
SME(s)	Small-to-Medium sized Enterprise(s)
SNIP	*Syndicat National de l'Industrie Pharmaceutique* (French Pharmaceutical Manufacturers' Association)
SPC	Supplementary Protection Certificate
SPCs	Summary of Product Characteristics
TCSDD	Tufts Centre for the Study of Drug Development
TEU	Treaty on European Union
TTM	Time-to-market
VAT	Value-added Tax
VFA	*Verband Forschender Arzneimittelhersteller* (German Association of Research-Based Pharmaceutical Companies)
VZBV	*Verbraucherzentrale Bundesverband e.V.* (Federation of German Consumer Organisations)
WTO	World Trade Organisation

Tables and figures

Tables

2.1 Top ten pharmaceutical products by global sales, 2003   23
2.2 Top ten pharmaceutical companies by global sales, 2003   24
2.3 Competing pharmaceutical policy interests   31
2.4 Selected Community pharmaceutical legislation (medicines   39
for human use), 1965–2004
4.1 Principal national-level actors and policy objectives in the   76
pharmaceutical sector
6.1 Perceived pros and cons of a potential European medicines   124
agency (prior to the EMEA)
6.2 FDA 'priority review' versus EMEA 'innovation' criteria   140
(centralised procedure)
8.1 Evolution of the Supplementary Protection Certificate policy   184
network
8.2 Evolution of the European Medicines Agency policy network   187
8.3 Evolution of Commission strategies over pricing and   190
reimbursement policy (multiple networks)

Appendix A   Pharmaceutical expenditure in EU member states   206
(1980–2002)
Appendix B   Summary of approaches to the regulation of   207
pharmaceutical prices in EU member states
Appendix D   European pharmaceutical legislation: medicinal   209
products for human use, 1965–2004
Appendix F   Selected actors and affected interests in the EU   214
pharmaceutical sector

Figures

2.1 Structure of supply and demand in the pharmaceutical sector 21
2.2 National versus Community concerns in EU pharmaceutical 42
      policy
4.1 Overlapping policy interests in EU pharmaceutical regulation 82
4.2 A typology of the 'politics of policy' 85
5.1 Number of NCEs discovered (Europe versus US), 1980–2003 99
8.1 The 'politics of policy' as applied to selected elements of the 184
      Community medicines framework

Appendix C   Employment in the pharmaceutical industry, 1980– 208
      2002 (EU versus US)
Appendix E   Domestic research & development spending 213
      (US$ million), 1990–2002 (EU versus US)
Appendix G   EMEA centralised procedure 215
Appendix H   EMEA decentralised procedure 216

Acknowledgements

As the decision to write this book on EU pharmaceutical policy has proven easier than the pursuit itself, I wish to express my gratitude and appreciation to several individuals who helped me redress the gap between the two. Considerable thanks are due to Professors Paul Taylor and Elias Mossialos of the London School of Economics & Political Science who supervised the original research as a doctoral dissertation. I am also obliged to the latter for advice and, along with colleagues at LSE Health & Social Care, for allowing me time to finish this project (sometimes in relative neglect of other duties). This book has further benefited from the constructive comments of two anonymous reviewers and the considered feedback provided by the EPRU series editors. Their suggestions have much improved the final draft. Here I am particularly grateful to Professor Simon Bulmer for his backing from the outset and confidence throughout. Much credit must also go to the team at Manchester University Press, most notably to Lucy Nicholson and Rachel Armstrong who endured my time management skills with admirable forbearance and understanding, and to Frances Hackeson, whose attention to detail smoothed my inelegances and ensured a consistent and readable text. Notwithstanding such extensive help and expertise, all errors remain mine alone.

I would also direct a quick word of thanks the way of TM for his support and camaraderie. And, as it is unlikely that this project would have been embarked upon, far less completed, without the encouragement and sympathetic ear of AM, I am enormously grateful for her counsel.

To Maria – who has put up with me through two versions of this project with unflappable patience and grace, providing emotional reassurance and an oft-needed 'kick in the pants' in just the right measures – what do you think of an update?

1

EU pharmaceutical policy: towards an understanding of the issues

In the context of modern medicines regulation the period of the late 1950s and early 1960s was a watershed. Under tragic circumstances the drug *Thalidomide* focused attention on the potential harm inadequately regulated medicinal products could cause. Originally released on the West German market in 1957 as a prescription sleeping aid in the treatment of morning-sickness for pregnant women, *Thalidomide* (*Contergan* in West Germany) was hailed as a breakthrough. But the subsequent births of tens of thousands of babies with congenital anomalies across scores of countries, as well as the affliction of many pregnant women with peripheral neuritis – a severely de-generative nerve disorder which can result in irreversible damage – saw the drug's removal from most of the major markets in 1961.[1] And although the damage had been done, policy-makers across the globe set about reviewing the nature of drug registration and regulation to ensure that it would not happen again.

Having long-recognised the potential toxicity of medicinal preparations, most western countries had various regulations in place before the tragedy. These were primarily administrative, however, pertaining mainly to drug quality, advertising and promotion, i.e. regulating what claims manufactur-ers could make about their products. With the exception of the Nordic coun-tries and the United States (US), until the early 1960s most had no indepen-dent safety and efficacy testing protocol for new drugs whatsoever. Begin-ning in West Germany,[2] therefore, came a wave of new medicine laws in many countries regarding the safety evaluation of therapeutic drugs. And as the US was the only major western market to not approve the drug, the *Thalidomide* disaster forced European policy-makers in particular to look to the American regulatory framework.

Pharmaceutical manufacturers in the US had since the late 1950s been obliged to provide reliable and accurate information in their packaging in-serts (particularly regarding any adverse effects), such that doctors and health professionals could make informed decisions on a drug's use. This was not yet the case in Europe where patients did not pay directly for their medicines and pressure for proof of efficacy was thus not as strong. The US also had a federal regulatory office for pharmaceuticals, the Food and Drug Administration (FDA), which in 1958 had been empowered by the US Congress to license medicine manufacturers subject to their meeting certain safety standards. It was on the basis of such safety and efficacy legislation that Frances Kelsey, medical officer at the FDA in charge of new drug applications, had delayed granting *Thalidomide* US market authorisation.

With the development of clinical pharmacology during the 1960s and 1970s (as a result of the tragedy), safety and efficacy slowly became widespread authorisation criteria in Europe (Dukes 1985). Aware of the need to regain public confidence, most European countries also introduced stricter liability standards, though the US example of an independent body to assess medicine applications took longer to become standard. The United Kingdom (UK), for example, created the Committee on Safety of Drugs (CSD) in 1963. And although companies were required to submit their data to the CSD for assessment, there was little direct government control until the 1968 Medicines Act.[3] And in Germany the 1961 drug law was accompanied by the compulsory registration of all new medicines with the *Bundesgesundheitsamt* (Federal Ministry of Health). But it was only in 1967 that proof of effectiveness became an approval criterion – this was strengthened in 1971 to include approval based on clinical trial evidence. Nevertheless, it is as a direct consequence of the *Thalidomide* tragedy that pharmaceuticals are today perhaps the most highly-regulated of all consumer goods.

Pharmaceutical policy and the supranational context

In western Europe, where negotiations over a six-country economic co-operation and cross-border trade regime had been concluded a year earlier,[4] the *Thalidomide* disaster also made it clear that a broader level of control was required. Thus, in 1965, and towards establishing public health protection guidelines for medicines, the European Community (EC) agreed Directive 65/65/EEC on common authorisation requirements for new drugs. Guidelines for the pharmaceutical sector were likely to have been an inevitability under the common market banner, but the disaster kick-started the process. Since the first piece of legislation, the European Union (EU) has been actively involved in pharmaceutical policy, and there have been numerous further instruments covering issues from guidelines on price transparency and good manufacturing practice, through to the licensing, advertising and labelling of therapeutic drugs in the Single European Market (SEM).[5]

More recently, and perhaps most significantly, since 26 January 1995 there has been an independent EU agency for the regulation of medicines. The European Medicines Agency (EMEA)[6] oversees a (Community) market approval process for new drugs based on the safety and efficacy criteria laid down in 1965. But more than that, according to the European Commission press statement released at the time of its inauguration, the agency's establishment was 'an important part of the overall strategy for the creation of a single market for pharmaceuticals' (CEC IP 1995). A Community market approval process had been in place since 1975, but the EMEA brought a more streamlined authorisation protocol, speeding the time needed for new medicines to reach the market. This would facilitate their 'free movement' within the single market, and represents a function which goes beyond the more limited, primarily information-dissemination role of most other EU agencies. The empowerment of the medicines agency in this way, indeed its very creation, reflects equally the growing regulatory role of the EU as it does the specific needs of the pharmaceutical sector in Europe.

The Community's regulatory history in pharmaceuticals is considerably longer than for other industrial sectors, and relates to both the product and the market. Yet, despite being one of the most highly-regulated sectors at European level – and ten years having passed since the opening of the EMEA in London – there is still no single European medicines market. The reasons for this are numerous and interwoven. They relate to certain unique characteristics of the pharmaceutical market and the nature of the EU's competences which result. Nevertheless, there is a broad-ranging regulatory framework for medicines in place – in which the EMEA is a central element – and the incomplete market has not precluded the Community from acquiring considerable regulatory powers. The purpose here is to examine this framework, to consider its development and orientation, and to address several important issues not dealt with in the existing literature about how pharmaceutical policy has been made in the EU.

Unique issues and the regulatory impasse

It is first necessary to set out some of the issues relevant to any examination of pharmaceutical policy. Foremost of these is the widely-acknowledged point that the pharmaceutical market is 'peculiar' in comparison to other industrial sectors in developed countries.[7] Although the reasons for this are detailed later, several points bear mention. First is the unusual market dynamic where the consumer is reliant on a prescribing doctor for most of the medicines she consumes, and the state (or health insurance funds) is the largest purchaser. Indeed, with the exception of defence, no industry is financed to such a degree through public expenditure. Second is that governments are responsible for protecting public health. This results, thirdly, in a heavily-regulated sector where governments have an unusually large say in the market because of both the public health issues at stake, and because medicines are directly tied to social security and healthcare budgets. As just three of the features which serve to distinguish pharmaceuticals from traditional products and markets, the policy issues they raise represent a constant challenge for decision-makers.

For it means that there are three different policy inputs in medicines regulation: public health (drug quality, safety and efficacy); healthcare (financing and reimbursing medicines); and, in some countries, industrial policy (ensuring a successful and productive pharmaceutical sector). National governments thus seek to ensure their citizens the best possible access to the highest quality medicines, along with keeping healthcare costs down and drugs affordable. At the same time, many are interested in supporting local industry and generating employment. These objectives are not always complimentary. Moreover, they invoke numerous actors and interests beyond the state, and the result is often a balancing act or trade-off; in particular between healthcare policy on the one hand, and industrial policy on the other.

Reconciling such sensitive interests at EU level is particularly complex. For although the EU has a clear Treaty-based public health mandate (Article 152) the policy trade-off exposes a gap between the Community's legal and policy frameworks.[8] It translates into a dissonance between the principle of subsidiarity on the one hand – a Treaty-based legal stipulation whereby policy competence lies at the lowest level at which it can be effectively undertaken[9] – and the free movement goals (of goods, persons, services and capital) of the single European market on the other. The former enables the member states to determine the healthcare policy elements of pharmaceutical policy, while under the latter pharmaceuticals are treated as an industrial good and fall within the Community's scope of competence under the SEM. Specifically, they are the remit of the European Commission's internal market or industrial affairs office, the Directorate-General for Enterprise.[10] Responsibility for pharmaceutical policy is thus divided between the EMEA and DG Enterprise at Community level, and the individual member state governments at the national level.

In practice, this clash in frameworks means that while the Commission legislates over (single market) industrial policy issues such as common standards for advertising and package labelling, it has no authority over healthcare matters such as the pricing and reimbursement of medicines which remain national competences. The implications of having EU policy-makers take decisions over national healthcare budgets and social insurance systems, along with the potential accountability questions which would arise, are such that member states refuse the Community a wider regulatory remit. And though national healthcare policy competence is also enforced under the Treaties – Article 152 requires the Community to 'respect the responsibility of the Member States for the organization and delivery of health services and medical care' – this is not to say that the EU has no influence or input here. By granting the Community an explicit public health role, Article 152 itself has an indirect influence on national healthcare priorities, as does the EMEA in deciding on authorisations for new drugs. There are also other articles, pertaining to the environment, or workplace health and safety for example, which impact on healthcare.[11] Additionally, many aspects of healthcare policy are relevant to the single market's free movement provisions (Article 100), as several rulings delivered by the European Court of Justice (ECJ) have demonstrated (Hancher 2004). In many ways, therefore, healthcare is not the sole purview of the member states.[12] Nevertheless, it is because of subsidiarity and the Community's limited healthcare policy competence that the European Commission has not been able to take the harmonisation process for pharmaceuticals forward as it has done in other sectors.

For instance, harmonising national pharmaceutical regimes under EU law along the lines of 'minimum content in programming' legislation in the EU television sector[13] is not possible. As it was completed through a slow and deliberate process to which medicines cannot be subject, neither is the integration of the EU telecommunications sector a comparable case.[14] For not only are national pharmaceutical sectors very divergent, but so too are member state health systems, and differences in speed of integration between national markets would create imbalances in access to medicines and further price differentials; something neither the Commission nor the member states could defend. Beyond the Commission's limited remit, the continued fragmentation of the EU pharmaceutical market along national lines also harks back to the *Thalidomide* tragedy. Member state regulatory regimes have since evolved in parallel though in relative isolation. Each has developed its own approach to maintaining a regulatory equilibrium between public health, healthcare and industrial policy interests, reflecting particular national circumstances and requirements. In a climate of increasing healthcare costs the divergence has become even greater, hardening national policy-makers' resolve over restricting Community influence. And this divergence is compounded by the lack of a single EU healthcare regime.

Although bringing these national regimes together under a supranational framework has been an expressed goal of the European Commission since its original 1985 White Paper on the Internal Market (CEC 1985),[15] the result has been that EU pharmaceutical competences have developed on an ad hoc basis rather than reflecting a particular strategy. As a consequence, the ECJ plays a major role. Exercising no regulatory capacity per se, by delivering decisions in respect of many issues relating to healthcare policy, competition policy, and pharmaceuticals specifically, it has nevertheless contributed to the environment in which pharmaceutical policy decisions are taken.[16] This too represents a complexity to be taken into account when looking at how the EU medicines framework has evolved.

Conflicting agendas

Beyond their concerns over public health and the organisation and financing of their healthcare systems, another reason for the member states' unwillingness to devolve the healthcare elements of pharmaceutical regulation to the Commission is the contribution that the sector makes to national economies. Medicines are an extremely profitable industry and one which generates a considerable number of jobs. As a single medicines market would mean industry rationalisation and job losses[17] – undoubtedly favouring the more established and globally-oriented member state industries – European governments are unwilling to gamble over this potential winners and losers scenario; hence their invocation of subsidiarity (ostensibly on healthcare grounds). This might, initially, seem to defy much theorising about the EU as a 'regulatory state' (McGowan & Wallace 1996); the 'spill-over' of Community economic regulation into social regulation (Leibfried & Pierson 1995); and the European Commission's growing regulatory remit (Majone 1996), but the reasons clearly relate to the national interests at stake.

Because of the sensitivities involved, therefore, pharmaceutical policy at EU level is a highly politicised arena. And it is one in which there are four main policy actors pursuing their own, often conflicting, agendas. Consumer/patient interests are primarily concerned with efficacious medicines; the pharmaceutical industry seeks a propitious regulatory environment to remain profitable and competitive; the Commission is pushing for a more integrated market and globally competitive industry while nonetheless preserving jobs; and the member states face the parallel challenges of ensuring access to quality medicines, cost-containment, and (in some cases) providing support for a local (high-employment) industry. These potentially incompatible goals are developed at a later stage, but they mean that co-operation between stakeholders is not always forthcoming. So while the Commission and industry may favour easing the ban on medicine advertising in the Community in order to promote the industry, many governments and consumer organisations are opposed on the basis of potential negative public health effects.[18] Another example is the parallel importation of branded medicines resulting from price differences for the same medicines between member states.[19] The practice is supported by consumer groups, the Commission, and several member states as a means of keeping healthcare spending down and ensuring access to medicines. But as it dents profits on the implicated products, it is contested by the companies producing them and those governments whose industries are affected. The point to be stressed from the outset, therefore, is that EU pharmaceutical policy is an inherently political arena in which interests (and actors) converge or clash depending on the issue at hand, with economic, social and ethical arguments all competing for attention. This book will analyse these clashes and the nature of the policy outcomes they generate.

Community pharmaceutical policy is thus characterised by a conflict between subsidiarity and national healthcare competence on the one hand, and the free movement principles of the SEM and Community industrial policy competence on the other. It is this disharmony, along with the actors' conflicting interests, which currently hinders further harmonisation. The dissonance also has a bearing on how and what sort of policy can be agreed. And while this point has been recognised in much of the literature, it is more observation than analysis. In looking at the expansive, even if incomplete, supranational regulatory framework for medicines, this study aims to go further. It considers the Community framework against the backdrop of how the healthcare–industrial policy balancing act is played out, and explores the development of EU competences for pharmaceuticals,[20] particularly since the early 1990s, to the continuing impasse which precludes completion of the single market.

Pharmaceutical policy-making in the EU

Within these parameters certain questions and issues which have generally not been dealt with in the existing literature are raised. Noting the subsidiarity-free movement clash, or highlighting that pricing and reimbursement is the main sticking-point, does not help us to understand the development of the regulatory framework. Nor how, in practice, policy has been achieved within the clash. For instance, it has not been asked why, if the Community is in essence empowered to act only in those (industrial) policy areas associated with the single market programme, has it been possible to establish a European licensing agency which is responsible for deciding on the safety and efficacy of new drugs (what is essentially a public health role with healthcare implications). With the exception of Shechter (1998), how the Community agreed exceptional patent protection for medicines in 1992 – given that longer patent times impact on drug prices – has only been described rather than critically analysed. And if pricing is the sticking-point, how is it that one of the pre-single market pieces of legislation is in fact a Directive on pricing and reimbursement transparency? It is also worth considering whether the need for a successful pharmaceutical industry in Europe has had any bearing on the type of regulatory policy outcomes achieved. These questions hint at some important political considerations in regulatory policy-setting for medicines at EU level, and suggest that insufficient attention has been paid to issues surrounding the accommodation of the often divergent interests of the stakeholders.

The role of 'politics'

A reason for this is that the political dimension of EU pharmaceutical regulation is generally mentioned only in passing. Discussions on Community pharmaceutical policy have for the most part focused on the economic and the legal aspects. This has primarily taken the form of textbooks on pharmaceutical and health economics, sector and management studies undertaken by private consulting companies, or as issue-specific chapters/articles published in edited volumes/law and economics magazines. There are few articles about the EU sector to be found in political science or public policy journals, and even fewer expressly political analyses.[21] And while specific aspects of the wider regulatory regime have, occasionally, been looked at, such pieces have tended to be more descriptive, historical or legal than analytical. The tendency to examine only the economic determinants (and implications) of policy out-comes may not seem surprising given the free movement goals of the single market. And the preponderance of economic and legally-oriented research has been valuable in discerning certain industry and sector issues, not to mention helping understand the (global) context in which policy is made. But this fails to acknowledge the complexities of EU policy-making generally, and for pharmaceuticals specifically.[22] It should not be forgotten that the EU (and European integration itself) is in fact driven primarily by political impetuses.

What has been missing, therefore, is an explicit examination of policy-making and the 'politics' of the sector. That is, research which looks at policy outcomes given the subsidiarity-free movement dissonance, and the sector's competing tensions: governments struggling to keep healthcare costs down and yet retain local industry; European companies seeking to remain profit-able and competitive (*vis-à-vis* the US and Japan in particular); and the Euro-pean Commission pushing for at least some degree of (price) harmonisation. In addition, patients and healthcare professionals are increasingly demand-ing access to the best available medicines, and elements of the industry are fighting amongst themselves over how best to tackle declining global com-petitiveness. As these all carry clear political implications and represent com-peting and overlapping objectives, it would seem crucial to understand how these tensions have contributed towards establishing the current EU frame-work.[23] As such, it is a political and policy-making perspective which this book proposes.

Inter alia, this involves analysing or understanding the special characteris-tics of the pharmaceutical market; the policy context in which EU pharma-ceutical regulation is agreed; the trade-off between industrial and healthcare policy interests, and the place of public health considerations; the priorities and requirements of the main actors (including what harmonisation and a single medicines market might mean in terms of their own interests) along with the role they have played in pursuing and achieving policy outcomes; and the nature and dynamics of the policy process. The study thus assesses the politics behind the regulatory framework in order to understand how policy has been made. No conclusions on how to breach the impasse towards completing the single pharmaceutical market are proffered. Indeed, beyond changing the Treaties to reconcile the subsidiarity-free movement dissonance it is not clear that anything can be done.

Bearing in mind the broad objectives mentioned, the study has a more specific and twofold purpose. This is, first, to elucidate a theoretical frame-work or lens which enables us to develop the wider policy-making understanding of the sector that we seek. And, second, to test a contention which appears to run against the established view that consumer interests prevail over pro-ducer interests in EU regulation (Young & Wallace 2000). For it is posited that the pharmaceutical industry (rather than consumer or patients' interests) is the main beneficiary of the current EU regulatory framework for medi-cines. The two aims are reinforcing in that it is via undertaking the former that the latter can be pursued.

Aims and objectives
The contention is based on the claim that industry and industrial interests dominate the EU pharmaceutical policy arena, and the study posits three reasons for this. First, that there is a natural confluence between industry's interests and the Commission's industrial policy priorities. Second, the insti-tutional leaning within the Community framework – where the Commission has industrial but not healthcare policy competence – supports industry arguments. And third, the fragmented nature of the market enables the in-dustry to exert undue influence within the policy arena. This latter point is perhaps the most contentious and it may even seem paradoxical. For if the market is fragmented it ought to be more difficult for a single actor to domi-nate. But as will be shown via the theoretical framework, not only is the industry the most stable actor within the policy process, and with a consistent set of demands, but because of certain informational asymmetries which characterise the sector it has generally been able to convince policy-makers of its arguments. Indeed, a theme throughout this study concerns the part played by the industry in the policy-making arena, along with the role of information.

The role of information in the policy process has long been identified as an important factor in establishing outcomes. But with access to pharmaceutical industry information (particularly data) notoriously difficult to come by, it seems especially important here.[24] As a high technology and high investment industry, companies are understandably reluctant to share information on their activities, often citing commercial secrecy as grounds for not doing so. Verifying what they may make available, such as data on research and devel-opment (R&D) costs, the focus of investment, the results of clinical trials, or time to market periods for new drugs, is therefore also difficult. Additionally, much important information is in any event only accessible to those with specialised knowledge: understanding clinical trials data requires medical or scientific training. This 'informational monopoly' is of concern. For the in-formation on which decision-makers and regulators tend to base their poli-cies is generally that provided by the industry itself. While the issue of infor-mational asymmetries in the sector could constitute a study of its own, it is dealt with here within the context of the policy process more generally.

The question of a potential industry-favouring regime is an important one from a social standpoint. For, despite all their shortcomings, the member states' regulatory frameworks have been developed primarily as a means of protecting patients rather than serving industry's needs (Anon 1991a). In one way or another, all were a consequence of the *Thalidomide* disaster. So al-though the Commission may claim that the EU framework and policies de-signed to foster a single pharmaceuticals market are a benefit to the European patient first (e.g. CEC IP 1995, CEC 2000), as this is predicated on the assumption that quicker market access for new drugs automatically means a health benefit, it seems more intuitive than empirical. More drugs do not necessarily mean more or better health, and Edmonds et al. (2000) have shown that, in comparison to the Community's earlier authorisation protocols, there is no evidence patients have actually benefited from the European Medicines Agency's quicker approval times. It has even been argued by an ex-member of the agency's Committee for Proprietary Medicinal Products (CPMP),[25] which undertakes new drug assessments on behalf of the agency, that industry interests prevail in the work it has carried out to date (Garattini & Bertele' 2000). Simply saying that any inclination towards industrial policy reflects the Community's comparative lack of health(care) capacity, or is the unintentional result of the push towards the single market, is a somewhat superficial conclusion which does not adequately explain how this situation was reached.[26] It is important to stress that the aim here is not to attempt a proof that public health is compromised by the europeanisation of regulatory policy for medicines, rather it is to consider whether or how the regulatory framework may be skewed in favour of industry interests and industrial policy.

In order to test whether the regulatory framework is indeed industry-leaning, it is important to first understand how EU pharmaceutical policy is made, and whether it is the case that industry has undue influence within the policy process. The approach adopted must be able to take into account the complexities and policy-making constraints already raised, along with the roles of the stakeholders. This returns us to the other aim, of offering a different lens through which to view the development of supranational competences than is currently found in much of the literature; one which would allow for a more complete picture of how the sector operates and is governed at European level. Here it will be shown that although existing theories of European integration and policy-making offer important insights, they are unable to offer a complete picture of how and why the framework for medicines regulation has developed in the way it has. Macro-theories are precisely that, *macro*: integration theory can thus be used to identify broad influences and to establish the policy environment for an EU sector such as pharmaceuticals, but it does not really help us to assess how policy is made. Meanwhile policy-making theories are able to explain sectoral dynamics, and may provide insight into a given decision, but do not really help to explain the wider Community 'approach' to pharmaceutical regulation. Further, they are often process-oriented, and thus unable to take the actions of individual actors in specific circumstances into account. This is not to deny the respective value of both approaches, but simply to point out that on their own they do not answer certain questions raised.

What is needed, therefore, is a meso-level or policy-making approach.[27] Here the umbrella of public policy theory provides more specific levels of analysis, particularly in terms of institutional and actor behaviour, the analysis of problem definition, agenda-setting, the role of preferences, and implementation – approaches which have already been transposed to the supranational context. Given the purpose of this study, the policy network has been identified as the most useful from within this literature.

Theoretical approach and outline

Specific to an examination of those policy processes which characterise an EU sector, a framework which is able to analyse decision-making with respect to political interactions (institutional or personal), 'pressure politics', and the balancing of economic and social priorities, is crucial. The stakeholders and their relationships in the pharmaceutical policy clash also make it clear that the approach must be able to account for their interests. And it needs to be flexible enough to accommodate both institutional and inter-actor behaviour and ought to be based on verifiable (observed) examples within various empirical settings. Such an approach is being advanced as public policy scholars continue to develop the field of policy network analysis. Acknowledging that there are other relevant approaches from which important findings could be gleaned, including a lobbying or interest group perspective (Mazey & Richardson 1993), or even a (new) institutionalist analysis (Armstrong & Bulmer 1998), a brief explanation of policy networks – and justification for using them to underpin the theoretical approach – is necessary.

Using policy networks
The policy network concept has attracted much attention in both the national and EU contexts. Although there is disagreement over its value, by focusing on actors and interactions in the policy process, it is a valuable approach which can take meso-level factors into account. Hence its extensive use as analytical tool for the study of policy-making which '… allows a more "fine grain" analysis by taking into account sectoral and sub-sectoral differences, the role played by private and public actors, and formal as well as informal relationships between them' (Börzel 1997a: 10). More specifically, as an approach which links actors because of shared concerns about a substantive policy area – actors whose preferences and actions must, therefore, be taken into account (Josselin 1994) – it is one which is clearly applicable to the EU pharmaceutical sector given the interests at stake, and necessarily close involvement of the primary stakeholders. Again, these are the member states, the industry, the European Commission and consumer interests. Additionally, because of the challenge in balancing the public health, healthcare and industrial policy inputs, pharmaceutical policy can also be seen as an arena of 'antagonistic cooperation'[28] between the stakeholders. That is where, despite sharing certain common goals which must be pursued collectively (implying a degree of mutual dependence), each has its own agenda. The study thus views EU pharmaceutical policy from the perspective of (network)

configurations of the four main stakeholders with the locus on the interest-intermediation rather than governance application of networks.[29]

Adopting this line requires us to understand the grounds for the stakeholders' behaviour, particularly given the competing interests already outlined. Here the study looks to Wilson's (1980) 'politics of policy' framework which characterises regulatory policies according to the perceived costs and benefits they bring to involved parties, and the type of politicking which results. Wilson differentiates between economics and politics in regulation. Consumers' wants from the economic marketplace are shaped by external factors, while politics (and politicians) not only provide these wants, but actually determine them. It is argued that this framework – which is developed later – helps to explain actor behaviour within EU pharmaceutical policy networks by showing how political factors can shape, if not decide, regulatory outcomes (and even preferences).

The study acknowledges that the policy network approach is not without its problems or detractors.[30] It is not an entirely novel one in examining the place and role of actors or interests in policy-making. Similar concepts such as 'policy communities', 'sub-governments', 'iron triangles', 'issue domains', and their linkages to systems or structural analysis, as well as to exchange network theory and sociological network analysis have all preceded it. There are also more contemporary constructs such as the 'epistemic community' or 'advocacy coalition', which encompass similar premises in addressing inter-actor or interorganisational behaviour and relations. Nevertheless, it should also be noted that such differences are not definitive and that the applicability of any given theoretical approach is often a largely subjective question. An approach which may not function in a particular context though works in another cannot be deemed without merit simply because it is not all-encompassing. The debate between the broader political science concepts of pluralism and (neo-) corporatism, or the persistence of the realism/idealism schism in international relations theory, remind us of the difficulties in studying policy-making – there are no fixed rules and certainly no one theoretical approach is wholly satisfactory. It may be the case that 'while networks certainly have an intellectual pre-history, there is no conscious continuity' (Jordan 1990: 320), but so too must it be left up to the individual student to formulate their own interpretation and application as to the approach's viability – as something both distinctive and relevant to their area of analysis. Thus, in using policy networks alongside broader theories, and in conjunction with Wilson's framework, the aim here is to provide a more integrated conceptual understanding of policy-making in the EU pharmaceutical sector. The book can therefore also be seen to contribute to the debate on the validity of the approach by providing a further application in an empirical setting. These are mutually reinforcing in that the chosen setting, the EU pharmaceutical sector, is one which is not often studied from a political (science) perspective.

Proposing a multi-dimensional approach is not to attempt a *telos* or single theory of EU pharmaceutical policy-making and regulation. Rather, it is to elucidate a lens through which to better analyse the shape and development of supranational policy for the sector. And, importantly, one that allows us to test the claim that industry is the main beneficiary of the EU regulatory framework.

Policy networks and European pharmaceutical policy: empirical questions and case-studies
In so doing, the discussion seeks to understand the positions of the stakeholders generally and their actions in particular instances specifically. With these actions interpreted through a policy network lens, it is necessary to consider what the practical effects of the stakeholders' actions were, how they were brought to bear, and whether or not the final policy outcome reflected their preferences. As an examination of all EU pharmaceutical policies is not possible, in-depth case-studies in three instances are laid out. Attention is given to the Community's 1992 decision to grant medicines a special intellectual property protection regime; the establishment of the European Medicines Agency in 1995 and its operation since; and the continued intractability of medicine pricing and reimbursement policy at Community level. Within the latter, the various attempts made by the Commission towards promoting price harmonisation (or at least liberalisation) and the reactions of the other stakeholders are analysed.

The representation of the stakeholders' positions generally, and their involvement in the evolution of the three policies specifically, is based on a review of the relevant official documentation. Commission communications and draft documents as well as the final legislative instruments; press releases; speeches by Commissioners and other key EU officials; internal Commission memos (where available); member state government (ministry) papers; minutes of European Parliament sittings and members' questions as put to the Commission; letters exchanged amongst EU officials, other stakeholders and interested parties; and records of discussions held during various EU committee meetings, have all been consulted. So too have position papers, press releases, published interviews and other primary source material put out by the stakeholders themselves, as well as minutes of important meetings. Such material offers a clear indication of the stakeholders' interests and actions, and reviewing it over a twenty to twenty-five-year period enables a historical perspective on their arguments. Supplementary and supporting material was gleaned from secondary sources, including articles taken from specialist trade publications and magazines, reports by interested parties such as non-governmental organisations (NGOs), and studies undertaken by private firms; these often provided information on discussions and meetings which took place behind closed doors and for which minutes or transcripts were not available.

The three case-studies have been selected as they represent separate and crucial policy initiatives within the broader EU medicines framework, and ones which implicate the three policy inputs: public health, healthcare and industrial policy. Moreover, in involving difficult relations amongst the main stakeholders they give a clear indication of the complexity in making policy at this level. Each is therefore treated as its own policy network (as the third case-study involves looking at several initiatives, these are presented as individual networks). Other, wider issues which factor into the discussions include transparency and access to information, parallel importation, industrial competitiveness, and the place of public health interests in the policy process. These too reflect political agendas within the sector. Further questions are therefore developed in relation to the broad theoretical rubric proposed. If, as mentioned, traditional theories of European integration do not fit, what then is their relevance to understanding harmonisation in the sector, and what do they reveal about the health–industrial policy clash? How do policy networks operate in the sector, especially within the constraints posed by the regulatory context? Does the composition of the networks affect the final policy outcome; does the nature of the policy at stake affect the type of settlement reached, or both? In what way can the industry be said to be the most 'stable' actor within the policy networks? And, does the theoretical lens provide a clearer understanding of the policy process?

Consequently, it must be noted that this study is not about EU (economic) regulation per se, and a detailed examination and application of regulatory theory is not relevant. But as the discussion does centre around the Community's regulatory competences in a particular sector, a brief consideration of the unique nature of Community regulation is provided as a necessary part of the theoretical discussion. The emphasis will be on explaining how certain interests are galvanised around specific issues into policy networks where EU (regulatory) pharmaceutical policy is concerned.

With the empirical element of the study being an analysis of stakeholder interactions at supranational level, this involves examining the behaviour and preferences of the European Commission, the member states, the industry, and consumers *vis-à-vis* certain policy issues (within the context of harmonising the market).[31] These are the primary EU-level policy actors for pharmaceuticals, and understanding how they push their agenda, how their agenda may (or may not) change given the issue at hand, and how these agendas are (or are not) reconciled in any final policy decision represents an important part of the project.

Although the focus is on the four stakeholders, the study does not aim to develop graded assessments of their interactions in policy discussions, nor does it attempt to quantify the relative strength of their relationships. Josselin (1994) has suggested a statistical analysis of policy network involvement in a sectoral context towards further developing the applicability of the approach at EU level, but it is too complicated in the context of the pharmaceutical sector. This is in part because of the earlier-cited lack of transparency. Independent data and information (i.e. non-industry sourced) about the industry is difficult to come by. Moreover, policy negotiations involving the industry, national governments and the EU, given the sensitive interests at stake, tend to be very secretive. The opaqueness and secrecy of the policy process means that it is difficult to establish with any certainty which links were or are strongest, let alone when and why. In addition, the sheer number of further actors, their interests, and the varying nature of their influence, along with the multitude of structures and avenues relevant to the policy process in the EU, would all seem to preclude a numerical representation of the policy-making frame. The practical difficulties of quantifying or valuing one inter-action over another in a given network situation are too considerable to be overcome. As such, qualitative case-studies of policy outcomes are employed instead.

Structure of the book
Broadly, the study consists of four parts. The first part comprises Chapters 1 and 2, and builds on the initial discussion here. It identifies the issues surrounding the EU pharmaceutical market and examines the sector and its peculiarities. The second comprises Chapters 3 and 4 and develops the theoretical framework, tying it to the stakeholders and their agenda. The third section represents the crux of the study and consists of the three empirical case-study chapters (5, 6 and 7). Each relates to a specific policy area within the EU regulatory framework for medicines and is examined as an individual policy network. Chapter 8 represents the final part of the study, and offers selected conclusions in view of the case-studies and the theoretical application.

More specifically, Chapter 2 discusses certain unique features of the pharmaceutical sector and profiles the issues involved in regulating medicines at member state and EU levels. This includes not only the need to balance the three policy inputs, and the trade-off between healthcare and industrial policy concerns at national level, but so too the dissonance between subsidiarity and the free movement principles at EU level. It also outlines the EU's competences, highlighting the gaps in its remit resulting from the Commission's constrained role. The policy issues raised thus set the stage for the remainder of the study by developing the backdrop to the discussions and divisions between actors which are highlighted.

Chapter 3 assesses the value of European integration and policy-making theory in understanding the ad hoc development of Community pharmaceutical competences. It traces the evolution of the regulatory framework, and initial insights from a macro-perspective are drawn. The chapter shows the contextual value of such an approach in relation to elements of accredited theories, arguing that a more encompassing understanding is, however, only gained through the addition of a meso-level line of analysis which looks at actor behaviour. Chapter 4 then makes the case for such an analysis, outlining the more salient aspects of policy network theory to show the approach's relevance to the study. Given that wider political dynamics can affect policy outcomes in the sector, the discussion also examines the nature of regulation in the Community. The main stakeholders and their agendas within the sector are then outlined, and here Wilson's 'politics of policy' approach is applied. This is used towards providing a wider contextual framework of regulatory policy-making, and is shown to have repercussions for networks in terms of when and how they can form over specific issues. With this wider view of regulatory policy-making in place, the study goes on to focus on the three specific policy areas which form the case-studies.

The three case-study chapters relate to the development of the Supplementary Protection Certificate, which concerns the extension of patent coverage for therapeutic drugs in the Community (Chapter 5); the rationale behind the creation of the European Agency for the Evaluation of Medicinal Products and what its mandate reflects in this regard (Chapter 6); and an examination of the impasse over pricing and reimbursement policy (Chapter 7). Wilson's framework is applied to each case within a policy network context, showing how the stakeholders' often competing interests were or were not reconciled, and what role each played. The case-studies reveal the depth of disagreement amongst the stakeholders, which precludes further market harmonisation.

Chapter 8 closes the study from both theoretical and empirical perspectives. It recaps the main arguments and condenses the findings from the case-studies, drawing out the main points and delivering some concluding remarks on the future of EU pharmaceutical policy within the single market. The chapter also looks at the study's theoretical lens, and assesses its merits and restrictions as they relate to the discussion. By way of conclusion, potential further research and lines of enquiry are suggested.

Finally, it must be stressed that although the study focuses on the EU regulatory regime for pharmaceuticals, it does not aim to assess it beyond showing industry as the prime beneficiary. Instead, it simply aims to answer the seemingly simple question of 'how did we get here?' As will be shown, however, the answer is not nearly as straightforward as the question.

Notes

1   At its height, *Thalidomide* was estimated to have been available in 46 countries and sold under 50 different tradenames (TVAC 2000).
2   The German medicines law, the *Gesetz über den Verkehr mit Arzneimitteln* (or *Arzneimittelgesetz*), was established in 1961.
3   In 1989 the CSD was replaced by the Medicines Control Agency (MCA), which has since merged with the Medical Devices Agency in 1993, becoming the Medicines and Healthcare Products Regulatory Agency (MHRA).
4   Plans for the European Economic Community (EEC) and European Atomic Energy Community (Euratom) were agreed in the 1956 Spaak Report.
5   The terms pharmaceuticals, medicines, medicinal products and (therapeutic) drugs

are employed interchangeably throughout this book.

6   Formerly the European Agency for the Evaluation of Medicinal Products.

7   For instance Pharma Info (1982), Scherer (1996), Mossialos & Abel-Smith (1997), Schweitzer (1997) or McIntyre (1999).

8   The EU has also initiated numerous multi-year health-related programmes since 1987 and, as of 1 January 2005, has an Executive Agency for the Public Health Programme to oversee the latest programme (2003–2008).

9   Article 3(b) of the 1992 Maastricht Treaty, the subsidiarity principle, specifies that the EU may act 'only if and in so far as the objectives of the proposed action cannot be sufficiently achieved by the member states and can therefore, by reason of the scale or effects of the proposed action, be better achieved by the Community'.

10 Before the establishment of DG Enterprise in 1999, Directorate-General V (Industrial Affairs) was responsible for pharmaceutical policy. Prior to that, the responsible office was DG1A, the Directorate-General for the Internal Market.

11 For example, Article 138 (ex 118) pertains to the prevention of occupational accidents and disease, and occupational hygiene; or Article 174 (ex 130r) concerning the protection of human health within the context of Community environmental policy.

12 Mossialos & McKee (2001) have argued that, via a growing number of ECJ rulings, an EU health framework is emerging.

13 Directive 89/552/EEC on the coordination of certain provisions laid down by law, regulation or administrative action in Member States concerning the pursuit of television broadcasting activities.

14 Directive 90/388/EEC on competition in the markets for telecommunications services.

15 The White Paper specifically cited pharmaceuticals as a problem area regarding the removal of barriers.

16 See Kanavos (2000) or Hancher (2004) for a discussion.

17 The Commission's first report on employment identified the pharmaceutical sector as an industry where rationalisation was likely in view of a future single market (CEC IP 1989).

18 Direct-to-Consumer (DTC) advertising of medicines is an extremely divisive topic with a host of research providing 'evidence' of both positive and negative impacts on health. It is banned in the EU under Directive 92/26/EEC.

19 Parallel importing involves the purchase of branded medicines by a distributor (generally from wholesalers) in a less expensive member state, and their export and resale at a lower than market price in a more expensive member state. Typically, they are sold on to local wholesalers or directly to pharmacies.

20 Although not looked at, the framework also covers biotechnology products, veterinary medicines, orphan and 'traditional' medicines.

21 Notable exceptions include Mossialos et al (1994a,b), Mossialos & Abel-Smith (1997), Shechter (1998), Abraham & Lewis (2000), Lewis & Abraham (2001) and Feick (2005).

22 There has, however, been a growing number of policy-oriented publications examining EU regulation in practice, specifically with regard to the number and speed of new drug approvals, often in comparison with the US FDA (e.g. Abbassi & Herxheimer 1998, Lewis & Abraham 2001, Redmond 2004). These are

relevant to this study and are taken up at various stages. But even so, most of this research is concerned with the basis for drug authorisation rather than how regulatory policy is made.

23 This gap in the literature exists primarily because research into EU healthcare policy has been a somewhat neglected field. Although this is changing as the effects of the integrationist dynamic on the national healthcare environment are increasingly being recognised, (e.g. Mossialos & McKee 2001 or Steffen 2005, particularly given the ECJ's role in pushing the agenda (Palm et al. 2000), it still remains an under-examined area.

24 For instance IJRSM (1996), HAI (1997), or Abraham & Lewis (2000).

25 Now the Committee for Medicinal Products for Human Use (CHMP).

26 A leaning towards industry at EU level has long been noted by consumer and patient groups (e.g. BEUC 1991, NCC 1994, Presc Int 2002), but has not generally been considered from a policy-making standpoint. An exception is the work carried out by John Abraham and Graham Lewis. They have argued a 'neo-liberal corporate bias' in European medicines regulation and remain critics of the industry's influence in drug authorisations (e.g. Abraham & Lewis 1998, Lewis & Abraham 2001).

27 Our use of the term 'meso-level' is based on Parsons' definition (1995:82): 'Meso analysis is the way in which issues and problems are defined and agendas set. "Meso" – or a level of analysis which cuts across or through various phases of the policy process – explores approaches which link the input side of the policy-making process with the policy/decision-making and output process by focusing on the relationship between the "pre-decisional" dimensions of policy-making and its decisional and post-decisional contexts.'

28 'Antagonistic cooperation' is a term coined by Marin (1990) with regard to public policy-making over social welfare issues.

29 See Chapter 4 for an elaboration of this division in the policy network literature.

30 For instance Jordan (1990), Kassim (1994), Mills & Saward (1994) or Dowding (1994, 1995).

31 The positions of other actors involved in the EU policy-process, such as the European Parliament and various consultative committees, are also referred to where relevant.

2

Regulating the European medicines sector

The opening chapter asserted that the pharmaceutical sector has certain unique features compared to other industries, resulting in complex regulatory issues. Divided into three sections this chapter develops the point in order to enable an appreciation of the policy considerations faced by decision-makers in Europe. The first highlights unique issues pertaining to the product, market dynamics, and the structure of industry. The second section considers medicine regulation in the EU member states, and outlines governments' competing interests in catering for health(care) and industrial policies. The final section examines the place medicines occupy in the EU frame in terms of the institutional setting and the nature of the regulatory regime. The Community's role is shown to be obfuscated by the clash between its legal and policy frameworks, particularly in relation to certain competing priorities between the member states and the European Commission. In explaining how the industry operates and where regulation is applied, the discussion also suggests the extent to which political considerations can, and do, determine policy outcomes in the EU sector.

Pharmaceuticals: an unusual industrial sector

According to Scherer (1996: 336) 'All industries are different, but some are more different than others. The pharmaceutical industry fits the latter category'. This stems from the fact that 'The pharmaceutical industry resembles no other industry, first, as to the nature of its products, and second, as to economic structure and development' (Pharma Info 1982: 9). The wider social implications that medicines carry, and the unusual economic conditions they generate, further result in a sector subject to regulatory influences unlike those in other industrial domains, particularly so with respect to issues of product quality.

A unique product

Medicines are manufactured to provide and ensure, if not create, health. They carry disease and debility-easing effects, often with a direct bearing on 'life or death'. Few other industrial products can make the same claim. Indeed, this contrasts them from related products such as vitamins, cosmetics and food supplements. And while other healthcare products such as medical devices also impact on health, the discussion will show that the market conditions generated by pharmaceuticals differentiate them.

Medicines are generally divided into ethical or prescription, and over-the-counter (OTC) drugs. Ethical medicines require a doctor's prescription and their availability differs by country according to criteria established by governments or health bodies. They are divided into proprietary – generally sold by brand-name – and generic medicines. The former enjoy patent protection and represent the most profitable market segment, with Germany, Sweden and the UK as the main EU producers. A generic has the same active ingredient as an existing brand-name product and is interchangeable with it where patents or other legal regulations no longer apply. It is marketed either under its own brand-name, or by the internationally-approved non-proprietary scientific name (INN), and many are available for consumer purchase. Generics can be with or without patent coverage, and differ with respect to therapeutic value and price. Germany, France and Italy are the main generic producers in the EU. OTC drugs meanwhile, are bought directly by consumers from a variety of outlets (uptake differs amongst the member states), generally without the need for a prescription. They offer a wide range of choice and are procured from multiple producers. Medicinal value and dosage tend to be very similar between products within therapeutic categories, and prices – because they are generally set by governments in Europe – are also more or less equal. Unlike for prescription drugs, the EU permits the direct-to-consumer advertising (DTC) of OTC medicines.[1]

There is a further category of drug known as the 'me-too' product. This refers to a new proprietary pharmaceutical with the same, or close to the same, therapeutic value as a product already on the market. So while it differs in chemical composition from the original product, its target group remains very similar (if not identical) and it too enjoys patent protection. Not many industrial products have such nuanced differentiation between their sub-sectors and this is an important consideration when looking at the sector.

The focus of this study is the prescription drugs sector. For, in addition to being the most profitable market segment, unique issues pertaining to patent protection, R&D, pricing, consumer access, market structure and therapeutic value, raise important policy questions; particularly in Europe where prices are directly influenced by governments. Further, as prescription medicines are in essence supplied by the state (via the healthcare system), the market reflects several unusual characteristics and imperfections which represent the second reason for designating the sector as peculiar.

Atypical demand and supply

The demand structure for prescription medicines is unique compared to other industrial sectors. The consumer does not usually choose the product,[2] nor do they generally choose to be sick. Demand comes from the prescribing doctor (so-called 'proxy-demand'),[3] and there is a third party – generally the state via some form of medical scheme or insurance – which pays. This three-tier structure has been well-documented, and is one wherein doctors (and to a lesser degree consumers) make up the demand-side of the market and industry the supply-side (Figure 2.1).

Figure 2.1 Structure of supply and demand in the pharmaceutical sector*

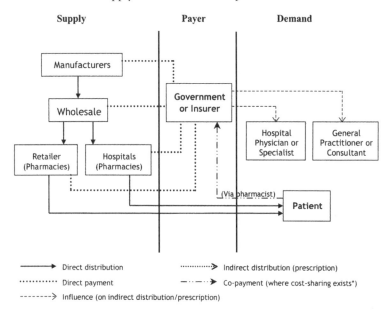

Source: adapted from Moore (1997).
* Cost-sharing is a healthcare financing mechanism whereby part of the cost of medicines is passed to the patient e.g. prescription charges.

This market imperfection results in a second unique feature of the demand structure, namely that medicines are very price-inelastic. First, 'because drug outlays are often covered at least in part by insurance', and second, because 'many physicians place little weight on price and much on good past thera-peutic experiences in their prescribing decisions' (Scherer 1998: 205). Consumers thus have especially low cost-awareness, and particularly when ill. Under the principle of solidarity they simply expect the best treatment possible (Belcher 1994). And this is often affirmed in the political rhetoric of the day, where a heavily-subsidised system of healthcare provision may be seen as a vote-winner. Price thus tends not to affect demand as it would in other industries. It may affect prescribing patterns, and does factor in government's healthcare calculations, but it does not influence consumer demand per se. As the general premise of 'health having no price' is a pervasive one – particularly in Europe – this price-inelasticity underlines the fact that medicines are not subject to traditional supply and demand forces.

Central to the demand–supply dynamic are certain informational asymmetries, representing a further market imperfection.[4] Consumers' lack of knowledge about medicines results in their reliance on doctors and pharmacists. However, as healthcare professionals are themselves often unable to properly assess the clinical value of a drug, treatment is generally based on the expectation that the assigned medicine will provide the health required. A further asymmetry lies in the fact that the public authorities who decide on licensing are dependent on the information provided to them by the industry. In seeking regulatory approval for their products, companies are required to submit detailed files demonstrating the proposed drug's safety, efficacy and quality as measured in controlled conditions over certain periods of time (see section on research and development below). These are tests which governments often have neither the expertise nor the resources to undertake themselves.

The supply structure too is unusual in that there is considerable fragmentation of the market. This takes place not just in terms of traditional market segmentation, but more with respect to the numerous sub-sectors of therapeutic category within product groups. Medicines serve different needs, often specific to individual cases, and are not interchangeable in the manner of other goods; there can be no direct competition between drugs designed to treat different conditions. Competition is therefore at its most pronounced within, rather than between, therapeutic categories (or traditional market segments).[5]

Market structure: the 'high profits–low entrants' enigma
Another unique feature lies in the so-called 'high profits–low entrants' enigma. That is, while industry profits are very high – both on their own terms and compared to other manufacturing sectors – there are very few players. This is especially in the ethical segment where ten companies made up 47.9 per cent of the global market in 2003 (Wood MacKenzie 2004), but may seem surprising when the top selling drugs in 2003 together had over US$48 billion in sales (Table 2.1).

This is partly because medicines do not conform to traditional price-elasticities, but also relates to an R&D process that is extremely costly, and which is longer and more intensive than for traditional consumer goods (see section on research and development below). In specific therapeutic categories, therefore, several companies have achieved near monopoly positions. In 2002 for instance, the global market for statins saw Pfizer's *Lipitor* and Merck's *Locor*

Table 2.1 Top ten pharmaceutical products by global sales, 2003

Rank	Product	2003 Global Sales (US$ billion)	Company
1	*Lipitor* – cholesterol-lowering	10.3	Pfizer (US)
2	*Zocor* – cholesterol-lowering	6.1	Merck (US)
3	*Zyprexa* – antipsychotic	4.8	Eli Lilly (US)
4	*Norvasc* – anti-hypertension	4.5	Pfizer (US)
5	*Erypo* (Eprex/Procrit) – antianemic	4.0	Johnson & Johnson (US)
6	*Ogastro/Prevacid* – antiulcerant	4.0	Abbott (US)
7	*Nexium* – antiulcerant	3.8	AstraZeneca (UK)
8	*Plavix* – antiplatelet	3.7	BMS (US)
9	*Seretide/Advair* – bronchodilator	3.7	GSK (UK)
10	*Zoloft* – antidepressant	3.4	Pfizer (US)
Total	Top 10 products	$48.3	8 companies

Source: adapted from IMS Health (2004).

with 42 per cent and 32 per cent respectively (Simons 2003). This is not the case, or at least not to the same degree, in more traditional industries where product substitution and market segmentation are more easily defined. It also raises the contentious question of competition in the pharmaceutical marketplace: 'Taking a static approach there are high concentration ratios, high prices and profits, a small number of large companies dominating a large number of smaller companies and a considerable lack of price competition … with a dynamic approach the impression is of cut-throat competition not only through product competition and differentiation, but through prices' (McIntyre 1999: 66).

The dynamic approach holds that as there is strong competition between brands within therapeutic categories, companies not only have to ensure that their products are affordable but that they are more innovative or efficacious than those of their competitors. And, because of economies of scale, it is suggested that only a small number of large firms will ever be able to afford the R&D required for new drug discovery in the first place. Here the argument focuses on cost-effectiveness as a natural market element, one which ensures sufficient (if not significant) competition. Market concentration is thus seen as the product of a natural evolution given the sector's peculiarities – driven mainly by the dynamism, costs and risks associated with R&D – and high profits are regarded as a just reward given the outlays and risks. The static approach meanwhile is reflected in Davis's assertion (1997: 84) that 'On closer inspection, however, it soon becomes evident that competition of this kind is more apparent than real'. The degree of competition between products in a class may be high, but this is not the same thing as saying the marketplace enjoys high levels of competition; particularly not when only two or three products dominate. Additionally, the limited number of (globally-dominant) companies is seen as a situation of oligopolistic structure at best and monopolistic structure at worst, and one which represents an uncompetitive market generally because of the power wielded by so few players. Table 2.2 lists the top ten global pharmaceutical companies and their global sales. According to Scherer & Ross (1990: 592), 'The moral to be drawn is that under conditions like those found in pharmaceuticals, first movers have natural product differentiation advantages that permit them to charge high prices and retain substantial market shares – the essence of monopoly power'.[6] And McGuire et al. (2004) note that the industry does have monopoly power at certain times in particular markets. Other voices are often less measured, suggesting the over-pricing of products by a cartel of multinational companies.

Assessing in detail the respective merits of these two positions is beyond our aims here. Indeed, many analysts have already done this.[7] And, in relation to Porter's (1980) widely-cited work on the analysis of industrial competition, Permanand (2002) has argued that, even if not intentionally enforced by the existing players, there are significant market entry barriers in the sector and that they are higher than in other industries.[8] What is important here, however, is the question of R&D. For not only does it represent a unique feature of the pharmaceutical market in its own right, but it lies at the heart of many issues concerning the industry and its regulation, particularly at EU level (it is central to the policy discussions examined in later chapters). These

Table 2.2 Top ten pharmaceutical companies by global sales, 2003*

Company (home country according to HQ)	Global sales (US$ billion)
Pfizer (US)	39.63
GlaxoSmithKline (UK)	29.82
Merck (US)	22.49
Johnson & Johnson (US)	19.50
Aventis (FR)[+]	18.99
AstraZeneca (UK)	18.85
Novartis (CH)	16.02
Bristol Meyers Squibb (US)	14.93
Wyeth (US)	12.62
Eli Lilly (US)	15.58
Total: 10	208.43

Source: Sellers (2004).

* The top ten companies marketed a combined total of 47 products that each made over US$1 billion in sales in 2003.

[+] In 2004 Sanofi-Synthélabo took over Aventis in a hostile bid for US$62.6 billion.

include market structure, profits, competition and market barriers (dynamic versus static approaches), and healthcare and welfare gains (or losses). It should be stressed that much of the data cited here, even if from apparently non-industry sources, are in fact the industry's own.[9] As mentioned earlier, this (necessary) reliance on industry for data is one of the informational asymmetries which characterise the sector. It is therefore advisable to treat such figures with some caution.

Research and development: pressure or smokescreen? The modern R&D process for therapeutic drugs is unlike that in any other industry. Companies must first discover and patent new chemical entities (NCEs) as the basis for their medicinal preparations, before harnessing these compounds to produce new drugs and treatments. They are then required to test these for safety, efficacy and quality before demonstrating the results to national authorities in the prospective market. Public/regulatory bodies then carry out their own reviews, also against the three public health criteria (often against cost-effectiveness as well). This culminates in a market approval process which, depending on the source, can take up to fifteen years.[10] No other sector is characterised by such a lengthy and strictly controlled market authorisation process, far less such a research-intensive and costly one (Danzon 1997).

As mentioned, the process of discovering new medicines is extremely high technology-oriented and expensive. Industry sources show that as the number of new discoveries is on the wane, R&D costs have been rising steadily since the 1980s, doubling in the last ten years alone. The European industry currently claims that bringing a new drug to market costs €868 million and along with the risks – only one or two products out of every 10,000 substances synthesised in a laboratory are said to pass all the tests and make it to market as a new drug (EFPIA 2004) – this sees companies under intense R&D pressures. Sub-markets in which new and innovative firms can acquire expertise and specialisation, as often characterise other industries, do not exist in the pharmaceutical sector; many companies may also be active in biotechnology, but this is a different sector entirely. There are different therapeutic categories in which companies can concentrate, but the research platform is high across the board. Established market-leaders thus enjoy an aggregate of latent knowledge which they understandably wish to safeguard. Moreover, it is on the basis of such knowledge accumulation and its protection that the industry justifies its market shares, and counters any charges of a lack of competition or excess profits. Looking at health outcomes research in chronic disease for instance, 'such studies can take 5–15 years, require thousands of patients, and cost millions of dollars. When firms that are established in a chronic therapy market (e.g. hypertension) invest in such research, they … raise the ante for any newcomer wishing to enter the market [and] they create a "time-buffered" competitive advantage' (Gelijns & Dawkins 1994: 169). The knowledge-base developed by the established firms thus gives them a considerable advantage over new competitors, especially in the future acquisition of knowledge. The expense and duration of R&D leads to the claim that it is the cost and potential lack of return on investment which discourages new entrants. R&D is here regarded as a pressure, and a natural feature of the market (others regard it as a barrier to entry), making it unlikely that the market could bear any more than a handful of players.

According to industry officials, the consolidation of the sector over the past few years is in large part due to these pressures. As in other industries, drug companies seek to streamline their operations, improve the product pipeline, and eliminate overlaps. Between 1999 and 2002 there were some 1341 mergers, acquisitions and strategic alliances in the global pharmaceutical sector. And in 2003 alone, because of an unusually high number of smaller deals, there were 568 transactions (PWC 2001, PWC 2003). Even in the so-called US$172 billion 'merger of equals' – Glaxo Wellcome and SmithKline Beecham in 2000 – and Pfizer's US$60 billion merger with the Pharmacia Corporation in 2002, amongst the rationale offered by company officials was the improvement of the research-base and product pipeline. Thus, not only do industry representatives expect to see sufficient gains to make their R&D investment worthwhile, but as drug development is almost exclusively carried out in the private sector, they seek government incentives and an unfettered environment in which to operate. As regards intellectual property protection, the global industry's lobby has been especially energetic, with success in extending medicine patent times in all major markets i.e. the EU, the US, Japan and South Korea.

Nonetheless, industry's claims about costs and risks, as well as the data it employs, are coming under increasing scrutiny. The fact that the public sector cannot afford to undertake drug development is not disputed by critics, nor is the relationship between costly research and new medicines. But to what extent R&D is actually a pressure, given existing profits, is questioned, and it has been noted that the major research-oriented companies have generally spent more on promotion and marketing than on R&D (e.g. Wertheimer & Grumer 1992, Davis 1997). Moreover, the R&D cost data cited by the industry may include a host of inputs which do not directly apply to the generation of any single product. Often included, for instance, are post-approval research spending, the costs of NCEs which were not/could not be synthesised into a new drug, as well as products which failed clinical testing (i.e. the industry's claims of only one or two of every 10,000 NCEs making it to market). The industry's figure of €868 million for a single drug is thus disputed, with many experts putting the actual cost considerably lower (e.g. Henry & Lexchin 2002). And it is important to note that, in both Europe and the US, while healthcare spending has been rising as a share of gross domestic product (GDP), so too has pharmaceutical expenditure as a share of total health spending gone up over the past twenty-five years. The industry can, therefore, also be seen as getting an increasingly bigger slice of an increasingly bigger pie (see Appendix A). For those who criticise the market's dominance by a limited number of players, not only does industry thus 'spin' its statistics, but its R&D claims are used as a smokescreen in pursuing favourable government policy.

One of the arguments here is that wide-ranging intellectual property rights consolidate the position of the market-leaders, and that mergers and alliances are thus more about profit than staying competitive (or because the research pipeline has dried up). Indeed the 'new' companies are themselves often mergers between previously merged enterprises (e.g. GlaxoWellcome and SmithKlineBeecham becoming GlaxoSmithKline in 2002, or Ciba-Geigy and Sandoz creating Novartis in 1996), or else are the product of multiple mergers (Pfizer buying out Pharmacia in 2004, having taken over Warner-Lambert in a hostile takeover in 2000). Smaller manufacturers must overcome a comparative lack of financial as well as informational resources if they are to become competitive, and the result is that they often sell their own (sometimes incomplete) research to the market leaders. Or else, they are simply amalgamated in this consolidation of the industry. This only widens the knowledge gap, further cementing the position of the few global leaders. So while the R&D task (cost and knowledge accumulation) clearly is a pressure, industry's claims about increasing costs, decreasing discoveries, and the need to consolidate – along with the data used to make their case – should not be unquestioningly accepted. Nor should it be forgotten that despite these claims, the top ten pharmaceutical companies in 2003 had 47 products between them which amassed over US$1 billion in sales (Sellers 2004), and that profits for the major companies remain high with total growth rates for the sector as a whole remaining around 10 per cent (IMS Health 2004).

Oligopoly or quasi-monopoly?   Irrespective of in which of the 'high profits–low entrants' camps one sits – adopting either the dynamic or static view – it remains the case that the structure and operation of the market is in contrast to higher levels of competition in other sectors. Greater demand and choice, and possibility for new entrants to exploit niche markets, as exists in other industrial domains, does not characterise the sector. Traditional arguments about start-up costs, capital and marketing are alone not responsible for the dominance of so few firms. Ignoring the earlier arguments as to whether this reflects an uncompetitive industry or not, what it does reflect is a structure which is less competitive than it could be.[11] And while many analysts argue that the dynamic approach is the more valid,[12] this still accounts mainly for competition amongst those already in the market rather than why there are so few companies in the first place.

In combination with the economic contribution and profitability of the sector, this lack of competition underlines the influence wielded by the industry where any regulatory policy may be concerned. Moreover, as patients (or the state) are obliged to pay high prices in order to secure a health benefit, the pharmaceutical industry has been characterised as 'extraordinary ... for the amount of monopoly power held by sellers of important new products' (Scherer 1998: 204). McIntyre (1999) prefers the term 'multinational oligopoly', while McGuire et al. (2004: 131) see it as 'characterised by an oligopoly structure, with monopoly power in particular markets and particular times'. This is not say that companies necessarily behave in monopolistic fashion – although there have been legal cases in both Europe and the US which have found the industry to be guilty of cartel-like practices in areas such as pricing or in influencing the prescribing patterns of doctors[13] – rather that the conditions under which this can happen do exist. Consequently, it is perhaps more accurate to deem the pharmaceutical market 'quasi-monopolistic'. And since the leading companies are powerful in public policy terms (because of the importance of medicines to society), the market structure should be of concern generally.

With respect to the EU specifically, a quasi-monopolistic view of the industry is important in the context of aims to complete the SEM. For where there are prevalent market barriers, economic theory suggests oligopolistic behaviour by the established players. An example would be predatory pricing where established companies exploit their cost advantages to bring medicine prices down to levels at which prospective entrants would be unable to recoup R&D expenditures. Squeezing out competition in the EU market in this way could be particularly egregious. Medical research is dependent on not just quality of research, but also quantity. The more firms (and member states) engaged in medicines research, the better the chances of breakthroughs. And an increased number of medicines within a given therapeutic class means lower prices and, in turn, increased competition. Ideally, more competition also means a better quality of product. An EU-wide market concentrated in the hands of a few multinationals is not going to inspire confidence in the provision of drugs for any other sake than profit (and profit for only some companies and some countries).

A further concern for the sector is the continuing consolidation of the industry. More mergers and alliances in the sector will strengthen the industry, and may therefore compromise the Commission's position *vis-à-vis* its continued efforts at harmonisation and an equitable balancing of interests. For despite the Commission's duty to act as a non-partisan regulator, a profitable and globally-competitive European pharmaceutical sector is in its interests. This raises the prospect of 'regulatory capture'. It is a concern in any industrial domain, but takes on especial significance where medicines (public health) are involved. Indeed, the strength of industry and its influence on policy-makers is an important consideration given this study's contention that the current EU regulatory framework already favours the industry.

Regulatory capture   Regulatory capture is well-established in both theory and practice, particularly in the US where the regulatory tradition has hinged on the state's market corrective interventions rather than it assuming a leading role in macroeconomic stability as is the case in Europe. Capture stems from a dichotomy between the public and private interest theories of regulation. The former is premised on a tension between producer and consumer, and asserts the common good or public interest in regulation. As patients and governments depend on the industry to deliver quality medicines, to what extent this tension exists in the pharmaceutical sector is debatable. But it is clear that companies aim to make a profit at the same time as consumers want the best possible medicines. The latter theory is widely associated with Stigler's famous assertion that 'regulation is acquired by industry and is designed and operated for its benefit' (1971:3). In the context of medicines where the public interest is in fact public health, there is clear potential for harm in terms of inefficacious or over-priced medicines. Moreover, private interest regulation would imply reinforcing an already well-performing industry, one which is not necessarily delivering therapeutically important medicines ahead of profitable ones. Worrying, therefore, is that the market structure of the EU pharmaceutical sector does reflect several characteristics which make it amenable to capture.

Its quasi-monopolistic constitution and the atypical role of the member states as purchaser and regulator (along with the Commission) mean that independent, objective regulation is difficult to achieve. This is compounded by the position of strength held by the industry in relation to three points in particular. First is the ethical argument that medicines research *ought* to be promoted given the direct health benefit that newer and better therapies can bring. Second is the argument that newer and more efficacious drugs will mean decreased healthcare expenditure, especially for long-term or chronic illness. Third is the industrial policy argument focusing on balance of trade and employment concerns. With pharmaceuticals representing one of the few high technology industries where Europe is a global leader, this carries especial weight amongst policy-makers, and the industry's arguments are reinforced by the informational asymmetries which characterise the sector. With the public sector hardly involved in the development of medicines, it is reliant on industry both for the provision of new drugs and the information which public bodies use to make their assessments. This makes the market further susceptible to capture on two fronts. These are the potential for information being selectively provided or strategically employed, and the potential for collusion between companies. Here the industry can either be seen as simply presenting a unified front in trying to maximise its interests – which, as will be shown, it does – or, more worryingly, such co-operation may allow companies to pressure or influence the regulators (whether at national or supranational level). Without proffering an opinion on industry operations – as its influence is examined in subsequent chapters – the point to be made is that the quasi-monopolistic structure of the market also warrants regulation, particularly as capture is a possibility.

So, why regulate?

This section sought to show why regulation in the pharmaceutical sector differs from that in other industrial arenas, and several reasons have emerged. First, pharmaceuticals are a unique product. Medicinal preparations are researched, designed and sold for profit, but also in order to bring a positive health effect in the event of illness (whether cure or control). Other industries are required to take consumer safety into account – with some specialising in this area – but consumer safety is not public health. Governments need to ensure that medicines are safe, efficacious and of high quality. And as drugs are costly, governments have a further vested interest in regulating to ensure affordable prices. Next, the atypical supply–demand dynamic requires regulatory oversight given the market imperfections it creates. Additionally, as most medication in Europe is reimbursed under health insurance, a fear of illness can provoke a demand for medicine often irrespective of cost considerations. Governments must intervene to control the costs of programmes which serve to ensure access to medicines. The informational asymmetries which result from this demand–supply configuration themselves necessitate regulation. This relates to patients' reliance on doctors given their inability to make independent, informed decisions on a product's use, and doctors' reliance on pharmaceutical companies for information on the therapeutic value of specific drugs. Governments and national regulatory authorities are also dependent on industry for scientific information.

The market structure too warrants regulation. The imperfections mean that traditional market forces are unable to ensure normal levels of (beneficial) competition and that entry barriers are especially high. Moreover, given the quasi-monopolistic structure of the market, governments' role in ensuring that this does not affect the provision of affordable medicines is crucial. Manufacturers should not be able to collude in such a way that maximising profits takes precedence over the delivery of required therapies. With a strong patent system in place, governments also need to ensure that companies do not behave in a monopolistic manner with regard to the prices they charge.

As a final point, there exists an ethical imperative which is stronger than in other sectors. And governments are socially bound to ensure that business interests do not override it. To what extent this imperative actually prevails is debatable, and represents a pervasive theme in discussions about the industry.

Regulating medicines

Turning to the health(care)–industrial policy clash raised in the opening chapter, a brief overview of the role of national governments *vis-à-vis* the regulation of their own medicines markets is necessary. This is important because it reveals, by comparison, the incomplete nature of the EU framework, and because it affords us our first look at why, unlike in the domestic context where health interests have a higher priority, the EU framework is said to serve the interests of industry first.

Pharmaceutical regulation in practice

Governments' role in pharmaceutical regulation is a multi-faceted one, and has been well-summarised by Orzack et al. (1992: 850): 'Public bodies determine which drugs can be provided to the public, exercise surveillance over production processes, limit distribution systems, control how patients obtain medication, establish standards for advertising as well as for printed inserts in packages, and often specify prices, insurance coverage, and reimbursement methods'. The remit is therefore broad-ranging and diverse, and involves regulating not simply demand and supply, but so too the product, market structure, industry conduct, and includes taking into account the wider social aspects of medicines. Indeed, as governments are generally responsible for a nation's health, and are both regulator and purchaser of drugs, this means ensuring that the safest and most efficacious medicines affordable within social security budgets reach the market. Given the economic contribution of the industry – and the fact that a successful industry is a prerequisite for high quality medicines – so too must policies be conducive to good business. Industry representatives argue that the two need not be incompatible,[14] but as governments have different priorities, there is no model. This creates a policy

Table 2.3 Competing pharmaceutical policy interests*

Healthcare policy	*Industrial policy*	*Public health policy*
Cost-containment and improving efficiency in health services and care	Promoting local research and development capacity	Safe medicines
Cost-effective medication	Intellectual property rights protection	High quality preparations
Regulating doctor and consumer behaviour *vis-à-vis* medicines	Supporting local scientific community	Efficacious treatments
Generic promotion and/ or substitution	Generating and protecting employment	Innovative cures
Improving prescribing	Promoting small and medium enterprise policies	Patient access to medicines
Ensuring access to medicines	Contributing to positive trade balance	
	Sustaining the university research base	

* This is a simple listing and does not indicate priority.

overlap where regulation must enable manufacturers sufficient returns to produce high quality medicines, but must also serve to keep the prices of these drugs as low as possible. It meshes public health, healthcare and industrial policy requirements (Table 2.3).

It is with an eye to meeting and balancing these policy interests that governments regulate both the product and market aspects of the sector. Bearing in mind the quasi-monopolistic market structure already discussed, regulatory officials must also ensure that industry structure and conduct are enabling good economic performance (Scherer & Ross 1990). As methods amongst the EU member states vary (at times considerably), the discussion turns now to how governments regulate the sector.

Product and market regulation: balancing policy goals
As noted, medicines must pass three regulatory 'hurdles' before they are granted market approval. The first is that manufacturers are required to prove the quality, safety and efficacy of new substances in terms of delivering a therapeutic benefit to patients under specific conditions and at a particular dosage (the 'public health test'). These assessments involve up to ten years of pre-clinical and clinical evaluations. The second hurdle is review and approval. Regulatory authorities assess the *dossier* of a new drug submitted by the manufacturer after completion of the trials. The *dossier*, or New Drug Application (NDA), contains the detailed results of the tests, outlines the purpose and target group of the proposed drug, and specifies under what conditions it can be administered. Review and approval can take several years after which, if the regulator is satisfied that the public health test has been met, the medicine can be registered and marketed. The final hurdle is pricing and reimbursement, and is 'the most contentious issue in pharmaceutical production and one where health policy objectives clash directly with the objectives of industrial policy [as] it is the public bodies' intention to achieve the highest outcome with the lowest possible cost' (Kanavos 1998: 77). Manufacturers engage in negotiations, generally with ministries of health, regarding the price of their new product and its inclusion in national formularies (lists of those medicines reimbursed under health insurance). Such discussions usually take place behind closed doors and, as all EU governments (save Germany) directly influence pharmaceutical prices, are crucial to both industry and health interests.

In addition to setting the public health test, governments are responsible for managing the market – the need for which, given the market structure and welfare issues at stake, is perhaps greater than in other sectors. Market regulation involves supply and demand-side measures, both of which are geared towards promoting healthcare and industrial policy goals. The former implies regulating industry *vis-à-vis* prices, the latter involves regulating consumers or healthcare providers with regard to demand for drugs. Methods have become more sophisticated as EU governments have sought to manage ballooning healthcare costs since the 1980s.[15]

Healthcare policy and cost-containment   Cost-containment has generally been the priority for most member states. As supply-side measures play on popular opinion which holds that if not medicine prices, then manufacturer profits are too high, it proves politically more viable to regulate the industry rather than consumers. Price controls are thus favoured by most EU states. These generally take the form of direct controls on individual products; profit controls or other limitations on industry; and reference pricing formulae (which involve setting benchmark prices by grouping similar products together and establishing a relative price for reimbursement by insurance). There are further methodologies (Appendix B) and most governments use a combination approach. With the EU member states exercising such varied types of control, it is the harmonisation (or at least standardisation) of national pricing regimes which the Commission has long pinpointed as the foremost obstacle towards harmonising the market (Bangemann 1997a).

As the member states' different policies mirror differences in health systems and health culture, this contributes to price differentials within the EU for the same product. In the southern European states, particularly Italy, Portugal and Spain, medicines are relatively inexpensive compared to their equivalent prices in northern states such as Denmark, Germany and the UK. This accounts for the former group of countries' general preference for price controls and the latter's use of reference pricing schemes.[16] It also reflects a range of national variances in health and economic concerns, including structural differences in healthcare system and drug reimbursement mechanisms; drug consumption patterns; variations in tax systems and value-added-tax (VAT) rates on medicinal products; doctors' prescribing habits; and the type and development of local pharmaceutical sectors. A single market for medicines would have to overcome (or accommodate) such national differences.

Although governments may see medicine price controls as an effective manner to cut back on costs incurred by health systems,[17] there is no consensus on their impact. Proponents point to lower prices, decreasing drug expenditures and a tighter rein on a market where traditional market forces do not necessarily guarantee competition. Opponents claim that price controls reduce innovation by limiting the returns companies can put into R&D, and are awkward to implement and manage. Moreover, that they may create scarcities (real and artificial) and have no clear impact on the national drug bill as this is also dependent on prescribing habits and consumption patterns. A detailed discussion of the relative merits of price regulation, including the complex variations which exist in Europe is neither desirable nor necessary here. But it does serve to underscore what potentially needs to be addressed if the single market is to be completed.

Considering demand-side measures, cost-sharing (specifically co-payments) is generally the most popular system in the EU. This means shifting some of the price for medicines to the consumer and usually involves a flat-rate payment for all prescription drugs. The premise being that patients are encouraged

to think more cost-effectively. However, as cost-sharing has equity implications i.e. welfare being based on the ability to pay, the unemployed or elderly
are generally exempt, while those in employment pay the same flat-rate (or
percentage) irrespective of their earnings. Thus, it is also a policy which has
been said to discriminate against those more able to afford. In addition, as
with price controls, there is no firm proof that co-payments are actually effective in containing costs. Mainly this is because savings depend on the nature and size of the exemption group. Still, it proves a popular option given
its relative simplicity to implement. When combined with a system of budget-
ing for doctors, cost-sharing can also affect prescribing and in turn consumption. User charges and financial incentives for doctors are also employed as
means of engendering price awareness and sensitivity to prevent induced demand and increase cost-efficiency. Such measures allow governments to not
only affect drug costs – albeit indirectly – but also to retain sufficiently high
prices to incentivise the industry.

This ability to influence indirectly relates to the use of prescription drug
lists (formularies). Positive lists identify those medicines which are reimbursed
under national insurance systems, while negative lists include those which
are not – these are subject to co-payment charges. Again, there are questions
over the effectiveness of lists in reducing drug costs; positive lists often cover
only cheaper drugs, while a change in a patient's course of treatment may
involve switching them from a negative to positive list medicine. Nevertheless, all EU member states currently employ either a positive or negative list,
sometimes both, and here too national differences are considerable, with the
financing aspects of healthcare systems directly implicated.

A final demand-side measure necessitating mention given its increased use
is generic substitution. While countries such as France, Italy and Spain may
not yet have well-established generic markets,[18] and implementation can sometimes prove difficult, the policy of substituting branded medicines for generic
equivalents is widely regarded as an easy way for governments to cut costs
and promote competition. This, despite doctors generally being against the
practice arguing that it undermines their professional autonomy (Burstall
1997). And although the Commission has strongly supported the use of generic policies in the member states (i.e. substitution, promotion, prescribing),
with healthcare beyond its scope of influence, it cannot enforce this.

Industrial policy   National regulatory systems are also designed to serve governments' industrial policy objectives. The specifics of these goals differ between member states, even amongst those with a domestic manufacturing
industry. In general, however, all are keen to support the industry for the
economic rewards it brings. This is especially so for those countries with a
research-oriented sector. In the UK for example, pharmaceutical production
was worth some €27,144 million in 2002 (EFPIA 2004). In terms of the EU
economy as a whole, pharmaceuticals represented the fifth-largest industrial

sector in 2000, representing some 3.5 per cent of total industrial production (Gambardella et al. 2000), and was worth an estimated €170,000 million in 2003 (EFPIA 2004). And the combined European industry (the EU plus Switzerland) contributes almost 37.5 per cent of the world's total output of pharmaceuticals (ex-factory prices), which is higher than the US at 35.5 per cent (EFPIA 2004). Much of the value of EU production is via exports – particularly to the US where medicine consumption is much higher than in Europe – and this contributes to the Community retaining a favourable trade balance.

As mentioned, medicines are an extremely research-intensive and high technology industry. In 1997 for example, Pfizer's R&D spending was some US$1,710 million on one product alone: its much-vaunted impotence drug *Viagra*. Although the drug did then achieve sales in excess of US$400 million in just its first three months of being on the market (Kanavos 2000), such returns are not the norm. The considerable investment required of medicine R&D is therefore important in the domestic manufacturing context. Moreover, the industry is a major employer across a range of sectors. The UK industry not only employs some 60,000 people directly, but it generates a further 250,000 jobs in related industries (ABPI 2001a). And the European sector as a whole directly provides around 588,000 jobs (EFPIA 2004). It should also be noted that the number of jobs provided by the industry grew at a steady average of 2 per cent per year throughout the 1980s (EUROSTAT 1998), representing a healthy increase considered against employment rates for other EU manufacturing industries (and when compared to the US and Japanese industries). And while this tapered off slightly in the 1990s, it has risen by some 9 per cent since 2000 (EFPIA 2004).[19] As this is something that European policy-makers are understandably keen to maintain, the industry and the Commission continually stress employment in all supranational policy discussions on the sector. In employment, investment and balance of trade terms, therefore, the success of the pharmaceutical industry is crucial to national economies, and many governments are keen to promote R&D capacity in particular.

It is unsurprising then that governments seek to keep pharmaceutical firms on home soil. Recent murmuring by several of the larger European multinationals about relocating their R&D elsewhere (specifically to the US where the research environment is said to be more conducive) has seen not just the member states, but so too the Commission, seek to placate the industry on a number of levels e.g. intellectual property rights and preferential tax arrangements. This has led to accusations of bias and unfair competition from several fronts, not least of which is the generics industry which feels that the research-oriented companies already enjoy favoured conditions. Where both a generic and research industry is present (e.g. Germany), governments have to strike an even more delicate balance. Nevertheless, the reason for the Commission's supportive approach to the industry in general is clear. The pharmaceutical industry is a major contributor to the European economy.

Regulatory diversity in Europe

Before turning to the supranational context it should be noted that the differences in member state regulatory approach stem from country-specific factors. Different healthcare systems mean that health spending and relative government shares of total drug expenditures are considerably different (Appendix A); the number of products available in national markets is therefore not the same. This may also reflect the subjective nature of therapeutic judgements (Dukes 1985), resulting in one country granting market approval to a given product and another not – in turn reflecting medical differences in both training and practice. Ethnic and cultural factors, along with demography and relative wealth have also contributed to the evolution of individualised systems. So too have national attitudes towards medicines, and medical requirements (not all countries have similar patterns of disease). Economic performance has also helped to mould distinct pharmaceutical regulation practices and systems in Europe. Such socio-economic or medico-historic differences pose a considerable obstacle to be overcome if the EU is to regulate over a single medicines market.

These national differences have been increasing since the early 1990s. Beyond their different industries, other contributory factors include growing pressures on healthcare systems; patients' changing drug consumption and lifestyle patterns; the realisation that current systems are inadequate in controlling costs; and – despite the establishment of a European medicines agency – the lack of a truly comprehensive European regulatory scheme. The result is that some member states are now looking to favour volume controls on pharmaceuticals in addition to price controls, others are working to stimulate the local industry, and yet others continue to tinker with their co-payment systems. More recently, debate about combining clinical-effectiveness with cost-effectiveness as a so-called 'fourth hurdle' has arisen in several countries. Again, this is because EU countries do not have the same history and experience with pharmaceutical regulation, nor do they have the same resource and administrative capacities dedicated to the purpose. Having seen how governments balance the sector's competing interests, the discussion now turns to the supranational level to look at how the EU has addressed these issues.

The EU regulatory framework for medicinal products

In looking at EU regulatory competences, a far less reaching role than at national level can be seen. This is perhaps surprising in light of not only the volume of European legislation pertaining to pharmaceuticals (Appendix D), but also a Commission whose role has been deemed as 'entrepreneurial' in expanding Community regulation (Laffan 1997). It also reflects not simply the member states' interests in pegging the Commission back, but their ability to do so under the subsidiarity principle. In order to better understand the Community's competences, along with what is at stake at supranational level, the discussion turns now to the context in which EU pharmaceutical policy is made.

A complex policy environment
In looking at the policy environment for the EU sector, important is the global nature of the industry: 'Few industries are as multinational as pharmaceuticals' (Schweitzer 1997: 2). This may seem self-evident given that the leading producers are multinational enterprises, several of which are household names. But in practice it means that medicine manufacturers must remain abreast of economic globalisation (one reason for the number of mergers and acquisitions), despite their activities being decided predominantly by national interests (resulting, for example, in different prices for the same product in Europe). So while this international dimension has seen the EU industry benefit from global trade liberalisation measures such as the General Agreement on Tariffs and Trade (GATT), and now the World Trade Organisation (WTO), or through the emergence of free trade areas including the North American Free Trade Agreement (NAFTA) and the EU single market programme, industry activities are nonetheless framed within national policy interests and subject to domestic influences.

For European policy-makers this means balancing the industry's global concerns with the member states' national requirements. Consequently, arguments about maintaining a strong European industry are more involved than they might initially sound. For instance, although several of the world's leading research-based companies are European, this is not to say that they necessarily carry out their business in Europe. They may be headquartered in the EU (though even this is not clear in terms of corporate versus operational headquarters), but as multinationals they seek to exploit cost and location advantages so, where possible, much of their activity is outsourced to foreign affiliates. Additionally, European companies generate most of their profits outside of Europe, particularly in the American market. This is mainly due to a combination of cost-containment measures by European governments (especially price controls) and low tax rates and higher profit margins in the US. The more important issue, therefore, is to what extent the companies' R&D activities are undertaken in Europe. Domestic R&D spending has been slowing since 1990, with the US being the main beneficiary in this shift in research expenditure (Appendix E).

It is this apparent declining competitiveness of the European industry (and the potential cost in employment terms) which has seen the Commission and member states push for strong industrial policy incentives. As mentioned, western Europe (i.e. including Switzerland) currently accounts for 37.5 per cent of the global market in production terms and enjoys a €36,000 million trade surplus in pharmaceuticals (EFPIA 2004). These domestic versus global concerns are especially complex given policy-makers' attempts to balance national industrial and health concerns, and have contributed to the current shape of the EU regulatory environment.

Official EU competences in pharmaceuticals
In looking at the competences which make up the EU framework it is striking that the Community's role is limited mainly to industrial policy concerns such as product licensing, marketing and sale, and patent protection (Table 2.4).

The table is limited to selected Directives and Regulations as binding instruments,[20] and hints at the breadth of Community competence more generally. More importantly, it captures the flurry of activity around the time of the single market programme. So while the Community's leaning towards economic and industrial policy competences may seem logical given the aims of the SEM, it belies the fact that market harmonisation has progressed under a political banner, one which is equally responsible for the impasse over completing the market.

Another important point to be noted from the table is that, despite the number of policies listed, it shows what is missing from the EU's role. Beyond Directive 89/105/EEC (and, indirectly, Regulation (EEC) 1768/92 on patent protection and Regulation (EEC) 2309/93 creating the EMEA) there is nothing pertaining to healthcare policy. Again, this is because of the Community's formal exclusion from healthcare matters, both in relation to Article 152 and the member states' use of subsidiarity. Unlike in the member states, therefore, market harmonisation motivations rather than health interests per se have led to the establishment of most EU responsibilities in the sector.

Institutional capacity vis-à-vis *medicines policy*
The EU bodies charged with overseeing the pharmaceutical sector are, primarily, the European Commission – specifically, the Pharmaceuticals Unit ('F2') of the Directorate-General (DG) for Enterprise – and the EMEA. Together the two work towards promoting the free movement of medicines. In addition, DG Enterprise, along with the European Court of Justice, is responsible for seeing that the legislation listed in Table 2.4 is applied. It should be noted that, unlike for public health and healthcare (Article 152), there are no Treaty references to pharmaceutical products.

What is important here is that pharmaceutical policy befalls the Directorate-General responsible for industrial affairs and promoting European competitiveness. This has been the case from the outset when pharmaceuticals were the domain of the industrial affairs DG1A and then its replacement, DGIII. The DG for Health and Consumer Protection (DG Sanco) has no formal authority; just as its predecessors DGV for social affairs and DGXXIV for consumer affairs had no direct competence. Although there is consultation between the two offices, this imbalance and neglect of the health policy dimension contributes to the industrial policy leaning of the Community framework. It is also one of the sources of criticism of the EU's role, particularly as the EMEA itself is located within DG Enterprise.[21] By comparison, the US FDA is the responsibility of the Department of Health and Human Services. Nevertheless, it would also be inappropriate for DG Sanco to have sole authority.

Table 2.4 Selected Community pharmaceutical legislation (medicines for human use), 1965–2004*

	Legislative Tool	Year	Purpose
Pre-Single European Market	Directive 65/65/EEC	1965	Approximation of provisions relating to proprietary medicinal products
	Directive 75/318/EEC	1975	Approximation of laws relating to analytical, pharmacotoxicological and clinical standards
	Directive 75/319/EEC	1975	Approximation of provisions laid down by law, regulation or administrative action relating to medicinal products
	Directive 83/570/EEC	1983	Amending Directives 65/65/EEC, 75/318/EEC and 75/319/EEC
	Directive 89/105/EEC	1989	Relating to the transparency of measures regulating the pricing of medicinal products and their inclusion within the scope of national health insurance systems
	Directive 91/356/EEC	1991	Laying down the principles and guidelines of good manufacturing practice
Post-Single European Market	Directive 92/25/EEC	1992	On the wholesale distribution of medicinal products
	Directive 92/26/EEC	1992	Concerning the classification for the supply of medicinal products
	Directive 92/27/EEC	1992	On the labelling of medicinal products and on package leaflets
	Directive 92/28/EEC	1992	On the advertising of medicinal products
	Directive 92/73/EEC	1992	Widening the scope of Directives 65/65/EEC and 75/319/EEC … and laying down additional provisions on homeopathic medicinal products
	Regulation (EEC) No 1768/92	1992	Concerning the creation of a supplementary protection certificate
	Directive 93/39/EEC	1993	Amending Directives 65/65/EEC, 75/318/EEC and 75/319/EEC in respect of medicinal products
	Regulation (EEC) No 2309/93	1993	Laying down Community procedures for the authorisation and supervision of medicinal products and establishing a European Agency for the Evaluation of Medicinal Products
	Regulation (EC) No 540/95	1995	Arrangements for reporting adverse reactions, whether arising in the Community or in a third country
	Regulation (EC) No 541/95	1995	Concerning the examination of variations to the terms of a marketing authorisation granted by a competent authority of a member state
	Directive 1999/83/EC	1999	Concerning testing requirements and introducing the notion of 'well established medicinal use'
	Regulation (EC) 141/2000	2000	On orphan medicinal products
	Directive 2001/20/EC	2001	Approximation of the laws, regulations and administrative provisions of the Member States relating to the implementation of good clinical practice in the conduct of clinical trials on medicinal products for human use.
	Regulation (EC) No 726/2004	2004	Laying down Community procedures for the authorisation and supervision of medicinal products for human and veterinary use and establishing a European Medicines Agency
	Directive 2004/27/EC	2004	Amending Directive 2001/83/EC on the Community code relating to medicinal products for human use

Source: adapted from EudraLex Volume 1: Medical Products for Human Use.

* The complete listing can be found in Appendix D.

Its mission statement is to 'ensure a high level of protection of consumers' health, safety and economic interests as well as of public health at the level of the European Union'. The last of these is undertaken by its Public Health Unit (Directorate 'G') whose main responsibilities are the analysis, co-ordination and development of policies and programmes in the field of public health – particularly those involving health promotion, disease surveillance, and matters of health and safety at work.[22] Still, it is clear that DG Sanco should have a more formalised role. And its predecessor – DGV (Employment, Industrial Relations and Social Affairs) – traditionally had to fight for its voice to be heard in pharmaceutical policy discussions.

This question of which office should regulate is further complicated by the fact that health issues play an important, even if indirect, role in many Community areas e.g. the Common Agricultural Policy (CAP), VAT policy and e-commerce. There are numerous other EU offices with a role or interest in the Community's health and social policy objectives as well, and these too are potentially affected by or have an effect on pharmaceutical policy. A survey prior to the 1999 reform of the Commission showed that of the old twenty-four Directorates-General, at least sixteen had a 'significant involvement' in matters related to health (Merkel & Hübel 1999). This is also part of the problem in forming a comprehensive European public health policy (Mossialos & Permanand 2000) and, according to Hancher (1991), creates difficulties with the resulting 'horizontal multi-regulation' of the EU medicines sector. This multi-layered structure is made more problematic by the 'public health article' of the Treaties. The 1992 Treaty on European Union introduced Article 129 and the provision that 'health protection requirements shall form a constituent part of the Community's other policies'. This was bolstered under Article 152 of the Amsterdam Treaty where 'A high level of human health protection shall be ensured in the definition and implementation of all Community policies and activities'. Responsibility here falls to DG Sanco.

In terms of how the Community exercises regulatory policy over medicines, the Commission has several legislative instruments at its disposal. It is empowered to propose, and later adopt, proposals for Regulations, Directives, and Decisions (all which are binding on the member states), as well as providing Recommendations and Opinions (non-binding). Unlike Regulations, which have to be incorporated into national law as they are, Directives allow the member states considerable leverage in their implementation. Given this discretion and latitude, it is not surprising that the majority of EU pharmaceutical legislation (indeed EU legislation in general) consists of Directives. For with the sensitivities involved, the member states are unwilling to countenance the complete replacement of their national pharmaceutical frameworks with rules from the Commission. This creates difficulties with respect to enforcement and, in conjunction with Treaty stipulations, exposes some gaps. Consequently, the European Court of Justice continues to have a prominent role in the pharmaceutical field.

Although not empowered to act in a regulatory capacity per se, as the guardian and interpreter of European law, the ECJ does establish certain 'rules of the game'. By insisting that national legal systems comply with European legislation, the development of European law complements the regulatory function of the Community (Majone 1996, Stone Sweet & Caporaso 1998). From relieving national decision-makers of certain responsibilities, to being integrated in full into national legislation, it also shapes domestic legal systems and policy interests. Unsurprisingly, therefore, the Court has at times been accused of undue judicial activism. Decisions are sometimes said to impinge on the member states' decision-making sovereignty by underlining the principle of 'direct effect' and the 'doctrine of supremacy'.[23] Nevertheless, the Court fills the gaps where the harmonisation of national provisions are concerned and where national and EU legislation are not concordant. Further, in making clear any outstanding issues within the context of the single market – in the case of pharmaceuticals this has to do with the clash between Article 3b (subsidiarity) and Article 100a (free movement of goods) – it has helped establish the working rules of the SEM. Indeed, the ECJ's 'constitutional' role in establishing the supremacy of European law as a *sui generis* system has had a major hand in advancing integration in Europe generally (Wincott 1996).

As will be shown later, via numerous rulings the ECJ has had a considerable effect on shaping the Community's market/free movement approach to pharmaceutical policy, and in promoting the evolution of a European healthcare policy more widely (Mossialos & McKee 2001). With the Commission unable to make use of the public health related elements of Community competences to address pharmaceutical regulation, it has, under other aspects of European law, concentrated on the harmonisation of national legislation through the dismantling of barriers to free movement. And the Court has delivered numerous pharmaceutical rulings aimed at facilitating the internal market.[24]

In summary, therefore, the institutional capacity for pharmaceutical regulation in the EU is clearly stilted. This is the direct result of the health-industrial policy trade-off as it manifests itself in the dissonance between subsidiarity and the single market programme, and the horizontal multi-regulation structure within the Commission. And this has given the ECJ an unduly prominent role in establishing policy in an industrial sector. It now becomes necessary to examine this clash more closely, and to elaborate how the health(care) and industrial policy interests of the EU in the pharmaceutical sector are played out.

National versus Community interests
In view of the overlap between policy interests at national level, the picture which emerges in the Community context is even more complex. The reason being the dissonance between Articles 3(b) and 100(a). Figure 2.2 depicts the policy deadlock arising from competing national and supranational interests

Figure 2.2 National versus Community concerns in EU pharmaceutical policy

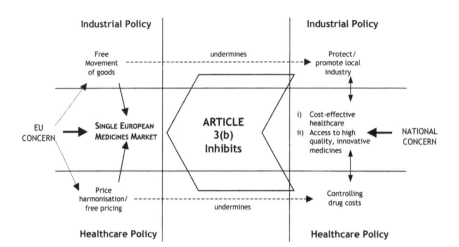

and frameworks for action in the sector. It shows the division between healthcare and industrial policy in both contexts, along with the result. More specifically, it shows why, despite sharing the Commission's interest in a strong pharmaceutical industry, the member states are unwilling to accept a single market as the means towards achieving this.

Important in the centre of the figure therefore is Article 3(b), the subsidiarity principle. For while the Community has pursued its designs for the sector under the banner of the single market, the member states have been able to opt out given the derogations to the SEM permitted under subsidiarity. Here the Community's free movement goals clash directly with the member states' own industrial policy objectives, particularly as a single medicines market would render jobs in several member states' sectors as superfluous capacity. Subsidiarity also hampers the Commission's goal of reducing intra-EU price differentials for medicines. This would compromise the member states' authority to set their own pharmaceutical prices, as well as impacting on the manner in which they organise and finance their healthcare systems. Cost-containment may be a common goal, but the manner in which the member states regulate their pharmaceuticals markets towards this end is not. And of course, because of the uncertainties about a single pharmaceuticals market, each member state is wary of the potential 'winners–losers' scenario which might result.

What is not included in the figure is the place of public health in this equation. Public health interests are obviously part of medicines regulation on the national side, but as the EU has limited competence in the area, it does not formally fall within the framework of pursuing a single medicines market.

The diagram is limited to showing where national and EU interests collide over EU pharmaceutical policy and that, because of this and the subsidiarity principle (not to mention Article 152), the result is the impasse over completion of the market.

Taking the discussion forward

This constricted remit over pharmaceutical policy appears to defy contemporary theorising about the nature of Community regulation. For it is generally held that the jurisdiction of EU regulation is not simply bound to the economic – market-correcting – aspects of the single market. Indeed regulation has been seen as a new form of governance in the Community, with the so-called 'regulatory state' view perhaps the most developed expression of this.[25] The regulatory state model is looked at later, but its mention here serves to emphasise the fact that the EU's function *vis-à-vis* regulation is a complex one, and one which otherwise includes a considerable social policy element as well. Yet, even with such a broad-ranging role in regulation generally, and the volume of pharmaceutical legislation in force specifically, the Commission is unable to force the pricing issue, far less wider harmonisation.

The EU's regulatory competences thus extend principally to the market aspects of EU integration. Since the SEM, the Commission has sought a market-oriented approach to the pharmaceutical sector. The emphasis has clearly been on liberalisation and the securing of an interventionist regulatory role towards ensuring the free movement of goods underpinnings of the single market, rather than outright harmonisation. It is supported by a considerable body of European law which, in this case, is mainly concerned with freeing impediments to inter-EU trade. More recently, the Commission has concentrated on promoting the competitiveness of EU industry (see Chapter 7), and its first major move in this direction was the publication in 1994 of a Communication on an 'industrial policy' for the pharmaceutical industry (COM 1993). There have been a spate of further initiatives since then. These have taken the form of meetings, advisory groups, commissioned studies, and policy papers by different EU offices. The most recent was the establishment of the High Level Group on Innovation and Provision of Medicines (or G10) in 2001. Made up of what DG Enterprise considers key stakeholders, the G10 was to devise a policy framework which would promote industry's competitiveness as a means of serving healthcare goals, and reflects the Commission's current thinking (see Chapter 8).

Here, it is interesting to note that fostering the competitiveness of EU industry (and promoting industrial policy in general) was not a Treaty-based competence until 1992. Article 130 of the Maastricht Treaty outlined the Commission's industrial objectives and enabled it to initiate and adopt policies towards this end, the only restriction being that such policies would not in any way distort competition or undermine single market objectives. As already noted, the question of competition – more specifically a lack thereof

– is important in the context of the pharmaceutical sector. Although not dealt with specifically in this study, it is worth considering whether the current industrial policy focus of the EMEA, and the EU framework in general, thus poses a threat to what is already a case of limited competition.

As the Community's competences are limited, it is unsurprising that the Commission has pursued its industrial policy mandate with some vigour. This is both as a means of breaching the impasse and in order to ensure a strong European presence in the pharmaceutical arena. Indeed, both the liberalisation and competitiveness approaches are ultimately aimed at achieving a single market, but represent different paths given the limitation imposed by subsidiarity. However, the sector still suffers from the lack of a singular EU policy direction. Strachan Heppell, former Chairman of the EMEA Management Board, recognised this several years ago when he asked whether the industry is 'to be taken in a healthcare context or in a single market context [for] the answer to that question will determine the sort of regime which develops' (Heppell 1994: 44). The Commission may be interested in pursuing the latter, but not only do the member states appear unwilling to support this unequivocally, the approach is insufficient. The healthcare and single market contexts are not so easily divisible where medicines policy is concerned.

With the issues now laid out, the study can address its more specific aims. The next chapter seeks to understand how the EU regulatory framework for pharmaceuticals developed from a theoretical point of view, and why an integrated analytical approach is necessary to address the research questions and hypothesis raised in the opening chapter.

Notes

1   Unlike in the US, the marketing and advertising of prescription medicines in Europe does not take place in the public domain. Direct-to-consumer advertising of drugs has been banned since 1992 under Directive 92/26/EEC.
2   Patients do demand specific products in the case of OTC, but their choices are often based on a doctor or pharmacist's recommendation.
3   This proxy-demand framework in Europe is changing. Although the direct-to-consumer advertising of medicines is not permitted, within the context of the recently-completed review of EU pharmaceutical policy (CEC 2004) the Commission proposed that drug companies be allowed to provide information on their products if requested (for AIDS, diabetes and asthma drugs only) (COM 2001). Although not passed in the final legislation, this was in part driven by concerns over consumers increasingly turning to the internet for health information – much of which is unregulated – or else looking up specific medicines on company websites, and may indicate a readiness to slowly liberalise advertising (see Chapter 8).
4   For a wider discussion see Davis (1997: 145–9).
5   In the OTC market, because of the lack of consumer knowledge, this may have the negative effect of actually leading to competition between products not

designed to treat the same condition.

6 The authors make the point that this monopoly power can be 'eroded' or 'undermined', though only when consumers have sufficient financial incentive to make cost-saving decisions, and providing that objective product information is available.

7 For example Scherer & Ross (1990), Schweitzer (1997) or McIntyre (1999).

8 Porter's (1980) seven barriers typical of traditional markets are: economies of scale; product differentiation; capital requirements; switching costs; access to distribution channels; cost disadvantages (independent of scale); and government policy (pp. 7–17). The industry rejects the idea that barriers are any more significant than in other sectors, see: www.pfizer.com/pfizerinc/policy/stake.html.

9 For instance, many commentators rely on data produced by the Tufts Centre for the Study of Drug Development (TCSDD) at Tufts University. The centre receives considerable sponsorship from several of the major pharmaceutical multinationals who themselves use TCSDD data to support their own positions. This is not to say that the centre's work is inevitably compromised, but rather to point out that even 'independent' sources of information are not necessarily without industry links.

10 For example Matthews & Wilson (1998), EFPIA (2001a) or TCSDD (2001).

11 With manufacturers focusing their activities in specific sub-markets and a few therapeutic categories, their power (and market concentration) may be greater than might initially appear.

12 See for example Feldstein (1988), Grabowski & Vernon (1994) and McIntyre (1999).

13 For example, in June 2001 the US Federal Trade Commission launched an investigation into complaints about companies having paid generic competitors to keep lower-priced drugs off the market. And in Europe, German drugs company Bayer has been fined by the Commission for uncompetitive practices regarding distribution of its cardiovascular drug *Adalat*.

14 For example Lawton (2001).

15 For a detailed discussion see Mossialos & Le Grand (1999).

16 The UK is an exception within this group. For although medicines are expensive in comparison to the rest of Europe, prices are regulated in secret between the Department of Health and the industry through the Pharmaceutical Price Regulation Scheme (PPRS), and are based on manufacturers' profits through sales via the National Health Service (NHS).

17 Though supply-side measures are the most popular method of cost-containment (and not just in Europe), member states are increasingly using a combination of supply and demand-side measures.

18 This is due to pharmaceutical prices being considerably lower than in other member states, such that the need for cheaper generics is not necessarily an issue.

19 See Appendix C.

20 Although not listed in Table 2.4, the Community also has competence with regard to immunological and homeopathic medicines, radiopharmaceuticals, medicines derived from human blood or plasma, and patent protection for products derived from plants.

21 For instance Garattini & Bertele' (2001), de Andres-Trelles et al. (2002).

22 Since 1 January 2005 there is an executive agency in place to oversee DG Sanco's

latest public health programme (2003–2006).

23 Cases C-26/62 *Van Gend en Loos* v. *Nederlandse Administratie der Belastingen* [ECR-1], and C-06/64 *Costa* v. *ENEL* [ECR-585]. Direct effect means member states must enforce European law such that it requires no additional implementing legislation. The doctrine of supremacy established the precept that, in the event of discordance, national law is to cede to European law.

24 See Kanavos & Mossialos (1999), or Hancher (2004).

25 For instance Majone (1994, 1996) and McGowan & Wallace (1996).

3

Theorising the development of Community competence in pharmaceuticals

It has been argued that the clash between health and industry interests over pharmaceutical policy at national level is not simply mirrored in EU policy-making, but is in fact manifest in the inability to harmonise the market. Yet there are numerous Community Directives and Regulations pertaining to medicines specifically, and a wide-ranging regulatory framework does exist. To explain this the chapter first examines the 'europeanisation' of pharmaceutical regulation, showing the historical lack of a comprehensive pharmaceutical 'strategy' at EU level and how, consequently, policies have developed on something of a piecemeal basis. The discussion reveals that predominantly market harmonisation motives rather than health interests have driven policy in the sector, leading to the (incomplete) regulatory framework. The second part of the chapter analyses this within the parameters set by wider theories of European integration and EU (regulatory) policy-making. This is to underline the study's use of a policy network approach in analysing the politics involved in setting Community pharmaceutical policy.

The development of European pharmaceutical regulation: a synoptic history

Casual observation might suggest that the focus of EU pharmaceutical regulation is on improving the market authorisation process for new drugs (and promoting the industry's competitiveness). Indeed, revising the approval regime has, historically, been the most common element in policy. In accepting that national divergence in member state pricing and reimbursement regimes precludes harmonisation, much (recent) analysis – particularly since the establishment of the European medicines agency in 1995 – has also focused on 'time to market' (TTM) periods for new drugs.[1] This, however, belies the fact that public health concerns first prompted Community and member state interest in medicines regulation. As mentioned in the opening chapter, the *Thalidomide* tragedy crudely exposed the need for stricter medicines testing and market authorisation mechanisms.

In reviewing the EU's history of pharmaceutical regulation, it is useful to divide it into four phases: i) the initial establishment of Community rules for medicines beginning with the first piece of legislation in 1965; ii) multiple state market authorisation commencing in 1975; iii) the need to address increasing international competition and the 1986 Single European Act; and iv) a Community licensing agency since 1995.[2]

Establishing Community rules for medicines

In September 1963 the European Commission convened a meeting of industry representatives, trades union officials, pharmacists, doctors and consumers to discuss the prospective harmonisation of national pharmaceutical legislation. However, as disagreement emerged over whether proof of a drug's 'therapeutic potency' was to be a necessary criterion for market authorisation, no consensus was reached. The Commission's subsequent press release noted that 'the doctors', pharmacists', consumers' and trade union representatives took the view that the requirement was indispensable. The representatives of the industry ... disagreed' (CEC IP 1963). Notwithstanding this early hiccough, Community guidelines for the sector, and rules for medicines registration in particular, were an inevitability as European policy-makers sought to bring their countries together under the common market. Indeed, two years later, in addition to having established stricter guidelines at home, the six member states of the then European Economic Community (EEC) agreed Community-wide controls and standards.

Directive 65/65/EEC was the first piece of Community pharmaceutical legislation. It represented official recognition of the need for a separate policy area for medicines and laid down two important definitions. A medicinal product was defined as: 'any substance or combinations of substances presented for treating or preventing disease in human beings or animals or any substance or combination of substances which may be administered to human beings or animals with a view to making a medical diagnosis or to restoring, correcting or modifying physiological functions in human beings or animals.' And a proprietary medicine was defined as 'any ready prepared medicinal product placed on the market under a special name and in a special pack'. These definitions have underpinned all Community drug legislation since. Equally important were the rules regarding the development and manufacture of medicines and guidelines for post-market monitoring of drug safety (pharmacovigilance) which the Directive set out. As these were agreed within the context of the free movement principles of the common market, rules for authorisation were also elucidated. A product was to be granted market approval only if it was accompanied by documentation providing evidence of the product's safety, efficacy and therapeutic benefit, as verified by the signatures of accredited experts. The Community was thereby setting out the criteria against which the safeguarding of public health was to be measured in order for a drug to be launched. And though some member states initially baulked at the 'proven therapeutic benefit' criterion on the basis that it was too strict (Hancher 1990), the proposal was eventually accepted in 1965.

Additionally, the Directive established the important precept that medicines could not be released onto the market of another member state without the prior agreement and authorisation (by relevant public medical authority) of that state. Community guidelines for the authorisation of medicines with respect to quality, time requirements, and decision-making procedures were also delineated. The emphasis was decidedly on product safety and efficacy, and European industrial policy interests were to be balanced against national health policy concerns. The Community's initial move into pharmaceutical policy had thus been spurred by a common health threat, which in turn prompted a pro-active approach fully endorsed by the member states.

Early European authorisations

With progress on tariff elimination in other sectors progressing, the Commission's next step was to facilitate the intra-Community movement of medicines. Thus, in 1975 came two new pieces of legislation. Directive 75/318/EEC created the mutual recognition or Committee for Proprietary Medicinal Products (CPMP) procedure. A product that had been granted market authorisation by the regulatory authority of one member state could now be granted multiple authorisations to five other member state markets without undergoing additional assessments – previously applications had to be made separately to each national authority. Directive 75/319/EEC set out the original Community rules governing the conduct of clinical trials towards product quality and safety, and harmonised the conditions for granting manufacturing authorisations based on the mutual recognition principle.

Comprising representatives of each member state, the CPMP was to act as a single authorisation body for the EC market. It would review all drug applications on the basis of the Community's 1965 safety, quality and efficacy standards, and then issue an opinion on marketing approval. The Committee was also to arbitrate should a member state object to a product being granted automatic access to its market via the new procedure. However, as the Committee's opinions were only advisory, the member states could, and generally did, choose to ignore them. The sensitivity of healthcare concerns for national governments, and the resulting derogation to the free movement rules under Article 30 (ex 36) of the Treaty – where products could have potential negative health effects – meant that the new rules did not speed market authorisation as envisaged. The opposite in fact resulted, and there were major delays as the member states regularly raised objections. Quite simply, the national governments were unwilling to accept each other's assessments.

Towards overcoming this, in 1983 Directive 83/570/EEC introduced the multi-state procedure under which the minimum number of countries to which authorisation would be extended was dropped from five to two. Manufacturers were thus no longer bound to seek approval in more than two markets unless they so chose. More successful than mutual recognition in terms of the number of applications submitted, the multi-state procedure nonetheless proved cumbersome as well. In 1994, its final year of operation, objections by one or more member states were registered for every product put before it (CPMP 1994). Although all three Directives made a point of underlining that health matters were of primary concern, they were clearly aimed at progress towards a unified medicines market. This would become the Commission's main agenda for future initiatives, especially following the Single European Act (SEA).[3]

A divisive issue to emerge during this period was parallel trade in medicines. Beginning in the 1970s it had become widespread by the mid-1980s (Macarthur 2001) and has continued to grow since. Price differentials for the same products were up to 10 times between EC countries in the mid-1980s (BEUC 1989), and European wholesalers and sellers of bulk pharmaceuticals became active parallel traders. Some member states supported this *arbitrage* for the healthcare savings it brought, while others opposed it as it damaged local industry. Consumer and patient groups were in favour as the practice ensured cheaper and quicker access to high quality medication, while those companies whose products were affected disputed it because of their lost earnings. With the practice burgeoning, it was contested by the affected companies before the European Court of Justice on numerous occasions, but was essentially sanctioned in the 1976 *de Peijper* case.[4] The ECJ ruled that national medicine licensing rules were not to be regarded as a restriction on intra-Community movement until full market harmonisation in pharmaceuticals was attained. This position remains unchanged, and has in fact been given more scope in several rulings since then.

The Single European Market programme
The Single European Act of 1986 elaborated a vision to establish a Single European Market for the free movement of all goods, services and capital by 1992. This was the Community's response to the need to compete more effectively in global markets, especially with the US and Japan setting up free trade areas of their own. Despite derogations again pertaining to sensitive areas such as public health and national security, the measures laid down by the SEA demanded member state compliance. Policy decisions thus came to be taken within the context of meeting the 1992 deadline.

Also in 1986, a retired Commission official, Paolo Cecchini, was appointed to lead an investigation into the costs of 'non-Europe' (to underline the benefits of a single European market). Despite its optimism over the market liberalisation process generally, the resulting 1988 Cecchini Report pointed out areas which required attention. And in an echo of the 1985 White Paper, pharmaceuticals were cited as a problem in being 'irretrievably linked to public health'. Nevertheless, with the 1992 deadline looming it was clear that future policy for medicines would now be taken under the auspices of the SEM rather than on the basis of public health requirements. Just as the push towards the single market has affected the nature of Community health and healthcare competences (Theofilatou & Maarse 1998), so too has it impacted on pharmaceutical policy.

In 1987, once more with a view to improving the authorisation process, Directive 87/22/EEC was agreed. The Directive created a new process, the concertation or centralised procedure, which was applicable only to biotechnologically-developed and other high technology products. Manufacturers were required to simultaneously submit their applications to the CPMP and one member state (the intended market), and once both had completed their evaluations, together they facilitated discussions between the applicant company and the other national authorities regarding access to their markets. This was a new approach by the Commission, as the 'competent authorities [were required] to consult with each other systematically within the framework of the CPMP, from the moment an application was received' (Hankin 1996: 11). Although biotechnology policy falls outside our discussion, the Directive's mention here is to underline the Commission's agenda. With biotechnology at the time an emerging field, the Commission was seeking harmonised standards even before they had been created (Vogel 1998). This obviously was with a view towards 1992 and the need for a single evaluation procedure. And by limiting the products subject to the procedure, the Commission was also seeking a more general transfer of regulatory authority from the member states to the Community (Friedel & Freundlich 1994). The member states were thus not so much losing authority as the Community was gaining it.

Parallel trade remained a problem in the post-SEA period, though now in terms of a future single market. Growing price differences between the member states on single products had only consolidated the practice and, via rulings in cases such as *Stephar* (1981),[5] the ECJ continued to permit it. In this somewhat unsettled environment, Directive 89/105/EEC, the 'Transparency Directive', was agreed. This obliged the member states to adopt 'transparent, objective and verifiable criteria' in setting medicine prices and their inclusion in national health insurance systems (see Chapter 7). Further legislation pertaining to labelling and packaging, advertising and sales promotion, and wholesale distribution followed.[6] And in 1992, Regulation (EEC) 1768/92 – the Supplementary Protection Certificate (SPC) – established a certification of extended patent protection for those drugs deemed to have had too short a period of coverage compared to the costs of their development (see Chapter 5). This was (and remains) a controversial issue in the area of medicines policy more widely. But it too was taken within the context of meeting the provisions of the SEM.

Despite the Community agreeing such wide-ranging and important measures, it remained unable to tackle the pricing question. Its proposals for a second, or at least amended, Transparency Directive were shelved in 1992 due to a lack of member state support. The intractability of the pricing issue – in terms of even reducing intra-EU price differentials – led in 1996 to the publication of a Communication on the development of an official EU 'industrial policy' for pharmaceuticals.[7] Agreed after several years of negotiation, the Communication was another major turning-point. It represented an acknowledgement by the Commission that there still remained considerable barriers to market harmonisation and that the requirements of the single market were not being adequately served.

Eight years prior, the Cecchini Report had concluded that '[regulation of] the market registration procedure for new products and price controls [is] the most important from the standpoint of the European market' (Cecchini et al. 1988: 66). Yet by the mid-1990s there was still no effective centralised authorisation process – the recommendations of the CPMP were not binding under either the multi-state or concertation procedures, and unanimity was seldom. Because of the failure of the former in particular, the Commission instigated a series of extensive consultations from the late 1980s onwards regarding the need for a new and more independent authority capable of binding decision-making. The end-result, some five years later, was a Community medicines agency designed to function as a centralised authorisation office for medicinal products within the single market. Despite little real progress on further 'europeanisation' since the establishment of the agency, it is clear that the SEM had a major influence on the direction of EU pharmaceutical policy. And that single market issues rather than health concerns per se, were going to dominate the Commission's future approach to the sector.

An agency approach to market authorisation
Established in 1995 (via Regulation No (EEC) 2309/93) as the European Medicines Evaluation Agency, the EMEA represented the coming to fruition of many years of political wrangling. Ruling on applications for market authorisation, the agency is mandated the task of product assessment and approval for all prospective new medicines aimed for the Community market. Accompanying the EMEA was Directive 93/39/EEC under which the multi-state procedure was replaced by a binding decentralised process, with applications made directly to the agency. The member states would only be able to query the agency's recommendations on the grounds that they could be shown to have a negative public health impact. The CPMP was to remain the arbiter where a member state may disagree with the agency's decision (though in practice applications rarely get this far).

In looking at much of the literature on the EMEA, one could be forgiven for thinking that its role lies simply in the issuing of market authorisations for new products. Yet this is only one element of its wider official remit to decide on which drugs are safe, efficacious and of high enough quality to be granted (and maintain) market access. The agency is not, however – as some thought or feared it might become – a European version of the US FDA. It is not responsible for anything beyond therapeutic medicines, and it lacks the FDA's executive powers to penalise – beyond levying fines – any derogation from, or misapplication of, its rules. Further, healthcare considerations are beyond its remit (although, by deciding on which drugs are to be sold in the EU, it does have an indirect effect on member state's healthcare policy). And unlike the FDA, which is a federal body, the EMEA regime co-exists with national procedures, it does not replace them. Still, given the clout it carries in terms of the Commission's reliance on its recommendations, it does represent the only quasi-regulatory body of its kind in the EU.

Ten years since its launch debate about the agency continues. As will be shown later, the official rationale offered by the Commission at the time of the EMEA's inauguration were not those invoked during the late 1980s when the plan for a medicines agency was still in its formative stages. And despite general satisfaction expressed by the Commission, the member states and regulatory officials, it continues to draw criticism (e.g. Abraham & Lewis 2000, Garattini & Bertele' 2001). The point to be made here, however, is that since the SEM and the creation of the agency, there has been a new decision-making approach to medicine policy in the Community. The use of an American-style regulatory authority reflects an acknowledgement by both the Commission and the member states of the need for independent regulation of industrial sectors within the single market. While the actual operations of the EMEA will be analysed later, its inclusion in this history serves to indicate the direction of Community thinking and objectives *vis-à-vis* pharmaceutical regulation.

The lack of a coherent EU pharmaceutical 'strategy'
At this stage several points require reiteration. First, the history of EU pharmaceutical regulation is an inconsistent one. The earliest medicines legislation was passed in 1965 in the wake of the *Thalidomide* tragedy and addressed public health concerns. Since then most competences have fallen under the industrial policy frame, having been enacted primarily in relation to the single market programme. And while this reflects the Commission's lack of healthcare competences, two major pieces of legislation with healthcare impacts – the Transparency Directive and the EMEA – have been agreed. Second, although the SEM may have prompted much policy initiation from the Commission, policy has been generated by other factors as well. Obligations under international trade agreements such as the GATT have meant loosening the national protection of the industry in Europe. And mounting pressure to address the question of affordable access to medicines for the world's poorer countries has seen the member states agree to the suspending of drug patent rights in the case of a public health emergency.[8] Other European institutions have also had a hand, even if indirectly, in shaping the regulatory framework. Most notable has been the ECJ which, through various judgements in relation to healthcare, competition and the free movement

principles, has affected the policy environment in which pharmaceutical policy is set.

Despite Community involvement in pharmaceutical regulation since the mid-1960s, therefore, there has not been a consistent strategy. There have been major steps forward in grounding EU-wide standards in some areas, but stalemate and even backward steps in others. Because pricing and reimbursement remain national level matters, the result for the Commission are competences made up primarily by industrial policy concerns. This is in contrast to related sectors such as biotechnology or medical devices where the Community's regulatory history is much shorter, but reflects a clearer purpose and powers (Altenstetter 2001). The lack of a singular strategy has also meant that policy developments have often been in response to particular requirements or obligations. Competences have been developed as necessary or even, as will be shown, when pushed for by specific actors.

Having highlighted that pharmaceuticals lack a clear status within the Community's range of competence, the discussion now turns to the process of European integration and the EU's policy-making dynamics in order to help make sense of this. The question is whether such theoretical approaches are able to explain or offer any insights into the evolution of the EU regulatory framework. And to see if they help to elucidate how and why industry is the main beneficiary of this regime as the study posits.

Medicines and traditional integration theory

European integration and policy-making theories provide ideas and themes which are helpful towards understanding where and why specific EU pharmaceutical policies developed. Acknowledging the distinction made by Hix (1994) between theories of European integration in *stricto sensu* and what he terms the 'politics of the EU policy-process', these ideas and themes relate to both the macro- and meso-levels. We begin with the former.

Neo-functionalism: pharmaceutical policy as 'spill-over'
Depending on their point of departure, the early integration scholars of the 1940s tended to follow one of two main lines. The federalists and functionalists were led by the visions of Jean Monnet and the work of Mitrany (1966) respectively. Their focus was on the end-product of integration, i.e. what form the integrated Europe should take. The transactionalists meanwhile, headed by Deutsch (1966), sought to understand the conditions requisite for political integration to be possible in the first place. Both approaches served to generate the academic debate that would later culminate in the development of neo-functionalism as the then leading theory of European integration.

During the 1960s neo-functionalism became the theory of choice, particularly amongst American social scientists with Haas (1968) at the fore. By combining the competition element in the political process of traditional pluralist thinking with the gradual nature of political change understanding proffered by Mitrany, the neo-functionalists sought to show how the European integration process was as much dependent on political action as economic determinism. Central to this was disproving the functionalist idea of a distinction between functional or technical policies (i.e. involving economic interests), and those which were more political or constitutional. Pharmaceutical policy proves the point given its inextricability from the healthcare context. For while other industrial commodities may, from the EU standpoint at least, comply with the functional/technical category, medicines do not. The market remains unharmonised precisely because of political factors. The health and industrial policy implications mean that pharmaceuticals are both a constitutional and functional matter, and member states are therefore particularly sensitive where any European policy is concerned. Nevertheless, via what is arguably its best-known premise, the concept of 'spill-over', neo-functionalism does prove useful with regard to explaining the impetus behind the Community framework for pharmaceutical regulation.

Central to the spill-over premise – where 'pressure in one sector could demand integration (or changes in standards) in order to complete the process of policy change' (Church 1996: 17) – was the idea that the integration process would prove self-sustaining. Developing this as an inheritance from Mitrany, the neo-functionalists attempted to gauge the relevance of the new EC institutions in the integration process. They argued that as supranational constructs, these bodies could (and did) foster integration of their own accord. The role of the ECJ as guardian and instigator of Community law (superseding national legislation) may have been the embodiment of this idea, but some member states were not entirely comfortable with a dynamic that they might not be in control of. Here, the 1966 Luxembourg Compromise represented a watershed and put paid to any illusions those who sought a federalist European 'super-state' might at the time have had. Without engaging the specifics of the Luxembourg Compromise – especially as it has not frequently been invoked – it served to underline that the integration process was not self-sustaining without member state support, and was in part responsible for the 'eurosclerosis' of the 1960s and 1970s.[9] The SEA revived the integration process and a new brand of spill-over emerged. This related to establishing a common European market by 1992.

The SEM demanded the elimination of inter-Community tariffs and other access to market barriers and, notwithstanding that there is still no single medicines market, it was earlier shown that most aspects of the Community's regulatory framework can in fact be attributed to the pursuit of the SEM. As Table 2.4 earlier highlighted, legislation pertaining to the standardisation of packaging guidelines for medicines, the type and manner of presenting information on package inserts/leaflets, and common rules on the advertising of medicines, all reflect priorities related to the single market, having evolved as spill-over from other provisions relating to the '1992 programme'. The SEM not only coincides with efforts to establish a single market for medicines, but in fact defines much of the regulatory framework.

Nevertheless, spill-over is not the sole influence on the EU's competences in the sector. As mentioned several times, important questions relating to the pricing and reimbursement of medicines have not been addressed at EU level, making it clear that spill-over is not pervasive and that the member states retain considerable autonomy. It was earlier established that this can be attributed to the explicit exclusion of healthcare from Community competences under the Treaties. So although neo-functionalism may explain developments within the industrial side of the policy dichotomy, it cannot explain why spill-over from the SEM did not generate healthcare competences (as it had done for social policies in other areas). That European integration does not proceed without member state support – that spill-over is not an unchecked momentum generated by supranational institutions – is one of the key tenets of intergovernmentalism as the other classical theory of European integration.

Intergovernmentalism: no Community role in healthcare

Developed out of the realist position in international relations theory with Hoffmann (1966) its leading proponent, intergovernmentalism offered a check on spill-over by showing that the member states, via the policy-making structure and procedures of the Community, remained firmly in control of both the pace and direction of integration. There are numerous variations on intergovernmental theory,[10] and although a considerable simplification, their shared premise of national self-interest being at the heart of the integration process does account for why the healthcare aspect of medicines regulation has not become a Community competence, i.e. why subsidiarity plays such a major role. Governments are neither practically nor ideologically prepared to have the EU legislate over national healthcare policies as would be required of a single medicines market; pricing and reimbursement thus remain the sticking-point.[11]

Also relevant from within intergovernmental approach is Hoffman's (1966) distinction between 'high' and 'low' politics. The former encompasses security, defence and foreign policy, while the latter is concerned with welfare and economic policy. The argument was that it could not be taken as a foregone conclusion that the member states would accept integration in high politics areas simply because they were (more or less) agreed on low politics concerns i.e. single market tariff elimination and any resulting social policy implications. This is certainly the case over pharmaceutical policy where, although a low politics area for the Community (i.e. a single market matter), in being tied to healthcare policy, it is a high politics matter for the member states. Consequently intergovernmental agreement is with regard to not mandating the Community a wider role rather than doing so. Community policies thus exist where economic priorities are at stake (low politics) but do not involve the exercise of executive powers related to healthcare (high politics). This reflects the policy clash in the sector, resulting in competences being shared between the member states and the Commission, and the fact that the EU has to date only been able to legislate in areas relating to industrial policy.[12]

At this stage two important points are to be noted. First, neo-functionalist spill-over is perhaps more intuitive than it is empirical (Pollack 1997). Institutions may matter in the integration process – indeed, there is an increasingly impressive body of literature, particularly under the banner of 'new institutionalism'[13] – but neo-functionalist theory is not really able to go beyond suggesting a *de jure* link between them. Second, the intergovernmental focus on member state self-interest may serve to elucidate their behaviour in the integration process generally, but it does not necessarily explain policy outcomes. And both theories fail to account for circumstances which exert integrationist pressures from outside the immediate Community frame; where policy decisions are taken neither on the basis of 'simple' member state self-interest, nor the result of an inherent supranational dynamic.

Liberal intergovernmentalism: domestic priorities and supranational policies
Recognising this failing, more recent work has focused on how member state agendas are shaped. Here, Moravcsik's (1993) liberal intergovernmentalist perspective concentrates on links between national decision-making and international co-operation. Integration is seen in supply and demand terms, where the demand for integration is shaped within the domestic context, and is then supplied through intergovernmental negotiation and bargaining. Hence Moravcsik's argument that understanding domestic politics is a 'precondition' for analysing member state behaviour. This is especially as the member states do not necessarily have fixed preferences; these change just as governments change. (Also, as the priority for any government is to remain in office, this too influences the demand-side in any intergovernmental bargaining on the supply-side). In asserting the pre-eminence of national governments, the theory recognises that common goals – even if deriving from differing national circumstances – may also promote integrationist tendencies. Here, one can look to the pressures exerted on domestic politics by the global trade liberalisation regimes of the WTO. Or else, it may be because of the local effects of negative externalities such as air and water pollution that the member states agree common environmental standards. Pertaining more specifically to pharmaceuticals, the International Conference on Harmonisation (ICH) and the Pharmaceutical Inspections Convention (PIC) – both of which push for global standards[14] – exert pressures on European governments individually and together within the context of the SEM. There is, therefore, no inherent supranational dynamic within this view.

Liberal intergovernmentalism holds that EU governments are willing to co-operate towards further integration, both in order to fulfil domestic requirements and as a manner of consolidating their position relative to each other. On the one hand they will agree to the concession of authority over issues where they feel the Community is more likely to be able to conserve their interests – particularly in a redistributive manner – on the other they remain steadfast over issues where national interests are at stake. Since the member states accept that certain aspects of pharmaceutical policy, such as market access and advertising (i.e. those matters relating to the single market), are better regulated on their behalf by the Community, there is intergovernmental co-operation. Areas which are more sensitive, such as the pricing of medicines, they continue to guard jealously. And although all countries may be agreed on not conceding pricing and reimbursement competences to the Commission, their reasons stem from domestic considerations. Their respective lack of interest in a consolidated medicines market – and indeed the variance in their support for specific initiatives – are based on national concerns. These may in many respects be common concerns e.g. cost-containment, but they are not necessarily shared given each country's particular requirements.

Although there are several critiques,[15] Moravcsik's assessment flounders primarily in respect of the degree to which it minimises the role played by the European institutions. In their examination of the Single European Market, Armstrong & Bulmer (1998) argue that Moravcsik also neglects the comparative politics literature on agenda-shaping. Indeed, as the later case-studies will show, while the European institutions have played a considerable part in shaping the EU's regulatory framework for medicines, so too have the member states' interests and priorities affected outcomes; the impasse over completing the market is at member state insistence. Moreover, medicines policy cannot simply be slipped into a two-level analogy. Specific regulatory policies may be shaped by national circumstances, which member states seek to protect at EU level, but common health threats and wider duties regarding criteria for market authorisation and medicine testing, are in all their interests.

On their own, therefore, the neo-functionalist and intergovernmentalist theories are incomplete in accounting for the development of EU pharmaceutical policy.[16] While the former (spill-over in particular) is relevant to understanding the economic rationale and industrial policy nature of the majority of Community pharmaceutical policy (single market-related), it fails when the healthcare aspect is invoked. The latter can explain why healthcare policy concerns, including pricing, remain a sticking-point, but does not necessarily explain policy outcomes. And the 'liberal' version can (to a degree) account for exogenous factors in influencing integration and promoting member state co-operation, but cannot sufficiently account for the roles of the ECJ and Commission in shaping the framework. So although such macro-theories tend to lose their explanatory power when it comes to policy decisions (Peterson 1995), as integration is an 'inherently dynamic, expansionary process which serves, amongst other things, to construct and reconstruct the contexts in which governmental choices and intergovernmental bargaining takes place' (Stone Sweet & Caporaso 1998: 119), they do establish certain contextual issues. As this is particularly with respect to where the EU is able to act, they have been shown to be useful in understanding the development of the EU pharmaceutical framework.

Multi-level governance and contemporary perspectives
Because of this lack of explanatory power, and particularly since the 1992 Maastricht Treaty on European Union (TEU), there has been a shift away from these broader perspectives. The internal dynamics of the Community polity in particular have attracted attention e.g. the 'agenda-setting' role of the European Commission (Peters 1996); interest group activities in driving policy (Mazey & Richardson 1993); the de facto integration role of the ECJ and European law (Wincott 1996); and the dynamics of comitology (Wessels 1998). There has also been a renewed focus on the Community institutions and institutional actors, such as the Parliament, in pushing an integrationist agenda in their own right – new-institutionalist theory – though in a less assumed manner than expressed under (neo-)functionalism. This reflects an acceptance of the EU as a new system of governance,[17] and one which does not readily lend itself to any singular theoretical categorisation.

The most widely-cited of these perspectives is that of multi-level governance (which Börzel (1997a, b) relates to the governance school of policy networks). It forwards the notion of a blurring between domestic and international politics, and portrays the Community as a *sui generis* form of policymaking:[18] 'a series of multi-level games fought out between an increasingly large number of policy actors – public and private – who exploit the many opportunities presented by different policy arenas' leading to the conclusion that 'there is some kind of internal dynamic which has the capacity to generate new policy proposals over time' (Richardson 1997: xi). This differentiates it from either the state-centric or supranational model (Hooghe 1995), with the Community assuming the lead role by fostering co-operation amongst member states (Marks et al. 1996). By highlighting the role of national and subnational actors, it also focuses on the policy-process rather than integration per se.

Critiques of this internal gaming view of the EU polity centre around it offering a good description but being limited as an explanatory or analytical perspective (Pierson 1996). For our purposes, however, the conception of the EU as a new form of governance is of interest insofar as it *is* descriptive. Multi-level governance captures the dispersal of power within EU policymaking, and accommodates the argument that medicines regulation at EU level results from the interplay between many (embedded) actors spanning both the healthcare and industrial policy communities. In other words, that it is not a simple case of intergovernmental bargaining. Consequently, it is the fact that such a criss-crossing of actors and interests does characterise the policy-process – not whether or not this amounts to a predictive view thereof – which is relevant to this discussion; particularly as it is at the level of policy analysis that the evolution of EU pharmaceutical competences can be best understood. Accordingly, the next element of the discussion is how the EU regulates or sets policy within the multi-level governance conception. This provides further insight into how EU regulatory competences for medicines have developed.

Medicines and regulatory policy in the EU

The continuing 'encroachment' of Brussels into many areas of national public policy has seen EU regulation become an area of much academic attention. In particular, the Community's shift from controlling the economic reins of the single market to exercising a role which encompasses wider and more complex social policy responsibilities has generated much research. While this may conform with the spill-over logic of neo-functionalism, it does not necessarily sit with an intergovernmentalist perspective. How this transfer of authority is taking place when so many national politicians are, at least publicly, keen to keep the 'Eurocrats' out of domestic affairs, has driven much of the research. Indeed, the practice of regulation by the Community has been central to the integration process, especially since the SEM.

Regulatory governance and the 'regulatory state'

The increasingly broad nature of EU regulation can in part be traced to the long histories of the European state being responsible not only for the market, through public ownership of enterprise and centralised administration, but also for social control. It is a tradition that helped give rise to the post-Second World War welfare democracies and which many countries are now struggling to maintain. This European approach is distinctly opposed to statutory regulation in the US which involves the use of independent agencies exercising legislative and administrative functions beyond state control. And while American regulation has developed primarily as a means of correcting market failures through a restrained state function, in Europe the state has been at the heart of macroeconomic stabilisation by serving a redistributive function in society. The emergent EU 'model' appears to incorporate aspects of both traditions. On the one side Community regulation involves a direct hand in the operation of the single market and, consequently, certain social responsibilities which result. On the other, the EU has turned to a variety of quasi-independent agencies to oversee particular policy areas. This trend mirrors developments in some member states themselves (e.g. France and the UK), and there are now sixteen such agencies.

In light of this changing regulatory environment, and the Commission's constrained remit, pharmaceutical policy would appear to defy contemporary theorising about the nature of EU regulation more widely. For it is generally held that the jurisdiction of Community regulation is not simply bound to the functional aspects of the single market, but also the 'broader regulatory concerns of the European Polity' (Joerges 1997). This view holds that the Commission's role – abetted by ECJ decisions – is predominantly concerned with 'the shaping of market processes i.e. with defining the conditions for market access and market operation (old or classical regulatory theory); and second with curbing negative external impacts on the public or workforce from productive activities and individual consumption (new regulatory policy)' (Héritier et al. 1996: 9). Accordingly, it ought not to be surprising that EU regulation has extended beyond an economic remit to cover social areas as well (at least insofar as they are related to the single market).[19] Nor should one be surprised at the ever-growing volume of Community law being generated as a result. Seeing the EU in this light helps to account for the increasing pervasiveness of Community influence in member state affairs. It is also a view which holds that Community legislation can be equated with more or less the same thing as public policy (Radaelli 1998), and has given rise to the perception of regulation in the EU as a new form of governance.

Perhaps the most developed expression of this *sui generis* system of governance is the 'regulatory state' model first set out by Majone (1994). This shows the development of Community regulation as something distinct from both the American system of statutory regulation and the European *dirigiste* state, though acknowledging the influences of both. As the EU does not undertake redistribution and stabilisation functions in the manner of nation-states (lacking the primary functions of government), it must rely on (and seek to expand) its regulatory competences in order to establish its authority. And it does so via the Commission. Regulatory policy is perceived of in demand and supply terms, with the European Commission on the supply-side and organised interests (including member state governments) on the demand-side. And three variables are seen as responsible for the growth of Community regulation: 'the tightness and rigidity of the Community budget; the desire of the Commission to increase its influence by expanding its competences; and the preference of multinational firms for dealing with a uniform set of rules rather than with [twenty-five] different national regulations' (Majone 1994).

The perception of the EU as a regulatory state is thus said to offer a plausible clarification of the on-going proliferation of Community regulation despite intergovernmental processes being at its heart. The willingness of the member states to empower the Community in this way – a transfer of economic powers without a complimentary transfer of political powers (Tsoukalis 1998) – also means that the regulatory state is in essence a manner of deregulation at national level. This is not only in instances where the member states feel that the EU may be better placed to oversee certain interests, but also where 'European measures are a useful scapegoat, a way of avoiding direct political responsibilities in difficult areas like cutting back industries with excess capacity ... or structural readjustment of public finance' (Radaelli 1998: 5). With the Council of Ministers taking all final policy decisions, this helps unravel the paradox of national politicians complaining over excess bureaucracy being imposed by Brussels at the same time as they appear to embrace it. And this is supported by Wilks's (1996) argument that, because of chronic budgetary difficulties in the EU, thereby limiting the possibility of continually developing new spending programmes, regulation in fact provides the best (and cheapest) means by which the EU can make (public) policy.

The regulatory state view is thus applicable to the EU pharmaceutical sector on two fronts. First with regard to the role played by the Commission in establishing the framework as currently exists (supply). This is evident in its continuing pursuit of an 'industrial policy' for pharmaceuticals and its attempts to shore up support for addressing the pricing issue within a single market context (see Chapter 7). Additionally, the Commission's role reflects its interest in increasing its authority in pharmaceuticals specifically, and regulation more widely. And second, in terms of both the lobbying the Commission is subject to from medicine companies, and the pressures exerted by the member states (demand).[20]

Negative versus positive integration: Which way for medicines?   Related to these broader views on EU regulation is the question of process. By setting 1969 as the date for a European common market, the 1957 Treaty of Rome invoked the political dynamics of 'positive' and 'negative' integration. Negative integration involves the elimination of national barriers to the free movement of goods and services (old regulatory policy), while positive integration is concerned with the establishment of common economic and social policies to define the conditions under which EU markets operate (new regulatory policy). The former involves liberalisation and the rescinding of national authority to the Community through tariff and quota reductions, and is the more straightforward process given Treaty obligations (supranational). The latter requires the active harmonisation of national regulations and goes through the Council of Ministers (intergovernmental). Both processes were envisaged to run concomitantly towards achieving the common market, but the Luxembourg Compromise that unanimity be achieved in the Council meant that negative integration came to the fore. As arbiter over matters involving the single market, this in turn accorded the ECJ a prominent role in the integration process. Through the considerable amount of case law generated between 1970 and 1985, the Court has in fact been credited with giving rise to the SEA via negative integration (Stone Sweet & Caporaso 1998).

At the same time, numerous legal decisions in social policy fields have granted the Community a greater mandate than was perhaps envisaged in 1957, and accorded the ECJ a positive integration role as well. Expansive rulings in some cases have ensured the Court (and the Commission) a major say in areas such as gender equity and social or environmental protection. Pierson (1996) has shown this 'regulation-creating' ECJ role to often result in changes on a national level which would otherwise have taken considerably longer to occur; thereby promoting integration. Rulings in the field of environmental protection and green policies for business have even resulted in completely new legislation in the absence of earlier national regimes (Majone 1996).

Since they support the earlier arguments regarding spill-over and intergovernmental bargaining over sensitive policy areas, positive and negative integration are also relevant to understanding Community pharmaceutical policy. The former applies to the industrial policy dimension of pharmaceutical regulation, and the latter to the healthcare dimension. And as regards the Court's role, issues such as parallel imports and trademark exhaustion confirm a pro-active mandate in pharmaceutical policy. Here it was the Court which established Community policy, not the Commission or other EU institutions via spill-over, nor the member states rescinding authority of their own accord.

Product versus process regulation: Healthcare versus industrial policy?
The new and old regulatory policy distinction also gives rise to 'product' versus 'process' regulation. Product regulation involves the establishment of common standards on goods and services (negative integration) and characterised early Community legislation. Intergovernmental agreement can be expected because differing national requirements over product safety and quality would undermine the market harmonisation goals of the SEM.[21] Despite derogations in sensitive areas,[22] it is thus assumed that member states will reach agreement on product regulation because of their common interest in a single market. This is not the case for process regulations which affect the more social and externally-impacting factors involved in regulating economic activity, and where a pro-active hand is required e.g. occupational safety requirements. Here the absence of a Community regime may see member states cut back on national standards to increase their own competitiveness. As the incentive to raise standards, whether individually or jointly, is thus limited, the rationale for the member states to pursue harmonisation is to avoid having to compete on an unequal footing with those with laxer standards. It was only with the SEA, for example, that EU regulation in areas such as environmental policy became possible. Even then it was up to the Commission to ensure that a situation of social and ecological dumping in some member states did not take place (Scharpf 1996). Positive integration can thus be linked predominantly with progress in the harmonisation of product regulation, though it has had a much weaker impact on harmonising process regulation.

Product regulation has dominated the pharmaceutical policy agenda. Most regulatory policy is 'old' as spill-over from the single market programme. Only perhaps the Transparency Directive and the establishment of the EMEA – both which have a healthcare and/or social policy dimension – can be seen as process regulation. Unsurprisingly, these two policies required considerably longer to be agreed, and involved difficult negotiations amongst the stakeholders. Pricing and reimbursement also relate to process regulation, where member state fears over what a single medicines market may mean in terms of their own authority over healthcare matters and local industry, prevents agreement on mandating the Commission a greater or process regulation role. Again, this is in contrast to other industrial sectors where there has been more consensus on a broader Community function.

As the focus of this study is not EU regulation itself, this précis has simply served to show that by virtue of the single market, the EU is able and required to regulate in both an economic and social capacity. It also shows that under the SEM, member states lose much of their ability to regulate over their own national markets and that the Court has had a major hand in pushing integration and promoting the consolidation of the regulatory state. The ECJ has been especially active in the pharmaceutical field given the gap in Community competences.

Making pharmaceutical policy within the regulatory state

The regulatory state model can thus be used to establish a framework which contextualises policy decisions generally, and those over pharmaceuticals specifically. A Commission relying on regulation to increase its authority is applicable to the pharmaceutical framework in light of the impasse over the single market. Policy is made wherever it can be achieved, resulting in much 'old' regulatory policy and an ad hoc framework. What the regulatory state model does not do, however, is to show why Community regulation exists in specific cases though not in others. As mentioned, the policy network, as a meso-level approach, is especially valuable here. And it can be tied into the regulatory state view. For the relationship between a Commission supplying regulation and demand-side actors vying for influence not only means a blurring of the public and private, but also that groups of (competing) actors form over specific proposals.

The discussion on the regulatory state also makes clear several further points important to the study. First, it fits squarely within the multi-level governance view by offering insight into the unique dispersal of authority in the EU frame, and shows that '"state" capacity at the EU level is overdeveloped in the area of regulation and underdeveloped in terms of redistribution and stabilization functions' (Rosamond 2000: 154). Hence the Community's regulatory framework for medicines being heavy on single market industrial policy concerns and light on healthcare policy competences. Second, the model accounts for the Commission's function as supplier of regulation (supported by the ECJ), such that various demand-side actors lobby to have their interests met in EU policy. While relevant to all policy fields it is especially so for pharmaceuticals, both in terms of the Commission acting as regulator over private and public interests,[23] and with regard to the healthcare versus industrial policy bargaining scenarios in which it is involved. The Commission has often found itself at odds with both the industry and the member states, not to mention with the host of variegated interests in between e.g. wholesalers and distributors, pharmacists, doctors' and patients' groups, etc.

With the emphasis on negative integration, therefore, it is not surprising that the Community's medicines framework leans towards support of the industry. (Single market) policy is simply easier to agree and implement, and the Commission is generally seeking to increase its powers wherever possible. This results in it being susceptible to influence, and contributes to the framework being heavily shaped by the interests of the industry – those of the research-oriented companies in particular. This is also because of a similar bias in countries with a strong innovative industry (the UK, Germany and Sweden), and a Commission which is seeking to promote an 'efficiency regime' to 'meet the political objectives of a single European market and the commercial agendas of transnational pharmaceutical companies' (Lewis & Abraham 2001: 53). Furthermore, despite the Commission being 'totally biased towards policy entrepreneurship' (Radaelli 1998: 4), the single market–subsidiarity clash precludes it taking harmonisation forward of its own accord.

Where positive integration is to be achieved, therefore, it is posited that pharmaceutical policy is often driven by networks comprising the Commission and other actors (including the member states) whose interests are from both the healthcare and industrial policy spheres. These form over specific policy proposals to see to what extent they can influence the final outcome.[24] Indeed, even if not specific to the pharmaceutical case, the unique system of EU regulation and governance leads to the view that 'The EU, with its sectoralization, the functional differentiation and fragmentation of policies, as well as the dominance of corporate actors in a horizontal web of interorganizational relationships at the negotiating level, appears the most ideal area of application for policy network analysis' (Héritier et al. 1996: 7). This has as much to do with the nature of the EU policy process as it does with a particular conception of policy networks. So although Héritier et al. take a seemingly specific and exclusive definition of networks, the increasing body of theoretical and empirical literature on the EU as new form of policy-making (and the role of networks therein) would lend support to such a view.

Adjusting the lens
The aim here was not to provide a single theory of EU pharmaceutical policy developments; assuming that this would actually be possible. Instead, by assessing the relevance of more accredited theories in view of the trade-off in policy interests which defines the sector, it was to provide an initial theoretical perspective on how EU competences have developed. Acknowledging that the body of theoretical literature continues to evolve, the discussion has nevertheless contextualised the emergence and evolution of the regulatory framework and why, therefore, there remains a policy impasse over completion of the single market. It has shown to what extent macro-level influences can shape the EU's capacity to make policy for medicines, and equally, where this level of analysis falters. Moreover, it outlines the boundaries which frame the

behaviour (and indeed, effectiveness) of the policy networks at the meso-level. This adds cogence to the point that politics and political factors have moulded the regulatory framework as currently exists.

The study thus keeps with the dynamic, multi-level gaming view of EU policy-making outlined above. For it is argued that the nature of current EU pharmaceutical policies and the ad hoc framework which has resulted, stem in large part from the competing interests of the main stakeholders. And while it is clear that the framework which governs medicines in the EU has been predominately shaped by old regulatory policy, so too is it obvious that the healthcare dimension, as a member state competence, precludes all policy being made by the Commission. The former is driven by the single market and the latter is dependent on meso-level policy outcomes achieved amongst networks. As it is necessary to understand how policy has been made within this environment, the remainder of the study concentrates on what Hix might term the 'politics of the EU policy-process for pharmaceuticals'. This accommodates the fact that there is a host of inputs into European pharmaceutical policy, and is able to contextualise the role of actors within such an environment. It is also compatible with the wider European integration theories, as it recognises the roles played by spill-over as well as the European institutions and member states.

Notes

1 For instance Walsh (1999), Hennings (2000) or Redmond (2004).
2 The recently-completed review of Community pharmaceutical legislation (CEC 2004) may now mean a fifth phase, but it is currently too early to assess whether this is the case. Moreover, given the Commission's continuing lack of healthcare competences – and judging by the Directive and Regulation agreed in the context of this review – it is unlikely to bring any fundamental changes in the regulation of the sector.
3 From 1986 onwards, legislation pertaining to the manufacture, assessment, and sale of various other types of medicinal product were also set down, each by separate Directive e.g. immunological products, veterinary products, homeopathic products, etc.
4 Case C-104/75 *Officier van Justitie* v. *de Peijper* [1976] ECR 613.
5 Case C-187/80 *Merck* v. *Stephar* [1981] ECR 2063.
6 Directives 92/27/EEC, 92/26/EEC, and 92/25/EEC.
7 Resolution 96/C136/04.
8 This was a crucial outcome of the World Trade Organisation's November 2001 meeting in Doha. Whether it would have gone through without the Anthrax scare in the US following the 11 September 2001 terrorist attack on the World Trade Centre buildings in New York is perhaps unclear.
9 'Eurosclerosis' refers to the slowdown in measures to facilitate European integration from the mid-1960s through the late 1970s. This followed French President de Gaulle having precipitated a constitutional crisis over the use of qualified majority voting for decisions affecting the common market. Known as the

'empty chair' crisis because of France's refusal to take its seat in the Council, it was resolved by the Luxembourg Compromise the following year, with agreement on the need for unanimity to pass legislation where 'very important [national] interests are at stake'. Defence, national security, health and welfare policy fell within this qualification.

10 For a discussion see Haltern (1995).

11 It is for this reason that the member states insisted on the exclusion of healthcare from Community competences and sought a clear, Treaty-based expression of this at the 1996 Intergovernmental Conference (IGC) in Amsterdam. The unambiguous language of Article 152 of the Amsterdam Treaty compared to that in the Maastricht text (ex 129), makes clear the strength of their resolve.

12 This competence-sharing reflects Weiler's (1994) view that European law is supranational while policy-making is intergovernmental. As European legislation on the single market finds its constitutional basis in the Treaties, much of it supersedes that of the member states. Infringements against Treaty stipulations can result in sanction, though the development of EU policies/competences within the framework set down by the Treaties first requires each member state to agree in the Council of Ministers. Pharmaceutical policy finds itself in the grey area of the middle. The industrial policy side fits within the SEM, and is therefore supranational (law), while its healthcare aspects ensure that policy-making remains an intergovernmental matter.

13 A stream in political science which reasserts (through a redefinition of) the role and place of 'institutions', which includes structures, treaties, legislation, etc. Policy-making does not simply take place via such institutions as neutral vehicles, but rather they contribute to the policy environment, thereby affecting outcomes e.g. Armstrong & Bulmer (1998), Bulmer (1997, 1998), Checkel (1998) or Warleigh (2001).

14 The ICH seeks to negotiate common standards for the regulation of pharmaceutical preparations in Europe, the US and Japan in order to speed the market approval process. It is co-sponsored by the national regulatory bodies and medicine companies' trade organisations in each country. The PIC seeks the mutual recognition of inspections of pharmaceutical manufacturing companies.

15 For a wider discussion see Rosamond (2000: 136–47).

16 It is acknowledged that since macro theories delineate the pattern and impetus for integration, neither neo-functionalism nor intergovernmentalism makes any claim to be able to explain all elements of EU policy-making.

17 For instance Sbragia (1991), Peterson (1995), and Scharpf (1999).

18 For instance Marks et al. (1995), Risse-Kappen (1995, 1996), Cram (1996), Héritier et al. (1996), Kohler-Koch (1996), Christiansen (1997), and Richardson (1997).

19 See for instance Majone (1996) or Young & Wallace (2000).

20 For a discussion of lobbying in the EU pharmaceutical sector, see Greenwood and Ronit (1994) or Shechter (1998).

21 Articles 28 and 39 (ex 30 and 34) read: 'Quantitative restrictions on imports and all measures having equivalent effect shall be prohibited between member States' and 'Quantitative restrictions on exports and all measures having equivalent effect shall be prohibited between member States'.

22 Article 30 of the Amsterdam Treaty (ex 36) reads in part: 'The provisions of

Articles 28 [ex 30] and 29 [ex 34] shall not preclude prohibition or restrictions on imports, exports or goods in transit justified on the grounds of public morality, public policy or public security; the protection of health and life of humans, animals or plants; the protection of national treasures possessing artistic, historic or archaeological value; or the protection of industrial and commercial property. Such prohibitions or restrictions shall not, however, constitute a means of arbitrary discrimination or a disguised restriction on trade between Member States.'

23   The regulatory state model also captures the normative and positive theories of (economic) regulation. The former cites protection of consumer interests (from a host of potential market failures) as the rationale for state intervention in the market. The latter regards the purpose of regulation as protecting the interests of the regulated industries themselves.

24   The Court plays a positive integration role here as well.

4

Networks and the 'politics of policy'

The previous chapter teased out certain insights into EU pharmaceutical policy-making from broad theoretical perspectives. And it argued that in order to understand policy development – particularly as the EU regulatory framework for medicines is a unique one – these insights needed to be supported with a more focused level of analysis. As it can account for the interests at stake, and would allow us to test the hypothesis of an industry-favouring framework, the policy network was advanced as an especially useful approach. It is the purpose of this chapter to develop this line of analysis, first providing a brief review of the policy network concept before considering the interests of the sector's four primary stakeholders who comprise the networks that develop around pharmaceutical policy issues at EU level. Since networks do not act in a vacuum – the broader insights gleaned from Chapter 3 having made this clear – Wilson's (1980) 'politics of policy' typology of regulatory decision-making is then introduced as the link between the meso and the macro. It is shown to help establish a policy environment, not only in which the networks operate, but one which can influence outcomes for the sector.

Meso-analysis: focusing on actors

As mentioned earlier, there is no single view of policy networks. Moreover, there is no unanimous support for the approach's value. The respective failings of pluralism and (neo-)corporatism as complete models – at least their fading significance in the face of evolving policy-making dynamics in western societies – have resulted in a host of actor-oriented public policy theories of which policy networks are just one. Nevertheless, in offering a more fluid and relevant view of how actors interact within different levels of the policy-process than either pluralism or neo-corporatism, policy networks continue to be employed by those seeking a meso-level understanding of policy-making, and there is broad consensus over the approach's relevance at this level. For our purposes, therefore, it is argued that, in comparison to other public policy approaches, policy networks are best suited to helping us understand the dynamics at play in setting EU regulatory policy for pharmaceuticals. This, as the approach can accommodate the sector's inherent peculiarities, the complexity of the interests at stake, and the (often) competing interests of the stakeholders.

Posing the question as to whether policy networks are best seen as a structure, model or theory, Börzel (1997a, b) distinguishes two schools: a *model of interest-intermediation* and a *mode of governance*. The former sees the policy network primarily as a generic representation of state-interest (bargaining) relations, while the latter defines it in terms of political resource mobilisation in instances where such resources are shared or dispersed between public and private players.[1] It is immediately apparent that the difference is not always going to be a clear one, and this is particularly so in empirical terms (indeed, this division would appear to lie at the heart of contemporary discrepancies in conceptualisation and should be consulted in order to help clarify them). Still, the division appears a legacy of the pluralist–neo-corporatist debates, with the former conforming to the structural notions of pluralism and the latter relating to the more dynamic interpretation proffered by neo-corporatism. Without engaging the minutiae of the literature, a précis of some of the more widely-cited conceptions makes Börzel's point.

Contemporary policy network application: structure, model or theory?
According to Kenis & Schneider (1991: 25–9), the policy network concept is an 'analytical toolbox' which we can use to understand actor relationships and their consequences in issue-specific decision-making. Others see it more as a diagrammatic model of interest group mediation which helps fill the gaps left by pluralism and neo-corporatism (Marsh 1995). A further view is of the policy network as less a tool for analysis than a tangible construct unto itself: 'an arena for the mediation of interests of government and interest groups ... [wherein] clusters of actors representing multiple organisations interact with one another and share information and resources' (Peterson 1995: 76). Citing these definitions is not to imply that the concept has an accredited understanding, for there is a plethora of further interpretation even within each school.

As examples of the more widely-cited theoretical perspectives, these definitions show that the spectrum of views on both the construct and applicability of policy networks covers inclusively all ground between a structural/descriptive and summary-providing approach (interest-intermediation) to an analytical and operational perspective (governance). This has spawned criticism that the approach suffers from a lack of substance (Jordan 1990) and, consequently, one of its main exponents has bemoaned the fact that the policy network is 'becoming ubiquitous ... it is most commonly used as a metaphor ... is infrequently used with precision ... [and] it is rare for it to have any explanatory value' (Rhodes 1990: 293). Yet the concept undoubtedly holds currency, and not simply because of its popularity. And in terms of its application, the student's focus of analysis will decide the choice of approach – each is valid in its own way.

For our purposes the interest-intermediation view is the more useful. First, there is a clear impetus for an actor-based clarification of the policy-process given the lack of transparency in the EU pharmaceutical arena.[2] Even a crude understanding of the policy-making architecture based on the use of networks would be germane to understanding the political forces shaping policy outcomes. In using networks to capture the dynamics of policy-making in the sector, and the structure of relationships between the main actors, this contributes to understanding outcomes as they manifest themselves in specific policies. It also helps merge the (politics of) decision-making with the regulatory policies which result. This use of policy networks further allows us to test the study's hypothesis. If it can be shown that the industry can dominate the networks which form over EU pharmaceutical policies/issues, this will help us to understand both the development of policy and the reasons for an industry-favouring framework. This is not to decry the value of the more fluid understanding of the governance school, but rather to keep within a manageable and relevant frame of analysis.

Using policy networks to depict the policy-process: interest-intermediation reviewed

As the earlier and arguably more prominent of the two schools, the interest-intermediation view offers the best indication of the theorists' disenchantment with the pluralist–corporatist debates. Networks are employed primarily at the sectoral level where balancing the needs and resources of state and (private) civil interests is most apparent, and the level where pluralism and corporatism would both seem to have failed. By constructing various typologies of policy networks and then applying them to particular empirical case-studies, scholars such as Wilks & Wright (1987), Rhodes (1988), Atkinson & Coleman (1989), and Jordan (1990) formalised the concept's theoretical foundations.[3] That their typologies differed has caused some to question the approach altogether.[4] But it remains the case that they paved the way for scholars from both schools to develop and apply their own conceptualisations.

Leitmotifs and relevance Reviewing several of the better-known interest-intermediation typologies reveals three common leitmotifs relevant to EU pharmaceutical policy-making. First, the policy network is treated as an analytical tool which can account for meso-level factors, particularly in terms of actor relationships and interactions in policy outcomes (Börzel 1997a). This is a valuable level of analysis when looking at competing actors in a multi-level (governance) EU polity. Not only does the pharmaceutical industry span both sectoral and sub-sectoral levels, but the interplay between institutionalised interests and actors is considerable given the overlap between healthcare and industrial policy areas. The (corporatist) blurring of the public–private divide is of especial importance here given both the issues at stake, and with respect to the structure of the pharmaceutical industry and influences upon the market.

A second thread is that policy networks allow for the development of (re-source) dependencies between network actors, resulting in the establishment of stable relationships over time. According to Wilks & Wright (1987: 299), actors seek to 'balance' and 'optimise' their 'mutual relationships' via re-source exchanges, and 'A policy network describes the general properties of the processes by which members of one or more policy community interact in a structure of dependent relationships'. Based on the stability ascribed the interest-intermediation construct, it can be inferred that the policy network itself does influence the policy process – especially given that some actors develop a certain degree of clout within it. Notwithstanding the 'fluidity, openness and largely unpredictable nature of the EU decision-making pro-cess' (Josselin 1996), it is the case that EU level interests develop (resource) dependencies in a relatively stable manner. Indeed, risk aversion for fear of failure compared to other actors or interests often precludes any attempts to be innovative in either pushing one's own agenda, else forwarding a new policy idea. Instead, a type of status quo prevails with actors more or less content in the stability of their existing relationships; and this will be shown to apply to some elements of pharmaceutical policy. This has led to the appli-cation of 'path-dependency' theory to the EU context. Without going into detail, as it generally asserts a type of evolved 'institutionalisation' amongst actors (which also sets their future preferences), it too is applicable to the EU pharmaceutical sector. The incomplete regulatory framework is the result of an impasse which cannot be broken by the main players within their current constellation of decision-making patterns and relationships. These dependen-cies are strong as constructs in themselves and in the stakeholders' relation-ships with other actors. The subsidiarity-free movement clash ensures that the nature of their relationships and future policy actions remain very much fixed.[5]

In noting the relevance of these perspectives, the aim is not to offer a (new) institutionalist examination of EU pharmaceutical policy-making. Instead it is to understand the policy-process from a more complete perspective; one which acknowledges an institutionalist framework in showing how the regu-latory environment – even if in part a result of path-dependency – can affect outcomes. The point being that the unique regulatory issues associated with the pharmaceutical sector, in combination with the Community's (incom-plete) regulatory functions, have an impact on what sort of outcomes can be agreed through the policy networks.

A final point to be gleaned from the interest-intermediation school is that policy networks are valuable in reaching difficult consensual policy decisions where other forms of interest mediation fail. Here the network is understood as a 'web of relatively stable and ongoing relationships which mobilize dispersed resources so that collective (or parallel) action can be concentrated toward the solution of a common policy problem' (Kenis & Schneider 1991: 36). Although related to path-dependency, for our purposes it underscores the salience of actor relationships in the policy-process and accommodates the single market–subsidiarity clash. The Commission is unable to push through policy without the support of the member states, whose interests are conditioned as much by budgetary and public constraints as industry and private requirements. The degree of interdependence between the actors in the sector is therefore very high.

Policy networks and the EU policy-process: scepticism? The relevance of policy networks to EU policy-making is not a view shared by all scholars: Kassim (1994) discusses policy networks as something different from the 'network model' – the former having grown out of the pluralist-corporatist debates in political science, and the latter finding its origins in international relations theory – and argues that neither can be applied to EU policy-making. This division relates to Börzel's distinction between the interest-intermediation and governance schools, but she in fact claims that both are relevant to the EU – the one to policy outcomes and the other to European governance.

Kassim's critique is based on three grounds: 'elusive fluidity', a lack of attention attributed to institutions, and the 'boundary problem'. The first refers to the near impossible task of capturing the fragmentation of the EU policy-process under a single conceptualisation. The second reflects his view that both the policy network and network model fail to account for the institutional architecture through which EU policy is made. And third is that both are predicated on being able to delimit networks, but that this is not really possible in the supranational context. Although valid concerns, perhaps the main problem here is actually the terminology in light of the overlap with looser concepts such as the policy community and the issue network, but also between the interest-intermediation and governance conceptions.[6] Nevertheless, his conclusion that 'the search for a framework for analysing the policy making processes of the EU must continue' (Kassim 1994: 25) remains current. Others sharing this sceptical view include Mills & Saward (1994), Thatcher (1995), and Dowding (1994), who perhaps sums it up best when he suggests not to 'stretch a good idea too far'. Their scepticism is over policy networks as a new form of governance or as a complete framework cum theory of policy-making.

Detailing such arguments is not our purpose, and it must suffice that they have been raised – especially as numerous scholars maintain the validity of the governance view at EU level (given the multi-level gaming structure which characterises it). But it should be reiterated that this study understands and uses networks mainly to capture the nature of the EU pharmaceutical policy-process, not as a mode or emerging theory of governance in the EU. In other words, as an apparatus of process, rather than a theory thereof. Perhaps

some of the governance scholars come close to proposing the network approach as a theory of policy-making, but even they do not hold up the approach as an authoritative model for understanding the EU policy-process
(e.g. Windhoff-Héritier 1993). Within this study the approach is simply accepted as a manner of conceptualising policy-making in the EU, and the
interest-intermediation view is employed insofar as it fits with multi-level
governance, not because it helps define it.

Employing policy networks – taking the approach forward
What appears to be lacking in the interest-oriented conception, however, is
its linkage to wider frameworks. The approach has, for the most part, been
used at a very focused level of analysis and can perhaps justly be criticised as
either too context-specific, else taking insufficient notice of what happens
outside the networks themselves. This has led some to deem the approach as
overly-descriptive (e.g. Jordan 1990). In noting this failing, Marsh (1995: 3)
argues the need to take the strong influence of the 'economic, political and
ideological context in which the network operates' into account.[7] In showing
the development of the EU regulatory framework for medicines as not solely
the result of what transpires in the networks, our approach supports this idea
that the environment in which a network develops and operates is central to
understanding how it works. Indeed, as the earlier discussion on liberal
intergovernmentalism has shown, external factors can and do influence actor
behaviour with regard to their pursuit of specific policy outcomes in the sector. And the EU's policy and legal frameworks ensure that negotiations and
outcomes are confined to specific arenas.

Furthermore, given our aims, Chapter 3 argued the need to tie the network approach to a wider theoretical perspective in order to understand how
the nature of the issue at hand can influence the policy-process. By way of
strengthening our use of the policy network, the study turns to Wilson's (1980)
'politics of policy' cost-benefit framework of regulatory policy-making. This
represents the liaison between the broader theories and the policy network
approach, and accounts for actors' interests and bargaining within networks.
Mentioned earlier, this allows us to forward a wider and more integrated
manner of examining the development of EU pharmaceutical competences
than a simple application of meso-level analysis. This level of analysis is developed later, thereby reinforcing the network approach and giving rise to a
broader theoretical context within which policy networks can be examined.

The purpose of this section has been to introduce the policy network concept, highlighting in particular the applicability of the interest-intermediation literature to the study. Above all, the discussion has made it clear that the
adoption of policy networks to analyse EU policy-making in the pharmaceutical sector is in keeping with a meso-level, actor-based approach. Wider theories provide an important level of analysis but are too sweeping to explain
outcomes. They offer a contextual understanding of the broader influences at

work in shaping policy for the sector and have shown the difficult environment in which policy is to be made, but they are not able to explain the more localised dynamics involved. Consequently, it is as a means of supplementing the insight provided by the wider theories that the study turns to networks.

As they pertain to the EU pharmaceutical sector then, policy networks are treated as meso-level constructs with established (institutionalised) relationships existing between the constituents. With relations in the sector taken as interest-based towards achieving particular policy outcomes, identification of the major interests and actors, as well as their relations and role within the policy-process, falls within the remit of such an analysis. This forms the next part of the discussion.

Constituent interests and EU pharmaceutical policy

A delineation of all actors involved in the EU pharmaceutical sector, along with an assessment of their respective interests and influences on the policy-process, is beyond the scope of this book. Not only are there are so many implicated, but the health–industry duality means that their interests tend to be quite specific and disparate. Table 4.1 identifies several of the main national actors and their general policy objectives, while Appendix F presents a selected listing of the more salient individual actors and their vehicles for expression at EU level. Although simple indexes, they provide an idea of how many interests and actors are involved and affected – in large measure reflecting the public health and healthcare issues.

An additional difficulty in looking at the sector from an actor-based perspective is in deciding on which are (not) important within the context of multi-level governance, for this risks the possibility of omissions. As such, the study focuses on what are the sector's four main actors at EU level – consumers, the industry, the member states, and the Commission – and employs the term 'stakeholder' (used several times to this point) in order to capture their vested interests and the nature of their involvement and interdependencies in a sector where traditional industrial relationships between consumer, producer and regulator do not feature. Other actors or groups of aggregated interests are also involved at EU level e.g. doctors' federations, non-EU industry associations, and international pharmaceutical standards groups such as the ICH. But as they are not directly involved in the policy-process, analysing them falls outside of our aims. It is the interests and interactions of the four primary stakeholders which thus represent the focal point for the remainder of the study.

Pharmaceutical stakeholders: interests and priorities in pharmaceutical regulation
Treating the four actors as stakeholders gives additional elucidation to the peculiarities of the sector, particularly with respect to the fact that: a) at national

Table 4.1 Principal national-level actors and policy objectives in the pharmaceutical sector

Sector	Entity	Policy objectives
STATE	*Ministries*	
Regulation	health	• adequate supply of safe, quality and effective medicines
Funding	finance	• minimise tax-funded health expenditure
Delivery	service	• maximise access to care for those most in need
Economic	trade, industry	• encourage local industry, employment, exports
INDUSTRY	*Firms*	
Innovation	research	• maximise profits and safeguard research base
Reproduction	generic	• improve competitive position
DISTRIBUTION *& INSURANCE*	*Firms*	
Distribution	wholesalers	• improve margins
Insurers	companies	• segment market to best advantage
PROFESSIONS	*Associations*	
Prescribing	medicine	• maximise autonomy and meet patient needs
Dispensing	pharmacy	• enlarge professional role and meet client needs
HEALTH SERVICE	*Organisations*	
Primary	practices	• maintain local visibility and community support
Secondary organisational	hospitals	• maintain market share and visibility
Regional	health systems	• meet requirements of key stakeholders
OTHER	*Various*	
Consumers	associations/ patient groups	• **ensure access to safe and effective drugs**
scientific community	journals	• advance knowledge and academic freedom
Media	firms	• enhance or maintain market segment

Source: adapted from Davis (1997: 21). Primary stakeholders are highlighted in bold type.

and subnational level there are many more players involved in pharmaceuticals than other sectors (recalling the direct link to healthcare and (public) health policy); and b) at European level this results in a difficult and complicated (regulatory) role for the EU – this is less the case in other industrial sectors within the framework of the Internal Market. Importantly here, the concept of stakeholder-oriented actors clearly fits with the use of policy networks, for the nature of the relationships it assumes is certainly true of the pharmaceutical sector.

In concentrating on the primary stakeholders, the actions of the Commission, the industry, and the member states are the most important in policy-making terms. While consumers are the critical element in that it is their interests which underlie policy, as they are generally not involved in the decision-making process directly, there is no vehicle for assessing their role beyond the positions expressed by patient or consumer organisations (usually from outside the policy-making arena). The member states (and to a lesser degree the Commission) do represent an element of the consumer view within their own aims, but in terms of any single consumer actor having a major say in the policy-process, there appears to be none. As it is less the case at the national level where patients' organisations and even doctors' associations have at least some degree of say, the exclusion of consumers has often been highlighted as a major failing of the EU medicines policy-process.[8] And while the Commission often claims to engage the patient's perspective via dialogue with representative groups, it appears more a case of lip-service than a real commitment to involving them in a meaningful way. Nonetheless, in order to understand what a single medicines market might mean in practice, the consumer (patient) perspective is paramount. So although patients are generally not involved in the decision-making per se, their positions and priorities require elaboration alongside those of the other main stakeholders.

Consumers: medicines to bring public health benefits   Although not formally represented in the EU policy-making process for medicines, consumer interests are not neglected. If a medicine is to sell it must work, and for it to work it must pass strict safety, quality and efficacy tests. These pertain not simply to 'consumer safety' as in other sectors, but more specifically to public health. Still, consumers are the most marginalised of the stakeholders, primarily because, as a group, they have the least influence, compounded by the poorest access to information. As noted earlier, their position within the market's demand structure where they simply want the best medicines, irrespective of cost, and demand is via an intermediary, also means that they are unable to affect the market on their own.

Nonetheless, consumers are becoming increasingly educated about medicines and healthcare costs. Notwithstanding the amount of inaccurate, outdated and unregulated information to be found, the Internet in particular has helped improve consumer awareness.[9] Consequently, a host of patient groups, disease-specific organisations and lobbying bodies have sprung up in recent years, and doctors are increasingly reporting that patients come with requests for specific treatments or medications (Spurgeon 1999). This development is in part due to growing pressure on the industry to provide information, but so too is it the result of a greater appreciation of healthcare concerns and industry activities. And as doctors and other health providers are becoming more involved in the debates about cost-containment, especially cost-effective prescribing, consumers are no longer as uninformed as they were even five years ago. But it remains a paradox of the pharmaceutical arena that consumers have so little market power over a sector which deals in their health.

Regarding a future single European medicines market, as there is so much uncertainty surrounding what form it would take and what benefits or costs it might bring, the consumer position is unclear. Access to the same products at the same price across the Community may seem a good and fair idea, but questions regarding pricing and a lowest common denominator approach to quality qualify this. Patients in the UK and Sweden may, for instance, be envious of the comparatively low out-of-pocket expenditure on medication and health insurance of their southern Mediterranean neighbours, but the reverse may be the case in terms of access to newer and more innovative preparations, or simply more choice. Chances are that neither would be willing to compromise the benefits they currently enjoy under their national framework. What they are likely to agree on, however, is that any further movement on completing the market be based on public health requirements to the same degree as other, primarily industry, interests.

Industry: a regulatory environment conducive to business   As a collective stakeholder, industry is often said to put profits ahead of public health. Research-intensive manufacturers are also frequently accused of seeking increasingly exclusive patent rights while baulking at the prospect of increased competition. Acknowledging that generic and research-oriented manufacturers have different priorities, balancing profits with escalating research costs, increasing government price controls to restrain healthcare budgets, and growing consumer demand (quantitative and qualitative), is no mean task. So while industry representatives may accept that their profits seem high relative to other industries, they argue that these are still not always in proportion to the costs which go into developing a product (and companies of course have a duty to their shareholders as well). According to the European Federation of Pharmaceutical Industry Associations (EFPIA), the EU research industry's trade body, these costs have risen at a more or less constant rate through the 1980s and 1990s (EFPIA 1998, 2004). And they stress that such returns are necessary to the production of high quality medication. Consequently, drug companies (research-oriented manufacturers especially) seek government incentives and push for what they view as the fair (market-based or free) pricing of their products.

But fair prices are a subjective matter in any sector generally, and here they are dependent on whether one adopts a health budget or shareholder perspective. Nonetheless if the research industry's claims on decreasing effective patent times, rising R&D costs, only a tiny number of NCEs synthesised in a laboratory being marketed as a drug, and European companies losing out to US manufacturers (Lawton 2001), are to be taken at face-value, then perhaps the industry does have a case regarding its future competitiveness. For it is the case that the origin of the top ten medicines (by worldwide sales in 2002) now favours the US on a ratio of 8:2, versus 6:4 for Europe in 1992. And European NCE discoveries have declined relative to the US since the late 1980s to early 1990s (OECD 2001, IMS Health 2004, EFPIA 2004). It should again be stressed that such data comes from the industry – even if it is also released as 'official' figures by the EU's statistical office EUROSTAT – and that they have been cited here to indicate those arguments industry brings to the table.

Simply put, industry seeks a regulatory environment which fosters and rewards innovation, where natural (as possible) market forces prevail, and in which the national governments and EU plays as minor a role as feasible. Here member state cost-containment measures which target the supply-side are often regarded as impediments to industry performance (EFPIA 1996), and Agrawal et al. (1998) have argued that a country's economic and regulatory environment impacts considerably on drug manufacturers' competitiveness. Still, as there is an appreciation that the relationship is one of co-dependence, the industry often proclaims that it is complying with, for example, demands for greater transparency in its operations e.g. the provision of information on clinical trials and testing (Sykes 1998). Whether the new regulatory system and conditions ultimately envisaged under a single market would meet industry's interests is not clear. And as is shown in the following chapters, the industry is concerned about what the future holds in this respect. If increased EU regulatory competences impinge on industry's competitiveness (and affect profits), the industry may simply push to retain the status quo of a fragmented EU market.

The European Commission: pushing for a successful 'euro-industry' Ostensibly the European Commission's responsibilities are as much to the consumer as they are to industry. As the only supranational stakeholder it also has an additional responsibility to the wider integration process. This means not only trying to balance industrial and health(care) questions, but equally, to reconcile economic and political interests towards fostering completion of the Internal Market.[10] In 1997 the Commission identified its priorities as:

- better medicines for all EU citizens, with fast access to innovations, better information and involvement in decisions affecting their health;
- continued provision and funding of medicines by Member States and

Insurance Funds with necessary safeguards on expenditure achieved with the minimum of legislation and regulation;

- development of informed customer-supply negotiations on both prices and volumes, which provide a basis for enhanced competition;
- a steady stream of valuable innovative medicines from Industry and a thriving generic sector, both of which will make a supply-side contribution to a genuinely competitive market;
- an attractive European investment environment in the biosciences and biotechnology for the R&D based Industry which will assume a prominent position for European Industry in world markets. (WG I 1997)

These priorities remain. And in order to achieve any or all of them, the Commission mandate will require more formalised establishment in terms of specific competences. As noted earlier, it is currently institutionally incapable of fully regulating the medicines sector. Given the proliferation of Community regulation, the Commission has in fact been shown to suffer from a management deficit more generally (Laffan 1997). It will have to develop further competences which, notwithstanding the EMEA, build on the member states' own roles. Aspects of healthcare policy are necessary if the EU is to eventually preside over twenty-five (or more) very different systems and traditions.

That said, as a completely harmonised market would mean equality of product (including branding and packaging), uniform (free) pricing, common reimbursement mechanisms, and equal access and supply of medicines in all member states, it would mean, first, a single market in healthcare.[11] The Commission has recognised as much: 'The problem is that the Community's health systems are not harmonised, and this is preventing completion of the standardisation process' (EUROSTAT 1998: 79). Complete market harmonisation is thus not necessarily the Commission's goal, at least not in the short to medium-term. Consequently, it has set about trying to improve the competitiveness of the industry as a means to increasing its own competences (related to the 'efficiency regime' referred to in Chapter 3) and towards pursuing some degree of price harmonisation. Moreover, it seeks to apply the free movement of goods requirements of Article 100 and to reduce intra-EU price differentials; in order to both diminish market fragmentation and to regulate towards a single market in some form. What this means in practice is outlined in later chapters.

Member states: protecting national interests   The final stakeholder – insofar as they can be grouped – is the member states. Pinpointing a set of finite interests for all EU governments requires some generalisation; each has different priorities with respect to its own industry or sector, and each has a different healthcare system. Nevertheless, common ground can be found in that national authorities must ensure a certain quality of health and healthcare for the consumer, along with maintaining control of medicines spending. They must equally make provisions for the industry in order to ensure both a high quality of product and national competitiveness. Governments' responsibilities are to industry, consumers, and the healthcare market, all within the context of the SEM.

This position is difficult in itself, but is hampered by the fact that governments' priorities for the pharmaceutical sector often have as much to do with electoral success as anything else. Keeping the voters happy is any government's primary concern. But how to do so when cutting costs through drug pricing controls may be a vote-winner on the one hand, but is seen as an impediment to a successful and contributing industry on the other? Failure to control expenditure leads to measures such as higher taxation or insurance contributions which are unpopular with consumers. Failure to meet the needs of industry means a potential loss of jobs and, perhaps, a decreasing quality of healthcare. With the Commission potentially looking to take the lead in the sector, this puts an added strain on national authorities who must still ensure the sustainability and success of the local sector. For as already highlighted, current Commission and industry goals, such as free movement and free pricing respectively, would undermine both. Furthermore, as some member states' industries would benefit from a single market at the expense of others, there is an added incentive to maintain the status quo.

The EU policy clash

We now have a more tangible understanding of what the clash means at EU level: a Commission interested mainly in promoting the free movement of goods, improving the competitiveness of European industry, and some degree of price harmonisation, whereas the member states are pursuing similar, national industrial policy interests (supporting the industry and promoting employment), along with local healthcare and public health objectives. The emphasis is on retaining control of healthcare spending, and subsidiarity enables them to do so. The industry is lobbying for its interests to be met at national and supranational levels. And although virtually excluded from the debate, the irony for consumers is that their interests are invoked by each of the other stakeholders to justify their own positions. As a result, the lack of clarity over what sort of regulatory regime will actually develop means that policy decisions (and the degree of consumer involvement in the process) will continue to be treated on an issue-specific basis.

Earlier it was shown how the dissonance between subsidiarity and free movement impedes the Commission's (regulatory) policy-generating role (see Figure 2.2). When the stakeholders' differing interests are added, this role is made even more difficult; especially as the EU's public health mandate is also limited (Holland et al. 1999). This is represented in Figure 4.1.

The figure captures the multi-faceted nature of the policy overlap. Each circle represents one of the wider policy spheres assumed in medicine regulation, while the numbered cells correspond to groups of specific policy

Figure 4.1 Overlapping policy interests in EU pharmaceutical regulation

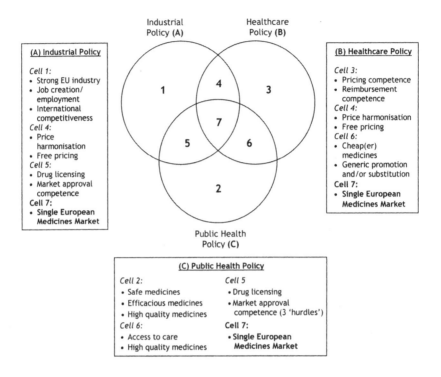

goals. The healthcare policy sphere (B) is the domain of the member states. Any policy interests that fall within it, even overlapping from another sphere, are subject to subsidiarity and member state approval i.e. Cells 4, 6 and 7. The public health (C) and industrial policy (A) spheres meanwhile, are areas in which the EU has some competence and where, therefore, the EMEA, DG Enterprise and DG Sanco play a role. The specific policy goals represented in the diagram are equally applicable in terms of domestic policy, but in the EU frame a single market would need to accommodate this structure for each member state; each has specific requirements and expectations corresponding to these goals, and none will permit any Community incursion into its healthcare sovereignty.

Looking more closely at the figure, while the Commission may be interested in price convergence from an industrial or single market point of view, because this impacts on national healthcare systems there is no progress (Cell 4). The same applies for the EMEA in that its mandate represents an overlap between public health and industrial policy interests (Cell 5), but it has no pricing or reimbursement authority. Cell 6 shows that the issue of quality medicines (and access), while clearly a public health matter and to some degree therefore a Community field, is nevertheless also a healthcare financing matter and beyond EU competence. Finally, the concept of a single medicines market is shown in Cell 7 to be an overlap of all three spheres, and one which is severely compromised given that Cells 4 and 6 show no prospects of being devolved to the supranational level. The result of this is the Community's ability to only involve itself in industrial – and to a lesser extent – public health policy concerns. Though, as the figure shows, its competences in the latter are also limited by the healthcare element.

With the differences in objectives of the primary stakeholders now clear, as well as the clash between free movement goals and the subsidiarity principle, it becomes necessary to see how they interact within the context of EU pharmaceutical regulation. Understanding how policy networks form around policy proposals and in what way the regulatory environment impacts on the type of policy that can be agreed is the next step. Industrial policies may dominate the EU regulatory framework, but as some of these impact negatively on interests in the health(care) policy community, it is important to see how they have been reached. It is here that meso-level analysis is valuable.

The 'politics of policy'

Our earlier discussion on the interest-intermediation application of policy networks made the point that networks do not operate in a vacuum. Instead, they take place within the constraints and boundaries of the policy environment. Thus, Marsh's (1995: 3) argument that 'Policy change is clearly not just a function of what occurs in the network: it is also strongly influenced by the economic, political and ideological context in which the network operates' is relevant to the discussion in that understanding the regulatory environment will help to explain why some policies have been agreed and others not. For although single market priorities resulted in the need to standardise packaging guidelines, advertising, and wholesale distribution among other issues, the sensitivity of healthcare matters have ensured that member states retain control over pricing and reimbursement concerns.

In order to address this, and to understand how policy has been achieved given the clash represented in Figure 4.1, the discussion now turns to the 'politics of policy' approach formulated by Wilson (1980). Mentioned several times to this point, it represents a framework of regulatory policy-making which characterises choices on the basis of perceived costs and benefits, arguing that the resultant configurations give rise to different modes of politicking. Having been used to show at what level lobbying can prove effective (Hood 1994), it has also been applied to explain EU regulation more generally (Majone 1996). Its use here is to show how actors behave within the networks which form around (proposed) EU pharmaceutical policies. Recalling the broader perspectives outlined earlier, this offers a clearer picture of how policy is actually made. Moreover, it enables the study's main contention – that industry is the main beneficiary of the regulatory framework – to be tested in relation to the case-studies of the following chapters.

Costs versus benefits: four scenarios

As a student of regulation in the US, it is not surprising that Wilson's politics of policy model was developed around the 'iron-triangle' conception of American politics of the 1970s and 1980s.[12] In helping to show how industry interests could come to dominate policy discussions and, indeed, outcomes, this represented a theoretical explanation of the earlier arguments made by other American scholars that regulation was designed by and operated for industry (e.g. Kolko 1963, Stigler 1971). Its incorporation of the trade-off between private and public interests within the policy-process, as opposed to seeing it as a by-product, is perhaps the main reason that scholars have sought to apply Wilson's framework beyond the American context. It also integrates lobbying by business interests into policy-making, rather than treating it as an external influence – something which, as already noted, is prevalent in all areas of EU policy-making. The 'politics of policy' is thus particularly relevant to the EU in that traditional pluralist and neo-corporatist configurations do not capture the dynamics at play in the Community's multi-level governance structure. Important is that it is compatible with the policy network approach which, as argued by Héritier et al. (1996), is itself ideally suited to the EU frame.

Wilson's assertion, quite simply, is that 'policy proposals, especially those involving economic stakes, can be classified in terms of the perceived distribution of their costs and benefits' (Wilson 1980: 365); that is, the trade-off price of implementation to the involved parties. These costs can be either (or both) economic or non-economic, and their value is changeable according to the political climate. It seems a sensible enough view but, in addition to qualifying regulatory decision-making according to the distribution of costs and benefits (concentrated or diffuse), he argues that for each of the four possible configurations this generates, there results a specific type of politicking via which outcomes are achieved. This goes some way towards supporting Lowi's (1969) earlier argument that the policy arena often determines the nature of the political processes within it. Figure 4.2 offers a matrix representation of Wilson's framework.

Figure 4.2 identifies the manner of politics via which different types of policy interest are resolved and, correspondingly, at what level this takes place. This is on the basis of what each player believes they have to gain or lose in a given policy scenario. As Wilson was concerned primarily with economic regulation at the national level, his stakeholders were industry, the state and the public, with the latter understood in terms of representing the 'common good'. The multi-level governance conception implies a host of further actors, and policy-making in the pharmaceutical sector is a case in point. However, as we are here concerned with supranational policy, our focus is on the

Figure 4.2 A typology of the 'politics of policy'

		BENEFITS	
		Diffuse	*Concentrated*
COSTS	*Diffuse*	Majoritarian politics	Client politics
	Concentrated	Entrepreneurial politics	Interest-group politics

Source: Majone (1996), based on Wilson (1980).

industry (particularly the research-based industry), the European Commission, the member states, and consumer interests (in whatever format or group represents their interests) as the main stakeholders. This allows for further inter-actor divisions where the policy issue at hand may provoke disparate reactions.

Wilson's model is relevant for two main reasons. First, it represents a more targeted decision-making framework which can be tied in with the integration and regulatory theories already profiled; thereby strengthening our conceptual approach. And second, it establishes the fact that policy networks operate within certain constraints. The politics of policy matrix thus fixes a set of parameters within which networks can operate, as well as acting as the liaison between 'meso' and 'macro' environments; it is in fact able to accommodate both.

Majoritarian politics According to the framework, in instances where the costs and benefits of a proposed regulatory policy are both diffuse, as there is little incentive for those involved to collaborate, the likelihood of a policy outcome is slim. The question of who pays, or more specifically, who is willing to pay what for a limited share of the benefit, means that resolution will only take place where there is sufficient political will and popular support. With unanimity required, any policy outcome will only be achievable via *majoritarian politics*. In the EU context, where the issue is about extending supranational regulatory authority, this means that all the stakeholders will have to consent to bearing some of the costs of a policy which will benefit the others as well; costs may be extremely high, at least in the short-term. Majone (1996) has cited social policy as one such example and the slow implementation of the 1993 Working Time Directive,[13] for example, would seem to bear this out.

In light of the wide distribution of both costs and benefits, matters involving member state healthcare systems and the provision of health also fall into this scenario. The Commission may favour an increased Community role in health matters – though this needs centralising given that several Directorates-General affect matters pertaining to health policy (Merkel & Hübel 1999) – but the member states remain very much against in view of not simply the potential economic costs, but so too the political consequences. Relating this to EU pharmaceutical policy highlights why the healthcare policy dimension of drug regulation remains a national level concern.

Client politics   Over issues where costs may be diffuse but the benefits concentrated, only a small group (or groups) stands to derive the most gain. As there is considerable incentive for one or more of these small groups to collaborate in order to influence the policy-process in their favour, this creates conditions enabling the emergence of *client politics*. This is the classic business lobbying profile. And success in such cases is bolstered by the costs being so widely distributed that the per capita price becomes negligible to those who might otherwise oppose the policy. The potential dominance of industrial lobbies under this scenario is usually countered by the use of independent regulatory bodies. But where such agencies do not exist, or else lack the clout necessary to enforce their views, the 'producer-dominance model' results (regulatory capture). Industry may thus receive favourable treatment by government via subsidies or simply a laxer regulatory environment.

Industry lobbying over specific policies has characterised the EU pharmaceutical market even before the SEM, and has for the most part been successful. This success is in part due to the market's fragmentation, but also the nature of the Community's multi-level governance structure which offers multiple levels for lobbyists to target. In addition to its ability to organise, industry success is also because the issues at stake tend to be similar across national boundaries, and the multinational nature of the industry has enabled it to gain significant lobbying experience in a host of environments (Greenwood & Ronit 1994).

Entrepreneurial politics   As *entrepreneurial politics* characterise policy decisions involving a wide distribution of benefits and more concentrated spread of costs, there is likely to be little support for the proposed policy. First, the small group responsible for bearing the costs is opposed, and second, the gains to the beneficiaries are too diffuse to mobilise their support. This may be the result of a lack of knowledge, or it may simply reflect a general disinterest in that the relative per capita gain does not warrant mobilising. With there being little incentive to support such legislation, Wilson proposes that a 'policy entrepreneur' is needed to take the issue forward. This is an actor able to animate public support and undermine any arguments the policy's opponents (those bearing the costs) may present. It generally does this by dramatising an issue or associating the benefits of the proposed (corrective) policy with values or the common good. For example, by revealing environmental mismanagement by companies and associating them with things such as children's health, a policy entrepreneur can engender support for (costly) sustainable environmental protection policies such that they become law.

At EU level the Commission often fulfils this entrepreneurial role. As policy initiator, it is able, and has a responsibility, to galvanise support on a host of issues, primarily on the basis of the widespread Community benefits they could offer.[14] It has done this over EU environmental issues and workplace health and safety policies for example. Here, the benefits of stricter standards are to be enjoyed by the member states' populations (diffuse), with private enterprise generally bearing the costs through financing and implementing them (concentrated). When broken down into individual policy fields such as air or water pollution, the costs become even more concentrated, and the need for an entrepreneur even greater. This is also the case where the costs of a given policy may disproportionately affect one or two member states, such as under the CAP. As for medicines, given the difficulty in sourcing information on the industry and the informational asymmetries which characterise the market, it is clear that a policy entrepreneur is needed to bring the issues, along with their costs and benefits, into the open. It should be noted, however, that the entrepreneur may not be a completely objective party. More often than not it will have its own agenda (as we see of the Commission in the pharmaceutical sector).

Interest-group politics   Finally, a policy offering high benefits to only a small number of interests, and at the expense of an equally small number of others who will bear the costs, gives rise to *interest-group politics*. In an industrial setting government subsidies or other incentives will usually favour one segment of industry while disadvantaging others (this may even be with regard to single companies). As noted of the pharmaceutical sector, priorities differ between generic and research-based companies, with one side usually standing to gain from the other's loss i.e. stricter intellectual property rights. Accordingly, the motivation for both sides to organise in order to influence the policy-process becomes acute. The result is a multitude of groups representing a kaleidoscope of specific interests all campaigning to ensure their own welfare as much as pushing a particular proposal: the few on the basis of the benefit they stand to derive, the majority on the basis of the cost they may have to bear. Since both the costs and benefits are concentrated, the question of the 'public good' is not normally raised. The gains and losses potentially implicated by such policies at European level means a variety of bargaining scenarios, often involving member states competing against each other, and disagreement with European institutions. EU Structural Funds, where the emphasis is on the redistribution of (and competition for) financial support, is such an area. Given the interests at stake, and the stakeholding nature of actor relationships, this dimension is clearly relevant to EU pharmaceutical regulation as well; discussions and bargaining between the primary stakeholders is a defining characteristic of the sector.

These four scenarios are the basis for Wilson's framework. Given the regulatory state conception of EU policy, wherein the Commission, the industry and the member states are all doing their best to preserve their own interests as much as they are trying to improve their respective positions, its relevance to the pharmaceutical sector is immediately clear.

The politics of policy: recasting Community pharmaceutical regulation
Wilson's framework is not perfect (see Chapter 8). It is very much a 'black or white' view grounded in the American rational actor tradition. There will be intermediate cases, and the high–low (concentrated–diffuse) measurement is inevitably a relative one. However, this does not diminish the conceptual value of the approach. As politics is not an exact science, and a degree of generalisation is usually necessary, discussions over perceived costs and benefits can be made within reason. And as the study uses the framework in conjunction with other analytical approaches – rather than claiming that it alone provides all the answers – its application to selected policy issues will be shown to be extremely useful in elucidating stakeholder interests within networks as they form over given policy proposals. These case-studies reflect not simply the relevance of the typology, but more the fact that supranational policy-making where medicines are concerned is extremely sensitive, with an appreciable effect on the stakeholders' interests. That various aspects of the EU regulatory framework correspond to different configurations within Wilson's typology reflects this. For while regulatory policy in more traditional industries might apply to only one or perhaps even two of the scenarios, it certainly does not involve all of them.

The first case-study looks at the successful industry lobby over intellectual property rights in the early 1990s and argues this as a case of client politics. The industry's claims that the patent protection rights accorded medicines were not sufficient to sustain their R&D costs resulted in the Supplementary Protection Certificate legislation of 1992 extending the protection period accorded new medicines in the Community. The second case-study concerns the establishment of the European Medicines Agency. As mentioned earlier, the EMEA is a unique body, and is the office responsible for granting drugs EU market approval. The discussion will show its establishment as a case of entrepreneurial politics within the policy network, though the industry's subsequent influence has perhaps shifted this towards client politicking. The third case-study is the pricing and reimbursement debate. Commission initiatives to overcome this impasse are looked at, as are the reasons for why this has remained such a sticking-point. Given the continuing deadlock, it appears that majoritarian politics apply. For with all sides having to agree, this helps explain why there is no progress.

Wilson's typology has four dimensions. The interest-group cell concerns a small group seeking to protect their interests in the face of benefits being accrued by another group. The respective win–loss trade-off, and strength of bargaining it generates, means that policy is extremely difficult to agree, if at all. Consequently, it would appear that an integrated EU medicines market corresponds to the interest-group scenario. Some of the reasons for this – most notably the winner–loser division which would emerge amongst the member states – have already been raised. Also, as there is too much uncertainty for the stakeholders over what a single market would mean in practice, who will benefit more (which countries, which industries) and by how much, the interest-group scenario cannot really be tested empirically. There is no one policy which fits. However, rather than compromising the applicability of the approach, not developing the fourth cell in fact strengthens it. For the inability to attain a harmonised market reflects the impasse and extent of the constraints. There are many actors, representing a panoply of interests, all trying to ensure that they do not have to bear the very high costs in order for another party to benefit i.e. not just the main stakeholders are involved. Chapter 8 provides a more detailed discussion.

Outlining Wilson's approach here was to introduce the politics of policy typology as an important level of analysis which can be integrated with a policy network approach in analysing the Community's formulation of pharmaceutical policy. Not only can it be tied into both the multi-level governance and regulatory state perspectives, but it does not preclude the involvement of outside actors or external influences on the policy-process (such as the ICH or WTO). And there is no reason to suggest that the predominately clarifying (and positive integration) role of the ECJ does not fit either. Regarding policy networks specifically, the politics of policy establishes a context which will affect the nature of outcomes. For the cost-benefit configuration can determine whether networks will form and, to a degree, determines in what cases they might be successful. Wilson's model can thus supplement the interest-intermediation approach by showing how the nature of the issue at stake can impact on the manner in which policy is or is not developed.

Nonetheless, on its own it cannot reveal the nature of interactions within the styles of politics it distinguishes, nor can it account for instances where a policy issue changes i.e. where more interests and actors join the political fray, or where externalities force decisions. Network analysis provides insight into the former, while integration theories can account for the latter – the 'politics of policy' sits in the middle. And it is precisely herein that its value is to be found. It can be used to link the macro and meso (and within the broader understanding of the EU as a regulatory state subject to the dynamics of multi-level governance).

As noted earlier, although the study does not offer an institutionalist analysis, path-dependency within certain structural arrangements does characterise policy-making in the sector. Here again Wilson's framework would seem to sit easily. As Rosamond (2000: 115) notes, 'Rational choice institutionalism tends to define institutions as formal legalistic entities and sets of decision rules that impose obligations upon self-interested actors', and this is clearly the broader environment which contextualises the study.[15] The case-studies characterise the stakeholders' choices in large part on the basis of costs versus benefits, and subjects these to the formal decision-making dynamics of, for instance, EU voting rules within the Council of Ministers. And it is clear that this in turn will affect any policy outcome. That said, the study keeps within the politics of policy approach, focusing on policy networks and the meso-level. The analysis is very much oriented around what each stakeholder in a given network perceives it has to gain or lose over a specific policy proposal (and whether the status quo might in fact be perceived as the best option). Wilson's typology is thus used as a framework which provides important insights into the policy network-oriented policy-process(es) of the case-studies which follow. Further, it enables a testing of the contention that the industry dominates the networks such that the regulatory framework favours its interests. So although in some ways perhaps conforming to a new institutionalist framework, the study acknowledges this rather than seeking to detail or elucidate it in any way.

Notes

1   As used by the interest-intermediation scholars, the policy network is considerably modelled after the earlier (primarily American) iron triangle and sub-government concepts. For the governance theorists meanwhile, the primary influence has been sociological network analysis.

2   Criticism of a lack of transparency is also levied against the EMEA. Based on the secretive nature of national-level pharmaceutical policy-making (particularly in pricing matters), European policy-makers are under pressure from both supply and demand-side actors to ensure that the same does not happen at supranational level. This would undermine any legitimacy that the arguments in favour of EU-level regulation of the sector might espouse. See for instance Abbasi & Herxheimer (1998) and here, Chapter 6.

3   Another early contributor was Katzenstein (1978), who sought to use policy networks in the context of international relations theory.

4   As the typologies often differ 'according to the dimensions along which the different types of networks are distinguished' (Börzel 1997b: 8), it may be that language is often the cause of discrepancies in usage (see note 6 below).

5   This may be related to Scharpf's (1988) 'joint decision trap' view of European integration and policy-making, where the development of institutionalised policy-making arrangements at EU level results in 'sub-optimal' outcomes from the member states' perspective. But given the members states' exercise of subsidiarity, it is not clear whether the impasse really is a sub-optimal policy outcome.

6   Dowding (1995: 140) for example writes: 'I will use the term "policy network" as a generic category and "policy communities" and "issue networks" as subsets'. Jordan (1990: 327) essentially argues the opposite: 'The policy community

is thus a special type of stable network … the policy network is a statement of shared interests in a policy problem: a policy community exists where there are effective shared "community" views on the problem'. Both are referring to the role and place of a specific level of interests in policy-making. But their differences have more to do with whether it is the policy network or the policy community which is the more overarching concept, than whether the approach itself is applicable.

7   Marsh sought to align the policy network with wider theories of state–civil society relationships in order to demonstrate the concept's applicability within a macro-frame of analysis. Specifically, he undertakes an evaluation of the concept's relevance to 'elitism', 'pluralism' and 'marxism' as comprehensive political ideologies.

8   For instance Orzack (1996), Abraham & Reed (2001) and Garattini & Bertele' (2001).

9   However, many health and health-related websites – including those providing disease and medicine information – are sponsored by the pharmaceutical industry. This raises questions as to the impartiality of the information provided given the fine line between information and marketing.

10 One of the key issues on the Commission's agenda is how best to adapt the current framework so as to integrate the healthcare markets of the accession countries.

11 Recent ECJ rulings in cases such as C-158/96 – *Raymond Kohll* v. *Union des Casses de Maladie* and C-120/95 – *Nicholas Decker* v. *Caisse de Maladie des Employés Privés* (on the cross-border provision of medical services), or Joint Cases C-157/99 *Geraets-Smits* v. *Stichting Ziekenfonds* and *Peerbooms* v. *Stichting CZ Groep Zorgverzekeringen* (on the reimbursement of hospital costs incurred outside the country of origin) are, however, setting the stage for some harmonisation.

12 The iron triangle in American public policy theory referred to the relationship of interdependence between the state (or agency), a Congressional committee or subcommittee, and an interest group.

13 Directive 93/104/EC.

14 Laffan (1997) in fact characterises the Commission's role as that of 'policy entrepreneur'.

15 Rosamond (2000: 109–22) highlights the diversity in the institutionalist literature and posits 'historical', 'rational choice' and 'sociological' institutionalism as the main variants.

5

'Client politics': the Supplementary Protection Certificate

Intellectual property rights are generally regarded as central to the activities of highly research-intensive industries, and pharmaceuticals are no exception. The costs and length of time required to develop a new medicine are considerable. Moreover, the period from identification of the new molecule to the launching of a derived product represents a much longer registration and market approval process than is found in other sectors. Less clear, however, is what the appropriate robustness of this intellectual property protection should be. Particularly when bearing in mind consumer interests, healthcare costs, (generic) competition and, in the EU, the principle of free movement of goods.

Notwithstanding that pharmaceuticals fall under the auspices of the 1973 European Patent Convention (EPC), in legislation enacted in 1992 the Community appeared to deliver its own answer to the question of adequate robustness. The Supplementary Protection Certificate (SPC) was introduced to extend the protection period accorded new medicines in the Community. Manufacturers were granted a five-year post-patent expiry extension,[1] or fifteen years total protection from the date of first *market authorisation* in the Community. This was as opposed to the twenty years from first *patent application* under the EPC. The SPC thus represented a derogation to both the European Patent Convention and the free movement of goods principles of Article 100.

This chapter examines how this piece of legislation came to pass, what the interests and roles of the stakeholders in the policy network which developed around the patent extension issue were, and what the politics of policy framework tells us about the policy-process. Beginning with a brief overview of patents in Europe, the discussion turns to protection expressly for medicines. An outline of the arguments in favour and against patent-term extension then contextualises an examination of the political interactions behind the SPC. It is expected that such an analysis will not only show that actor (inter-institutional and even interpersonal) relationships and resource dependencies via a policy network configuration played a considerable role in this process, but will also indicate how industrial policy interests came to the fore. Specifically, the discussion agues that the Commission came to be influenced by the research industry on the basis of a client politics configuration (*vis-à-vis* the policy network's other stakeholders).

Protecting intellectual property

Pharmaceutical manufacturers place considerable emphasis on the role of intellectual property legislation as a means of securing rights and ensuring returns. A patent accords the holder the right to the exclusive use of an invention (product or process), and provides legal grounds for preventing its unauthorised use. Given the R&D process, along with the costs and registration periods, the role of patents and the security they afford medicine manufacturers is regarded as a 'make or break' issue, perhaps more so than for other sectors. Moreover, industry representatives are often at pains to point to a causal link between a prospering European pharmaceutical sector where 'adequate' intellectual property protection is in place, and better healthcare.[2] As noted earlier, however, this proves a tenuous link in practice.

Patents in Europe
Before looking at pharmaceutical patents, the general nature of European patent legislation requires mention. This underlines just to what extent the SPC is a unique piece of legislation. The origins of patent protection stem from the 1883 Paris Convention for the Protection of Industrial Property. Trademarks, patents, tradenames, and even regulations pertaining to unfair competition were covered. In Europe specifically, patent protection is legislated for under the 1973 European Patent Convention (EPC). The EPC set down the principles of a Europe-wide patent for single applications for all industrial products/processes, and is currently in force in twenty-nine European countries. It grants the patent holder the same rights as would be accorded under a patent granted nationally. A single application is given multiple country accreditation, but is nevertheless subject to the national legislation of the individual countries. The term of coverage for all industrial patents is a standard twenty years from the date the application has been registered. Subject to several exceptions including certain biotechnology applications, medical (surgical) procedures and computer programs, patents under the EPC are granted to new inventions which incur a significant 'inventive step' and which could be commercially exploited by parties other than the inventor. There are a host of internal definitions, clauses and conditions within this simplification, but they are too detailed for consideration here.

Co-existing with the EPC is the Community Patent of the European Union. As the EPC covers several countries outside the EU, the European Community has long sought to establish its own patent system. The principle of a

Community-wide patent was to provide an alternative (not a replacement) to individual national patents in the member states. It represents an adaptation of the EPC, and was designed within the context of removing obstacles to the free movement of goods and services in the single market. Several of the more notable measures under the Community Patent include:

* a single patent applicable in all EU member states;
* a process whereby an application approved in one member state becomes effective in the others following a so-called 'transitional period';
* national authorities retain the ability to invoke national legislation in the granting of compulsory licences;
* making available the option to pursue a single country patent to applicants; and
* protected products to be subject to the free movement of goods and services principle of the single market.

Originally called for at the Luxembourg Convention on the Community Patent in 1975, and despite numerous amendments by the European Parliament, several Green Papers, compromise agreements at several councils, a Commission proposal in 2000, and a deadline on agreement for the end of 2001 set at the March 2000 Lisbon European Council meeting, the Community Patent is still not in force. The reasons for this, according to ex-Internal Market Commissioner Frederik Bolkenstein, are because of 'vested' and 'protectionist' interests on the part of the member states (CEC Memo 2004), and its implementation therefore remains high on the agenda for European policy-makers.

The benefits of a single EU patent include uniformity and Community validity with a central jurisdictional authority; the obsolescence of the requirement that in order for a patent to be recognised in a country it must first be used there; and the removal of fees payable separately in each country for patent renewal. There are also drawbacks, including that a challenge or infringement in one member state becomes relevant to all, and may result in an EU-wide patent revocation; companies with the same patent in several countries (on an individual basis) will no longer be allowed to let it lapse in one or more while maintaining it in others; and the administrative (including translation) and transaction costs of a Community patent may be higher than for individual patents in each country. The aim in pursuing an EU patent system is to 'eliminate the distortion of competition, which may result from the territorial nature of national protection rights. It should also ensure the free movement of goods protected by patents' (EP 2001). Once this legislation is finally enacted, it will have a considerable impact on pharmaceutical patents in the Community.[3]

Pharmaceutical patents

For medicines, the purpose of patents is 'to stop competitors selling: the identical product, a similar formulation of the active ingredient, or a product incorporating a "me-too" active ingredient for as long as possible' (Wright 1997: 19). Companies argue that, particularly in less-developed countries, 'patent infringements resulting from lax laws allow local generic companies to reap undeserved financial rewards. Multinational pharmaceutical companies lose revenue and market share' (Ganorkar & Korth 2000: 77). As they also incur considerable legal costs in contesting infringements, the patent-holding companies are keen on stricter intellectual property rights. Medicine patents are thus intended to lower the profitability of imitation by enhancing that of innovation. In principle such rationale are no different than in other sectors. But in practice the intellectual property protection afforded drug producers is unlike that in other industries.

Pharmaceutical patents apply to the discovery of new chemical entities and afford the holder the exclusive right to make and market drugs using that compound for the lifetime of the patent. In addition, multiple patents apply to any given medicinal product covering, most notably: substance, compound, formulation, usage and process. SmithKline Beecham's antiulcerant drug *Tagamet*, for example, carried some twenty-six separate patents (EGA 2000a), precluding research into any of these areas. The breadth of this protection is a consequence of the earlier-mentioned costs and registration times for new drugs, as well as the knowledge-accumulation on which they are based. It is also controversial in that such protection may preclude potential advances or discoveries. Not just the length of protection accorded patent-holders, therefore, but the fact that patents cover the discovery and any prospective application of a new chemical entity represents a situation not seen in more traditional manufacturing sectors. With this already the case, why then have drug manufacturers in most major markets (the EU, the United States and Japan) sought, and been successful in securing, longer patent terms than are offered other products?

The reasons relate to the unique nature of the product, namely that pharmaceuticals are both an industrial good and healthcare commodity. Recalling that under the EPC patent-life is the length of time between the original application for a patent and when the patent expires (twenty years), the three criteria of safety, efficacy and quality which new products seeking market authorisation must fulfil, mean that a considerable amount of this protection period is lost even before the product makes it to market. Consequently, 'effective patent life' is used to denote the period of time a product is covered by a patent while on the market. The length of the approval process not only compromises the duration of the effective patent-term, but industry argues that since so many parties in addition to the innovator are in fact involved, patent protection should nonetheless apply during such assessment periods (REMIT 1996). And as approval and testing times are not as long in more traditional industries, it does perhaps seem somewhat inequitable that products subject to such strict and important pre-marketing requirements receive shorter patent protection terms than products which are not.

As already noted, rising R&D costs in the sector have been commensurate with the amount of time it takes to develop a new product – the so-called golden age of drug discovery of the 1950s and 1960s has long passed. New compounds are less forthcoming, and the earlier breakthroughs in areas such as antihistamines, steroids, and penicillin appear to have run their course (Sharp et al. 1996). Industry officials currently put the cost of bringing a new drug to market at y868 million (EFPIA 2004)[4] and argue that this expense alone justifies exceptional patent considerations. In addition, the complexity of current genome research has led to claims that the cost of researching a single medicine is set to increase by more than one hundred per cent over the next few years.[5] Although pharmacogenomics is a relatively new field and will actually only apply to a small number of drugs in very specific therapeutic indexes (Pirmohamed & Lewis 2004), this growth in research expenditure perhaps reflects the industry's strongest argument for patent-term extension, and it is perhaps not surprising, therefore, that the Community has legislated in this area. Nevertheless, as mentioned earlier, some see industry's claims as a smokescreen in the pursuit of increased profits and market shares. They question whether medicines truly warrant exceptional coverage. New medicines can, after all, achieve up to US$1 million a day in global sales (Vogel 1998) and, despite increasing R&D costs, pharmaceuticals continue to be one of the most profitable of all industries (Scherer 1996). Furthermore, critics counter the industry's complaints about unduly long registration times as a worst-case scenario, with many more drugs making it to market more quickly than before. It has also been the case that the patent-holding companies release their own generic equivalents following patent expiry on their branded product – the earlier-mentioned antiulcerant *Tagamet* being an example. As one commentator put it 'the industry in totality seems to have fared pretty well in spite of the encumbrance of "inadequate" [sic] patent cover' (Paltnoi 1998: 55).

As with the issue of the market's competitiveness, pharmaceutical patents are thus generally viewed from two camps. The pro-industry view holds that stringent intellectual property rights on medicines act as an incentive to industry *vis-à-vis* innovation,[6] thereby promoting public health, healthcare and welfare (EFPIA 1996). Those who cast a more dubious eye over industry claims argue that extended patent-terms are sought to boost companies' profitability by insulating the holders from competition, moreover, that they result in higher drugs bills and welfare losses. For more products, even in specific classes, leads to lower prices and increased competition. The former hails from an industrial policy position and the other primarily from the health(care) vantage-point. These competing perspectives, along with the uniqueness of pharmaceutical patents, should be borne in mind as the background to our discussion on the Community's decision to extend patent times in 1992.

Having hinted at the rationale, and pros and cons for (extended) pharmaceutical patent protection, the point to be stressed is that it is not clear whether long(er) protection periods serve either healthcare or patients' interests or not. Protecting innovative medicines may indeed help companies recoup their investments, and it may provide them with a tangible incentive to continue the search for new and better drugs, but as there is no definitive correlation between extended protection and (quality of) health, it is a question which remains unanswerable. The relationship nevertheless underpins the research industry's (ongoing) arguments for extending protection. As regards the Community's 1992 extension of patent-terms for medicines under the SPC, it is perhaps surprising, therefore, that the Commission should ultimately deliver a proposal so clearly in favour of the research industry.

The Supplementary Protection Certificate
The Supplementary Protection Certificate became effective on 2 January 1993 and applied to drugs granted market authorisation in the EU after 1 January 1985.[7] A synopsis of its main terms reveals just to what extent it represented a major boost to Europe's research-driven companies.

First, the SPC extended the effective patent life on new and innovative medicines by five years.[8] The certificate provides a longer period of coverage than previously available – a maximum fifteen years 'effective monopoly' from the date of the medicine's first market authorisation within the Community. This prolongs the 'profit-life' of covered products as it is during the period of marketing exclusivity that drug sales are generally at their highest (IMS Health 2001). Second, it prevented 'unauthorised third parties' (generic companies) from engaging in R&D prior to patent expiry. Generic manufacturers had previously been able to begin their own testing and research from the date of the original patent submission, potentially releasing their copy on the day the patent on the original had expired. By preventing generic research during patent coverage, a longer shelf-life for the branded products was ensured. The legislation thus shields the research industry from the more traditional levels of competition seen in other sectors. More importantly, the total coverage period of fifteen years was more generous than what was available in the US and Japan at the time – as will be seen, the Commission had in fact originally proposed a ten-year SPC with up to thirty years coverage – helping boost the research industry's position in the global market.

An example of the degree to which the research companies benefit from the SPC comes from Eli Lilly's antidepressant *Prozac*. In the UK *Prozac* came to market in 1986 and the patent expired in 1995 (around nine years effective patent life). The company applied for the extra coverage, which was granted until the end of 1999. According to IMS Health (2001) data, *Prozac* achieved approximately 80 per cent of its total sales between 1990–99 in the final five years alone i.e. during the extension period granted by the SPC. This was the situation in the UK. Eli Lilly was granted certificates on *Prozac* in eight other member states (any company seeking an SPC is required to submit an individual national application for each market). With *Prozac* achieving UK sales in the vicinity of £100 million a year, the overall benefits to the company on this one product alone have been substantial. Two years after the enactment of the SPC, one analyst commented that 'The pharmaceutical industry, owners of patents covering successful commercial products, have been trying to get the highest profit from the EC Regulation and National Laws [sic]' (de Pastors 1995: 192).

How was it, therefore, that Regulation (EEC) 1768/92 was agreed, especially as it is clear that mainly the research companies stood to gain from any extension? Again, there is no verifiable link between more drugs and better healthcare (it depends on what is being researched and licensed), but there is a correlation with increased drug prices. Moreover, 'Although the additional patent protection period clearly helps the innovative industry, it may not necessarily encourage innovation; it may simply create inertia and a disincentive for rapid innovation and transition to a new product cycle' (Kanavos & Mossialos 1999: 324). So given that patents on medicines clearly impact on national healthcare financing – and bearing in mind the EU's lack of competence in healthcare policy – how did the SPC come to pass?

Extending medicine patents in the Community: initial dialogue

Because of the issues already outlined, passing the legislation was not an easy affair. The emergent policy network reflected disparate views and interests. Consequently, the Commission was subject to intense lobbying and detailed representations by the primary stakeholders (and, later, by other actors as well), particularly after publication of the formal proposal document. A preliminary draft proposal of September 1989 was soon followed by the official version in April 1990 (CEC 1990a). After some revisions, based also on the Parliament's reading (EP 1991a), the Council Common Position was published in February 1992 (CEC 1992a), and the final text was agreed and adopted by Regulation (EEC) 1768/92 in July 1992 (CEC 1992b). It was a decision which openly favoured the research industry though, as the discussion will show, prior to the amendments the Commission's proposals had actually gone even further. An examination of the stakeholders' actions during the policy-process reveals to what extent the Commission was influenced with regard to the content of the new Regulation, why in the final legislation the Commission's proposals were diluted and, ultimately, why the client politics scenario is therefore invoked to characterise its passing.

'Industrial policy' and the research industry lobby: the case for an SPC scheme
During the 1980s the European industry began its campaign to have patent terms on medicines increased. This reflected shortening effective patent life terms since the 1973 EPC, and the fact that both the US (1984) and Japan (1988) were introducing patent legislation of their own. Manufacturers felt that because of growing R&D costs, the lengthening of pre-market testing

Figure 5.1 Number of NCEs discovered (Europe versus US), 1980–2003*

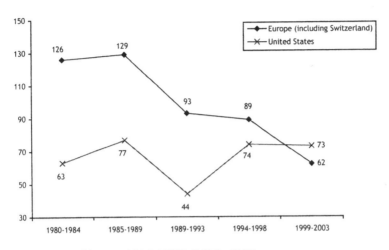

Source: OECD Health Data (2001), EFPIA (2001b, 2004).
* Data for 1980–84 and 1985–89 are for New Chemical Entities and since 1989, for New Chemical or Biological Entities; note overlap at year 1989.

periods, and extended registration times, they were not earning sufficient returns on their products to warrant their expenditure. The industry claimed that as the number of new chemical entities being discovered was diminishing, the length of the discovery and approval processes (and hence their own costs) were increasing, in turn compromising European competitiveness. The industry held that stricter licensing procedures in the member states, and growing pressures to look into then (in some cases still) untreatable conditions such as HIV and cancer, were behind these trends. A 1996 report commissioned by the European Commission estimated that R&D intensities in the main drug-producing countries rose from between 7–8 per cent to 10–12 per cent between the 1970s and 1990s, with the main causes being increased regulatory requirements combined with the difficulty of testing drugs for chronic long-term diseases, and diminishing returns to drug discovery (Sharp et al. 1996). Figure 5.1 shows that NCE discovery in Europe dropped in the mid-1980s commensurate to the US closing the gap. As mentioned earlier, however, the issue of R&D is not quite so clear-cut – companies may be spending more but it is difficult to ascertain just how much of this is purely R&D expenditure.

The fear expressed by many politicians and commentators was that Europe was losing its leading position in the sector, and that research-bases would be relocated to the US where innovation was better rewarded. As this applied mainly to member states with an innovative industry, the statements by Lords Butterfield and Hacking during an April 1991 House of Lords debate on the UK industry makes the point (Hansard 1991a):

> *Lord Butterfield:* I am for British industry and I am for the pharmaceutical industry. I have a nightmare in which the West Germans, the French, the Americans and the Japanese run our pharmaceutical industry off its legs. (1326)
>
> *Lord Hacking:* What then should the government be doing? They should certainly not be dithering. Perhaps I may gently suggest that they should adopt the posture of supporting their industries. They should support their research-based industries; they should support skilled scientists who work in such industries and, above all, they should encourage investment in the United Kingdom. (1320)

It was with similar justification, and to attract foreign direct investment, that both the French and Italian governments were unilaterally introducing their own national 'supplementary protection' legislation in 1991 (France proposed seventeen years effective protection and Italy eighteen). However, as it was obvious that such national approaches would have ramifications for the single market, the need for a binding Community-wide policy was recognised. But rather than this policy emanating from the Commission, the impetus for the prolongation of patent protection on medicinal products in fact came from the industry.

The European Federation of Pharmaceutical Industries and Associations (EFPIA), the research companies' EU trade association since 1978, took up the baton. At the time of the SPC, the association represented eleven of the twelve member state organisations (excluding Luxembourg) along with those of five European Free Trade Area (EFTA) countries: Austria, Finland, Norway, Sweden and Switzerland. EFPIA's job was to ensure that the industry's interests were heard in the European arena, and this it did through the organisation of meetings, the drafting of reports and position papers and the running of information seminars. More importantly, the association was the industry's official representative in negotiations with the European institutions. EFPIA was created 'to bargain with the EC's institutions over the precise forms of regulation and self-regulation compatible for example with the Community's drug information policy, harmonization, pricing and patent law' (Middlemas 1995: 468). This led to it being targeted by individual firms seeking to lobby in Brussels (Abraham & Lewis 2000), and in 1997 it was restructured to account for this. Membership is now held by twenty-nine national pharmaceutical industry associations,[9] and by forty-three of the world's largest research-driven firms. Organisationally, EFPIA consists of four committees: Economic and Social Policy; External Trade Policy; Scientific, Technical and Regulatory Policy; and Intellectual Property Policy, which are responsible for issuing its recommendations and positions on relevant issues.

From as early as 1988 EFPIA and its members were lobbying the Commission over patent-term extension (SCRIP 1287), and the association outlined its vision for the sector in a booklet entitled 'Completing the Internal Market for Pharmaceuticals' (EFPIA 1988). As patent extension was an issue affecting the European industry as a whole, EFPIA felt that it could be most effectively handled in a centralised Community manner, rather than on a member state basis. In lobbying the Commission, however, EFPIA's initial contact did not go well. In mid-1997, EFPIA's Director-General, Nelly Baudrihaye, met with Berthold Schwab, Head of the Competition Directorate-General's (DGIV) Unit for Intellectual and Industrial Property, to discuss the issue. She found that he did not see this as a matter for the Commission (Shechter 1998). As noted earlier, pharmaceutical policy was the domain of the Industrial Affairs DG, and the Commission could, therefore, only act where industrial policy issues are at stake. Mr Schwab recognised that patents on medicines impact on national healthcare financing and did not see how DGIV, far less the Commission itself, could take the issue forward. The industry's calls for a Community response to the question of inadequate protection were thus rejected at the first hurdle.

The industry regrouped, altered tack, and aimed to sell the idea from an industrial policy stance. EFPIA now centred its arguments around the idea that current patent protection terms were beginning to starve innovation, and that this could potentially have negative effects on the Community's industrial competitiveness. They turned their attentions to DGIII (Industrial Affairs), and pinpointed Fernand Sauer, then head of the Unit for Pharmaceuticals and Cosmetics (DGIII/E/F), aiming to convince him of the merits of their case.[10] In the course of their discussions it seems that a deal was struck. In exchange for DGIII's support on the patent issue, the industry would drop their objections to proposals on Community pricing rules; or at least they would be willing to engage in dialogue over the matter. DGIII/E/F was at the time trying to secure support for Community rules on medicine pricing transparency (what was to later become Directive 89/105/EEC), which the industry had until then regarded as an interference in their affairs (see Chapter 7).

Discussions about Community rules on the transparency of drug prices were at a fairly advanced stage at this time, and Shechter (1998: 83) has stated that 'He [Mr Sauer] then promised a trade-off – if the industry accepted the Price Transparency Directive, the Commission would take the initiative with regard to the SPC issue'. Not only did Mr Sauer make no mention of this when asked about the Commission's stance on the SPC in a 1993 interview, but his answer: 'We are neutral' (Koberstein 1993: 32) does not seem to tally with the clear pro-research industry recommendations made by the Commission in the 1990 proposal (see below).[11] This concession or trade-off by EFPIA appears to have been a successful one as DGIII then helped to make the industry's case within the Commission, and Mr Schwab amongst others came on board. With influential insiders now embracing their cause, EFPIA then set about lobbying the other Community bodies and sought also to curry support amongst the national associations.

Creating the Commission's proposal document
With the Commission pushing the idea at EU level, DGIII's discussions with
EFPIA now turned to the specifics of an official proposal. How was the Commission going to sell this industrial policy slant to the European Parliament
and Council, and on what grounds; especially when its own initial reaction
(under DGIV) had been negative? It was going to need 'proof', and EFPIA
was thus requested to provide substantial evidence as to their claims of patent
time erosion.

Wasting little time, a special group was set up within EFPIA to deal with
the Commission's request for evidence. It was charged with drafting a report
to demonstrate diminishing patent periods for several hundred products across
a host of therapeutic categories. The Association of British Pharmaceutical
Industry (ABPI) played a leading role as the UK industry had already raised
the matter at home; highlighting declining exports and growing imports in
Europe compared to the US, and criticising the UK government's lack of initiative to address this (e.g. SCRIP 1291, HoL 1991a). Additionally, a high-
profile campaign providing data and detail on all aspects of the industry, and
the economic costs associated with patent protection, was launched. *Inter
alia*, the companies cited a six-year registration and approval process in some
member states – which, when substituted from the twenty-year protection
accorded by the EPC, resulted in a much diminished effective patent life compared to other products – as a major impediment to their operations. In Germany the effective period was around eight years at this time, and in the UK
the effective period of protection on some drugs was cited as only six years by
the ABPI in a memorandum to the House of Lords (Hansard 1991a). EFPIA
members also pointed to the revised patent legislation in America and Japan
to support their case. Europe was not only losing out, they argued, but patent-
term restoration in these countries could be linked to their closing the competitiveness gap. This could be measured in terms of total sales, employment,
R&D spending and, as Figure 5.1 suggests, the number of new discoveries
being made.[12] Closer to home, EFPIA was also able to use France and Italy's
earlier pursuit of patent extension measures for their own industries as further indication of the pressing nature of their claims. The special group produced a study entitled the 'Memorandum on the Need of the European Pharmaceutical Industry for Restoration of Effective Patent Term for Pharmaceuticals' which spanned 1960–86, and EFPIA presented it to the Commission in
early 1988. Apparently in need of no further convincing, the Commission
drafted its 'Proposal for a Council Regulation Concerning the Creation of a
Supplementary Protection Certificate for Medicinal Products' (CEC 1990a)
on the basis of EFPIA's memorandum, and presented it to the European Parliament, the Council of Ministers and the Economic and Social Committee in
April 1990 for their consideration.

After the initial hiccough over DGIV's lack of interest, things had very
much gone EFPIA's way. The Commission had adopted an industrial policy

(rather than competition-oriented) view on the issue, and had drawn up a proposal which reflected the industry's demands. Although shortened in the final legislation, indication of the Commission's commitment was reflected in the call for a ten-year SPC with thirty years maximum patent coverage. This was much more generous than the periods agreed in other countries' patent-term extension laws. Both the 1984 Hatch-Waxman Act in the US and its 1988 equivalent in Japan allowed for (up to) a five-year extension and maximum twenty-five years protection. And whereas these contained provisions for generic competition – the Hatch-Waxman Act included a 'fast track' procedure for generics, and the Japanese legislation was agreed in a climate of cost-containment – in the case of the SPC the Commission essentially sought to stifle it. Generic companies were to be prevented from engaging in research during patent coverage on the branded product. In the US it has been claimed that 'The robust generic industry owes its very existence to the [Hatch-Waxman] act' (Mossinghoff 1999: 54), and this was noted in the Opinion of the Parliament's Economic and Monetary Affairs and Industrial Policy Committee on the issue: 'what is striking, of course, is that this competition-boosting aspect of the US legislation is totally absent from the Commission's proposal' (EP 1990a). In light of the implications such a one-sided position carried, it is not surprising that an opposition lobby emerged during Parliament's discussions of the proposals.

Adopting the proposals

Until now the Commission and EFPIA had been working together behind closed doors, (Shechter 1998). But with the proposals leaving the Commission for a wider readership, the other stakeholders were to get their say. For as part of the Parliament's reading procedures, it is required to consult numerous committees and outside groups. And as the Council of Ministers must deliver a response which reflects the position of all member states, it too must consult with a broader constituency. As might have been expected with the proposals now under scrutiny from a wider range of interests, the more sceptical position on patent extension was formally voiced for the first time. With the generics industry, the national governments and consumers/patients now involved in the policy-process, a policy network emerged around the SPC issue. And as these latter stakeholders were to bear the costs of the research industry's gains – with no immediately apparent benefits to themselves beyond the anecdotal evidence on improved innovation given to the Commission by EFPIA – they were understandably critical.

Debate and amendment

With the Council the real decision-making authority, the agreement of the ministers was crucial if EFPIA was to have its way – the Proposal was assigned to the Internal Market Council. However, several of the member governments had concerns. Their primary interest was in controlling healthcare costs and it was felt that patent extensions could delay the introduction of cheaper generics, thereby keeping drug prices high. Not all member states had identical interests within this broad objective. While those with generic industries (or no real indigenous industry per se) such as Greece, Portugal and Spain opposed the proposals outright, countries such as the United Kingdom and Germany, which have major research-based industries, were reluctant on other grounds.[13] As cost-containment was a political priority at home, their reservations concerned the potential effects any changes to patent times might have had on pharmaceutical prices. The UK Minister for Industry and Enterprise, Douglas Hogg, noted that 'In its *Fiche Financière*, the Commission suggests that the proposal would have no effect on the EC budget. While this may be so, there are implications for the prices of and expenditure on drugs, which the Government are currently considering' (HoL 1991a). Although both the UK and German governments supported the revised proposals in the end, this uncertainty amongst the member states meant that EFPIA would have to convince the Parliament. Indeed, this would be crucial. For since the Single European Act, Parliament had become a central player in the formal decision-making process of the Community.

Previously MEPs were granted just a single reading of proposed legislation – under the 'assent' and 'consultation' procedures – the conclusions of which the Commission and Council could effectively ignore. Under the SEA, and via a new 'co-operation' procedure, Parliament was accorded a second reading where the Council had rejected or disregarded the conclusions of the first reading. If the Council was again to reject the Parliament's views, it would now have to do so on the basis of unanimity.[14] With the SEA, therefore, MEPs had been conferred a substantial voice more in keeping with that of their counterparts in national parliaments, and which they were keen to exercise. This also meant that they were now much more a target for lobbyists than before. Regarding the SPC proposals, the Commission had based them on Article 100(a) – free movement and single market-related legislation – which had since been subject to the co-operation procedure. With Greece, Portugal and Spain opposed to the legislation and likely to vote against in the Council, EFPIA was thus going to need Parliamentary support. This was not immediately forthcoming as some forceful opposition was voiced during the MEPs' readings.

In May 1990 the document was assigned to the Parliament's Committee on Legal Affairs and Citizens Rights. The Committee on Economic and Monetary Affairs and Industrial Policy, the Committee on Energy, Research and Technology, and the Committee on the Environment, Public Health and Consumer Protection were also consulted. In delivering its Opinion, the latter committee in particular expressed reservations, questioning many of the Commission's assertions. The most notable of these pertained to the risks of R&D relocation, the discouragement of generic competition, and the supposed benefits to the European patient (EP 1990a). As one commentator noted from the outset: 'no company will give a commitment today to close down an R&D laboratory if patent-term restoration does not happen in Europe, any more than it will formally undertake to open a new one if patent-term restoration does come into effect. Nor can any firm or group of firms guarantee to discover more, or fewer, new medicines as a direct result of the outcome of this debate' (Albedo 1990: 16). The committee was in essence challenging the basis for the research industry's claims.

The European Economic and Social Committee (ESC) – which is granted a reading of proposed legislation – raised some crucial questions in its own Opinion (ESC 1991a). Handled by the Section for Industry, Commerce, Crafts and Services, the ESC Opinion opened by questioning the legal basis for the Commission's action: 'This proposal, which is based on Article 100A of the EEC Treaty, falls within the framework of a Community health policy or, more specifically, of an Internal Market for medicinal products'. This was the point Mr Schwab had raised in his meeting with the EFPIA Director-General, and was advanced again in a question tabled by an MEP, who queried the legal basis for the proposals (CEC 191/91). Although the ESC agreed with the Commission on the effects of patent-term erosion, and the need to remain competitive with the US and Japan, pointing out that 'A fair solution would be to align on US and Japanese patent protection laws so as to safeguard the competitive position of the Community's pharmaceuticals industry worldwide', it adopted a health policy line throughout its Opinion.

For instance, noting the specific claims about unduly long registration times, it pointed out that these were 'administrative procedures which are recognized as necessary precautions for the marketing of medicinal products. Furthermore, the effect of brand loyalty over longer periods should not be underestimated in the case of many products'. The Committee also voiced its concerns on the potential impact on the generic industry. It accepted the proposed ten-year extension as necessary to compete with the US and Japan, but stressed that 'The interests of generics producers, who have an influence on price competition in a number of market segments must also be borne in mind. In this connection, a balance must be maintained between the interests of this industry and pharmaceutical research ... The Committee urges the Commission to verify whether the direct interests of generic producers will be damaged.' Additionally, it asked the Commission to take into account the price increases which would result from extended patent periods. Notwithstanding such intense scrutiny of the proposals, the Committee gave its approval: with eighty-one members in favour and five abstentions. The irony in its doing so was that its justifications were concerned with the benefit to the European patient and healthcare policy in general, while the Commission's interest was in promoting the industry. As part of the rationale given for approval, the Opinion reads: 'The Committee recognizes that, in the interests of health protection, the marketing of medicinal products in the Community must be subject to stringent quality and therapeutic requirements ... Patent protection for innovation in the Community pharmaceutical industry can also be said to contribute to health protection.' However, as the ESC is only a consultative body within the legislative process, its calls for clarification were not taken on board by the Commission.

The Parliamentary Committee on Legal Affairs and Citizens' Rights, to which the legislation was formally assigned, gave its views in its Opinion of 29 November 1990 (EP 1990b). However, it wanted the SPC to be extended to include patents on plant protection research as well. The argument being that plant protection research was also central to improving public health (by helping ensure supplies of good quality food) and that as an R&D intensive industry, there was a danger that it too might be relocated outside the Community. This was not what EFPIA had in mind, and the Council in fact dropped the motion in its February 1992 Common Position. What should be noted, however, is that the Committee was also agreeing the legislation principally on health policy grounds.

EPC compatibility and agreement
At the same time, an important debate was taking place regarding the legality of the SPC proposals under the terms of the European Patent Convention. Article 63(1) of the EPC stipulated twenty years patent coverage from the date of patent filing, and the question was how to bypass this. Any changes to the Convention required the approval of three-quarters of its signatories (fourteen countries at the time), more than a quarter of which were not Community member states. An exception for only the EC countries was thus not likely. In addition, simply tacking on an extra five years to the EPC period would affect patents on all industrial products and would not result in the derogation EFPIA was seeking for itself.

Following pressure by the member states and the Commission, a meeting was called in 1991 to discuss the issue. The result was agreement on an addition to Article 63. This enabled any EPC contracting state to extend the terms of the European patent immediately following its expiry. This was applicable only where the subject-matter of the patent 'is a product or process of manufacturing a product or a use of a product, which has to undergo an administration authorisation procedure required by law before it can be put on the market in that state' (SCRIP 1993: 94). It was a compromise which suited all parties and the Commission could now advocate the SPC without fear of contravening the EPC.

With EPC compatibility secured, Parliament agreed the legislation on second reading subject to certain revisions in the Council Common Position. The first was that some member states were granted different implementation dates. A transition period was permitted for those countries that had opposed the legislation. Greece, Portugal and Spain were given until January 1998 to implement the SPC in order to protect their local (generic) industries.

The second was that the date of first authorisation for drugs after which an SPC could be granted would be different in some member states. The legislation covered medicines authorised as of 1 January 1985, but Germany was allowed until January 1988 on account of its introduction of a new reference price system which would have been affected by the legislation. Denmark too was permitted until 1988, while in Belgium and Italy the date was in fact pushed backwards rather than forwards, to 1 January 1982, in order that more drugs would qualify. The third amendment was a reduced SPC term. The Commission's ten years were cut to five.

Needless to say, EFPIA was disappointed with this latter revision. John Griffin, Director of the ABPI, was reported to have given a 'guarded welcome' to the decision, saying that the association would 'obviously have preferred the Commission's "imaginative and constructive" original draft regulation' (MARKETLETTER 1992a: 17). Still, the SPC was an obvious win for the research industry, and one which demonstrated its influence and resourcefulness within the policy network.

Health(care) policy interests and opposition

Generic manufacturers had been dead-set against the proposals. They would no longer be able to begin their own research and testing from the time of patent submission for the original product. Instead, they would have to wait until patent expiry, thereby further delaying the release of their own medicines. And while EFPIA's members viewed this as rectifying what they perceived to be an unfair competitive advantage, generic manufacturers saw it as threatening their business – they too faced growing research periods and rising costs. The generic producers sought to bring this to the Commission's attention and produced their own data, which showed that patent expiry did not mean an automatic end to a medicine's market life as the research-based industry was claiming (Anon 1990). They also tried to have the SPC limited to only the first drug in a new class of compounds, as was the case under the data exclusivity rules of the US Hatch-Waxman Act.

To make its case, the generic industry thus sought support from outside Europe, particularly from the US. For with much of the European generic industry's output being sold to American drug-makers as bulk pharmaceuticals, the SPC would negatively impact on the US industry (and healthcare costs) as well. When asked about the imminence of the SPC legislation in Europe, Dee Fensterer, President of the US Generic Pharmaceutical Industry Association, said: 'It's the same crazy battle we had here in the US in the early 80s, with the Pharmaceutical Manufacturers Association saying that US patent life was only about eight or nine years. And, of course, that was a horrendous lie' (Bahner 1993). Indeed, even European industry experts were sceptical of EFPIA's 'proof':

> it must be admitted that, at present, there are insufficient data to support the generalisations, particularly with respect to Europe. The more closely one

examines this putative evidence, the more one wonders if the data couldn't give rise to queries regarding the size of the samples in the studies and the comprehensiveness of the raw data ... Above all, the most striking feature of the current industry argument is the rather general tone of the statement that patent-term restoration will have a beneficial influence on the range and quality of products in the future. This still has the ring of assertion rather than demonstration. (Albedo 1990: 15–16)

Unsurprisingly, patient and consumer groups also rallied against the proposals, continuing to do so even after the legislation had been agreed. They expressed concerns surrounding the length of protection under discussion and, consequently, the speed of access to new products and potential for higher prices. In early 1991 the European Consumer's Organisation (BEUC) issued a statement claiming the proposals represented 'a blank cheque' for industry (BEUC 1991). In a memorandum circulated later the same year, the UK's National Consumer Council (NCC) was more specific: 'even if the erosion of patent life has been as large as the industry claims ... The expiry of patent protection does not mean an end of the drug's role in the market, or the return on the patentee's investment' (HoL 1991a: 23). More importantly perhaps, the NCC made the point that 'Increasing patent life passes the cost to consumers, or taxpayers. The balance on interests on patents is innovation, but not at any cost' (ibid: 24).

The Consumers in the European Community Group (CECG)[15] made similar representations. It argued that lengthy patents, as they limit the speed of access to new therapies, were more a public health matter than a simple industrial policy concern. Thus, and fearing higher prices, they felt that the Commission ought not to have taken a decision so easily. In a letter to the UK House of Lords they wrote that 'we believe that extending patent protection will undoubtedly restrict the production of generic drugs – which are cheaper than branded drugs – and therefore we oppose the Commission's proposals' (HoL 1991a: II–9). This view was not limited to the consumer organisations. At least one industry analyst warned against a 'price explosion', arguing that the only safeguard against it 'is the acceptance, indeed encouragement, of legitimate generic competition for products whose patent (and in future, Supplementary Protection Certificates) had expired' (Redwood 1992: 22).

Opposition continued even after the proposals were agreed. The CECG argued that 'increased protection should apply only to new molecular entities which represent a genuine therapeutic gain. CECG sees no reason why virtual copies of old medicines should receive extra protection and the production of cheaper generics be impelled' (CECG 1993: 28). This had been one of the generic industry's main points, one which the Parliament had also endorsed during its first reading. It had sought the inclusion of a provision limiting the certificate to products which are 'already protected by a patent and which provides for the effective treatment or diagnosis of a condition which has not hitherto been adequately treated or diagnosed by a medicinal product already on the market'. The fear was that extended protection across the board would act as an incentive for industry to research products which were more profitable than they were therapeutically valuable. And that it would have been more equitable to the generics industry to have the SPC limited to only the first drug in a new class of compounds, rather than including everything which might follow as well. Since the Commission ignored this, both the generics industry, via its trade association, the European Generic medicines Association (EGA), and the BEUC later called on the Commission to codify generic substitution as a quid pro quo for the extended patent-terms granted the research industry under the SPC (SCRIP 1993). Not only was this rejected by the research lobby at the time, but with no competence in healthcare policy, it was (and still is) beyond the Commission's remit.

Within this generalised opposition, there existed further differences in opinion and more specific interests *vis-à-vis* the Commission's proposals. Nevertheless, the one thing all had in common was the potential negative effects the SPC would have on healthcare policy and/or welfare. The problem, however, was that they either came too late, else were simply not strong enough. For example, there was no official European representation for generic producers. The EGA was only formed in early 1992, the very year the SPC legislation was passed; perhaps in part as a result of the SPC. Institutional opposition from generics companies as a unified group within the policy-process was therefore heard only after the Council Common Position was released in February. Consumer interests via the CECG, the BEUC and the Parliament were also tabled late on in the game. But, as highlighted in Chapter 4, compared to the other stakeholders, they in any event carry comparatively little sway.

Conclusions

It is clear that the path to approval of the SPC was a complicated one. The major stakeholders were not in agreement, as not all would find their interests served by the legislation. The policy network which developed was one in which the actors were scrambling to protect (if not maximise) their own interests. And it was one in which EFPIA had been spectacularly successful; not simply in putting the issue of patent-term extension on the Community agenda, but also in convincing the Commission to support and help push it through. This allows several conclusions to be drawn in support of the contention that the SPC policy-process was a case of client politics within the politics of policy framework.

Costs versus benefits
Wilson's cost–benefit configuration of stakeholders' interests is applicable. Patent-term extension was a policy issue which involved concentrated benefits for a small group, with diffuse costs to be borne by a wider constituency.

The SPC, in providing a longer market exclusivity period for innovative products, was going to benefit the research-driven industry. Not only does longer intellectual property coverage help make up the effective patent-life lost by the approval process, but it serves to keep the patent-holding companies' drugs at a higher price for longer, maximising their returns – *Prozac* was earlier shown to be an example. Such concentrated benefits induce co-operation between otherwise competing firms in pursuit of a common goal which would benefit them all. The gains to be made by collaborating outweigh those to be made, individually, by not. This can be seen in the cohesion achieved by the research companies during EFPIA's lobby.

The costs of the SPC meanwhile were to be fairly widely distributed amongst a larger group of actors. These include the generic companies, patients, and those member states interested primarily in controlling healthcare costs (particularly those with no domestic research industry to protect). Beyond granting the research industry an extra five years coverage, the SPC actually sought to constrain the generic industry by preventing any R&D until after patent expiry. This may also harm patients' interests by preventing cheaper products being made available, else inhibiting new, innovative and more efficacious treatments being made available more quickly, i.e. older products remaining on the market for longer. Not only does patent-term extension not offer a guarantee of better healthcare, but it is generally accepted to result in higher drugs prices impacting especially on those consumers who pay out of pocket. As higher prices tend to disproportionately affect the elderly and those suffering from long-term or chronic maladies, i.e. those most vulnerable and potentially least able to pay, it is perhaps somewhat ironic that it is particularly with regard to research into chronic disease and illnesses associated with ageing that the industry has argued for patents to be used as an incentive (Goldberg 2000).

Another potential cost (to the consumer) is that with extended patent terms, companies are likely to seek protection for those products which are most profitable. While this is only natural, these products are not necessarily in therapeutic areas which serve society's greatest needs. As shown earlier, this was noted by the consumer groups, the generics industry and the Parliament in their respective representations to the Commission. Along with higher prices and patents on drugs for chronic illnesses, this carries financial repercussions for national governments (and insurance funds) who pay for medicines, making cost-containment goals more difficult. It was for these reasons that Greece, Portugal and Spain opposed the SPC legislation in the Council, while Germany and the UK were, at least initially, hesitant.

As the prime beneficiary, therefore, the research companies were going to have to act strategically within the network. According to one commentator, this meant treading 'a difficult tightrope in simultaneously demonstrating its desperate need without scaring off support with fears of the likely costs' (Albedo 1990: 19). As shown, these 'costs' saw other actors express their objections to the proposed regulatory intervention. And although the need for the beneficiary/ies to act strategically clearly fits with the client politics scenario, the extent of the opposition expressed by those bearing the costs does not. The typology assumes that the costs to the non-benefiting actors are so diffuse and insufficient as to not warrant opposition; hence it is only the beneficiary who lobbies. That said, several mitigating factors resulting from the SPC for the opposition actors can be identified, such that the costs to each were eventually made more palatable.

For instance, while generic manufacturers were understandably concerned, they admit that the research industry requires incentives to invest. For without someone else doing the discovering, the generic industry has no business. At the time of the discussions, when asked about the response of the UK generics industry, Edward Leigh, Under Secretary of State for Trade and Industry, responded that 'The representations received from the manufacturers of generic medicines have covered a range of views. None has given unqualified support to the Commission's proposal; indeed, some have not favoured any supplementary protection. Most, however, have recognised the case for some supplementary protection, but have advocated a shorter period' (Hansard 1991b: 19). This is repeated even today. According to a discussion paper by the European Generic medicines Association: 'The EGA believes that pharmaceutical innovation is critically important to both European healthcare and industrial policies. Innovative pharmaceutical companies should be allowed to enjoy premium prices and market exclusivity under patent periods to reward them for the high cost of developing *genuine* [sic] innovative medicines' (EGA 2001: 12).

The CECG may have objected to the Commission's proposal document but it too will have been aware that a happy research industry is an innovative one, and that innovation is key to future cures. In a 1993 report following the SPC legislation, they wrote that 'Consumers have always accepted that, where a drug is genuinely innovative and required substantial research effort and investment by the manufacturer, it is right that there should be a stronger element of protection' (CECG 1993: 28). As far as consumers' interests went, even if choice may decrease, the financial impact of longer patent protection is minimal, as patients generally do not bear the true costs of the medicines they consume. It can be presumed that the potential for more and better products – and the potential long-term benefit to the European patient – was also in the minds of the Parliament and Council when they agreed the legislation. During the ESC's deliberations at least, the benefit to the consumer/patient was raised.

There also appear to have been several mitigating influences which softened the costs to the member states. First, increased patent protection helps to ensure a successful national sector where a research-driven industry is present and, theoretically (via the SEM), could result in the provision of better quality products within the healthcare system even where it is not. If patents do promote innovation and research into new drugs, they may also help to foster pricing competition among comparative products. They may also generate research into new drugs for chronic and long-term illnesses (areas in which governments are keen to make savings). These latter points are debatable, but a successful 'Euro-industry' is definitely in the interests of all member state governments. And as the SPC was expected to improve the European research climate, it is perhaps not surprising that the majority eventually supported it subject to the different implementation dates. Furthermore, all countries were aware that these discussions were taking place within the context of developing the Single European Market. The differing transition periods notwithstanding, the SPC would, in the long term, standardise medicine patent-terms and times across the Community, thereby helping to promote the free movement of goods and services.

Finally, a successful pharmaceutical industry was clearly in the interests of the Commission given its (continuing) aim to promote European industry and strengthen the European economy. At the same time, however, it may be argued that the SPC – in permitting different implementation times – complicated the pursuit of the single market as the Commission's other main goal. But perhaps the two cancel each other out. Or at least one can assume this from the Commission's push for the SPC legislation throughout the policy-process, and its earlier-mentioned trade-off over the transparency proposals. For the latter represented more of a problem within the single market framework than the former.

Collective action and capture
Another element of the client politics scenario is that the concentrated costs can bring the likely beneficiaries together. And further, that a relatively small number of these interests can, if sufficiently well-organised, come to dominate the policy agenda to their obvious gain. This is especially the case where a weak regulator is present, resulting in the 'producer-dominance model' or regulatory capture.

With respect to the SPC, the research companies clearly banded together under EFPIA's lead. This group included not just the major European companies of Germany and the UK but, ironically given the arguments for boosting the competitiveness of European industry, many of the American multinational drug producers with operations in Europe as well. The US firms were represented by their own umbrella group, the Pharmaceutical Manufacturers of America – now the Pharmaceutical Research and Manufacturers of America (PhRMA) – which had an office in Brussels, and this led to close collaboration with EFPIA over the SPC issue.[16] Such cooperation between otherwise competing companies has long been a feature of the pharmaceutical industry, reflecting its global nature. But here it led to a single face being presented to the Commission, and resulted in a Proposal document which could essentially have been drafted by representatives of the industry. For it echoed the industry's claimed link between stricter patents, further innovation and more drugs and, as a by-product, greater price competition amongst medicines designed for similar purposes. Intellectual property rights were not only deemed necessary to the delivery of new drugs, but they were justified as important in the context of global market competition. The small but well-organised EFPIA lobby had influenced the policy agenda to its benefit.

Again, Wilson asserts that within the cost–benefit scenario of client politics, the 'producer-dominance model' can result where a weak regulator is present. As the regulator in the SPC policy-process, the Commission may not have been weak – in fact the opposite is perhaps the case – but it clearly was steered by the industry lobby. It was earlier mentioned that information plays a crucial role in the pharmaceutical sector. Not only is independent information difficult to come by, but with the Commission's limited resources, it would have been an almost impossible task had Commission officials tried to procure such sensitive data as on patent-term expiry for medicines and R&D expenditures. Thus, the Commission virtually unquestioningly accepted and acted upon the information put to it by EFPIA in its 1988 memorandum. Through the strategic use of information, therefore, the industry was able to convince the Commission as to the merits of its case. According to the UK's NCC at the time of the initial proposals, 'the drugs industry has so far won the battle for the hearts and minds of many policy makers in Europe by default' (HoL 1991a: 24).

Just as important in the Commission's 'capture', however, was the fact that the industry's interests coincided with the Commission's wider agenda – the promotion of European industry and progress towards the single market. These are reflected in the Proposal where the sixth and fourth recitals read respectively:

> Whereas a uniform solution at Community level should be provided for, thereby preventing the heterogeneous development of national laws leading to further disparities which would be likely to create obstacles to the free movement of medicinal products within the Community and thus directly to affect the establishment and functioning of the internal market.

> Whereas medicinal products that are the result of long, costly research will not continue to be developed in the Community unless they are covered by favourable rules that provide for sufficient protection to encourage such research. (CEC 1990a)

Given the Commission's priorities then, the SPC represented the stone with which it could kill two birds. That the Commission not only endorsed EFPIA's position but effectively campaigned on its behalf, shows to what extent this agenda coincided with the industry's more detailed demands. Indeed, the Commission's support went a long way to convincing key individuals in the EU frame as to the merits of patent-term extension (Shechter 1998). And though the final Regulation fell short of what the industry had hoped for (or been promised), the Commission had, in the original Proposal, tried to meet all its demands. Recall that the Commission had initially sought a ten year SPC with thirty years total protection; an extension that was far more generous than in any other major market. It was earlier asked why the Commission delivered a Proposal so blatantly favouring the research industry. The answer is now clear. The SPC was a case of client politics in which the Commission, as regulator, was 'captured'.

Final remarks
Perhaps the most important factor behind the SPC legislation was the regulatory context in which it took place. The creation of the Single European Market by 1992 was the preoccupation in all areas of Community affairs. For EFPIA, therefore, the timing of its lobby was excellent. The Commission was not simply interested in promoting European industry, but it was more focused on removing market impediments across the board and, as the Cecchini Report had noted some years earlier, pharmaceuticals were an area in which comparatively little progress had been made. More than that, however, the Commission was seeking to maximise its own sphere of influence. Recalling that the proliferation of Community regulation can in part be put down to the Commission's attempts to increase its influence by expanding its competences, the SPC is a case in point. Irrespective of healthcare considerations, it took the view that medicine patents fall on the industrial policy side of pharmaceutical regulation – it was only by making this an industrial policy issue that the Commission could have competence. Thus, not only did DGIII handle negotiations, but the Commission in fact took a pro-active stance in selling the matter as an industrial concern to other Community institutions. Here it is again worth stressing that the Commission's move to enact the SPC as a Regulation was a strategic one. Regulations are binding legislative instruments across the Community (overriding any national measures), thereby giving the Community (the Commission) exclusive competence.

Early on, therefore, the Commission displayed its hand. In addition to sanctioning the research industry's arguments, by proposing the SPC as a Regulation, the Commission was saying that this was an industrial policy matter; that the Commission and DGIII in particular had competence;[17] and all member states would be obliged to implement the legislation in full. Given the prominence of the Commission's role one might be tempted to see this as a case of entrepreneurial politics. But despite the Commission's own interests, it is clear that the impetus came from industry. That the final Regulation reflects so obviously the industry's agenda shows just to what extent it was able to influence the Commission's thinking in a client-oriented manner. So although not a distinction to be found in Wilson's approach, it would appear that the Commission thus acted more as policy 'manager' than 'entrepreneur' (Laffan 1997).

Finally, the industry's successful campaign over the SPC shows two further things relevant to the remainder of the study. First, the dilution of the original

Proposal was the result of the interplay and exertion of pressures by cross-cutting interests amongst the stakeholders in a policy network configuration. Although initially sidelined, once the proposals were sent to the Parliament and Council, the other stakeholders were able to voice their interests. And secondly, that the policy network which developed around the SPC was constrained from the outset. Beyond having initially been excluded from the policy arena, patients, national governments and the generics industry did not have too much to lose (or at least the costs were diffuse and carried something in compensation). Accordingly, they did not (were unable to) oppose the legislation as intensively as they perhaps could have. The issue at hand, in involving concentrated benefits and diffuse costs, essentially dictated the outcome from the outset – client politics would result.

Notes

1 Although industry commentators see the SPC as a patent-term restoration, this chapter uses the term extension given the limits it set on generic research during the extra period. Because of these limits, other commentators regard the SPC as granting a period of 'marketing exclusivity'.
2 For instance EFPIA (1995) and Gilmartin (1997).
3 For an outline of the European pharmaceutical industry's views on the Community Patent, see EFPIA (1997).
4 Again, this is an industry figure, and one which includes a host of exogenous variables relating to R&D, risk and failure of other chemical entities and, furthermore, reflects the industry's unwillingness to acknowledge that there is a ceiling in innovation capacity.
5 EFPIA – 'Did you know?', available at: ww.efpia.org/2_indust/didyouknow.htm.
6 A study undertaken by the US Office for Technology Assessment (OTA) in 1981 concluded that 'The evidence that is available neither supports nor refutes the position that innovation will increase significantly because of patent-term extension. Thus, the net effects of patent-term extension on pharmaceutical innovation cannot be ascertained' (OTA 1981: 4).
7 The SPC came into force on 1 July 1993 for Austria, Finland, Norway and Sweden, and on 1 January 1998 for Greece, Portugal and Spain.
8 The time difference (in years) between the date of patent application and first market authorisation minus five years decides the length of the SPC period. If the product was approved within five years of patent application, then it does not qualify for the SPC. A period between five to ten years qualifies for a certificate, and anything longer than or equal to ten years receives a maximum five years extra SPC coverage.
9 These represent each of the EU member states save Luxembourg (Germany has two associations), plus Bulgaria, Norway, Romania, Switzerland and Turkey.
10 Interestingly, Fernand Sauer went on to become the first Executive Director of the EMEA before returning to the Commission in December 2000 as Director of the Public Health Unit (Directorate 'G') in DG Sanco.
11 Later in the same interview Mr Sauer refers to the SPC as 'clearly a message in favour of innovation' (34). This would seem to suggest a conscious decision by

the Commission to side with the research-oriented industry.

12 See also Appendices C and E.

13 Germany also has Europe's largest generic industry.

14 With unanimity always difficult to achieve, the proposals would have to go through 'conciliation', a joint Council-Parliament committee procedure aimed at resolving the deadlock. It should be added that the Maastricht Treaty introduced a fourth procedure, 'co-decision'. Under co-decision the Parliament and Council share decision-making in adopting proposals by joint agreement. In cases where disagreement remains after two Parliamentary readings and invocation of conciliation, MEPs are given a third and final opportunity to agree the proposals. If they do not (an absolute majority is required), the proposal fails and does not become a legal instrument. This essentially puts the Parliament on par with the Council over much normal secondary legislation, representing a major step towards an EU system based on bicameral parliamentary democracy. It is also noteworthy that Parliament is now able to introduce amendments during conciliation, a power it did not have prior to Maastricht.

15 The CECG is an umbrella group of UK organisations concerned with the effects of Community policies on British consumers.

16 This took place under the auspices of the so-called 'Dolder Group' (named after the Dolder Grand Hotel in Zürich, where representatives of the two groups held regular, informal meetings) (Scherer 2000).

17 In 1992 Spain challenged the use of Article 100(a) for the SPC legislation. Spain had voted against the Regulation and now argued that patent-terms on medicines were not a single market issue (something that the ESC had also raised). In its 13 July 1995 judgement, however, the ECJ dismissed the case finding in favour of the Commission (Case C-350/92 *Kingdom of Spain* v. *Council of the European Union* ECR I-1985).

6

'Entrepreneurial politics': the European Medicines Agency

Based in London, and responsible for granting EU market approval to new medicinal preparations, the European Agency for the Evaluation of Medicinal Products celebrated its tenth birthday on 26 January 2005 and was rebranded as the European Medicines Agency (EMEA remains the acronym).[1] Established via Regulation (EEC) 2309/93, the agency occupies a unique place in the EU frame. Unlike the guideline or recommendation issuing roles of the other EU agencies, by delivering specialised opinions resulting in Community decisions that are binding on the member states, the EMEA exercises a quasi-regulatory function.[2] It is perhaps something of an irony that such a body exists for the pharmaceutical sector, an area of EU policy for which there is neither a single market nor a coherent Community strategy; wherein the Commission has limited competence; where the EU's legal and policy frameworks clash; and where the member states have different interests which they nonetheless defend collectively in reference to the subsidiarity principle. At the same time, it is precisely because of this that an agency exists.

The idea of a centralised European medicines authority emerged in the mid-1980s. The Community authorisation regime was proving unpopular and it was clear that a more efficient and binding system was required. Yet the official explanations offered by the Commission for creating the EMEA had less to do with single market designs than they did with public health protection. The Commission's proclamation in the press release accompanying the agency's inauguration that 'The creation of the European Medicines Evaluation Agency is firstly a benefit for the European patient' (CEC IP 1995) does not sit with the preparatory work behind its establishment. In the words of one commentator, 'five years ago no one thought of seriously selling the idea as a patient benefit' (Albedo 1995a: 10).

In light of this, the aims of this chapter are threefold. First, to reveal that the rationale for the establishment of the agency had less to do with patients' interests than they did Community industrial policy goals. Second, to demonstrate that as a result the pharmaceutical industry is in fact the prime beneficiary of the agency, both in practice and by design. And third, to show that the regulatory policy represented by the creation of the agency was a case of entrepreneurial politics. The discussion first sketches the agency's functions and purpose to differentiate it from other EU agencies. Next, an outline of the stakeholders' positions on a Community medicines agency at the time of the original discussions is provided, before detailing how, given the differing views which emerged, the Regulation establishing the EMEA was agreed. This is followed by a critical examination of its public health role, and several points of comparison are made with the US Food and Drug Administration.[3]

Reassessing the Community authorisation regime

Earlier it was discussed that Europe and the US have different regulatory traditions: Europe with a strong state role, the US relying on the use of expert agencies. As this derogation of responsibility to independent regulatory bodies is frequently based on the state's lack of expertise in the area, such agencies are often granted judicial and executive powers to enforce the implementation of their decisions. Although most EU member states still rely primarily on public bodies for addressing the market, the American model has impacted on the way regulation is carried out in Europe at both the national and supranational levels. The use of independent regulatory bodies represents a break with the more statist traditions prevalent in Europe after the Second World War, especially in those member states with a corporatist or *dirigiste* history such as Austria and France, and there are now sixteen such independent Community agencies outside the central administration of the Commission.

The Community 'model' is not commensurate with that in the US, but 'is based on the quantitative expansion of EC jurisdiction, and might be seen at the same time as a qualitative change within EC policy-making through both horizontal and vertical co-ordination and co-operation' (Kreher 1997: 241). Consequently, there are calls for the development of further agencies in other areas of Community policy. Without comparing the EU agencies, it should be noted that although all regulate on the basis of information 'either by changing the structure of incentives of the different policy actors, or by supplying the same actors with suitable information' (Majone 1997: 265), there is no model. They are structured, staffed and financed differently and operate across the three EU pillars (Chitti 2000). Where the agencies are similar is that they 'owe their existence to a kind of paradox. On the one hand, increased uniformity is certainly needed; on the other hand, gradual centralization is politically inconceivable, and probably undesirable' (Dehousse 1997: 259). Their broadly-shared 'regulation by information' mandate is an attempt to account for this. But unlike the other agencies, instead of regulating by gathering and then sharing information, the EMEA has information provided to it (by the pharmaceutical companies). It then uses this in delivering opinions on market authorisation for new medicines. And rather than linking actors through information within the regulatory process – towards co-ordinating networks of actors – the agency in fact uses information to exclude them. This reflects the peculiarity of the sector and the agency's unique quasi-regulatory role.

The Community medicines agency: a unique institution
The significance of the EMEA should not be understated, neither in respect of its unique quasi-regulatory function in the EU generally, nor in terms of what it means for the pharmaceutical sector specifically. And its establishment elicited headlines such as 'A Drug Tsar is Born' (Anon 1994) and 'A Real European Milestone' (Albedo 1995b). Unlike previous attempts to create a unified approval procedure, this was because the authorisations issued by the EMEA are binding. A single process was to relieve the duplication of effort by (then twelve) different national regulatory procedures, thereby easing bureaucratic and administrative pressures on manufacturers and national administrations, and to speed the time required to bring new medicines to market; a review process which, as noted previously, is exceptional in terms of the time and detail required. Though the secretariat consists of only about 260 people providing technical and administrative support to the scientific committees and working parties, the EMEA brings together the expertise of some 3,500 experts from across the EU, including from Iceland, Liechtenstein and Norway (who are subject to the original 1965 Directive). Thus, it is national experts who carry out the assessments on the agency's behalf. This combined expertise also helps the less well-resourced national authorities keep abreast of technological advances in drug development. By streamlining the regulatory environment, not only has the agency contributed to the Commission's free movement goals, but it helps to make the EU a more attractive place to do business.

The emphasis may be on speeding approval times, but the safety, efficacy and quality criteria for authorisation as set down in the 1965 Directive have been retained. According to the Commission, the EMEA 'allows for a quicker and simpler access to the single market, with the guarantee of an evaluation of the highest scientific standard' (CEC IP 1995). It also has a role in post-approval regulation (pharmacovigilance). And though it is the Commission which delivers the final ruling on market authorisation, as it cannot do so without the EMEA's expert opinion, the EMEA's role is not only more imperative, but the agency is closer to an independent regulatory office than any of the other agencies. Without going into the intricacies of the EMEA approval processes – reviews of which are to be found elsewhere[4] – a brief précis serves to qualify the Commission's claim of it having been designed as a benefit first to the European patient.

New licensing procedures
Charged primarily with the task of fostering market access for new medicines, two new systems were put at the EMEA's disposal.[5] Subsuming the

CPMP (concertation) and multi-state (mutual recognition) procedures out-lined earlier, these are the 'centralised' and 'decentralised' procedures, and both are based on the Community's safety, efficacy and quality criteria as laid down in Directive 65/65/EEC. There have been some changes to the authorisation rules and procedures under the March 2004 revised medicines framework (CEC 2004) – which at the time of writing have yet to come into effect – but as we are concerned here with the original plans, the folowing discussion refers to the authorisation rules as contained in the original Regulation 2309/93 creating the EMEA.

The centralised route is an updated concertation (multi-state) procedure with approval by majority vote (Appendix G). Mandatory for all biotechnol-ogy-derived products, it is also optional for those conventional products with an innovative or high technology element.[6] Companies send an application to the agency in a standard format (*dossier*), which refers it to the Committee for Medicinal Products for Human Use (CHMP)[7] for review. The CHMP (like its predecessor the CPMP) is the body assigned the task of preparing the agency's opinions on medicines for human consumption (under the decentralised procedure as well). As the body responsible for deciding on behalf of the EMEA, the probity of the CHMP must be ensured. The commit-tee is comprised of one scientific expert from each of the member states who are nominated by their national administrations (plus one each from Iceland and Norway), and they are required to put aside any national sympathies or private interests;[8] the intent is to guarantee scientific decision-making of the highest quality.[9] The CHMP evaluation is undertaken by experts drawn from a list provided by the member states, and the committee has 210 days to carry this out. Since 2000 there has also been a Committee on Orphan Prod-ucts (COMP), made up of one member from each member state, two CHMP members, one from the EMEA management board, and three from patient groups. It assesses applications for granting a drug 'orphan' status,[10] although the CHMP retains authorisation responsibilities.

Towards ensuring an objective report, two assessment teams are appointed to undertake concurrent reviews (*rapporteur* and co-*rapporteur*). The evalu-ation – consisting of the committee's opinion, the assessment report, the Sum-mary of Product Characteristics (SPCs),[11] the text for labelling, and the pack-aging insert – is passed to the Commission, the member states and the appli-cant, along with a recommendation, and the Commission is then required to prepare a draft decision on authorisation within thirty days (it has three months to deliver its final decision). During this period both the member states and the applicant may raise concerns or query the committee opinion. Should a member state appeal against the decision, they must do so in writing within twenty-eight days and only on the basis of 'important new questions of a scientific or technical nature which have not been addressed in the opinion of the Agency' (CEC 1993a). The committee is required to take this into ac-count in drawing up a new opinion. Barring unnecessary delay, the process from application to final national decision was designed to take a maximum of 300 days.

The decentralised procedure is a revamped version of mutual recognition, designed to improve the member states' faith in each others' assessments (Appendix H). It applies only to conventional products and involves the company making an application for marketing approval to one of the national agencies, the Reference Member State (RMS). This is the initial target market, and if approval is granted other national authorities, the Concerned Member States (CMS), are expected to recognise the authorisation. A right of appeal exists should a CMS refuse the authorisation, with a formal arbitration procedure going through the CHMP. The committee's new verdict is reviewed by the Commission before it delivers a final decision. As was the case with its predecessor, however, the member states' commitment to the decentralised procedure has been sketchy. Brian Ager, EFPIA Director-General, is quite frank about this: 'Countries simply balk. Suppose you're a German regulator and someone comes along with a product approved in Greece or, once the EU is enlarged, Estonia – how are you going to react?' (Ross 2000a: 65). The CMSs thus continue to simultaneously assess applications themselves.

While not an FDA, the EMEA serves a combination of public health and industrial policy goals, as well as fulfilling economic and social policy interests – 'The EU's goal [in establishing the agency] was to transform the relationship between national regulatory authorities and those of the Union, thus finally creating a common market for pharmaceutical products' (Vogel 1998: 5). None of the other agencies can make a similar claim about the policy field in which it operates. Recalling the Community's history of regulatory competence in the pharmaceutical sector, the institution of a centralised agency is undoubtedly the most important achievement to date. And while it has been successful in changing the EU regulatory climate for medicines for the better – in terms of speeding the availability of medicines to consumers, granting orphan drugs priority, and serving industry interests – the EMEA and its authorisation procedures have not been free from criticism.

Before considering the grounds for such criticism, it is necessary to understand how the agency came to be. Beginning with the consultations of the late 1980s, we examine the path to adoption of the final Regulation in July 1993. The focus is on the stakeholders' positions and behaviour rather than the details of the legislative process. This provides insight into their preferences and what weight they carried in the policy network. Further, it supports the contention that the EMEA came about as the result of entrepreneurial politics.

Establishing the EMEA: putting a new face on medicines control in the EU

Notwithstanding more recent pronouncements regarding patients, the main rationale cited by the Commission during the deliberations over a potential European medicines agency was the need to improve the approval system.

There were several reasons for this. First, drug registration was slowing down in most European countries (CEC 1993b). A surging number of applications, a growing industry, and increasingly technical and complex scientific issues were contributory factors. Second, the CPMP and mutual recognition procedures were deemed slow and inefficient. Third, the '1992' deadline was imminent and it was clear that the sector was not ready. This was the most important consideration from the Commission's perspective, as the failings of the Community authorisation procedures represented a setback in its aims to promote the single market. Thus, it was in a 1988 report on the work of the CPMP that the Commission first raised the possibility of a single, unifying regulatory office for medicines (COM 1988).

The Commission agenda
The 1988 report is significant on several fronts. Having asked the member states and 'interested parties' what 'form any definitive system for the free movement of medicines might take (mutual recognition, a centralized Community system or an intermediate approach)' (COM 1988), it laid the basis for the Commission's later proposal for an agency. As the interested parties consisted of industry and consumer organisations, the Commission essentially established the policy network from the outset. Furthermore, since the report was issued by the Industrial Affairs DG without consultation with the Social Affairs DG, the nature of the relationships within the network were also set: consumer interests were secondary considerations. Indeed, the report concentrates primarily on the need to improve the system from an industrial rather than public health standpoint.

Perhaps the most important element of the document is that it reveals the Commission's agenda. The report reflects on the failings of the multi-state route, pointing out that the number of applications was 'very few in comparison to the hundreds of applications made separately each year in each Member State ... [and] it is unfortunate that, to date, every dossier has systematically been the subject of reasoned objections [and referred back to the CPMP], in spite of the obligation on Member States to take due consideration of the initial authorization, save in exceptional cases' (COM 1988). As the member states consistently raised objections to authorisations granted by other national authorities, the industry's pursuit of single market applications had thus continued unabated. With multiple national approval systems having been identified by the Cecchini study as an impediment to completion of a single pharmaceuticals market, the report concludes that:

> In accordance with Article 15 of Directive 75/319/EEC as amended, and also within the legislative programme set out in the White Paper on the Internal Market, in light of experience, the Commission must, before 1 November 1989, submit to the Council a proposal containing appropriate measures leading towards the abolition of any remaining barriers to the free movement of medicinal products within the Community. (COM 1988)

The Commission regarded an authoritative Community system as necessary to promote multiple market applications by the industry, and to overcome disparate national approval procedures (thereby eliminating varying authorisation times), both of which hampered the development of a single market. Underlying this was 'the assumption that many national regulatory standards are really disguised barriers to trade: their primary purpose or effect is to protect domestic producers from international competition' (Vogel 1998: 16). However, DGIII found that its priorities did not gel with the views of the other stakeholders, and that it would have to push for its agenda to be implemented.

Stakeholders' interests – costs versus benefits
In order to understand the positions within the policy network during the policy-process, an outline of several of the more important issues under consideration helps establish the backdrop. Table 6.1 generalises the stakeholders' concerns during the late 1980s when it was still unclear as to what form, if any, a new authority might take. All were agreed on the necessity of quicker approvals, but did so for different reasons and therefore had different hopes and concerns.

From Table 6.1's admittedly simplistic division between the then (perceived) pros and cons of what an agency might bring, the potential costs and benefits to the stakeholders – and hence their representations during subsequent negotiations – can be contextualised. The Commission's April 1989 compilation of responses document revealed the extent of this lack of consensus and the depth of scepticism (CEC 1989). These views would harden as discussions developed around more concrete proposals.

The drug companies appeared to think that they stood to lose the most from a new regime not directly geared towards industrial policy interests. It was felt that a single centralised procedure was unlikely to be able to adequately match their growing expenditure on new drugs with more efficient approvals. In the 1989 document EFPIA had said that its members were firmly 'against a fully centralized system with decisions being made by a European body', and suggested that not only would the workload prove too great (and approvals therefore too slow) but that there was a danger that any agency would be a political construct. EFPIA thus insisted that mutual recognition be made binding, arguing that companies should not be disadvantaged under a revised (centralised) Community regime because of political imperatives. The fear was of a 'Euro-FDA'[12] and of authorisations being politically-determined. John Griffin, Director of the Association of British Pharmaceutical Industry ABPI, thus referred to the Commission's early vision for an agency as a 'recipe for disaster' (MARKETLETTER 1989). Because of these fears (and the potential costs to be assumed) EFPIA even suggested that it be consulted and involved in all preparatory work for Community legislation in the area.

Table 6.1 Perceived pros and cons of a potential European medicines agency (prior to the EMEA)

Stakeholder	Pro (Benefit)	Con (Cost)
Industry	• a standard application format and single approval mechanism could ease companies' administrative difficulties *vis-à-vis* 12 disparate national procedures (in several different languages) and save costs • a system geared towards speeding the approval process may serve as a boost to industry generally, and help to promote small to medium sized companies specifically • quicker approvals (via a new body) would limit the erosion of the effective patent life for new drugs	• one EC system (via a centralised office) might mean higher levels of scrutiny across Europe, thereby undermining companies' ability to 'pick and choose' amongst national authorities according to perceived ease of assessment criteria or target market for pricing purposes • the potential for an overly-politicised body staffed by nominated bureaucrats, with decisions on marketing authorisation taken on political rather than scientific grounds

Member States	• a Community body would not have to preclude the continuation of a complimentary system of single country applications
	• might promote collaboration with other member state scientists and regulatory offices, and foster the exchange of knowledge
	• political, scientific and legal liability to be shifted from the national to the supranational level (Commission)
		• a loss of sovereignty – not just in political terms but with regard to:
		  i. the ability to decide on which drugs are appropriate for their populations
		  ii. healthcare financing autonomy and control of the drugs bill
		• a centralised mechanism for all companies irrespective of origin may harm local industry
		• loss of national responsibility for the health protection of its citizens; how would an EU agency be held accountable, and who would then be liable?

Patients/ consumer interests	• national approval procedures (often) relate to other political or economic goals, and can mean delays in the introduction of new medicines to the detriment of patients – an EU agency would not have such wider responsibilities • an EC system could overcome disparate member state approval procedures, eliminating differences between member states in approval times for the same products	• the potential for a 'lowest common denominator' approach to safety and efficacy guidelines i.e. those member states with strict approval procedures having to dilute them given a European 'efficiency regime' approach • resulting in a body in which they might have less say (compared to the national level) and one susceptible to regulatory capture because of a reliance on (European) industry fees for its financing

Although sharing an interest in preserving sovereignty and controlling healthcare expenditure generally, the 1989 document showed that the member states' views were not uniform. While some (including Ireland and Luxembourg) reflected on the merits of a single supranational license issued by a Community office, others (most notably France) favoured a revised mutual recognition procedure with national authorities retained at the heart of the system. And the UK's support for an agency in principle can be compared to Germany's outright opposition. The member states' differing views would later prove problematic in agreeing the legislation.

The consumer position was, and would remain, the most straightforward even if the least heeded. Responding to the 1988 consultation, the European Consumers' Organisation BEUC echoed the other stakeholders' dissatisfaction with existing arrangements. Its primary concern, however, was the persistence of different safety standards for drugs in the member states, and that existing authorisation procedures were therefore not necessarily the safest from a consumer point of view. For instance, while the drug *Halcion* – designed to treat sleeping disorders – was withdrawn from the UK market in 1993 on safety grounds, it continued to be marketed in other member states.[13] The BEUC felt that patients would be best served by a pan-European office with stringent approval standards – rather than continuing with twelve national regimes exercising different criteria – and thus endorsed the creation of a Community agency, in principle, providing that it would harmonise safety and quality standards upwards.

Despite the stakeholders' concerns, the Commission was not to be deterred. DGIII was wary of the 1992 programme and, after stressing in the 1989 document that a 'major transfer of executive competence' was necessary to complete the single market, the 'Proposal for a Regulation laying down Community Procedures for the Authorization and Supervision of Medicinal Products for Human and Veterinary Use and Establishing a European Agency for the Evaluation of Medicinal Products' (CEC 1990b) was submitted in November 1990. This was presented to the Council as part of a package of four 'future system' instruments representing broader plans for the free movement of medicines (COM 1990). But the discrepancy in the stakeholders' positions meant that it would only be in July 1993, after several important amendments, that the final text of the Regulation was agreed (and yet another two years before the EMEA became operational).

The route to approval

The Commission's proposals made clear its goals. An agency would be established to co-ordinate two new authorisation routes, and member states' objections to authorisations granted under the centralised procedure were to be permissible only for 'objectively defined reasons of public order or public policy', while under the decentralised procedure, the CPMP would arbitrate where bilateral agreement failed. The aim was to deliver authorisations within a timeframe of around 300 days. Given the clear internal market orientation of these proposals, the Commission put it to the member states that Article 100(a) of the Treaty – designed to facilitate completion of the single market through harmonising national laws – was the appropriate legal basis for establishing the system. But the German government disagreed and rejected the article's applicability. In addition, it claimed that subsidiarity precluded the Commission taking decisions on drug authorisations, and was, therefore, only willing to countenance a small 'technical secretariat'. According to Robert Hankin (then of DGIII), in his testimony to the UK House of Lords Select Committee on the European Communities, this was because of 'the German concept of federalism and the view that the role of the Community should be limited to decisions of principle while decisions on individual products are the responsibility of the individual Member States' (HoL 1991b). Other governments, including those of Ireland and Luxembourg, had no difficulties with the proposals generally, nor the use of Article 100(a) specifically.

More subtle views were revealed in the member states' answers to the Commission's December 1990 request for written responses to the future system plan. Denmark, Italy, the Netherlands and Spain were in favour of an administrative agency (retaining the member states' technical competence), while France preferred to continue with a strengthened mutual recognition principle. The French position was essentially that of its industry, as set out by Yves Juillet of the French industry association (SNIP) at a 1988 conference:[14]

> It is the view of SNIP that the operation of the future European system, harmonized with the two alternative procedures which may be used at the choice of the manufacturer, *should remain* [sic] in line with texts and procedures which already exist, with no break in the structures that are already set up … with the only changes being:
>
> – that States which make remarks or objections would have to justify their position
>
> – that the European Committee in charge of judging the validity of these refusals would issue a ruling which the Member States would have to respect. (Juillet 1989: 262–3)

Although in favour of an agency, the UK position was that if it were to rule on 'scientific issues' (i.e. drug approvals), then Article 100(a) was inappropriate for its establishment and that Article 235 was required instead. Article 235 – which allows the Council to take decisions on fostering the common market where existing Treaty provisions are insufficient for the Commission to do so – had already been invoked to create other Community agencies. Additionally, the UK government's official response was that 'ministers wish to reserve their position on the acceptability of any particular proposals until they can satisfy themselves that the proposals are capable of meeting satisfactorily the objectives set and of maintaining acceptable standards of protection

of public health' (HoL 1991b). In other words, it wanted further consultation with its industry, for the ABPI had already made clear that it was against
a centralised European agency (Griffin 1990).

In its 1988 policy document, 'ABPI's Blueprint for Europe', the ABPI expressed its preference for a single authorisation regime characterised by unambiguous data requirements and overseen by an independent authority, separate from the CPMP, which would reach decisions within 210 days (Abraham
& Lewis 2000). It wanted all biotechnology products to be scrutinised by this
new authority, though companies would retain the right to choose whether
to submit other products to this regime or to continue with mutual recognition. In the case of the latter, the Community authority would be empowered
to make binding decisions. This is very much the system which emerged,
albeit based on an agency with a revamped CPMP at its heart.

Not just the British, but the Belgian, Italian and Spanish governments all
saw Article 235 as requisite were the agency to be delegated any scientific
powers. Even if opposed to the agency, the German authorities also agreed
that this provided a more appropriate basis. The French view was more nuanced. Were Article 100(a) used for the creation of the agency, then the
centralised procedure would have to be based on Article 235. So despite both
the European Parliament and the Economic and Social Committee having
earlier endorsed the use of Article 100(a), it was decided at the Internal Market Council meeting in December 1991 that Article 235 would provide the
appropriate legal basis.[15] As this meant the consultation procedure in the
European Parliament (and unanimity in the Council), it may seem an odd
decision given Germany's clear opposition and France's scepticism. However,
since consultation only allows Parliament a single reading, the choice of Article 235 would also ensure that the MEPs had little say. The Parliament's
Committee on the Environment, Public Health and Consumer Protection,
which had been assigned the text, had already suggested numerous amendments with which the Commission was unhappy (EP 1991b).

As a forum where wider interests are given expression, the Parliament
focused largely on the fact that only tangential attention had been paid to
public health requirements. It suggested that 'medicinal products belonging
to specific pharmacological categories of particular social significance' be
added to the biotechnology and high technology designation of the centralised
procedure. This was to ensure that products designed to treat diseases or
conditions of especial concern would qualify for the quicker, multiple market
route. Unlike the Commission, the Parliament envisaged a sparing use of the
centralised procedure. The ESC too suggested that public health protection
feature more prominently (ESC 1991b). Recognising that 'The importance of
the Agency lies in the remit and role which will be assigned to it', the Committee asked whether the division between types of product qualifying for the
two procedures 'protects the interests of either the 'passive consumer' (patients) or the "active consumer" (the doctor who prescribes the drug and is

thus the real promoter of its consumption)'. The point being that drug approvals carry a wider social element not adequately addressed in the proposals. Prepared by its Protection of the Environment, Public Health and Consumer Affairs section, the ESC also stressed that transparency be a central element of the new agency, with the names of the national experts carrying out reviews on its behalf being made public. This did not happen – ostensibly in order to protect the experts' safety (Abraham & Lewis 2000)[16] – and the ESC's further calls for the agency to 'avoid interference from industry and intervention by the national authorities which would be incompatible with assessment duties' were similarly disregarded.

The industry did not impassively watch these debates unfold. There was potentially a great deal to gain from a revised regime, but EFPIA felt that as the CPMP procedure had not worked the first time, there was no reason to believe that an agency would make it any better. It criticised the Commission's call for further centralisation, reiterating its members' frustration at the lack of any real (i.e. binding) mutual recognition in practice: 'industry objected to the bureaucratic prolongation of approval processes, feared the creation of a centralised agency empowered to render final decisions that would override national regulations, called for effective mutual recognition of national decisions, desired quicker action from existing agencies, and hoped for close links between industry and regulatory bodies' (Orzack et al 1992: 860). More specifically, industry expressed its fear that the culture of mistrust between the member states would continue, leading to overwhelming use of the centralised procedure and resulting in the national authorities trying to outdo one another in terms of the strictness of approvals.

Beyond representations to the Commission and the national governments, industry representatives voiced their concerns more publicly. For instance, in clearly playing to the audience, John Griffin asked in a letter to the British Medical Journal at the time of the proposals: 'Is patient safety being put at risk in the decision making process offered by the Commission?' (Griffin 1990: 1537). He argued that CPMP members were not always medically or scientifically trained, and that the committee ought to be comprised of recognised scientists to ensure rigorous assessments. This health protection line belied the industry's underlying interest in ensuring that appeals would not go back to the same officials who rejected the authorisation in the first place. A further example comes from William Currie (1990: 388).

> There is little to support haste in the creation of such a European Institution. We must remember that currently the time to achieve market authorization in the Member States of the EC is not greater than that taken in other geographic areas and that comparable statistics reviewed periodically by the Pharmaceutical Manufacturers Association (PMA) of the US often show the European national performance in a favorable light.

Representing an American company, his agenda was slightly different from that of his European counterparts i.e. expressing a preference for the European status quo over the US system. But what is interesting is that his assertion contradicts EFPIA's position in its 1988 memorandum to the Commission on the need for extending patent protection periods (see Chapter 5). Then the argument had been that improved protection was necessary because of slower registration times in Europe. Now it was that European approval times were not less competitive than the US. Ultimately, industry was wary of a Community equivalent to the FDA and was prepared to try all lines of argument.

Nevertheless, the companies acknowledged that some type of Community authority was necessary, especially if they were to glean any benefits from the SEM. With the Commission set on an agency, EFPIA lobbied to ensure that authorisation decisions would serve industry's interests. It thus insisted on manufacturers' freedom of choice between mutual recognition or the centralised procedure, where the former – subject to the addition of certain procedural 'safeguards' in terms of ensuring that national authorities were bound to recognise each others' approvals – was to remain the heart of the 'future system', and the latter based on a fortified CPMP with the authority to enforce its decisions (especially regarding appeals). EFPIA was also adamant about companies retaining the right to choose the *rapporteur* in applications. Although this is very much the current system, the problem at the time according to Dulio Poggiolini, Chairperson of the CPMP, was that 'An improvement in the legal situation of the CPMP will only be possible if the Council of Ministers is charged with making the opinions of the CPMP mandatory and operational ... The acceptance of EEC opinions on marketing authorizations of new medicines implies a renouncing of sovereignty and sovereignty includes political and legal aspects' (Poggiolini 1989: 243). With the impending single market sovereignty was a concern for the member states generally. But the potential 'free movement of medicines' represented a particularly difficult prospect at a time when they were struggling to control health budgets – Community approval of expensive medicines could mean higher drug bills. Further, any loss of sovereignty was seen as potentially damaging to local industry, and public health concerns too could be affected.

Indeed, as the BEUC accused the Commission of being 'more concerned about promoting the recognition of other countries' medicines, despite differing safety standards ... Proposals for opening up the market take precedence over those which have to do with the quality of health care' (Orzack 1996: 20), so too was it sceptical of industry's vision. Irrespective of whether the member states would show more faith in each other's work, or of a binding mutual recognition route, the BEUC was against both the industry having a choice of procedure, and national agencies competing against each other. The worry was that this would 'create the strong possibility of a Community licensing system containing double standards ... medicines assessed by a newly created, highly scientific central body may be scrutinised more critically than those submitted to a less resourced and sophisticated national agency' (Currie 1989: 771). Were this the case, industry could be expected to turn overwhelmingly to the latter. The BEUC thus envisaged a policing rather than policy-making role for the national authorities.

The Consumer's Consultative Committee (CCC)[17] also insisted on a stronger public health protection element under any new authority. It argued that an agency should be able to assess medicines according to 'specific therapeutic advantages' *vis-à-vis* products already on the market (CCC 1991). This echoed the Parliament's call for products of 'particular social significance' to be granted centralised approval. To facilitate this, the CCC sought consumer representation in the CPMP, suggesting that its independence 'is not guaranteed, for research in the area of pharmaceutical products is largely funded by the industry'. The Commission ignored this, along with most of Parliament's submissions.[18] This single-mindedness is reflected in an unpublished May 1991 correspondence from a senior official in DGIII/E/F to Ricardo Perissich, then Industrial Affairs Commissioner: 'Thus at the present time it appears that the current proposals do provide a good basis for negotiation within the Council, and no fundamental review is required. Consideration needs to be given to the extent to which the Commission can accept "Communautaire" amendments from Parliament, bearing in mind that such amendments may provoke a counter reaction from Member States' (Anon 1991b). The official had foreseen that public health concerns would be raised by Parliament and was suggesting, if not recommending, that any prospective amendments be disregarded for fear of the policy being rejected by the member states. It would seem that patients were neither the Commission's nor the member states' primary concern.

Just two months after the ESC's July 1991 report, the Commission agreed an amended proposal for the agency based on Article 235. But Denmark now expressed reservations. Its authorisation criteria were seen as stricter than most of the other member states', and it was concerned that unanimity under Article 235 meant no possibility of opting out. Once the details of the centralised procedure had more or less been hammered out, Danish opposition faded and it looked a 'done deal'. However, at the 10 November 1992 Internal Market Council another obstacle emerged, now over 'headquartering' the new agency.

At Belgian and Spanish insistence, a Council Declaration stating that the agency would only begin operations eighteen months after its headquarters had been decided was agreed. It had been expected that the decision on the EMEA's location would – along with the new environment and internal market harmonisation agencies (the drug addiction monitoring centre, training foundation, and police force were themselves still homeless) – be decided via raffle at the December 1992 Edinburgh summit meeting. But under the Declaration the location of the EMEA would have to be decided by the leaders of the member state governments. And now that it was clearer how the agency and a centralised procedure would work, Denmark, Ireland, the Netherlands, Spain and the UK all launched campaigns to host it. A decision of the heads of state and governments on 29 October 1993 agreed London as the EMEA seat.

The reason for the bidding war was the perceived industrial policy gains to be accrued. When asked why the UK government had fought to have the agency in London, then Minister of Health Virginia Bottomley's response was unequivocal: 'The British pharmaceutical industry will have the advantage of easy access to the agency, which will be working in its language and will offer its products quicker access to the European single market, all of which means that there will be increased inward investment in the UK, more exports and more jobs' (Hansard 1995). Unsurprisingly, the ABPI had spearheaded the UK's campaign (Jackson 1993). And with then Prime Minister John Major stating that 'I and the British government support the pharmaceutical industry's initiative in proposing that the Agency should find its permanent home here' (SCRIP 1820), it clearly did so with full governmental backing.

What proved to be the final sticking-point emerged over the fees to be paid to the agency. Several member states objected to the proposed cost of new drug applications as too high compared to those charged by national authorities, fearing this would result in increased overall expenditure on drug regulation and a loss of national fee revenues. And while some governments sought Commission oversight of EMEA financing via Community subsidy, the UK favoured an agency funded solely by fees (as was the case for its own agency). This further delayed the opening of the EMEA's doors, especially as the Parliament had a vested interest here. All Community budgetary plans require Parliamentary approval, and MEPs wanted some control over agency financing (Gardner 1996). The end result was a 'half-and-half' agreement under Regulation (EEC) 297/95, but not before the Parliament and Council reduced the amount of the subsidy in late 1995, with financing to be reviewed after three years. As a consequence, the agency is now financed mainly through fees and, as will be shown, this has contributed to criticism of its role.

Differing industrial policy goals, and to a lesser degree public health concerns, were implicit in the member states' disparate positions throughout the policy-process, and all shared an uncertainty about the Commission's vision. Initially, most feared a squeezing out of their own regulatory authorities and that a streamlined authorisation procedure could mean rationalisation of local industry. This has not really happened in practice, though some national agencies are used more often than others. And, by working with the companies, the agency in fact helps to promote the aggregate European industry. Ultimately then, it seems that the costs to be borne by the member states were less significant than the gains – the amended proposals were endorsed in the Council on 23 July 1993.[19]

The Commission's new line
Following Council's adoption, the Commission sought to distance itself from its position of industrial policy first and health policy second, and set about

presenting the agency as a patient benefit. Dr Bangemann, successor to Mr Perissich, and known for his strong commitment to a single pharmaceuticals market, immediately adopted this new health protection line. Gone were his earlier references to the agency's role in consolidating the internal market (e.g. Bangemann 1991, CEC IP 1994), now he stressed that by improving market authorisation procedures, the new structure 'generates consumer protection thanks to severe test criteria' (Albedo 1995b). More recently, in an information booklet published by DG Enterprise, it is even claimed that the agency was established 'partly in response to demands from consumers' organisations, particularly the BEUC and the European Parliament' (CEC 2000: 7). It has already been shown that this was not the case. The BEUC may have endorsed the idea as first raised by DGIII, but it had a completely different vision. And most of the Parliament's amendments were ignored. What is true, is that the decision to draw up and publish the details of all products approved via the centralised route was the result of consumer and Parliamentary pressure for transparency. As stated at the outset of the chapter, 'no one thought of seriously selling the idea as a patient benefit', and there is in fact no proof that patients have benefited from the revised approval procedures under the EMEA.[20]

The Commission's new patient protection line reflects the criticism it drew both before and after the deal was done, especially as the policy network involved no consumer representation; after the initial consultation, patient/consumer interests were not solicited. The Commission thus sought to deflect criticism by insisting that the patient had always been the prime concern. Recalling Wilson's politics of policy framework, one of the characteristics of the policy entrepreneur is that it often aims to associate the proposed regulatory intervention with broader social concerns or widely-held values. Nevertheless, despite the Commission's new sell, it is clear that DGIII's single market preoccupation, along with industry pressure, had been the driving force. Further evidence of this comes from the agency's operation in practice, and the degree to which it works with the industry.

Grounds for criticism

As a unique body it should not be surprising that the EMEA has its share of detractors. But what is perhaps surprising given the Commission's insistence that the agency is designed primarily for European patients, is that its critics are primarily those with patients' interests in mind. Dissatisfaction relates mainly to the nature of the system, and criticism has generally been twofold. First is a perceived lack of transparency in the agency's work and that healthcare professionals do not have the access they perhaps should. Second is that the agency's operations (and even its remit) are therefore geared more towards the needs of industry (i.e. the applicant) than the patient. The point being that the EMEA's emphasis is on improving time-to-market (TTM) for new drugs rather than protecting public health per se. Quick access to new medicines is clearly in patients' interest, but the question is whether speeding TTM as an end in itself is sufficient. These are charges which reverberate particularly sharply with those interested in the public health side of medicines regulation, and they relate to the earlier discussion on how and why the agency was established.

Transparent, accessible?
The lack of transparency criticism is one which the agency has fought since its inception. Primarily through the maintenance of a detailed website, the EMEA has striven to make its activities open and accessible. The site posts an array of material, including a listing of all legislation pertinent to medicines in the Community, summaries of meetings and assessments of its operations, and pharmacovigilance 'alerts' regarding drugs already available on member state markets. Importantly, it also publishes two sets of documents. First is the Summary of Product Characteristics (SPCs) for new drugs which provide detail about individual products so that interested parties – primarily doctors and national regulatory officials – can obtain information about clinical effectiveness. Second are the European Public Assessment Reports (EPARs), which are detailed assessments of new applications for all positive opinions granted under the centralised procedure. Publishing such information is intended to demonstrate the agency's accessibility, but the nature and value of what is published has been questioned, and accusations of non-transparency therefore persist.

One of the most openly critical voices has been that of the International Society of Drug Bulletins (ISDB). Founded to promote 'the international exchange of information of good quality on drugs and therapeutics, to encourage and to assist the development of professionally independent drug bulletins in all countries and facilitate cooperation among bulletins', it has consistently questioned the extent of the EMEA's commitment to transparency. According to the ISDB, the material provided on the agency's website, along with the way it is presented, is opaque, often inconsistent, and even unhelpful (ISDB 2001). In a 1998 report assessing nine EPARs, the society characterises them as 'hazy and irrelevant' (ISDB 1998). The BEUC's view is also critical, but it sees the EPAR as requiring:

> a high level of technical knowledge about pharmaceuticals and is therefore adequate for professional use. Consumer organisations usually have very limited financial resources and it is hard to get experts with this kind of knowledge willing to work for small money. For the ordinary consumer/citizens the publication is not useful. It is too technical and very difficult to find your way around in for an unskilled person. (BEUC 2000: 3)

The ISDB report concludes that the major problem with the EPARs, however, is the 'lack of a clear and consistent policy on the reporting of the clinical trial data which influenced the decision on whether or not to license a new drug'. The group has even accused the EMEA of employing obscure and coded language in the presentation of these reports; that which diminishes the reliability of their content (ISDB 2001). The SPCs have also been criticised, and critics identify two main failings. First, doctors are expected to look up the SPCs on the EMEA website themselves (assuming they have the means and time) – national authorities have traditionally provided doctors with this information. Secondly, in the SPCs the drugs are described without reference to comparable preparations, let alone those designed to treat similar conditions. This hinders doctors' ability to make comparative assessments for prescribing purposes, raising questions about the value of the summaries as they are drafted.[21]

Beyond containing unclear information, a further concern is that the manufacturers are involved in writing the SPCs and EPARs, which are essentially public health documents (although the CPMP has final say over the text of the latter). Not only may this result in documents of variable quality,[22] but it may compromise their objectivity or accuracy.[23] For instance, even though the direct-to-consumer advertising of medicines is prohibited in the EU, it has been alleged that 'In practice, drug companies have failed to fulfil their duty to inform via the patient leaflets and SPC[s]. By completely blurring the dividing line between information and promotion, they have developed highly effective promotional tools and methods that ignore the very special nature and utilisation of the "merchandise" they produce' (Bardelay 2001: 4).

Another example of the potential for a lack of accuracy comes from a question tabled by MEP Nel van Dijk in 1996 (CEC 814/96). He asked why the package leaflet for the drug *Fareston* – designed to treat breast cancer – did not actually carry the word 'cancer', using the word 'tumour' instead. As 'cancer' features in both the EPAR and SPCs and is not interchangeable with 'tumour', he claimed that this was misleading to patients.[24] The Commission's response was that the leaflet text was in accordance with the labelling of medicinal products Directive,[25] which states that 'The competent authorities [CPMP] may decide that certain therapeutic indications shall not be mentioned in the package leaflet, where the dissemination of such information might have serious disadvantages for the patient'. This seems slightly odd given that cancer is such a widely-reported issue, but the Commission did concede that steps needed to be taken to ensure a higher degree of clarity. Noteworthy is that the Commission's response was given by Industrial Affairs Commissioner Martin Bangemann, rather than Social Affairs Commissioner Pádraig Flynn.

A further issue, particularly for consumer groups, has been improved access to the EMEA's work. The BEUC has long complained about the lack of patient representation in the CPMP, registering its dissatisfaction as early as 1986 that consumer groups were not formally included in discussions on drug approval under the multi-state procedure, while industry's views were in fact solicited (Orzack 1996). In France for instance, both industry and consumer representatives are permitted to make observations during scientific deliberations. And relating their own attempts to access from the agency what they felt was 'general information' that the average patient might be interested in, Abraham & Lewis (1998: 481) write:

> despite European Commission and EMEA support of greater freedom of information, the European procedures for medicines regulation remain opaque to public scrutiny. We found it impossible to get basic information from the EMEA about mutual recognition applications, such as names of products, RMSs [Referring Member States] and CMSs [Concerned Member States]. The EMEA referred us to the Mutual Recognition Facilitation Group of the national regulatory authorities; the chairman of that group, Dr D. Lyons, told us in a letter dated Sept. 5, 1996, that 'only the applicant, the RMS and CMSs need know' such details. Moreover, there is no public right of access to CPMP meetings or minutes.

According to the authors' more recent work, this situation has hardly improved (Abraham & Lewis 2000). While issues of commercial and industrial secrecy must be respected, this exclusion of the public from even basic information – far less the substantive discussions – does not inspire confidence where public health is concerned.

Appreciating the importance for increased transparency and access, not only does the agency hold yearly audit meetings to which numerous non-governmental organisations including the ISDB and BEUC are invited, but another series of annual meetings discusses specifically how it can work towards increased openness. At one such meeting, in June 1998, the ISDB put the findings of its study on the nine EPARs to Rolf Bass, then head of the agency's unit for the Evaluation of Medicines for Human Use. Acknowledging the need for improvement, he said that the agency's website would soon be carrying a full index of trials to accompany the EPARs, as well as the complete list of documentation generated in each drug approval case (HAI 1998). This was understood to include even restricted documents which, while remaining so, would at least acknowledge their existence. As a follow-up, Professor Bass issued a letter to the ISDB in December 1998 responding in detail to the group's study (Bass 1998). Based on consultation with the CPMP, he addressed the ISDB's complaints on a product-by-product basis, generally acknowledging 'shortcomings' and 'inconsistencies'. However, he refuted that the EPARs provided insufficient scientific data, arguing that 'in accordance with current legislation', only 'commercially confidential information e.g. pharmaceutical development details' were not included. Further, he claimed that the reports were a 'readable and digestible volume of text' based on the full study reports. And again, assurances were given with regard to improving the quality of the reports, particularly in relation to common standards under the International Conference on Harmonization with the US and Japan. In a follow-up report two years later, however, the ISDB complained that these assurances had yet to be met (ISDB 2000).

Still, the publication of the EPARs and SPCs, and the maintenance of an up-to-date website is, as even the critics admit, a laudable step. Few national agencies are as forthcoming (Dukes 1996). But given that much of this information is quite specialised, and assuming that transparency really is a priority, the operation of a website is not sufficient when the material posted remains selective and/or inaccessible to a broad readership. The charges of a lack of transparency and inaccessibility are not likely to dissipate soon.[26]

Favouring the industry?

Such failings have fuelled the second line of criticism: wider questions about what the agency's function really is. Despite regulating for the safety, quality and efficacy of new medicines, many commentators remain unconvinced that public health is the first priority as the Commission and agency representatives consistently stress. The basis for their concerns is the degree of co-operation extended to the companies. Co-operation which, it should be noted, is closer than the industry's equivalent relationship with the FDA in the US.

For example, the applicant is allowed to nominate one of the two *rapporteurs* in the assessment. The result is that they usually choose one of the better-resourced and 'quicker' agencies (see below).[27] Even before choosing the *rapporteur*, a company is permitted to seek scientific advice from the agency several years in advance of the application. This is to ensure that its clinical research protocols comply with the types of questions the EMEA is likely to raise during the evaluation process, so that the drug stands a better chance of a positive opinion (Ross 2000a). By contrast, the FDA is often involved in the whole development plan for a new medicine, which is aimed more at ensuring that the product meets approval standards than simply fulfilling licensing requirements.

More worrying is the access to the agency's evaluation work which the industry enjoys. Silvio Garattini, previously one of the CPMP members, has asked why the applicant companies are privy to the committee's consultation documentation (which includes preliminary votes) prior to the final decision (Garattini & Bertele' 2001). This gives manufacturers an initial 'feel', and allows them to either withdraw the product before assessment, else accept a preliminary negative decision to begin preparations for an appeal. Between 1999 and 2001 there were some thirty withdrawals prior to the CPMP opinion (EMEA 2002).[28] While negative decisions are now listed, the details for refusal are not published. Withholding this information, and not divulging the grounds for withdrawal – initially neither the names nor the types of drugs were made public – may keep the applicants happy, but does not serve public health interests. As noted by the ISDB (1999: 5) 'it is not by working hand in hand with drug companies to produce documents stamped "controlled" that drug agencies can make themselves most useful and credible'. This also compares badly with the US where, according to Gerald Deighton, formerly head of the FDA's freedom of information office, public access is permitted to around 90 per cent of the FDA's records (NCC 1993). Although secrecy and opaqueness are admittedly features of the national regulatory process as well, the EMEA leaning towards industry does remain in stark contrast to the member states' own regimes which reflect much more of a health protection mandate. Nevertheless, it should be noted that prior to 1995 (before the EMEA), information regarding the review process and applications under consideration was even less available than now.

One reason for the companies' close involvement is said to be because applicant fees represent the majority share of EMEA receipts.[29] Unlike the FDA which is majority state-financed with only 15 per cent derived from fees in 2003 (FDA 2003), the Commission subsidy to the EMEA represented 14.6 per cent of total receipts in 2003 versus 67.4 per cent derived from fees (EMEA 2004). And while FDA fee revenue goes mainly into human resources and manpower costs, the EMEA's fee revenues go towards evaluations, scientific advice, renewals and other EMEA services. The agency, the Commission and the industry refute any link between the fees paid and the agency's work – indeed, most national authorities are financed primarily by fees – but some commentators argue that this reliance may mean that the companies have influence, and that TTM is going to be the priority (e.g. Abraham & Lewis 2000, Garattini & Bertele' 2004). Evidence to support this comes from the FDA where, following the Prescription Drug User Fee Act (PDUFA) in 1992,[30] approval times declined by 51 per cent (TCSDD 2000).

That the EMEA's relationship with industry is an especially close one has been conceded by Brian Ager, head of EFPIA. In an interview with an American journal, he referred to it as 'not a case of the regulator versus those regulated when it comes to improving performance. It's a partnership' (Ross 2000a: 62). The interviewer expresses his surprise at this admission: 'That's a far more cooperative system than anything we have in the US … It strikes me that the EMEA has really made a tremendous effort to form a partnership with industry'. And this relationship has even seen the US government's General Accounting Office (GAO) ask whether 'the new European drug approval processes may provide some alternative approaches for improving the timelines of FDA's drug approval' (GAO 1996: 1). This is something which American industry representatives have themselves suggested, arguing that the EMEA 'tries to be client-friendly … the FDA, by contrast, is oriented towards compliance and comports itself like a police agency' (Miller 1999: 3). As Egan (1998) has already noted that an inherent danger in the EU's use of agencies (to monitor the internal market) is that firms can become dominant players within the regulatory regime, the EMEA's particularly close relationship with the regulators would seem to warrant particular scrutiny.

Recalling the Commission's insistence that the EMEA puts patients' interests first, and having examined its design, it is now necessary to look at its work in practice. This is particularly in relation to public health protection and in comparison to both the member state authorities and the FDA for which the *Thalidomide* tragedy had provided the impetus.

The EMEA and public health: working as 'firstly a benefit for the European patient'?

In an information document on the EU pharmaceutical market, DG Enterprise stresses that the EMEA's more efficient approvals ensure quicker access to new innovative medicines, thereby contributing to improved health protection (CEC 2000). The causality may be tenable, but contributing to 'the protection of public health' is the thrust of the EMEA's mission statement and its annual Work Programmes. This it does by:

> Mobilising scientific resources from throughout the European Union to provide high quality evaluation of medicinal products, to advise on research and development programmes and to provide useful and clear information to users and health professionals.
>
> Developing efficient and transparent procedures to allow timely access by users to innovative medicines through a single European marketing authorisation.
>
> Controlling the safety of medicines for humans and animals, in particular through a pharmacovigilance network and the establishment of safe limits for residues in food producing animals. (EMEA 2000b)

Without putting too much stock into the specific wording, the mission statement appears to have 'evolved' in respect of public health. The original Regulation 2309/93 claimed the agency would protect public health 'by mobilising the *best* scientific resources within the European Union [emphasis mine]'. The aim of promoting health care 'through the effective regulation of pharmaceuticals within the single European market' has also been dropped. Nevertheless, the question now is whether the agency's pursuit of this mandate warrants claims of a benefit firstly to the European patient?

A public health mandate?
One of the main concerns over the EMEA's function has been that a single approval process raises the possibility of authorisation standards being laxer at EU level than at national level (particularly as they already differ by member state). This is especially as the decentralised procedure leads to competition between the national agencies. With only the largest and best-resourced really benefiting (the RMS receives the largest share of the applicant's fee), this is mainly about who can turn applications over most quickly, rather than who has the strictest standards. The previous EMEA Executive-Director, Fernand Sauer, may claim that 'They [national agencies] really enjoy working together, and instead of worrying about sovereignty issues, they now feel a degree of competition to prove that they are able to do the work in the required timeframe' (Ross 2000b: 56). But others have expressed concerns

over a race to the bottom, and for the need to ensure that 'the rush of competition does not overwhelm the fundamental responsibility for safety and efficacy in drugs' (Gardner 1996: 62). It has also been suggested that national authorities are often less enamoured with this competition than Mr Sauer. Abraham and Lewis (2000: 147–71) for instance found that some German and Swedish regulatory officials concede to having accepted products approved via the agency which, under their own national safety standards, they would not otherwise have authorised. Technology is changing not only the development process, but so too the assessment procedure, and though some states are more advanced than others or have higher standards, the EMEA regime does not account for this.

The degree of health protection afforded via the centralised procedure has also been questioned. In a letter to Mr Sauer in 1997 asking about the marketing approval of certain anti-depressant medications, Charles Medawar of Social Audit Ltd[31] suggests that 'the scientific evidence on which the [national] authorisations have relied is so flawed as to leave open the possibility that even basic assumptions about safety and efficacy (and therefore benefit and risk) may be quite wrong' (Medawar 1997). This, he suggests, is due to the lack of transparency, no consumer or patient involvement in the regulatory process, and inherent conflicts of interest between regulatory authorities and industry. And he put it to Mr Sauer that 'these are serious shortcomings also in the EMEA/CPMP system'. This letter sparked a three-year exchange of correspondence and is too lengthy for examination here.[32] Its mention, however, is in the context of considering the extent of the agency's public health protection role.

Another area where the EMEA has no say, is in pursuing the 'need' element in drug registration i.e. helping to ensure that those drugs for which a clear need is established are granted approval. Although this is because the 1965 Directive stipulates safety, quality and efficacy as the only permissible approval criteria, ex-CPMP member Silvio Garattini argues the EMEA ought to be given the power to 'acquire the rights on drugs abandoned by the industry because of the lack of commercial interest despite their clinical importance' (Garattini & Bertele' 2000: 441). The companies (and member states) would never agree to this – albeit for different reasons – but were the agency able to pursue the development of such products, and then sell the licenses to companies interested in marketing them as generics, its commitment to health protection could be strengthened. With patient and consumer groups not involved in the CPMP's evaluation work, need is not a consideration in any form. The agency simply considers those products the industry puts before it.[33] As such, according to Chapman et al. (2004), in Europe there are more than twenty drugs available in the lucrative hypertension market, none of which is clinically superior to the others.

Table 6.2 FDA 'priority review' versus EMEA 'innovation' criteria (centralised procedure)

FDA (US)	EMEA (EU)
The drug, if approved, would be a significant improvement compared to marketed products [approved (if such is required), including non-'drug' products/therapies] in the treatment, diagnosis, or prevention of a disease. Improvements can be demonstrated by, for example: 1 evidence of increased effectiveness in treatment, prevention, or diagnosis of disease; 2 elimination or substantial reduction of a treatment-limiting drug reaction; 3 documented enhancement of patient compliance; or 4 evidence of safety and effectiveness of a new subpopulation.	Medicinal products developed by other biotechnological processes which, in the opinion of the agency, constitute a significant innovation. Medicinal products administered by means of new delivery systems which, in the opinion of the agency, constitute a significant innovation. Medicinal products based on radio-isotopes which, in the opinion of the agency, are of significant therapeutic interest. New medicinal products derived from human blood or human plasma. Medicinal products the manufacture of which employs processes which, in the opinion of the agency, demonstrate a significant technical advance such as two-dimensional electrophoresis under micro-gravity. Medicinal products intended for administration to human beings, containing a new active substance which, on the day of entry into force of the regulation, were not authorised by any Member State for use in a medicinal product intended for human use.

Sources: FDA Manual of Policies and Procedures (CDER) and List 'B', Annex, Regulation (EEC) 2309/93.

Qualifying innovation

Related to this is the lack of an official EMEA definition of 'innovation' which leads to clash between industry and patients' interests. Unlike the strict approval standards in place since 1965, criteria for the evaluation of therapeutic value have not been laid down. The agency instead enjoys the discretion to decide whether a product constitutes a significant innovative gain or not. Looking at the FDA's criteria for 'priority review', the EMEA's innovation criteria – while more technical in language – are vague by comparison; dependant very much on the 'opinion' of the agency (see Table 6.2).

Since innovative products qualify for the quicker and wider market access of the centralised route, the companies favour a definition which allows more of their products to qualify. This despite initial fears of backlogs (Griffin 1990). Industry representatives claim that stricter innovation criteria at EU level would have repercussions on reimbursement decisions in the member states (Mossialos & Abel-Smith 1997). But as national authorities do not employ innovation as a reimbursement criteria for their own markets, the industry's argument is perhaps something of a smokescreen. Meanwhile consumer groups would prefer a stricter elaboration so that only truly therapeutically superior products are granted centralised access. A review of the 129 products granted centralised approval by the end of 1999 found that about half were copies or 'me-too' drugs (Garattini & Bertele' 2000), and an audit of the EMEA's procedures found that 'only 37% of patient associations feel the availability of innovative products is satisfactory or very satisfactory, and their concerns are increasing as Governments seek to control the rising expenditure on health caused by demographic change and scientific developments' (Cameron McKenna 2000: 51).[34] Even earlier, MEP Adriana Ceci referred to the Community's 'discretionary structures' as potentially promoting the 'corrupt acceptance' of new medicines (STOA 1993).

Nevertheless, the Commission favours a high use of the centralised procedure. Not just with regard to promoting the single market, but also in making Europe more attractive for pharmaceutical R&D. Here, as 'The first aim would be to make an absolute priority of raising the number of innovative drugs produced' (Bosanquet 1999: 136), limiting what constitutes an innovation would prove defeatist. Indeed, a paper recommending clarification of the innovation criteria was put to the agency's management board already in December 1995 (SCRIP 2106), but was not acted upon.[35] It should also be recalled that the CCC's and Parliament's earlier demands for therapeutic advantage to be part of the EMEA's assessment procedures were disregarded by the Commission. And while an advisory role for the agency in conducting cost-effectiveness studies to help in differentiating products of similar therapeutic value might represent a contribution here, given Commission and industry interests it is unlikely. Moreover, as each member state employs its own criteria the imposition of a single model would in any event prove unacceptable.

It should be noted that since 2000, the EMEA, like the FDA, has a system for the quicker approval of orphan drugs – in the EU defined as those with life-threatening or very serious conditions, and affecting less than 5 in 10,000 people. The target time for orphan approvals is 210 days and, in 2003, the average was in fact 190 days for the 182 orphan designations. By way of incentivising manufacturers, orphan drugs are also permitted shorter and smaller clinical trials, are granted ten years post-patent expiry marketing authorisation, lower applicant fees, and are now compulsory for centralised approval. These are important measures, demonstrating a sympathy to certain public health interests, and will hopefully act as an incentive mechanism.

Other considerations

Other critiques of the agency's public health commitment relate to its role in post-approval regulation. Pharmacovigilance is part of its remit, but its role is weak compared to that of the FDA.[36] In addition to post-marketing surveillance, FDA functions include monitoring and reporting on medication errors (due to poor advice, incorrect labelling, etc); ensuring accurate prescription drug advertising and promotional labelling; evaluation of drug shortage situations (with plans to alleviate them); monitoring industry behaviour; and reporting on 'therapeutic inequivalence' – that is, evaluating reports of 'therapeutic failures and toxicity which might indicate that one product is not equivalent to another similar product'.[37] This reflects a mandate more dedicated to consumer safety and public health, particularly as the FDA has the power to punish any misapplication or derogation from its rules. The FDA is also regarded as less conservative, and in bringing more therapies to market – not simply more products – more needs-focused. Its willingness to review products in 'specialist areas' such as oncology for instance, can be compared to the EMEA's shunning of such therapies (Cameron McKenna 2000).

The agency's appointment procedures are also a cause of concern. Regulation 2309/93 stipulates that CPMP members be 'chosen by reason of their role and experience in the evaluation of medicinal products for human and veterinary use as appropriate and shall represent their national authorities'. This is a somewhat vague criterion for appointment. For despite members being required to sign a declaration of interests, it means that each member state can appoint according to its own view of appropriate 'experience'. There is also no common appointment protocol and no central EU accreditation for the net of experts used by the agency. Further, the EMEA has no internal mechanisms for quality assessment. An independent (internal) scientific review committee to assess the quality of the assessments undertaken by the experts ought to be a priority here, especially as not all experts are used with the same frequency and national authorities retain their own procedures and requirements. This relates to the earlier point that the companies generally choose *rapporteurs* they perceive most sympathetic to their needs. These tend also to be the best-resourced and most efficient (quickest) agencies. Although all member states should have 'equal opportunity' to be both *rapporteur* and co-*rapporteur*, the UK was overwhelmingly the companies' first choice, with France, Sweden and the Netherlands following (Cameron McKenna 2000, EMEA 2000a).

Unlike many national authorities, the EMEA has no say in the pricing and reimbursement of the medicines it approves; also not in terms of requesting or insisting a product be reimbursed. The preamble to Regulation (EEC) 2309/93 reads in part: 'The provision of this Regulation shall not affect the powers of the Member States' authorities as regards the price setting of medicinal products or their inclusion in the scope of the national health system of the Member States' authorities or their inclusion in the scope of the social security schemes on the basis of health, economic and social conditions.' The industry does not favour any Community influence on prices (unless to establish free pricing), while the member states often pursue industrial policy goals in their exercise of these measures, and will not therefore accept any impingement on their authority. And Article 152 rules out any Community involvement in member state healthcare systems. Pricing and reimbursement remains a matter between the companies and the national governments.

Notwithstanding the benefits a single mechanism brings in minimising protectionism and preventing the authorisation of new products being denied because of reimbursement concerns, the EMEA has had other effects for the member states. National cost-containment goals (healthcare policy) have been affected given the agency's role in deciding on approvals. Sovereignty more generally has also been affected as the states lose much of their ability to decide, according to their own (often historical and cultural) criteria, which medicines are appropriate for their market. A right of appeal exists, but the CPMP's recommendations are almost always followed (Ross 2000b). Also, with potential disputes referred back to the CPMP for resolve, this ultimately means that national regulatory officials are generally excluded from deliberations which directly impact on the health of their constituencies. The Commission's underlying assumption that 'the national regulatory agencies are more alike than they are different' (Kidd 1996: 201) is at best, therefore, debatable.

Finally, although not a failing of the EMEA itself, patients often face long delays between (supranational) market approval and (national) market availability.[38] Despite the centralised procedure, the availability of new medicines post-authorisation varies considerably between the member states (Edmonds et al. 2000). While the agency is not required to accommodate the circumstances specific to each market – and accepting that some of these delays are unavoidable given differences in marketing and pricing systems – this lack of a post-approval mandate begs two questions. What is the contribution the agency actually makes to a single market in pharmaceuticals? A single, binding approval regime without commensurate health(care) authority (such as over pricing and reimbursement) is on its own insufficient. And does speeding TTM represent a patient benefit in practice as opposed to simply in theory?

The discussion has shown the interests of the pharmaceutical industry to be at the fore of the EMEA's activities. Compare the public health oriented criticisms outlined with the fact that, after the first five years of operation, 92 per cent of applicants declared themselves 'satisfied' or 'very satisfied' with the work of the CPMP, and 83 per cent of those who received scientific advice from the agency felt that it was 'useful' or 'very useful' (Cameron McKenna 2000). While such satisfaction is due primarily to the EMEA's reduction in approval times for new products (Koberstein 1999), the Commission's claimed link between quicker approvals and improved health protection is contingent on numerous assumptions or conditions. These include that the drugs being

authorised are those which are most needed; that medicine licenses are actually sought by producers primarily to improve public health (rather than to
turn a profit); and that the authorising body is empowered to primarily serve
public health interests. As already evidenced, none of these hold. Instead, it is
far easier to see how industrial policy and industry interests are served by a
binding authorisation regime which, rather than assessing products against
stricter approval criteria than those employed in the member states, instead
emphasises turning around applications as quickly as possible. As noted, the
EMEA's limited mandate is in stark contrast to the FDA's more proactive
role. This is only compounded with no consumer/patient representation in
the work of the agency, and may intimate some degree of regulatory capture.[39] Here, further evidence comes from the Commission's review of pharmaceutical legislation document (COM 2001). Not only does it contain suggestions for speeding market access for new medicines, but the Commission
initially proposed a review of the agency's management board to include two
representatives from industry. This would not have been tempered by the
inclusion of two patient representatives to be chosen by the Commission –
especially when so many patient and disease groups are today sponsored by
the industry – but it was forced to drop this from the final legislation (CEC
2004).[40]

Conclusions

This chapter set out to examine whether the EMEA really was, as the Commission has claimed, a benefit firstly to the European patient. It has been
shown that this is the case neither by design nor in practice. Single market,
industrial policy rationale were the drivers for the Commission's revamping
of the Community's authorisation procedures, and industry is the prime beneficiary. The discussion also aimed to provide support for the contention that
the establishment of the agency was a case of entrepreneurial politics within
the policy network. Although this has in part been done through an examination of the positions of the stakeholders and the role of the Commission in
proposing and pushing the legislation, what requires brief explanation is why
the EMEA 'policy' came to favour the industry in the manner it does. For if
corresponding to the entrepreneurial politics, it ought to have been a regulatory intervention where the 'producer' loses out to the 'public interest' due to
the presence of an entrepreneur. As this was not the case, it is posited that
once the decision to set up an agency was all but taken, the policy shows
characteristics of client politicking.

Involving patient interests?
Evidence that patients' interests were unlikely to be the focus of the new
agency comes from the gradual freezing out of the consumer position from
the policy-process. Despite calls for patients (and the medical profession) to

be consulted before any final decision was reached (e.g. Mann 1988), consumer interests – with the exception of the CCC – were really only involved until mid-1989. The BEUC had been asked to comment on both the 1988 CPMP report and the April 1989 compilation document, but was not privy to a third document circulated in December 1989 which, according to Robert Hankin of DGIII 'had a slightly more limited circulation in that it primarily went to the governments of the Member States at that stage as the ideas were beginning to harden further into the beginnings of formal proposals' (HoL 1991b). Mr Hankin also stated that while none of the three documents was formally published by the Commission, 'they were as public as an unpublished document can be'. The cryptic nature of this statement aside, important is that the Commission's 1988 report had not even involved DGV's public health unit (DGV/F). Responsibility for pharmaceutical policy fell to DGIII's Pharmaceuticals and Cosmetics Unit, but the repercussions of inefficient approval procedures should also have been discussed from a welfare point of view – how patients could be better served under a revised regime. If interest in a future 'centralized Community system' had truly been based on concerns for the European patient, DGV ought to have at least been consulted before the report went to the Council. As mentioned earlier, this situation remains the case (and has been criticised), where the EMEA falls under DG Enterprise's scope of activity, with DG Sanco not formally involved.[41]

Moreover, it was shown that there is little consumer representation within the EMEA structure – there are only two appointments to the management board. As Vos (1999: 250) notes, this need not be the case: 'Although the EMEA increasingly seeks contacts with interested parties (as required by Community legislation), the way in which contacts are made depends on the goodwill of the Management Board and the Commission; they determine *who* may participate, *where* and *how* [sic].' By initially marginalising one of the stakeholders in the policy network in this manner – and by keeping them out of the agency's work since – the Commission made it clear that single market concerns were its priority.

The industry 'hand'
On the other side were industry's interests, and it has been shown that EFPIA made considerable representations to the Commission, relying on arguments about competitiveness *vis-à-vis* the US and the need to support Europe's industry, and was in fact involved throughout the policy-process. In assessing the extent of the industry's influence, therefore, one need only consider that the agency's structure closely resembles that of what was then the UK's Medicines Control Agency. As the MCA was seen as one of the most conducive to industry's interests in terms of approval times, industry officials forwarded it as the preferred model (Staples 1994). Unsurprisingly, this has meant that the MCA and its officials have been the most popular choice of *rapporteur* under the centralised procedure. Additionally, the final format of the authorisation

procedures reflected industry's wishes to avoid a single route along the lines of the FDA, which was seen to be unduly bureaucratic and excessively slow. The UK and French trade associations were particularly involved here. EFPIA's demands for a binding mutual recognition process (based on 'safeguards') and a loose definition of what constitutes an innovative product were also met. Furthermore, the companies' insistence on control over who was to undertake evaluations resulted in the centralised procedure being revised to include a co-*rapporteur* of the applicant's choosing.

The competition between national agencies brought about under the decentralised route – once it was clear that they would compete over speed of approval rather than strictness of criteria – also reflects the industry's interests and influence. For the ability to select the Reference Member State allows companies to exploit the disparate national regulatory systems to their advantage; for example, by putting their products on those markets first, which other member states who employ either a reference or average price system may use as benchmarks in setting their own prices. This allows the companies to indirectly affect the price of their products. Even the choice of location for the agency – London, with the UK as Europe's biggest investor in pharmaceutical R&D – can be attributed to industry pressure (NCC 1994). If one takes the view that this not inconsiderable influence played a major role in setting the agency's mandate, the establishment of the EMEA may, like the Supplementary Protection Certificate, be regarded as a case of client politics.

That said, the policy environment during discussion over the agency, and the commensurate pressures, were different from the SPC; so too was the Commission's role. First, there was a clear political element involved. A centralised approval process via a Community agency was viewed as a major step in promoting an integrated pharmaceuticals market, and in achieving it, the EMEA undoubtedly represents the Commission's biggest achievement in this direction. And while the agency's creation may therefore reflect elements of spill-over, a neo-functionalist explanation fails to acknowledge the Commission's efforts. Second, it was not the industry that put the matter on the agenda but DGIII – EFPIA in fact opposed the idea initially. And rather than dominating the policy network through the strategic use of information (which was the case during the SPC campaign), as industry's interests overlapped with the Commission's (and member states') single market priorities, it sought to frame the discussion within an industrial policy context towards having these interests served. That is, when the operational details of the new office were being finalised – in consultation with industry – and when the industry could therefore impress its views. (Industry data was less important and DGIII in any event had EPFIA's 1988 memorandum prepared during the SPC campaign). Finally, not only did the Commission introduce the idea of an agency, but it also had the fixed aim of a binding authorisation regime within the context of the SEM, and accompanying deadline. Indeed, complimentary to the provisions establishing the agency were four Directives pertaining to wholesale distribution, classification of the supply, labelling, and advertising of human medicines respectively.[42] Known as the 'rational use' package, these Directives were aimed at completing the internal market. The Commission was clearly entrepreneurial in pushing the EMEA agenda within this context, and the EMEA's first annual report in fact cites DGIII as primarily responsible for the preparatory work behind the agency's establishment (EMEA 1996).

In summary, in showing the Commission to have been entrepreneurial within the network, it should also be recalled that the entrepreneurial politics scenario involves a policy outcome in which a small group is likely to bear the (high) costs on behalf of a much larger group expected to reap the benefits. The likely 'losers' within the policy network are, therefore, expected to oppose the policy (whether publicly or behind the scenes). Meanwhile, because the benefits are so widely spread that individual gains will be fairly minimal, most people outside of the network are unaware of, or even apathetic to, the proposal. And as the benefits are simply insufficient to mobilise the potential beneficiaries to push for the regulatory intervention, it is for this reason that an intermediary or entrepreneur is needed to sell the proposed policy.

In this vein, as the EMEA – both in the run-up to its creation and in its work – reflects the clash between health and industrial interests in the sector, the Commission had to overcome initial disinterest amongst the stakeholders and, as mentioned, even hostility from the industry. For while the member states, industry and consumer interests were all agreed on the need for a revision of Community authorisation procedures, none perceived sufficient gains (versus potential losses) to actively push for an agency as a solution. In part playing to each stakeholder's interests, therefore, the Commission adopted the entrepreneur's role towards pursuing its own agenda. Thus, as noted by Robert Hankin of DGIII at the time, 'what is reassuring from the Commission's point of view is that there are no alternative proposals on the table ... it is more a case of being the job of the Commission ... to try to win them over' (HoL 1991b). Thus, not just the impetus, but so too the campaign for an agency approach to medicines regulation in the Community, was the work of an entrepreneurial Commission interested in attaining a single market for pharmaceuticals. And despite the pro-patient rhetoric which came later, industrial policy goals within the single market had clearly been the prime concern.

Notes

1   This was agreed as part of the 30 April 2004 new European legislation for medicines (CEC 2004).
2   Under the 'Meroni Doctrine' – resulting from the 1958 judgement of the ECJ in

Case C-36/56 – *Meroni v. ECSC High Authority* – European law prevents the Commission from delegating decision-making to any other party. But the Commission's reliance on the EMEA (see next section on the Community authorisation regime), suggests that the agency's role can be seen as (quasi-)regulatory.

3   The FDA carries regulatory authority for a wide range of consumer products beyond medicines. Its Center for Drug Evaluation and Research (CDER) is responsible for pharmaceuticals.

4   For example Kingham et al. (1994), Jeffreys (1995) and Cameron McKenna (2000).

5   Accompanying the new procedures were 'The Rules Governing Medicinal Products in the European Community', a six-volume publication (now nine volumes) which sets out common guidelines in areas such as pharmacovigilance and clinical testing requirements.

6   Vogel (1998) puts the inclusion of biotechnology down to its potential for economic growth, and because it was such a new field that there were few national testing infrastructures.

7   Until April 2004, the Committee for Proprietary Medicinal Products (CPMP).

8   This failed to prevent a scandal emerging around Dulio Poggiolini, former chairperson of the CPMP, who was accused of accepting up to US$180 million in 'gifts' from pharmaceutical companies during his 30 years at the Italian Ministry of Health.

9   However, the grounds for selecting and appointing these representatives differ by member state, and not all are necessarily free of industry connections.

10   Orphan drugs, as defined within the EU, are those aimed at diseases having life-threatening or very serious conditions, but which are so rare as to affect less than five in 10,000 people.

11   The SPCs – created via Directive 93/570/EEC – is part of the marketing authorisation and represents the scientific text which contains all of the important information on the product. The information leaflet is derived from the SPCs.

12   The FDA was seen by both European and American industry officials as overly-bureaucratic and slow in reaching decisions on market authorisations. See for instance Matthews & Wilson (1998).

13   The CPMP response to the UK's suspension and then withdrawal of *Halcion* in October 1991 was to commission two position papers (released in October and December 1991), both of which concluded that the drug was safe if used in accordance with the labelling information – this despite internal recommendations for its withdrawal throughout the Community.

14   At the same conference, Trevor Jones, head of the UK's Medicines Control Agency, argued that 'what is required for the future is an efficient, authoritative central agency which operates to a high standard of scientific and clinical understanding with a minimum of timescales' (Jones 1989: 255).

15   A switch from Article 100(a) to 235 would also prove the case for the Community Plant Variety Office.

16   This has since changed (see note 26 below) and the names are listed on the agency's website.

17   The CCC is a consultative body of the Commission which represents consumer

interests. Its views are not binding.

18 One amendment adopted by the Commission was that suspension of a drug be permitted only after assessment of the harm likely to be accrued during the wait for a Commission decision i.e. unless there were justifiable public health reasons for not waiting, the product could not be withdrawn until the Commission had assessed the reasons. While the Parliament's concern were governments' protectionist motives, the Commission saw the unilateral right of the member states to withdraw products as undermining its internal market goals.

19 Parliament conducted a second reading but its amendments (26 May 1993) were again disregarded.

20 For instance Cameron McKenna (2000) or Edmonds et al. (2000).

21 The types (and names) of new drugs under review, which would also be of interest to healthcare professionals, are not posted on the website.

22 This variability prevails despite the harmonisation of SPCs under the centralised procedure. And while the majority of medicines circulating in Europe pre-date the procedure, and thus already carry differing SPCs, the EMEA could make a more concerted effort to ensure that all drug reporting is more objective and to a high standard.

23 The counter-argument being that the applicants ought to have input given that they have conducted the clinical trials and are thus likely to be best-placed to comment on the drugs' indications.

24 In a letter to Fernand Sauer, Ellen 't Hoen (1996), then of HAI Europe, also queried the *Fareston* package leaflet: 'The use of Fareston (toremifene) is restricted to the treatment of breast cancer and is not indicated for benign tumours'.

25 Directive 92/27/EEC.

26 It is to be noted that the new legislation contains proposals for ameliorating EMEA transparency, with regard to both the availability of hitherto unreleased information and the increased posting of material on the agency website (CEC 2004).

27 Initially the *rapporteurs*, indeed none of the network of experts, were named on the EMEA website – 'largely at the behest of the UK which cites "personal safety" reasons' (Abraham & Lewis 2000: 107) – but now all are listed.

28 Concerns about the rising number of pre-CPMP opinion withdrawals saw the 1999 establishment of the Working Group on Withdrawn Applications.

29 Commission financing was initially designed to be phased out after 5 years, but represented 24 per cent of EMEA receipts in 2000 (EMEA 2000a).

30 The PDUFA is a scheme whereby the pharmaceutical and biotechnology industry pays 'user fees' to the FDA in exchange for it setting performance standards aimed at reducing approval times.

31 Social Audit Ltd is the publishing arm of the Public Interest Research Centre (PIRC). PIRC is an independent UK charity which aims broadly to represent the 'public interest' in pharmaceutical medicine, and is financed largely by the Joseph Rowntree Charitable Trust.

32 The full chain of correspondence is available on the Social Audit Ltd website at: www.socialaudit.org.uk.

33 Although not part of the centralised process and not bound by EMEA decisions, as a member of the European Economic Area (EEA) and thus subject to Directive 65/65/EEC, Norway had to drop its own need clause in 1994. The Norwegian

national centre for medicines control, the *Statens Legemiddelkontrol*, had used the clause since 1938 to limit the number of medicines available on the market. Serving public health needs had been its priority in this regard (Norris 1998).
34 In the same study, companies expressed their desire for an expansion of the scope of products covered by the centralised procedure.
35 The paper was prepared by Professor Gianmartino Benzi of the Italian Institute of Pharmacology and based on a five-point innovation capacity scale.
36 Beyond issuing product 'alerts' this role involves disseminating post-approval practice guidelines to be observed by the member states and market authorisation holders. For example, the 2001 position paper on pharmacovigilance regulatory obligations (EMEA 2001).
37 According to the FDA's CDER Handbook.
38 While this also has an affect on the companies, as they are used to engaging in lengthy post-approval discussions with national governments about pricing, their primary concern from the agency is quicker authorisation.
39 Vos (1999) suggests that there is a 'risk' of capture. Others, including Abraham & Lewis (2000), are more critical.
40 The new constellation is one per member state, two each from the Commission and Parliament, plus two representatives of patient organisations, one representative from doctors' organisations, and one from veterinary organisations. These latter members are to be appointed by the Council in consultation with Parliament, on the basis of a list drawn up by the Commission (CEC 2004).
41 To coincide with the Parliament's reading of the Commission's review of pharmaceutical legislation proposals, nine members of the CPMP wrote to MEPs asking that, amongst other things, responsibility for the EMEA be moved from DG Enterprise to DG Sanco (de Andres-Trelles et al. 2002) (see also Chapter 8).
42 Directives 92/25/EEC, 92/26/EEC, 92/27/EEC and 92/28/EEC.

7

'Majoritarian politics': the pricing and reimbursement of medicines in the EU

It has been mentioned several times that the major hurdle in the Community's efforts to establish a single pharmaceuticals market is the pricing and reimbursement issue. This is not just because of subsidiarity, but also the formal stipulation of Article 152 in the Amsterdam Treaty confirming healthcare as the exclusive purview of the member states. As drug expenditure in most EU countries is mainly reimbursed by social security systems, this has resulted in distinct national pricing and reimbursement regimes, with prices for the same preparations varying, at times considerably, between markets. Notwithstanding its exclusion from healthcare concerns, as differing prices are inconsistent with a single market, the Commission has made several attempts to introduce harmonising legislation. This chapter examines how and where it has done so.

The discussion focuses on three initiatives: Directive 89/105/EEC (the 'Transparency Directive' of 1989); the Commission's 1994 'Communication on the Outlines of an Industrial Policy for the Pharmaceutical Sector' (COM 1993); and the series of three 'roundtable' meetings organised under the auspices of the Industrial Affairs Directorate-General (DGIII) in 1996, 1997 and 1998. As these represent different Commission strategies to address price harmonisation, they have been chosen because they show just to what extent the Commission is handcuffed in this area. Since each can be viewed as its own policy network, the initiatives are treated as a mini case-studies of stakeholder involvement. As the only formal Community policy in the area of pricing and reimbursement, the Transparency Directive is given the most attention.

The chapter forwards two contentions. First, that what has been undertaken *vis-à-vis* pricing and reimbursement, as with the wider regulatory framework itself, has been driven by industrial policy interests. Second, that the Commission's inability to develop a common EU policy (or policies) enables the application of a majoritarian politics characterisation of the policy-process. Recalling that this involves diffuse costs and diffuse benefits (such that resolution takes place at the national rather than EU level), this suggests that there is little incentive for any actor, either singly or in co-operation with another, to pursue such a policy. The discussion will show how the other stakeholders have consistently rejected the Commission's initiatives on the basis of perceived costs. None (of the policy networks) have effected change here, and policy remains decided at the national level. In addition, as the ECJ plays a role in the absence of policy and 'has been most effective when its rulings have altered the balance of power in the policy-making process so as to facilitate the passage of legislation which might otherwise have failed' (Wincott 1996: 183), it is also relevant to the discussion. For even if otherwise exerting only an indirect influence on the broader regulatory framework, by establishing that national pricing and reimbursement systems are permissible under European law providing they do not conflict with the Treaty's free movement goals (Hancher 1991), it is argued that the ECJ has essentially consolidated pricing and reimbursement as an area of majoritarian politicking. Several of the Court's more important rulings are thus mentioned. Finally, conclusions are drawn with regard to outstanding issues and recent proposals.

Pricing and reimbursement – defence of national competence

As touched upon in the opening chapter, despite general recognition that price liberalisation is necessary for a single medicines market, governments are fiercely protective of their national systems and have consistently rebuffed what they regard as Commission interference. Considering the basis for this defence of their autonomy helps to put into context the positions expressed by all the stakeholders in the policy discussions outlined here.

Healthcare and industrial policy goals

The main reason for the member states' unwillingness to forgo any sovereignty over pricing and reimbursement – despite the host of legislation in other matters (including licensing) – is that the clash between healthcare and industrial policy objectives is here most difficult to reconcile. It is particularly acute in countries with a domestic R&D pharmaceutical industry, as governments' interventions to contain healthcare costs may tighten the regulatory environment. Nevertheless, pricing controls are implemented by all member states, with individual drug prices set to ensure the manageability of health expenditure and to promote industrial policy objectives. Thus, in the UK these are based on a system of profit control on manufacturers aimed at boosting local investment – the Pharmaceutical Price Regulation Scheme (PPRS)[1] – in Germany, medicine prices are 'reference-priced' against the lowest-price equivalent so as to enforce the prescribing of less expensive generic products,[2] and in France, price regulation has been used to protect the local industry. Reimbursement controls are similarly used – negative lists are used to cut expenditure, while policies such as linking reimbursement to a product's origin can advance local industry by 'discriminating' against imported products.[3]

As highlighted earlier, medicine prices are thus not based on market forces, but rather the type of product, the amount of innovation which went into its development, along with wider healthcare requirements and industrial aims. Further, they result from deal-making between governments and the industry. National authorities may be willing to accept companies' price demands in return for guarantees on investment; whether in terms of R&D or simply with regard to the location of production facilities. This is especially so in the higher-priced countries where the business rationale behind several of the large multinationals maintaining costly research laboratories might otherwise seem questionable (Marsh 1989). Such arrangements help to explain the continuing over-capacity in the EU pharmaceutical sector,[4] as well as why neither the member states nor the industry (nor indeed the Commission which is interested in promoting job creation) have raised the issue of (over-) employment in discussions about improving Europe's industrial competitiveness. It should also be noted that in the member states different offices are responsible for price-setting. While this duty befalls the Department of Health (DoH) in the UK – via its PPRS unit – it is the responsibility of the Directorate-General for Trade and Competition in Portugal; the Federal Ministry for Social Security and the Generations in Austria (in consultation with the Federal Economic Chamber and Federal Chamber of Labour); and in Germany, as the Federal Standing Committee of Physicians and Sickness Funds (BÄK) groups drugs under the country's reference pricing scheme, it indirectly sets prices.[5] This too reflects differing objectives and regulatory systems, and poses a further obstacle for the Commission to overcome.

Because of differing healthcare priorities, national reimbursement methods are as varied as price controls. Cost-containment is the priority for most member states, even for the UK, France and Germany where, as three of the world's biggest pharmaceutical exporters, national authorities are said to be 'ambivalent' compared to their other European counterparts (Burstall et al. 1999). Along with Spain, Germany has used positive lists since 1993, the UK employs a series of limited lists, while France introduced a set of compulsory reimbursement guidelines for doctors in 1994, the *Références Médicales Opposables* (RMOs). Since 1996 Italy has guidelines restricting reimbursement to specific cases, and Dutch and Finnish authorities employ pharmacoeconomic studies in deciding reimbursement. Cost-effectiveness analyses are increasing in popularity and may be a mechanism for replacing other approaches; particularly as there is more homogeneity between such approaches than between national reimbursement systems more generally (McGuire et al. 2004).

Despite the single market, differing priorities have seen member state pricing and reimbursement systems moving further apart rather than converging, and since the early 1990s a 'North–South' divide has emerged (Redwood 1992). The former have sought to implement controls on doctors, pushing them towards more economic prescribing (e.g. generics). This has contributed to higher prices for branded drugs as volume consumption has dropped. In the latter, volume consumption is higher as price controls on individual products (and hence lower prices) were implemented. Additionally, countries with a strong industrial base (e.g. Germany and the UK) tend to permit freer pricing than those with a comparatively weaker one (e.g. Spain and Italy), who instead execute a variety of price controls.[6]

Detailing each of the national pricing and reimbursement regimes is not possible here. Suffice it that the majority of countries employ either direct price controls or reference pricing mechanisms or both – the UK being an exception in operating a profit control system – and most use negative or positive lists with reimbursement often correlated to disease type or frequency (see Mrazek & Mossialos 2004 for a discussion). Although this generalisation belies a host of variables, the issue is that medicines are delivered via national healthcare systems and are often priced and reimbursed to serve industrial as well as healthcare objectives. The member states are therefore not prepared to renounce any autonomy over such a sensitive area.

'Filling the gaps' – the European Court of Justice

While such diverse national arrangements are, on the face of it, inconsistent with the free movement principles of the single market, not only does Article 152 give rise to them, but the ECJ has consistently sanctioned them. The Court has generally ruled that European law does not prevent governments from pursuing their own measures to contain health expenditures via price controls or reimbursement restrictions on medicines. The qualification being that such measures do not amount to 'quantitative restrictions' against imported products. This recognises the right of the member states to exercise healthcare policy as they see fit, and is in part based on the caveat of Article 30 (ex 36) which permits a derogation to the free movement of goods on the grounds of 'public policy or public security' and 'the protection of health' amongst others.

An example comes from the 1982 *Roussel* case[7] involving a Dutch system of price controls which distinguished between local and imported drugs. The Court ruled in favour of the Dutch government on the grounds that such a policy was not a de facto impediment to the marketing of the imported medicines. This was subject to the proviso that 'although such systems [national price controls] do not in themselves constitute measures having an effect equivalent to a quantitative restriction, they may have such an effect when the prices are fixed at a level such that the sale of imported products becomes either impossible or more difficult than domestic products'. The ruling clarified that only if 'material discrimination or disadvantage' was demonstrable would such controls be in breach of Article 28 (ex 30). This interpretation has also been applied to reimbursement policies, as in the *Duphar* judgment two years later.[8] The case again concerned a Dutch law, one which excluded certain drugs from the compulsory healthcare scheme on the basis that cheaper medicines with the same therapeutic effect were available. Such restrictions were deemed permissible if they promoted the financial security of the health insurance scheme. Aware that this might be seen as an indirect restriction on imports, the Court stressed that the choice of which medicines to exclude from reimbursement had to meet certain criteria, and that these had to be applicable without any reference to the origin of the medicines and verifiable by any importer. Medicines meeting these conditions could be imported providing that they were cheaper in bringing the same therapeutic effect as one already available. An important by-product of the ruling was that controls on doctors' prescribing behaviour – in terms of only certain products being reimbursable – was also deemed consistent with the Treaty. The *Duphar* judgment thus set the legal basis for the national implementation of negative and positive lists, and has since been widely invoked to underline that Community law does not detract from the member states' power to organise their social security systems (e.g. Palm et al. 2000).

Irrespective of the Court's free movement reasoning in such cases, permitting national pricing (and reimbursement) regimes causes difficulties within the context of the internal market. The most problematic of these is price variations between countries for the same product, which in turn has led to the controversial practice of parallel trade in medicines.

Parallel trade Earlier it was stated that parallel trade is one of the most vexing issues in the pursuit of a single market, and brings not only the clash between the Community's policy and legal frameworks to the fore, but also reveals the divisiveness of the pricing question where the stakeholders are concerned. Price differentials amongst the member states are the main reason for the development of parallel trade in prescription medicines, and can be seen as the natural product of an imperfect market. This does not occur to same extent in other sectors where the Commission has taken steps to harmonise prices. In the UK the retail price for the identical product often exceeds that in France or Spain by up to 100 per cent (Kanavos 2000). Currency fluctuations have contributed to this,[9] as have differing demand patterns and income differences between the member states. Distinct national regulatory systems have compounded the issue. But such *arbitrage* has flourished, in part because it is viewed as an acceptable manner of ensuring relatively equal access to the same medicines throughout the EU. Commentators have sought to underline its public health value in enabling national healthcare systems to afford otherwise expensive innovative products (e.g. CECG 1993, EAEPC 2001, or Macarthur 2001).[10] Another reason is that it can, in theory, help check what many view as excessive industry profits.[11] As industry is often accused of actively exploiting the differences between member states' regulatory systems, parallel trade is also seen as helping to provide a more level playing-field. According to Hancher (2000a: 82), 'It is probably fair to say that the truth of the matter lies somewhere in between these two poles:

the industry must continue to live with a scattergram of national policies on pricing and profit control, but is of course able to react to this situation in a number of ways, even if it cannot necessarily control it'. By promoting competition in the market – potentially leading to a greater range of choice for the purchaser – parallel trade also has cost-saving implications for those medicines provided and reimbursed via healthcare systems. Indication of this comes from the UK, where 'parallel traded' products are estimated to have an annual growth rate of 15–20 per cent (ABPI 2001b).

Given their divergent interests in pharmaceutical regulation generally, the views of the stakeholders on parallel trade is suitably nuanced. Because it affects profits, the research industry argues that it undermines their ability to recoup the expenditure necessary for R&D.[12] The claim is that it discourages innovation and reduces competitiveness. Generic manufacturers view it as a redressing mechanism towards improving competition in the sector (EGA 2000b). Consumer and patient groups are also supporters. Differing healthcare and industrial policy priorities mean that while the German and British governments share concerns about the negative affects on their domestic industries, Denmark and the Netherlands have actively encouraged it as a government regulated manner of reducing healthcare spending, and Spain is a net parallel exporter. Nevertheless, research manufacturers want the practice stopped and have adopted various tactics to prevent it. One of the most egregious is that companies withdraw products on non-health-related grounds – as AstraZeneca did in Finland in 2001 over its antiulcerant drug *Losec*. This has led to bitter complaints from several corners, most notably the EGA, that through such withdrawals the large manufacturers would be compromising public health (EGA 2000c). For the most part, however, companies have turned to the courts.[13]

Although European law prohibits restrictions on imports or measures 'having equivalent effect', Treaty Article 30 (ex 36) permits certain derogations including where the protection of industrial and commercial property is concerned. This is permitted insofar as it does not constitute a 'means of arbitrary discrimination or restriction on trade between Member States', and has often been invoked by the innovative industry as grounds on which to prevent parallel trade. However, the ECJ has generally ruled that once the manufacturer makes a medicine available in two member states, it cannot then employ this intellectual property exception to prevent any resale of that product between them. Additionally, its decisions have made it clear that intellectual property rights cannot be used to prevent parallel trade in medicines, despite such rights differing by country (itself a problem in the context of the single market). Further, the ECJ seems to have adopted the view that parallel trade *vis-à-vis* medicines is not only consistent with the SEM, but that it could help bring about closer market integration as well. The Court has also had to address other issues, including the extent to which parallel trade is in keeping with internal market priorities, and questions relating to competition.[14] And while the Court's decisions have primarily been based on the free movement principles, wider social concerns have also featured in its judgements. The most likely result is that parallel trade will continue for the foreseeable future.[15]

It is in the absence of Commission authority that the ECJ has been so involved. Moreover, the Court's role gives additional indication of why there is no supranational regulation in this area, and why it is therefore presented here as a case of majoritarian politics. Nevertheless, the Commission has constantly stressed the need to overcome the distortions caused by price differentials and, despite the ECJ's rulings, has tried to address the issue in reference to the free movement principles whenever possible. The most significant initiative in this direction was the Transparency Directive of 1989.

The Transparency Directive – the 'one step at a time' strategy

Directive 89/105/EEC represents the first explicit push for a European dimension to medicine pricing. The legislation, which came into force on 1 January 1990, sought to establish open and verifiable criteria in member state pricing and reimbursement decisions. This was to ensure that national policies on pricing, the range of products covered by insurance, and any controls on manufacturers' profits, did not inhibit the intra-Community trade of medicines. It was also to limit any quid pro quo pricing deals between governments and industry. In addition, the Directive called on the member states and Commission to co-operate towards developing future proposals to minimise the disruptive effects created by national controls. As Tony Venables, former Director of BEUC, noted in September 1987, 'the extent of price differences throughout Europe for the same pharmaceutical product is unheard of in other industrial sectors' (Clive 1989). The Commission was thus trying to kick-start the process of bringing pharmaceuticals in line with other sectors as required by the 1985 White Paper.

Community pricing and reimbursement transparency: 'take one'
There is much analysis of the Directive, most of which suggests that it has not worked as well as envisaged and that its effects are difficult to measure. Rather than assessing its impact, what is important here is that the formal proposal was much thinner than the 23 December 1986 original, wherein the Commission had proposed measures to promote price harmonisation (COM 1986a). Because of strong opposition, particularly from the member states, the Commission was forced to accept that this was not realistic and the provisions were removed. The preamble to the final text refers simply to 'further progress towards convergence' and the Commission acknowledged the Directive as a first step.

Published on 23 June 1987, the proposed 'Directive on the transparency of measures regulating the pricing of medicinal products for human use and their inclusion within the scope of the national health insurance system' (CEC

1987) contained thirteen Articles aimed at ensuring member states' pricing and reimbursement policies were not in breach of the internal market. *Inter alia* these involved:

- a time-limit for issuing decisions on pricing, reimbursement, any later price increases (with the need for written reasoning if not to be granted), and potential price freezes;
- the release of criteria relating to any controls on the profitability of manufacturers or importers;[16]
- publication of pricing and reimbursement criteria, and the reasons for rejection under the latter;
- the member states were to communicate to the Commission the 'therapeutic classification' used for reimbursement purposes, and their criteria for transfer pricing (the Commission envisaged two later Directives aimed at approximating national provisions regarding the former and on the fairness of the latter);
- the establishment of a 'Consultative Committee on Pharmaceutical Pricing and Reimbursement', chaired by a Commission official, and to ensure implementation and adherence of the Directive – each member state would contribute one member; and
- publication by the member states of a list of all products covered by insurance (subject to common guidelines laid down in the Directive), for communication to the Commission.

As if several of these were not already likely to draw criticism, even more controversial was Article 9 obliging the Commission 'in the light of experience' to 'submit to the Council a proposal containing appropriate measures leading towards the abolition of any remaining barriers to or distortions of the free movement of proprietary medicinal products'. Eventual price harmonisation was clearly the message,[17] and the draft had in fact been preceded by a communication pertaining to pricing and reimbursement specifically (COM 1986b).

This earlier Communication had set out what the member states were and were not able to do within the parameters established by the *Roussel* and *Duphar* judgments. More importantly, it provided the Commission's own view, including that pricing had to be 'realistic' and 'transparent', price controls specific to imported products were not permissible, nor could member states pursue measures to prevent or hinder wholesalers and retailers obtaining their supplies outside the national market. As for reimbursement controls, decisions had to be made on objective criteria which did not discriminate against imported products. This was the case in the UK where reimbursement was often linked to the product licence to 'stop pharmacists dispensing medicines made in other countries' (Marsh 1989: 935). And while financial grounds were not an acceptable basis for denying reimbursement, they could be applied where a cheaper product with equivalent therapeutic effect was already available.

According to Patrick Deboyser, then of DGIII/E/F and author of the Communication,[18] these views were 'non negotiable', for the Commission was trying to prepare a later directive on price harmonisation (SCRIP 1153). As if to reinforce this, the Commission brought two cases before the ECJ relating to aspects of the Italian and Belgian pricing systems which were said to be in breach of the guidelines.[19] The Court ruled against an element of Italy's regime which employed different criteria for local and imported medicines, but the case against Belgium's system of maximum prices was dismissed for an inability to show 'material discrimination or disadvantage'. In both the ECJ reiterated its position on allowing national controls.

Community pricing and reimbursement transparency: 'take two'
The focus of the proposed Directive was on preventing national favouritism by making the process transparent not only to the Commission, but the other stakeholders as well. Nevertheless, the initial responses of the member states were varied. The West German authorities were most opposed, though they felt that transparency was to be sought in principle. Based on free pricing, drug prices in West Germany were at the time the highest in the Community, and it was felt that other countries were maintaining artificially lower prices – greater transparency would reveal to what extent this was the case. For this reason the idea of a consultative committee seemed irrelevant – why should a body be established to monitor price controls when Germany did not use them? The UK government accepted the proposals (though wary of the effect on the PPRS), and the Department of Health and Social Security reported to a House of Commons Select Committee that implementation of the Directive would involve no significant financial implications.

Despite accepting the notion of increased transparency of national systems, the industry was wary of increased europeanisation of the sector, and was particularly unhappy with the transfer pricing and consultative committee proposals (EFPIA 1986). The former were seen as vague and a matter for the member states' fiscal authorities rather than the Community, and the latter as superfluous at best and intrusive at worst. It thus lobbied the Commission for the abandonment of the committee, highlighting the lack of member state support. This continued even after the Directive had been implemented (EFPIA 1992a).

Given industry's endorsement in principle, however, it is not surprising that the BEUC saw the draft as too industry-focused. And it had a point. According to the accompanying memorandum, the proposed Directive was to: 'ensure that the measures taken by Member States to control pharmaceutical expenditure do not pose a barrier to the creation of a genuine internal market for the pharmaceutical sector by 1992. However, the realisation of the internal market is not an end in itself but the means to the creation of a more favourable environment for stimulating enterprise, competition and trade' (COM 1986a). The Commission indicated its wider intentions as encouraging 'the future development of the innovatory pharmaceutical industry'; preventing companies from making 'excessive profits in dealing with national health services'; and preventing European patients from becoming 'dependent on research in third countries'. This was to be undertaken within Treaty competition rules taking into account 'the needs of the Member States in ensuring the availability of an adequate supply of medicines at a reasonable cost for their citizens'. The third recital even asserts that reimbursement 'should also be intended to encourage research and development into new medicinal products, on which the maintenance of a high level of public health within the Community ultimately depends'. The BEUC suggested that the result would be the eventual upwards convergence of prices. And while not in favour of a European pricing regime, the group argued that the Community had to implement measures which balanced the legitimate requirements of the research companies against those of the generic industry (including permitting parallel imports). Promoting price competition was a key point, and it was felt that the proposals were more a response to industry complaints than an attempt to address the more important issues, particularly the opaqueness surrounding prices. Not just pricing, but the BEUC had concerns regarding the structure of the market and the volume of drugs available (Anon 1988).

Based on the report prepared by its section for Industry, Commerce, Crafts and Services, the Economic and Social Committee also noted the document's pro-industry leaning. The ESC's primary concern was the lack of competition in the market, and felt that one of the aims of the Directive ought to be to help remedy this (ESC 1987). In its Opinion of 23 September 1987 it described the measures to increase the transparency of national systems as 'useful', but that: 'in order to achieve a clearer and more objective relationship between the pharmaceutical industry and the controlling authorities, the draft Directive must: (a) require firms to indicate the economic data and therapeutic properties of individual medicaments; (b) require the Member States to publish "transparency lists"; (c) urge the Commission to set up a data base covering the pharmaceutical market'. Giving further indication of its more consumer-oriented focus, the ESC proposed that since national negative and positive lists can create 'complications', 'In the interests of both manufacturers and of consumers it would be desirable to harmonise the systems of lists … the Committee, in the interests of clarity, would opt for a positive list'. The Commission did not incorporate this in its revised proposal. It had no authority to pursue such a line, but would in any event have been opposed by both the member states and industry.

On 15 December 1987 the report prepared by the Parliament's Economic and Monetary Affairs and Industrial Policy Committee was released (EP 1988a). Controversially, but clearly to allay some member states' industrial policy fears, it deleted several of the provisions opposed by EFPIA. These included that the Commission be later able to propose legislation on approximating national criteria on the fairness of transfer pricing policies, and harmonising national rules on classifying drugs by therapeutic category for reimbursement. Unhappy with these deletions, Dutch MEP Alman Metten sought numerous amendments, including that: companies be required to provide more data in support of any arguments for price rises (governments would be allowed to reject these if the data proved insufficient); that a Community medicines price databank was required to help improve competition in the sector and to promote the more efficient use of medicines; and that two years after implementation of the Directive, the Commission should submit a proposal towards ensuring that the 'necessary supplies' of medicinal products are 'available at the lowest possible prices'. Although Mr Sauer of DGIII/E/F invited Mr Metten and Pierre Lataillade, *rapporteur* of the committee report, for discussions on a compromise, the amendments were ultimately ignored and the Council agreed an informal text in November with the vague stipulation that companies provide 'sufficient information' to support any calls for price increases. With a Council text therefore virtually identical to its own, the economic affairs committee then adopted the report by twenty-seven votes to fourteen on 15 December. At Parliament's 19 January 1988 plenary, however, the debate was stopped mid-session because of a growing number of proposals for changes (including several of those proposed by Mr Metten), and the document was referred back to the committee.

Community pricing and reimbursement transparency: 'take three'
Only on 9 March did Parliament resume its reading, approving the committee's latest revision. The committee vote had again been an unconvincing endorsement (thirteen for, one against, and eight abstentions, with Mr Metten the lone dissenter), but the new draft contained several amendments (EP 1988b). Most controversial was the reintroduction of the databank. This was to include the consumption, prices and daily costs of treatment of the top 2,500 medicines in each member state, and was to be made available to public scrutiny. Not just EFPIA, but so too were several member states dead-set against such an initiative – notably France and Germany (Reich 1989). The industry's fear was that it would result in lower prices as governments could make comparisons more easily, and that the provision of such detailed information on products would facilitate parallel trade. And while some member states feared the Commission would use it as a mechanism to pursue price harmonisation, even evolving into a European pricing authority.

As a compromise, in its Common Position of 22 June 1988 the Council agreed the databank as a Declaration (SEC 1988). Not officially part of the legislation, the databank would nevertheless 'start becoming operational when the present Directive is implemented for medicinal products authorized in a majority of member states of the Community'. This acknowledged the strength of consumer pressures in the Parliament. Thus, knowing that MEPs would reject any draft which failed to include the databank, Fernand Sauer expressed the Commission's acceptance of this compromise (SCRIP 1321).[20] The economic and monetary affairs committee unanimously gave its support, noting that the Commission had incorporated all of the amendments from the first reading. And it recommended that Parliament accept the 'slightly amended' changes made by the Council (EP 1988c). It endorsed narrowing the brief of the consultative committee to (breaches in) the application of the Directive, and only acknowledged the Council's deletion of the databank from the main provisions asking how it would be set up. The consultative committee remained a sore point for EFPIA, as it allowed only the Commission and the member states direct access. But with Parliament's subsequent endorsement, the Internal Market Council finally (and unanimously) approved the draft legislation on 21 December 1988 with a view to member state adoption by 31 December the following year (CEC 1987).

This was not the end of the story. As envisaged under Article 9, the Commission's next step was to attempt a follow-up directive. After several years of political wrangling, however, this fell through. Detailing the intricacies of these deliberations is not possible here. But as it again involved all stakeholders, a brief summary of what was proposed and the reaction it elicited is informative. For the failure of the Community to adopt a second version is further evidence that pricing and reimbursement is a majoritarian politics issue.

Transparency revisited?
In January 1991 the Commission circulated a discussion document and questionnaire (CEC 1991a) to the member states, industry, and professional associations, seeking feedback on how to reconcile three conflicting goals:

* doctors' freedom to prescribe the 'most appropriate' medicine versus promotion of the 'rational use' of medicines i.e. limiting reimbursement to the least expensive products in each therapeutic category;
* promoting increased competition between companies versus supporting them in developing innovative products; and
* short-term controls on medicine costs versus long-term support of the industry (adequate R&D investment for innovative drugs, and ensuring it remains competitive compared to the US and Japan).

The document acknowledged divergence in national controls and noted the North–South divide. In a second document (CEC 1991b), which assessed application of the Transparency Directive in the interests of promoting the single market, the Commission outlined its intent to pursue increased price transparency and harmonisation of packing and therapeutic classifications. As there had been a flurry of national reforms after the Directive – several member states sought to recast elements of their pricing and reimbursement systems to accommodate growing cost pressures[21] – this resulted in numerous queries (and Parliamentary questions) as to whether the new or reformed systems were in keeping with the legislation. While the member states accepted the Commission's goals on price transparency, they were not keen on the ensuing proposal for a pricing Directive.

The proposed amendments – based on the fact that national measures to control medicine prices had not really led to lower expenditure, but instead had made the market more rigid by neutralising competition (Hodges 1997) – were gradually watered down over at least five drafts. At their most stark they had included: progressive dismantling of direct price controls towards promoting price competition; procedures for informing the Commission and other member states as to any planned changes to national systems; the need to clarify the concept of 'interchangeability' of medicines (towards establishing a system of comparing medicines with different active ingredients but similar pharmacological effects); and measures to introduce co-payments, generic substitution and increased transparency of information in the event that prices were liberalised. The early drafts of the original Transparency Directive had been criticised for similar proposals, and this time was no different.

The industry continued to voice its concerns about member state price controls and any europeanisation measures. In its comments on what was to become the final draft before the amendments were shelved, EFPIA highlighted what it saw as the inconsistency in the Commission's position: 'whilst the Commission continues to advocate *deregulation* [sic], it is also pursuing initiatives to *manage competition* [sic]' (EFPIA 1992a: 2). EFPIA stressed that what it wanted to see in a potential recommendation to accompany the amended Directive was 'a suggestion that Member States *eliminate any measures affecting competition* [sic] on the market place (such as encouragement to prescribe, or incentives to substitute, generics)' (ibid: 4). And the removal of proposals to inhibit member states' ability to set prices and reimbursement rates was a particular disappointment – twelve separate and heavily-regulated markets would remain.

The position set out by the BEUC was equally unequivocal: 'We do not believe that the harmonisation of price controls, or of prices or reimbursement systems would bring substantial benefits to consumers at this stage. There are many more important things to be done' (Albedo 1991: 16). Their position reflects their focus on the patient and follows from their earlier arguments stressing the need for not only common European standards, but a uniform review procedure for the withdrawal of old or superfluous drugs from national markets.

Finally, the member states – at least those who responded to the Commission's questionnaire[22] – again emphasised that they would not accept any Community infringement on their healthcare sovereignty. The UK opposed any suggestion that member states be obliged to inform the Commission of potential pricing measures at the draft stage. It argued that as its PPRS was a 'negotiated agreement with no legal basis', 'The UK could not accept revealing its negotiating objectives to the Commission, Member States and other 'physical or moral persons from the private sector' in advance of concluding an agreement' (CEC 1992c). And France opposed any formalisation of the prices databank saying that it saw no need for the reintroduction of this provision (ibid). Ultimately then, the stakeholders remained unhappy with the Commission's continued interest in price harmonisation.

Member states' objections in particular meant that the Commission's 'technical amendments' would not clear the Council, and they were dropped in December 1992. Commission Vice-President, Leon Brittan, put the decision to shelve the proposals down to the subsidiarity principle, which he saw as representing a formal limitation on the further development of Community pricing policy (Brittan 1992). Meanwhile, in the words of Fernand Sauer (while still head of DGIII/E/F) 'If we were only to please industry, we would have proposed it [a revised Directive] a long time ago, but it would be stuck ... because nobody would adopt it. We have to negotiate back and forth between industry and governments to get a consensus' (Koberstein 1993: 36). This represents an acknowledgement of the policy network at the time, along with its tensions: 'no one outside Brussels wants a sequel ... The overwhelming view of pricing and reimbursement is "Keep Brussels out!"' (Albedo 1991: 16). As the Commission was to find out with regard to subsequent initiatives, this view would continue.

An EU 'industrial policy' for pharmaceuticals – the 'shared interest' or 'competitiveness' strategy

In light of the disparities seen amongst the stakeholders during the Transparency Directive network, the Commission's next step was to identify an area of common interest to which it could tie pricing and reimbursement. It attempted this on 2 March 1994 with its 'Communication on the Outlines of an Industrial Policy for the Pharmaceutical Sector in the European Community' (COM 1993).

Co-operating with the industry?
Taking as its underlying assumption that a successful industry was in the interests of all stakeholders, the Communication set out measures to improve industrial competitiveness. Asserting that the European pharmaceutical industry 'is not well enough prepared to brace itself against stiffening competition and with the relentless rise in the cost of pharmaceutical research, and that its industrial competitiveness could prove insufficient in regard to its main competitors', the document focused on comparative industrial statistics and provided an assessment of competition policy and legislation in other major industries and markets. It acknowledged that the SEM had not 'radically

changed' the industry and argued that the continued fragmentation of the market was harming European interests.

Areas of especial concern included a lack of European presence in biotechnology and declining employment in the sector. The Communication cited 65 per cent of global biotechnology patents being American compared to only 15 per cent European, and 1993 was identified as a turning-point for the industry with the number of jobs having gone down for the first time in over ten years (by 1.3 per cent). It suggested that some 27,000 jobs could be lost by 1995 through 'delocalization' or the closing of research and manufacturing sites, resulting in massive disinvestment.[23] The Commission argued that a more integrated market with freer competition and price deregulation was required, and in the Communication set out its case that European-level policies were the remedy.[24] Several of the more important proposals were:

- consolidating and updating existing Community pharmaceutical legislation in a transparent manner (increasing accessibility for industry and health professionals, and to enable the member states to transpose and implement it easily);
- promoting the rational use of medicines by providing health professionals and consumers with sufficient information e.g. harmonising package labels and indications for use, and setting up the pharmaceutical prices database;
- quick introduction of the future marketing system (the EMEA) to achieve health(care) and industrial policy goals;
- enforcement and improvement of intellectual property protection for genuinely innovative drugs (to match that in other countries)[25] and creating a favourable environment for biotechnology;
- increasing competition in the market via improved price transparency;
- monitoring the (distortive) effects of member states' pricing and reimbursement controls and their implementation of Directive 89/105/EEC, with a view to adapting it 'in the light of experience'; and
- contributing to global harmonisation efforts to reduce R&D overlaps and facilitate the opening of external markets to Community medicines.

After the failure to entrench pricing and reimbursement within the Community's agenda – despite the Transparency Directive – the Communication was clearly a trade-off. The premise was that through the development of measures to maintain the industry's competitive position, it would be obvious to all stakeholders – especially the member states – that pricing needed to be addressed next. But it proved an ill-founded approach.

Reaction (and rejection)
This industrial policy strategy, one without any immediate attached conditions or proposals relating to pricing, was heavily criticised. The German

consumer association (AgV), complained that: 'In the communication, an industrial policy is drafted based on an analysis that it is oriented towards industry interests only. Thus the policy is disadvantageous to consumers' (AgV 1994: 3). The BEUC agreed, and reproved the Commission for not giving enough attention to fostering competition in the sector (BEUC 1994). In a speech to the Commission's June 1994 hearing on the Communication, BEUC's Director, Jim Murray, also attacked the proposals for paying too much attention to improving industry's competitiveness. He argued that lifting price controls as a means of improving competition was unrealistic, and disputed many of the conclusions drawn in the document. For example, accepting as 'clearly a matter of legitimate concern' that the number of new medicines originating in Europe was declining compared to an increase in Japan over the same period, he indicated that a closer look revealed that 'the majority of the increased Japanese share has come almost entirely from medicines which represent very little therapeutic advance; for the most part they are "me too" medicines and the increasing Japanese strength in this area has parallels in Japanese industrial development in other areas also' (Murray 1994).[26] This need for a closer look was echoed by the Parliament's Committee on the Environment, Public Health and Consumer Protection. Its draft opinion of 8 December 1994 points out that 'Progress in the pharmaceutical sector has produced savings largely in excess of the increase in its costs' (EP 1994: 4). Further, the report called for the rationalisation of promotion and advertising given the opaqueness which surrounds them, and argued against abolishing price controls.[27]

The reaction of the generics industry was predictably robust; arguing that the SPC had already worsened its competitive position and that the proposals would further harm generic interests. In a letter to the Social Affairs DG (DGV) seeking support, Greg Perry, Director of the European Generics Association,[28] complained about the existing restrictions on generic research and suggested that ' if the Commission's objective is to encourage greater competition within the medicines market ... then greater attention will have to be paid to those factors which affect both the demand and supply of generic medicines in the European market' (Perry 1993a).

Anticipating member state opposition likely to stem from such criticism,[29] the Commission argued its case at a special session of the Parliament's economic and monetary affairs committee (which had been assigned the Communication) on 27 September 1995. This was attended by MEPs, representatives of both industry segments, consumer groups and member state officials. Mr Deboyser of DGIII/E/F emphasised that the Communication was only about improving competition and industrial competitiveness, not public health or healthcare policy, and that it should only be examined in this light lest it prove a wasted opportunity to maintain European competitiveness. While this resonated with the research industry representatives, since industrial and health policy are not so easily separated as the Communication was suggesting, the other stakeholders were unmoved. Several members of the parliamentary committee were even said to have launched 'a string of largely hostile questions at the European Commission and the industry speakers, on jobs, on costs, on orphan drugs, and on the reliability of the data on which the Commission had based its policy document' (Anon 1995: 6). If not already clear that the proposals were in trouble, this showed just how far the Commission was from finding the common ground it sought.

The result was the tabling of some sixty-six amendments in Committee's 19 March 1996 report, most of which related to restraints on industry (EP 1996a). These included: increasing the cost-effectiveness of research rather than using subsidies to promote industry; enabling generic research and regulatory preparedness prior to patent or SPC expiry; concentrating on research into therapies for as yet untreatable diseases; and ensuring that national measures to cut the costs of using medicines were promoted (with safeguards against the development of monopoly situations). It also called for transparent Community procedures for switching prescription drugs to over-the-counter. This had in fact been raised by Hubertus Kranz, Director-General of the Association of the European Self-Medication Industry (AESGP), at the September special session. The report was adopted by a narrow margin of twenty-six to twenty-four, reflecting the difficulties inherent in the Commission's new 'competitiveness' approach.

Following the previous autumn's special committee meeting, Parliament attacked the proposals at its 16 April 1996 sitting. The Commission was accused of being 'out of touch with reality in claiming that normal market operation is feasible in the pharmaceutical industry and that it is merely necessary to cut back on government intervention schemes to achieve this' (EP 1996b). Calling for a more overarching view of the sector, MEPs made numerous suggestions from increasing R&D into areas which may deliver therapeutically beneficial new medicines, to generic promotion. These suggestions also included several outliers e.g. ethical queries regarding animal experiments, the uptake of homeopathic medicines, and it was suggested the Commission take a greater role in dissemination of the effects and risks of medicines. The MEPs' scepticism may have been warranted, but by tying industrial policy to such a wide range of concerns, their Resolution could not offer a way forward. This was precisely what Mr Deboyser had feared when he addressed the special session the previous spring.

The Council's (Internal Market) views followed a week later, and its 23 April Resolution was equally broad-ranging (CEC 1996). Passing reference was made to the peculiarities of the market and the need to balance health(care) interests against any industrial policy initiatives. Amongst the few workable suggestions, the Council called for measures to support small-to-medium sized enterprises (SMEs) in the sector. This, because SMEs have 'local knowledge' and 'specialised know-how' which would benefit competition as well as serving public health interests. However, given the perceived costs of its implementation, the Resolution was rebuked by all of the stakeholders (again, save the research industry). Having delivered little that could be enacted, there has been no policy follow-up to the Communication since the Council's Resolution.

Policy network exclusions
As with the legislation to establish both the SPC and EMEA, consumer interests appeared of secondary importance in the Communication i.e. it was implicit that they would be served by measures to promote the industry. Although this competitiveness approach had been a Commission initiative, the Communication was actually the product of the 'Pharmaceutical Industry Policy Task Force' – a joint industry-Commission group established by Industrial Affairs Commissioner Martin Bangemann in the wake of the aborted attempts to amend the Transparency Directive. According to the Parliament's Intergroup on Community Affairs (ICA), the underlying purpose of the task force was 'to explore [in] the broadest possible manner the whole range of factors which affect the international competitiveness of the European pharmaceutical industry ... [and] to identify in concrete terms the needs of the industry, and what role the Community can play in meeting them' (ICA 1993: 4). ICA was concerned that consumer interests would not feature in any conclusions reached by the task force, as their views had not been solicited. This fear proved justified, and not simply because of the document's clear pro-industry leaning.

Prior to the Communication's publication there had been a draft to which only the industry had been privy. In his response to the published version, Jim Murray of the BEUC said that 'It was apparently stated in a previous draft of the Communication, that pharmacists should be permitted to dispense the cheapest multi-source medicine when the prescription allows it but this positive sentiment seems to have been watered down in the current Communication' (Murray 1994). Not only had he not seen the previous draft, but one can assume that the provision he refers to was removed because of pressure from the research industry. For EFPIA had sent the Commission a memorandum in June 1992 responding to the Communication in which, in a section entitled 'avoiding pitfalls', it argued that 'Measures such as incentives or sanctions to prescribe or dispense the cheapest product ... pose a considerable potential threat to the continued viability of the research-based pharmaceutical industry and ... are anti-competitive' (EFPIA 1992b: 24). This also suggests that EFPIA was already involved with the pharmaceutical policy taskforce.[30]

Even clearer indication of the Commission's intentions comes from the fact that the EGA had not been consulted about the Communication. In a letter to Commissioner Bangemann, EGA Director Greg Perry claims to have received no reply from DGIII to two EGA submissions and protests that, 'Furthermore we were not even informed by your cabinet of the existence of the circulated version of the first draft Communication. When I phoned your cabinet to obtain a copy I was informed that the European generics industry was not entitled to receive one. I was subsequently given a copy by a source other than the Commission' (Perry 1993b). The Commission's commitment to 'intensify the dialogue already initiated in the pharmaceutical field', as stated in the draft, would seem to have meant excluding all but the research industry, else applied only post-publication when the document and proposals were a fait accompli. In his letter, Mr Perry went on to criticise the document for only vague references to promoting generic prescribing without addressing the real issue of market access as soon as possible after patent-expiry.

Beyond the lack of dialogue, what had proven even more controversial in the unpublished draft was that it was said to have included measures for the outright abolition of national price controls. It had recommended these be replaced by more indirect reimbursement mechanisms to contain national spending and that prices be actively converged (Anon 1994). This was presented as necessary to ensure the industry's further contribution to the Community economy (Hodges 1997). Dr Bangemann had often spoken of his wish to see pricing and reimbursement separated, particularly since the Transparency Directive, thereby endorsing industry's campaign for free pricing.[31] In consulting with the member states, however, the Commission was unable to secure support for such proposals. More importantly, price deregulation proved unpalatable to the Social Affairs DG (DGV). The fear was that freer pricing equated to higher prices.

Of especial concern were so-called 'break-through' drugs. If these new and innovative medicines were to be subject to free pricing, would the emergent 'market price' prove affordable? Companies would be expected to set high prices for such medicines (which had little or no competition i.e. the superiority of a single product in a given therapeutic category, else a medicine which essentially creates its own category), and this was not desirable from either the member states' cost-containment perspective, or DGV's public health and consumer protection viewpoint. DGIII was thus forced to drop the price deregulation proposals from the subsequent draft. According to one editorial 'the purge was engineered by Social Affairs Commissioner Pádraig Flynn, backed by President Jacques Delors and "half the commission"' (WSJE 1994: 8). It has even been claimed that there had in fact been at least ten previous drafts of the Communication (Mossialos & Abel-Smith 1997). As these seem only to have been shared with industry, comparing them is not possible. Nevertheless, the point here is that the final text – as with the transparency legislation – was very different from the initial drafts. The stakeholders' views were simply too disparate to be overcome in such a document, especially one which was about promoting industry first, and addressing other issues second.

The Commission had tried to sell this new approach on the grounds that improving industry's competitiveness would benefit all stakeholders. But it can perhaps better be seen as a concession to the research industry over the need to tackle other issues related to promoting the internal market, most notably liberalising prices. And its failure can be put down to the fact that the stated intent of the Communication 'to monitor the impact on the functioning of the internal market of national pharmaceutical pricing and reimbursement measures ... to assess the need to adapt [the Transparency] Directive in light of experience' did not assuage governments' concerns over cost-containment (Furniss 1997). With the Communication all but dead and buried, DGIII went on to claim that it had in any event been intended more as a means of facilitating dialogue than as a policy statement (Deboyser 1995).

The Bangemann roundtables – the 'dialogue' strategy

Viewing the Communication as but a minor setback, the Commission stuck with this competitiveness strategy. Accepting that price harmonisation was unlikely – at least not via a top-down approach – and that dialogue with all stakeholders, not just the research industry, was necessary, Commissioner Bangemann next organised (and chaired) a series of three 'Roundtables'. Rather than detailing each meeting, on the basis of the positions voiced by the stakeholders, the ensuing discussion teases out the main tensions.

Convening twice in Frankfurt (1996, 1997) and once in Paris (1998), the roundtables were closed-door affairs with restricted guest-lists, and the media was barred entry to the 1997 and 1998 gatherings giving rise to accusations of secrecy and deal-making (Furniss 1998).[32] Representatives of the Commission, the industry (EFPIA, EGA and individual company officials), national regulatory authorities and member state governments, professional and consumer groups, along with selected academic experts were invited. The first roundtable was sponsored by EFPIA with a grant from the Pharmaceutical Partners for Better Healthcare group (PPBH).[33] And although the next two were financed by Community grants, this may suggest that the agenda was already clear.

The underlying theme of all three meetings was liberalisation of the market generally, and the question of how to pursue a pricing regime which would meet the interests of industry, the member states and consumers in an equitable manner specifically. Topics discussed included how to overcome national price controls to relieve market fragmentation; the role of OTC and generic medicines; developing Europe as a strong R&D base; enhancing European biotechnology; taking advantage of advances in information systems and 'e-commerce'; and what EU enlargement would mean.[34] Impacting on all of these, parallel trade was thus a hot topic.

What to do about parallel trade?
As noted earlier, the Court has traditionally ruled in favour of parallel trade, and four days before the first round-table it did so again. In the joint *Primecrown* cases,[35] the manufacturer's (Merck) concern was that as patent

rights did not apply to Spain and Portugal before their accession to the EC, existing case-law allowed them to produce and export copies of original drugs. Merck thus argued for a re-consideration of existing case-law given both the increase in *arbitrage* since the *Stephar* ruling, and because the SPC would lose its meaning if parallel imports from the Iberian countries were to be permitted; price differences between Spain and Portugal and the rest of the Community were argued to be much greater than at the time of the *Stephar* case. Despite the Advocate General's recommendation that the patent-holder should be able to prevent parallel imports from the two countries, the Court stuck with its exhaustion of rights line from previous rulings. Its decision that price distortions resulting from different member state legislation were to be remedied 'by measures taken by the Community authorities and not by the adoption by another member state of measures incompatible with the rules on free movement of goods' (ECJ 1996) nevertheless permitted the patent-holders to continue using their patents to prevent parallel importing for a limited period. These rulings ensured that parallel trade would continue to be a major discussion-point at subsequent roundtables.

On the one side were consumer representatives who underlined the importance of the practice as a manner of ensuring affordable medicines, along with some national representatives who argued that it promoted sustainable healthcare financing. On the other side, the research industry along with DGIII (and officials from other member states) pointed to the distortions it created. They were supported by the European Association of Pharmaceutical Full-line Wholesalers (GIRP). Even if legal, GIRP argued that parallel trade did not serve efficiency, as the main cost savings in healthcare would come from a more efficient use of medicines (GIRP 1998). In any event, the Commission had already endorsed the ECJ's position in its 1998 Communication on a single pharmaceuticals market, stressing parallel trade as a 'driving force for market integration where there are significant differences in price' despite the inefficiencies it creates (COM 1998). And though some effort was made to bridge the sides, these efforts were described as more 'metaphorical and rhetorical than concrete and tangible' (Albedo 1998).

What to do about price differentials and national controls?
National pricing controls were the crucial discussion-point during the roundtables. While the recurring theme in all of Commissioner Bangemann's presentations was the abolition of strict controls (as they were disadvantageous to Community industrial policy goals), the other stakeholders were equally adamant over their own positions.[36] Recalling that the industrial policy Communication had earlier been watered down in part because of the intervention of DGV, Commissioner Flynn's submission to the 1996 roundtable reiterated the reasons for this. Namely that measures affecting price (de-)regulation could only be pursued within the broader context of public health policy and the development of member state health systems. Similar views

were expressed by Michael Noonan, Irish health minister. He acknowledged that while 'unrestricted free movement is not compatible with unrestricted governmental intervention in the domestic market ... member states *cannot* [sic] give ground on the prerogative to set health policy within their own jurisdiction'. The result of this paradox, according to the Danish health minister, Yvone Anndersen, was that member states' cost-containment measures had pushed the industry into pricing its products at high levels. Jim Murray of the BEUC thus asserted 'the fundamental challenge is to develop and maintain the necessary price sensitivity in the market for medicines, in other words to keep pressure on prices'. Unsurprisingly this was challenged by industry representatives, and Pierre Douaze of Novartis linked price controls to Europe's declining position in the global sector, arguing that the benefits to industry brought by Commission policies such as the EMEA and SPC 'have been more than outweighed by the negative impact of the combined effort of national cost containment, currency erosion and the spillover effect of such actions into other markets'. Such divergent views continued in the second meeting when two working groups set up after the first roundtable reported their findings. Group I had been charged with developing solutions to reconcile the free movement–national price controls clash from the member state perspective. Group II was to look at the pharmaceutical sector itself, considering the possibility for member state co-operation on pricing.

The report of the first group concentrated on balancing industrial and healthcare policy within the parameters of member state competence. One suggestion regarding pricing was to establish 'broadly based' contractual arrangements between member states' health services and individual pharmaceutical company suppliers (WG I 1997), the idea being that prices could be agreed which served both their interests, with companies trading-off lower prices for stability. The report also stressed improving the R&D environment to promote investment and innovation. The more market-oriented perspective of the second group saw it focus on competition. It concluded that so long as the member states were responsible for healthcare, there was no question that they should continue setting their own medicine prices (WG II 1997). A uniform pricing system applied centrally was deemed neither desirable nor practicable. And the group offered three alternatives but endorsed none:

i   continuing with the status quo on the basis that it was 'inevitable', and even 'desirable' in public health terms – although parallel trade had to be limited in this context;
ii actively seeking price convergence which would be 'desirable in an environment where all Member States are comfortable with the resulting balance between access and affordability on the one hand and innovation and industrial development on the other';
iii neither of the former two 'extremes', though member states should work

together on identifying and addressing those aspects of the market which were 'suitable' for price convergence.

Discussing these options, Jim Attridge, *rapporteur* of Group II and executive-director of the British Pharma Group,[37] admitted that there had been disagreement on several issues. The most divisive had been over the relationship between the current European regulatory environment and declining innovation and investment in the sector. The industry argued a clear link made worse by ever-stricter national controls, while some member states had refuted this on the grounds of insufficient evidence. Both groups were comprised of a mixture of Commission staff (DGs III and V), industry and government officials – no consumer representatives – and thus delivered compromise conclusions. Nevertheless, the results of the second meeting were described by Commissioner Bangemann as 'encouraging', with 'excellent' cooperation between the industry, Commission and member states (Bangemann 1997b). That translated into no conclusions but agreement on the need for a third roundtable, based again on what he called 'tripartite dialogue' i.e. minimal consumer representation. Dr Bangemann suggested that the Commission would work on an action plan or Communication in the meantime.

The final roundtable was possibly the least satisfying to the invitees. As the Commission's 'Communication on the Single Market in Pharmaceuticals' (COM 1998), which had been released a few days before the meeting, had pleased no one, much to the detriment of any substantive analysis of the pricing problem it became the focal-point. The Commission had intended it as a consensus-generating document, bringing together, on an equal basis, the views expressed by the stakeholders over the past few years – building also on the work of the two working groups. But it was roundly attacked: by representatives of the research industry for not going far enough with regard to promoting R&D; by generic representatives for not paying enough attention to their needs; and by member state officials and consumers for showing insufficient appreciation for healthcare and public health requirements. According to Herxheimer (1999: 25), 'It is not clear whether any of the participants knew much about health issues, but the text of the Communication suggests that none did. References to health amount to no more than superficial generalities, whereas industrial and economic issues were discussed in detail.' Any potential for serious debate at the final roundtable was ultimately compromised by the Commission's communication.

Much ado, but nothing
Considering the roundtables as a single initiative, while some degree of appreciation for each other's stances was achieved within the policy network, there appears little to suggest that any stakeholder changed its views as a result of the meetings. The evolution of the meetings shows DGIII to have become less dogmatic about price deregulation as the sole way to achieve

further harmonisation – endorsing a more gradual approach – but even this indirect manner to address pricing and reimbursement yielded no answers. No real policy decisions resulted.

Beyond the fact that the interests at stake are simply too sensitive to concede on, this was due to the parties having spent more time attacking each others' positions than they did actually explaining their own. The merits of a dialogue-oriented approach notwithstanding, the stakeholders were unable to agree on a way forward. Recalling the industrial policy Communication, this may in part be due to the Commission's seeming willingness to side with the industry – throughout the meetings Commissioner Bangemann stressed R&D requirements, the need to improve biotechnology in Europe, and made numerous references to electronic trade and free pricing – but it has more to do with the majoritarian politics nature of the issue. For even the conscious creation of a network, in the form of the roundtables, failed to achieve progress. Despite this, on 26 March 2001 a new network, the G10 High Level Group on Innovation and the Provision of Medicines, which again brought the stakeholders together, was set up by Erkki Liikanen, Dr Bangemann's successor at the then new DG Enterprise. As the issue of price harmonisation is only one element in its remit, a detailed analysis is beyond our purposes here (see Chapter 8).

Conclusions

As the discussion has shown, despite three major initiatives (and corresponding policy networks), the pricing and reimbursement question remains unsolved. There is doubt as to whether the question will be resolved given Article 152 and the cost–benefit implications for the stakeholders. But if the consequences of a spate of recent ECJ decisions on the compatibility of the free movement principles with national healthcare policy are anything to go by, the member states are being pushed into accepting increased European intervention in healthcare matters (Mossialos & McKee 2001). Not only that, but as the European industry continues to exert pressure on national governments and the Commission with regard to a loss of competitiveness against the US – both of which appear to be listening – Hancher (2001a: 20) suggests that 'The recent findings that institutional and regulatory factors might serve to protect and insulate the European industry from competition as opposed to forming barriers to the further expansion of what it usually viewed as one of Europe's most competitive sectors may well offer the Commission a new point of departure from which to tackle the vexed issue of price regulation'.

Here, EFPIA has stated that: 'We recognise, with the Commission, that competitiveness of the pharmaceutical market is an essential prerequisite for price deregulation' (EFPIA 1999: 2). But is the Commission really seeking this 'new point of departure'? The review of pharmaceutical legislation (COM 2001) called for under Article 71 of Directive 2309/93 creating the EMEA, and the establishment of the G10, are very much in keeping with an industry-focused, competitiveness approach. The former assesses mainly how EU market authorisation is working, while the latter can be seen as a formalised mini-roundtable in which pricing and reimbursement is a key discussion-point, but which again failed to deliver any substantial or workable policy recommendations (see Chapter 8).

Costs versus benefits

What the disparate views and reactions of the stakeholders highlighted in this chapter indicate, is that all are affected by the prospect of Community intervention in pricing and reimbursement. Although something of a generalisation of the complex issues already raised, it can be concluded that each stakeholder has something to gain and lose under a European pricing regime, such that both the benefits and costs of any 'policy' are widely dispersed. More specifically, each perceives the benefits to be insufficient to warrant bearing the costs (which may even be anticipated as high if the regulatory intervention proves unfavourable to their interests). Equally, incentives for co-operation in pursuit of a common agenda are lacking given the differences in interest.

There is also a considerable uncertainty surrounding what manner a European price or pricing system might take, far less what it would bring. For the industry, as a Euro-regime essentially amounts to higher or lower drug prices and thus higher or lower profits, it is keen to assert its interests. But as a policy which benefits only one stakeholder is therefore likely to do so at the expense of one or more of the others, all aim to defend their positions. The potential costs also mean that there is no real motivation for any actor to 'rock the boat'. All recognise that the issues are too complex and involved for a Community pricing and reimbursement regime and, as things stand, the status quo remains preferable. Indeed, this was one of the options presented to the 1997 roundtable by Working Group II.

Nevertheless, the main cost–benefit calculation is perhaps that of the member states. Despite their own national interests, they are unanimous in their opposition to Community 'interference' in healthcare. The potential costs to be borne in terms of their control over healthcare expenditure, loss of jobs, and the income redistribution implications raised by an EU pricing regime, all preclude any willingness to rescind authority. The Commission's view, therefore, is that national cost-containment should be addressed only from a reimbursement point of view – this is seen to be more consistent with a single market than price controls – and that European policies are required for the other industrial policy issues. But, this is not likely given that national interests span both healthcare and industrial policy matters, and there are many different systems in place to address this. Hence, with the Commission only able to address the industrial policy side of the market, the competitiveness approach is not producing results, least of all where pricing and reimbursement are concerned.

The problem is that this approach manifests itself in measures to promote the industry (mainly by innovative companies) without generating workable proposals to take the pricing and reimbursement issue forward. By comparison, the interests of the other stakeholders, particularly consumers, are neglected. Thus, irrespective of any new policy network constellations such as the G10, the majoritarian politics character of the issue will remain.

Overcoming majoritarian politics?
Two additional conclusions are to be drawn from this chapter. First, the Commission's 'competitiveness approach' since the Transparency Directive has tended to fragment the stakeholders. Consensus-building has been made more difficult and more actors have been brought into play, in turn complicating the formation of effective policy networks. The majoritarian politics nature of the issue has thus brought severe constraints on the Commission's ability to regulate. One reason for the numerous redrafts of the industrial policy Communication for example, was the split that emerged within the Commission between DGIII and DGV over proposals for national price deregulation. The final Communication was in fact signed by both Martin Bangemann and Pádraig Flynn – a first where pharmaceutical policy was concerned. The member states too were divided. Despite shared concerns about cost-containment and potential job losses, differences in national industry, market, and drug consumption patterns saw them voice different requirements both in favour and against the proposals.

Issues such as generic promotion – towards stimulating price competition – are equally divisive from the stakeholders' perspective. Indeed, this topic in particular has divided patients and doctors, two otherwise traditional allies in matters pertaining to European pharmaceutical regulation. For while patient groups such as the BEUC, Health Action International (HAI) and the UK Consumers' Association favour generic substitution from a health(care) policy perspective, the Standing Committee of European Doctors (CP) is more circumspect, believing that the choice of medication should lie with the doctor (CP 2001). The question of what to do about parallel imports has also firmly entrenched otherwise secondary stakeholders into the fray. The GIRP and association of European parallel trading companies can, for example, now expect to have their interests taken into account by national governments. This contributes to the member states' differing positions on pricing and reimbursement more generally.

Another conclusion is that consumer interests, at least in terms of formal involvement in the policy-process, have been excluded. Jim Murray's earlier-mentioned address to the special hearing showed that the BEUC had not been privy to the early draft of the industrial policy Communication; he was not even aware that by that time there had actually been several earlier versions. Even the roundtables, which ostensibly sought to bring the major stakeholders together, have been criticised for neglecting consumer concerns: 'To describe the occasion as a roundtable was perhaps misleading. The concept of a roundtable implies a meeting among equals, but that was not the impression created at this event' (Furniss 1997: 28). Although this exclusion compromises the Commission's ability to make any headway, according to Hancher (2001b: 24), 'The debate on how to tackle pricing can no longer be safely confined to a privileged dialogue between industry and governments and European bureaucrats. Nevertheless, it remains to be seen to what extent the Commission can ensure broad stakeholder involvement ... It is unlikely that consumers or health care providers could be closely involved in this assessment process.' Indeed, the selective membership of the G10, as the latest major initiative in the pharmaceutical arena, appears to underline her point.

Two lines of argument were set out at the beginning of this chapter as the threads which would tie together the disparate elements of the discussion. The first was that despite no Community pricing and reimbursement competence, what does exist of a supranational regulatory environment has been driven by industrial policy and industry interests, without equivalent attention paid to social policy or consumer considerations. The Commission's inability to tackle the healthcare policy aspect of the market has meant that it has been confined to the use of industrial policy measures – in part as a trade-off approach – which have inevitably involved promoting the industry.

The second contention was that pricing and reimbursement represents a majoritarian politics issue, where the prospects for supranational policy are constrained. This is both because of Article 152 and the actors' divergent interests. Unlike the entrepreneurial politics scenario where there is widespread apathy amongst the actors because of the diffuse costs involved, in the case of majoritarian politics all are heavily involved. Consequently, the regulator cannot take the lead and opportunities for (compromise) policies to be reached via policy networks are thus limited. This is clearly the case over pricing and reimbursement, where the exclusion of healthcare from the Community remit means that the Commission lacks the competence to take the issue forward. Thus it has relied on Articles 28–30 (ex 30–36) on promoting the internal market in order to develop proposals. That the Transparency Directive remains the only formal policy, and parallel trade continues, are testament to this. As one commentator noted when discussing why the proposals for amending the Transparency Directive were shelved: 'it would not be fair to blame anything than the complexity of the problem itself' (Faus 1997: 20). And as noted, particularly in respect of parallel trade, the ECJ has also helped to consolidate pricing and reimbursement as a national level competence, ensuring it as a case of majoritarian politics.

Notes

1 The PPRS regulates companies' allowable profit, permitting higher profit margins for those with larger sales and research investment in the UK.

2   The German reference-price system has been reformed numerous times since its enactment in 1989. Although it has resulted in a reduction in prices for patented drugs, this has been tempered by the number of prescribed medicines having increased over the same period (Giuliani et al. 1998).

3   Reimbursement controls are at the same time said to impact on the industry's R&D capacity by affecting sales.

4   Comparing employment statistics from the EU and US trade associations shows the US to have similar output to the wider European industry (i.e. including Switzerland), but with around half the full-time employed (see Appendix C).

5   Charging the BÄK with price-setting in this way has allowed the sickness funds to make considerable cost savings (Busse 2001), but this has been queried under both German constitutional law and European law. The question is whether the system infringes on European competition law. For a discussion see Kaesbach (2001).

6   France is an exception to the former group. As part of the latest 2003–2006 agreement between the industry and government, free pricing is applied only to innovative medicines as a counterbalance measure to the government's attempts to increase generic uptake.

7   Case C-181/82 *Roussel Laboratoria BV & Others* v. *Netherlands* (ECR 3849).

8   Case C-238/82 *Duphar & Others* v. *Netherlands* (ECR 523).

9   This has been mitigated by the introduction of a single currency in the Euro-zone countries.

10 Although parallel trade can be shown to have an effect on prices, any welfare gains are difficult to substantiate (Ganslandt & Maskus 2001). The only clear beneficiaries are the wholesalers who engage in the practice (Burstall et al. 1999).

11 The wider availability of parallel-imported medicines might also, eventually, bring about some degree of price convergence. It is unclear whether this will mean higher or lower prices; industry fears the latter, but some commentators have suggested the former (e.g. Towse 1998).

12 As with the intuitive welfare gains for consumers, to what extent parallel trade actually harms the research industry is also indeterminate.

13 Other industry 'tactics' include limiting availability via small batches; altering dosage by country (different licenses); supplying direct to pharmacies at reduced prices; and making different pack sizes or altogether different packaging.

14 For a wider discussion of the ECJ's role see Hancher (2000b, 2004).

15 Indeed, since 1998 parallel traders have their own EU trade association, the European Association of Euro-Pharmaceutical Companies (EAEPC), which lobbies on their behalf.

16 This was aimed especially at the UK's PPRS given not just its opaqueness, but that it was generally recognised as a means of promoting local industry as much as it was to control costs.

17 The provision that this was to be based on twice-yearly Commission studies on pharmaceutical prices across the Community was dropped from the first draft.

18 Patrick Deboyser is currently head of Unit D4 (Food Law and Biotechnology) in DG Sanco.

19 Cases C-56/87 *European Communities* v *Italy* (ECR 2919) and C-249/88 *Commission* v. *Belgium* (ECR I-125).

20 The elements to be listed for each drug in the databank were to include: the SPCs;

the ex-factory price; the retail price; the estimated cost of treatment based on daily dosage; and the cost and manner of dispensing. Many of these were already publicly available (although not from a single source), and the content of the databank was limited to this information because of industry pressure.

21 With regard to these reforms, Burstall (1992: 5), however, notes that 'the impact of the Transparency Directive is only one factor among many, and one that is difficult to separate from the rest … it would be difficult to prove that it was the major consideration'.

22 Only Denmark, France, Greece, the Netherlands, Spain and the UK responded.

23 Despite no legislative follow-up to the Communication, this predicted loss did not happen. According to the Community's own data, employment in the sector actually went up the following year (EUROSTAT 1998), and this trend has continued since (see Appendix C).

24 The background to this was the SPC (1992) and the EMEA (1993) which were in Chapters 5 and 6 respectively shown to have been driven by the Commission's industrial policy and single market priorities.

25 As Chapter 5 has shown, the SPC was in fact more generous than equivalent legislation in either the US or Japan.

26 Indeed, part of the European industry's 'decline' can also be related to the European recession of the early 1990s rather than better regulatory conditions in the US and Japan, as the Commission was suggesting.

27 The committee's role was only advisory since the document had been assigned to the Economic and Monetary Affairs and Industrial Policy Committee.

28 Now the European Generic medicines Association (EGA).

29 For instance, the reaction of the UK House of Commons Select Committee on European Legislation was: 'We consider that the following [aspects of the Communication] raises questions of political importance, but make no recommendation for its further consideration' (HoC 1994).

30 The memorandum also made the claim that 'The results will be measurable not only in terms of better healthcare – a significant achievement in itself – but also in economic terms' (EFPIA 1992b: 26).

31 For example Bangemann (1991).

32 Proceedings for all three meetings were subsequently published.

33 The PPBH is a an industry-financed pharmaceutical think-tank which researches healthcare reform.

34 This latter point was of especial concern to the industry, see EFPIA (2000, 2003). For a more general discussion regarding the anticipated impact of enlargement on the sector, see Forte & de Joncheere (1999).

35 Joint Cases C-276/95 and C-268/95 *Merck* v. *Primecrown* [1996] ECR I-6285.

36 The citations in following can be found in the official proceedings of the 1996 roundtable (IMS Health 1996).

37 The British Pharma Group then represented the interests of Glaxo, Fisons, Boots, SmithKline Beecham, Zeneca and Wellcome.

8

Conclusions

In concluding this study it is necessary to return to the major lines of enquiry identified in the opening chapter. Recalling the two main objectives: the empirical element was to address the question as to whether the pharmaceutical industry is the main beneficiary of the EU regulatory regime, while the theoretical element was the development of a framework which allowed us to both understand the nature of policy-making in the sector and answer the question. The discussion here begins by reviewing the theoretical element of the discussion in order to reiterate its application and what it has demonstrated. The case-studies are then revisited towards drawing some conclusions in a comparative format, and remarks on current Commission proposals for the sector are made in order to underline the arguments. Some final observations and conclusions are then offered by way of closing.

Theoretical considerations

Since the 1985 White Paper on the internal market (CEC 1985), the Community's aim for the pharmaceutical sector has been the eventual harmonisation of member state markets. Although considerable progress has been made, it has been shown that we have reached something of an impasse and that any further europeanisation is a difficult prospect. The interests of the European Commission, the member states, the industry, and consumers as the sector's main stakeholders, are too disparate for agreement to be reached over the outstanding aspects – most notably, pricing and reimbursement. And the clash between the EU's legal and policy frameworks – subsidiarity versus free movement – means that the Commission is unable to force an agenda as in other sectors. Additionally, Article 152 of the Amsterdam Treaty excludes the Community from direct competence in member state healthcare systems, and reflects a position over which national governments have been adamant. The implications of healthcare spending policies and income redistribution being made areas of Community authority remain unacceptable to all member states, as do any potential negative impacts on local industry, particularly regarding jobs. Here, the member states have concerns over potential 'winners–losers' scenarios which may result under a single pharmaceuticals market, and have been able to couch these in reference to healthcare sovereignty via the subsidiarity principle.

Although other EU policies, Treaty articles, and judgments by the European Court of Justice do impact on healthcare (and public health) concerns, the dilemma over supranational policy-making is clear. The EU is only able to legislate over the industrial policy dimension of the sector (i.e. within the remit accorded it by the SEM), while the healthcare aspects remain in national hands. Yet, as the discussion has shown, even if incomplete, a wide-ranging regulatory framework is in place, and it includes policies that do impact on both the healthcare and public health priorities of the member states. This study endeavoured also to ascertain how this came about, and here it turned to three important case-studies: the Supplementary Protection Certificate legislation, the creation and operation of the European Medicines Agency, and the continued intractability of the pricing and reimbursement issue. It is the question of market harmonisation and the divergent views of the stakeholders that ties these otherwise separate elements of Community pharmaceutical policy-making together. And for all three, the discussion sought support for the study's underlying contention that the industry would appear to be the prime beneficiary.

To test whether policies reflect an industry-favouring regulatory framework, the study approached the EU sector from a political perspective. The case was made for a theoretical lens which takes the wider policy environment into account in order to understand the preferences and actions of the stakeholders in the policy-process (meso-level factors), and which can be used to understand how Community pharmaceutical policy has been made given both the constraints faced by European policy-makers and the unique characteristics of the sector. This was then applied to the case-studies. In developing this line, both the value and failings of traditional (macro) European integration and policy-making theories – where the focus is often on the role of the member states and European institutions, or international organisations/influences within the international arena – were considered. Neo-functionalism was revealed to be useful in establishing the policy environment for pharmaceuticals, such as the integrationist pressure of the SEM (spill-over), and able to account for the industrial policy leaning of the regulatory framework. But it was unable to explain how the framework appears to have come to serve industry interests. The relevance of intergovernmentalism is in explaining sector dynamics in terms of supranational–national relations, and it can account for the fact that pharmaceutical policy is a divided competence between the member states and the Commission. But it could not explain outcomes in terms of actor preferences and interactions in the policy-process.

Thus it was necessary to ask how policies were agreed, which actors were involved in the policy-process, in what capacity, and a meso-level approach which focused on the four primary stakeholders was required.

From the relevant public policy literature, policy networks were chosen for several reasons. First was that the EU policy process and regulatory outcomes cannot be adequately captured by traditional pluralist or corporatist theories of interest mediation and bargaining. Variables such as the amount of resources, access to the policy arena, and the level of information which, while defining pluralist and corporatist analyses, have a different part to play here. In support of the claim by Héritier et al. (1996) of a 'sectoralised' EU polity, consensual decision-making is crucial at supranational level, where the gains to be accrued through compromise often outweigh the price of holding to an individualistic (e.g. national) position. It is also at this level that the relative power/influence of individual actors may be less cogent given wider considerations, and where interests tend to be more aggregated than at national level. Here, multi-level governance was seen as a natural theoretical ally in the use of policy networks. Accepting it as a descriptor of the dispersal of power within, and dynamics of, the EU policy-process, it offers insight into where and how policy networks can develop and operate. Other process-oriented views such as negative and positive integration, old versus new regulatory policy, were also tied into the discussion.

Another rationale for employing networks is that not enough empirical research has been done on transposing policy networks to the EU sectoral level (Josselin 1994). This may be because the approach suffers from the lack of a singular theory and, as Rhodes (1990) has lamented, is therefore mainly used as a metaphor. Or it might be because Kassim's (1994) 'elusive fluidity' view of the EU policy-process makes such application difficult. Nevertheless, policy networks do appear a useful line of analysis in their own right, and are valuable in examining cases of consensual decision-making. And as they enable the student to focus on actors and their interactions in the EU policy process (e.g. Josselin 1996, Börzel 1997a, b), where 'their function is to develop new measures in European policy' (Héritier et al. 1996: 7), it would seem an approach which lends itself to analysing and understanding EU policy-making for medicines. It is especially useful where groups of interests – often with different or competing agenda – come together in the making of policy which affects them all. With the interests of the European Commission, the member states, the industry and consumers not always convergent given the three policy inputs, this is clearly the case over pharmaceutical policy. The interests are such that any policy will carry a winners and losers effect, and the stakeholders' behaviour thus conforms to Rhodes's (1990: 42) view of the network dynamic where: '[actors] manoeuvre for advantage, deploying the resources they control to maximize their influence over outcomes and trying to avoid becoming dependent on the "other players" … [with] the relevant resources including constitutional, legal, organizational, political and informational'. Rosamond (2000: 124) argues that 'Policy network analysis only works when the institutional dimensions of policy-making are weak', and the constrained role of the Commission *vis-à-vis* pharmaceutical policy also fits squarely within this view.

Rather than joining the debate on the theoretical viability of policy networks, their use here was based on contemporary applications. Nevertheless, the discussion went beyond simply applying the accepted (interest-intermediation) conceptualisation. On its own the approach is somewhat uni-dimensional. It enables an understanding of actor relationships – institutional or otherwise – within narrowly-defined policy fields, thereby providing for a very focused analysis. This is particularly so at the sectoral level where actors and their interactions tend to be fairly fixed. However, this view does not sufficiently accommodate that network behaviour can be affected, even limited, by the external policy environment.

Ignoring this context may be a valuable exercise for the student seeking principally to map structural relationships between actors, but it may prove insufficient to explain how and why specific policy is made. The study thus engaged Wilson's (1980) 'politics of policy' framework in order to supplement the use of networks. By examining proposed regulatory interventions on the basis of actors' perceived gains or losses, the framework suggests that the regulatory environment must also have an impact on the type of policy agreed and, indeed, the type of politicking which will enable outcomes to be reached. That wider political factors necessarily influence networks in the pharmaceutical sector was discussed earlier – factors which impinge on the Commission's role in particular – so too that they can affect whether policy is achieved. Use of this typology allowed us to integrate policy networks into a broader frame of analysis, thereby strengthening the theoretical value of the concept and, in turn, providing a more inclusive basis for understanding regulatory policy-making in the sector.

Comparative network evolution and the 'politics of policy'

By establishing what type of politicking is required (or results) in instances of divergent views (amongst the network participants), Wilson's politics of policy framework goes some way to capturing why certain regulatory outcomes are successful and others not. Here, regulatory policy-making and the nature of outcomes is predicated on stakeholder preference and behaviour – on the basis of perceived gains and losses from the intervention being considered – resulting in four distinct types of politicking. These were 'client politics', 'entrepreneurial politics', 'majoritarian politics', and 'interest-group politics'. Recalling Figure 4.2, an application of the framework to selected elements from the Community's regulatory competences, including the case-studies, now gives rise to Figure 8.1.

Figure 8.1 The 'politics of policy' as applied to selected elements of the
Community medicines framework

Costs versus Benefits

Diffuse-Diffuse	*Diffuse-Concentrated*	*Concentrated-Diffuse*	*Concentrated-Concentrated*
• Pricing • Reimbursement	• Patent protection • European Agency for the Evaluation of Medicinal Products*	• Packaging, inserts and leaflets ←	• **A fully integrated single market for pharmaceuticals**
Majoritarian	*Client*	*Entrepreneurial*	*Interest-group*

Type of politics

Note: The arrow from 'entrepreneurial' to 'client' regarding the EMEA reflects the point made in Chapter 6 that, while initial proposals for an agency came from the Commission, the specifics of its mandate resulted in large part from industry pressures.

Reviewing the case-studies

The three case-studies were chosen as major elements of the regulatory regime, and each was treated as an area of regulatory policy-making over which policy networks developed. Looking at the networks in each case, their respective evolutions are represented in table format in Tables 8.1, 8.2, and 8.3. The issues at stake during each stage of the respective policy-process are corresponded to which stakeholders were involved at the time. Although an abbreviated re-telling of the story, the tables are useful on three fronts. First, they trace the development of the regulatory intervention in terms of 'who did what'. Second, they enable comparisons to be made between cases, in particular with regard to stakeholder involvement. Thirdly, and importantly, they reveal the industry to have been the most stable actor within the networks in each case. This stability has contributed to the strength of industry influence in the policy networks which emerge over individual regulatory policy issues. And it is this strength and stability which is now highlighted in reviewing the case-studies.

The Supplementary Protection Certificate network   The case of the Supplementary Protection Certificate provides the clearest example of how, by dominating the policy network which developed, the (research-based) pharmaceutical industry has been able to influence EU policy outcomes towards its benefit. Chapter 5 showed that it was the industry which set the agenda from the outset. Citing patent-term erosion as harmful to business, healthcare interests (and public health), and European competitiveness, it was able to appeal to both the member states' industrial policy priorities and the Commission's

Table 8.1 Evolution of the Supplementary Protection Certificate policy network

PHASES	STAKEHOLDER INVOLVEMENT	ISSUES
Pre-proposal (1) 1987	Research industry: EFPIA Commission: Competition DG (IV); Industrial Affairs DGIII	• Discussions begin about addressing patent-term erosion (EFPIA members already lobbying national governments) • EFPIA approaches DGIV, is rejected, and then convinces DGIII to take on the case
Pre-proposal (2) 1988	Research industry: EFPIA Commission: DGIII	• EFPIA presents 'memorandum' and begins serious campaigning • DGIII sets about 'selling' extended patent terms on medicines
Proposal and legislative process 1989–1992	Commission: DGIII Member States Research industry: EFPIA Consumers: BEUC; CCC; CECG Generic industry (Other European institutions: European Parliament and committees; Economic & Social Committee)	• Commission presents proposal document suggesting 10 year extension • Member states express differences; France and Italy seek their own patent extension legislation • EFPIA lobbying other European institutions, especially MEPs • With Parliamentary review, consumer/patient groups are able to voice their opposition to the proposals • The generic companies being to campaign against the legislation, but have no organised representation in the manner of EFPIA • Consultation and review of proposal – 10 years extra protection watered down to 5, and different implementation dates for different member states
Adoption of Directive and post-legislation 1992–	Member states: Council of Ministers (Internal Market) Research industry: EFPIA Generic industry Consumers	• Legislation is approved in the Council – Spain, Portugal and Greece vote against • EFPIA pressing for no subsequent legislation on improving conditions for generic producers • Generic companies form European Generics Association (EGA) • Consumers and generic companies call for mitigating measures e.g. generic substitution as quid pro quo (in view of public health needs and generic industry requirements), but Commission cannot/will not address them

single market aims. Moreover, Table 8.1 shows the industry to have been present at every stage of the policy-process.

EFPIA took advantage of the informational asymmetries which were earlier shown to characterise the sector and, using otherwise publicly-unavailable and commercially sensitive data, provided a detailed report to selected parties in order to make its case. This strategic dissemination led to Shechter's (1998: 98) finding that after meeting with EFPIA, one MEP who was known to be sceptical of industry's position 'was simply cut off ... Either [he] was to settle for information provided by the industry, or he was to face the difficulties of collecting information using his own scarce resources'. Despite some of the claims made in the report not being as clear-cut as DGIII took them to be when delivering its initial proposal for a ten-year extension, the lack of opposition and access to information within the network ensured that only EFPIA information featured in the policy-process. By contrast, the generics industry had no formal EU representative body to counter EFPIA's data and to make its own case, and consumer interests were scattered without a real voice. In fact, the consumer position was granted a formal say only after the proposal had been sent to the Parliament and the Council i.e. once the underlying decision to pursue a patent extension was taken and discussions turned to finalising certain details. Table 8.1 also shows that the other stakeholders were involved in the policy-process only after the Commission had made up its mind. Opposition was both weak and late.

Even if opposing 'evidence' had been presented, however – data was said to be available from the US where the generic industry had had a similar battle with the research-based companies in the early 1980s – it is unlikely that it would have changed the Commission's stance. For there was also a natural convergence between the industry's demands and DGIII's concerns about European competitiveness. This pro-industry approach was only compounded by a Commission wanting to be seen to be doing something in the field of pharmaceutical policy, and DGIII was thus not difficult to convince. Further, Mr Sauer's alleged 'deal' with EFPIA over its opposition to the transparency legislation showed DGIII to be a receptive vehicle to the industry's demands. It is clear that a client–politics scenario thus developed in the case of the SPC, with the research industry, via EFPIA, lobbying extensively and dominating the policy network primarily through the strategic use of information.

The European Medicines Agency network   In the case of the EMEA 'policy', although Chapter 6 has shown it to be a case of entrepreneurial politics, industry was again heavily involved throughout the policy-process (Table 8.2). The Commission's first point of contact was the industry – to ascertain its views and requirements. Here EFPIA's complaints about long registration times and the lack of binding decision-making resonated with the Commission's concerns over the 1992 deadline; current registration procedures were not

Table 8.2 Evolution of the European Medicines Evaluation policy network

PHASES	STAKEHOLDER INVOLVEMENT	ISSUES
Pre-proposal (1) 1988	Research industry: EFPIA national associations e.g. ABPI, SNIP, EFPIA Commission: DGIII	• Industry calls for quicker Community registration procedures • DGIII compiles report of CPMP outlining the problems and need for binding authorisation (circulated to all stakeholders asking for views)
Pre-proposal (2) 1989	Commission: DGIII Research industry: EFPIA, national associations Member states Consumers: BEUC	• DGIII publishes compilation of responses document • All stakeholders recognise problems with registration procedures, though for different reasons (EFPIA opposed to any centralised agency) • National governments with mixed responses – corresponding to consultation with national industry associations and cost-containment priorities • BEUC calls for independent, quicker approval process with high standards of health protection in evaluation criteria
Proposal and legislative process 1990–1993	Commission: DGIII Member States Research industry: national associations, EFPIA Consumers: BEUC (Other European institutions: European Parliament and committees; Economic & Social Committee)	• Official proposal document published • Political wrangling between governments over legal basis to establish agency (Article 100a or Article 235) • Member states consulting with national industry regarding pros/cons and divergent national responses to DGIII's wider future systems proposals • Parliament and ESC stress agency be based on public health protection grounds • BEUC (consumer perspective no longer consulted by DGIII) issues response criticising lack of public health element in proposal
Adoption of Directive and post-legislation 1993–	Member states: Council of Ministers (Internal Market) Research industry: national associations, EFPIA	• Council approves revised legislation • Bidding begins between member states to host agency (London agreed as site); only established in 1995 • ABPI instrumental in bringing EMEA to UK

serving single market priorities as the member states continued to reject each others' authorisations. Consequently, industry's demands helped to ensure an agency remit which, in many respects, is limited to speeding market approval rather than quality of assessment. Chapter 6 showed the degree to which the EMEA remit was shaped to accommodate industry's requirements. In particular, a revised mutual recognition regime under the decentralised procedure, one in which the choice of a *rapporteur* lies with the applicant, is a clear example.

Although involved from the beginning, the industry was not supportive of the idea of an agency from the beginning – the opposite was in fact the case. On the basis of an initial consultation document, the Commission found that the other stakeholders were equally sceptical. Although all recognised the failings of the Community's authorisation regime *vis-à-vis* their own interests, their respective cost–benefit calculations saw them express reservations regarding an agency approach. In order to overcome this, DGIII actively courted their views, appealing to those elements of a potential new agency that each saw as beneficial to its own interests (recall Table 6.1). Quicker, more efficient and Community-wide approvals with minimal member state interference would address industry's priorities in getting drugs to market more rapidly. Consumer interests would be served by the accelerated approval of important, innovative medicines. And faster registration could help governments control healthcare costs as well as support those with a local industry. In other words, the Commission's ante was that all would benefit, and in this regard it proved itself entrepreneurial in garnering the necessary support for its view of a European medicines agency.

In addition to industry's stability within the policy network and influence on the Commission's plans, another reason for the EMEA's industry-favouring mandate was the fact that, after initial consultation with consumer groups (the BEUC in particular), they were then frozen out of the substantive policy discussions (Table 8.2 reflects this). When talk turned to the operational aspects of the new agency, DGIII listened only to industry requirements and member state industrial policy priorities. In keeping national regulatory agencies at the heart of the system, thereby ensuring for the member states that their authority would be preserved (and that medicines approved centrally would not simply flood their market at unbearable costs), the Commission was able to secure their support. The Commission's aims, much like in the SPC case, were driven by how best to meet the requirements of the SEM – again the proposal went to the Internal Market rather than Health Council for a decision.

The agency thus represents – and was clearly intended as – a step forward in the Commission's search for an integrated pharmaceuticals market. And while Feick (2002) is correct to point out that the europeanisation of market approval is not necessarily detrimental to public health in terms of poor approvals, streamlining the approval process was more a means to standardise national authorisation regimes, serve national industrial policy interests, and address industry concerns (i.e. promoting a successful European industry and improving competitive advantage *vis-à-vis* the US and Japan), than it was to improve the quality of drugs available in Europe via more stringent assessment criteria. According to the German consumer association (AgV)[1] at the time, 'Centralization is supposed to lead to increased transparency of the evaluations in the single market ... Main aims of the EMEA have to be to define high standards of admission criteria i.e. quality, efficacy, and safety of products' (AgV 1994: 3). But as Chapter 6 has already shown, transparency is lacking and the EMEA has not sought to strengthen the authorisation requirements. The AgV also noted that instead of establishing strict registration criteria, the 'short duration and low costs of admission procedures are described as aims of the European Medicines Evaluation Agency' (ibid). Maintaining a high standard of health protection was implicit in the new regime, but definitely not its focus.

Pricing and reimbursement – multiple strategies and networks   As mentioned numerous times, the main reason for the incomplete pharmaceutical market is the lack of pricing and reimbursement competence at EU level. Despite the Commission's best efforts, it has not been possible to secure member state commitment on even gradual price deregulation towards lessening the effects of price differentials between countries. Not just the member states, but the industry and consumer interests are also sceptical about price deregulation (even if for different reasons), and are unlikely to support any moves in this direction unless there are guarantees which address their concerns. The extent of the divergence in interest between the stakeholders, along with the constraints on the Commission's regulatory role, are simply too substantial to overcome via entrepreneurial politics. This reflects a situation of majoritarian politics where the potential costs and benefits to the affected parties have to be reconciled if any policy is to be agreed, and is demonstrated by the different Commission 'strategies' discussed in Chapter 7. Table 8.3 compares the policy networks which formed around three initiatives in particular, only one of which resulted in a policy outcome, and even then it was not what had been originally envisaged by the Commission.

It is clear that in each initiative and at each stage of the process the research industry was present. Unlike in both the SPC and EMEA cases, however, it has at times been reluctant to impose itself, and in others unable to do so. The uncertainty over whether price harmonisation would be beneficial to its interests or not has seen industry accept the status quo; particularly as it is still able to use the differing national price control strategies and, indeed, price differentials, to its advantage. The views of the other stakeholders, especially the unwillingness of the member states to renounce their right to set their own medicine prices and reimbursement rates, has in any event meant that the issue remains unresolved. The Transparency Directive notwithstanding, the member states have refused to address the issue on the Commission's

Table 8.3 Evolution of Commission strategies over pricing and reimbursement policy (multiple networks)

		POLICY NETWORKS	
STRATEGY	Phase	Stakeholder involvement	Issues

Transparency Directive (& Amendments)

STRATEGY / 'one step at a time'	Phase	Stakeholder involvement	Issues
	Pre-proposal 1986	Commission: DGIII	· DGIII drafts COM document calling for member state pricing transparency and price harmonisation
	Proposal and legislative process (1) 1987–1988	Commission: DGIII Member States Research industry: EFPIA Consumers: BEUC (Other European institutions: EP & committees; ESC)	· 'Softer' official proposal presented (clause indicating eventual harmonisation remains a Commission priority) · Varied responses from national governments e.g. West Germany uninterested; UK in favour so long as PPRS was left untouched · EFPIA agreed on transparency, though adamantly against provisions which will impact on companies e.g. pricing databank · BEUC, although not consulted, begins campaigning to Parliament on the basis that the proposals missed the point · Parliament and ESC see the proposal as pro-industry; but Mr Metten's amendments are opposed by industry and refused by Commission
	Legislative process (2) and adoption 1988	Member States: Council (Internal Market) Research industry: EFPIA Commission: DGIII	· DGIII redraft proposal to incorporate some changes · Council agrees compromise with databank separate from main provisions · EFPIA gives its ok (suggestion of SPC 'deal' with Mr Sauer)
	Post-Directive 1989–1992	Commission: DGIII Member States Research industry: EFPIA Consumers: BEUC	· All stakeholders reject Commission's attempts at a revised draft; DGIII finally gives up in 1992

Industrial Policy Communication

'shared interest'	Phase	Stakeholder involvement	Issues
	Pre-proposal 1992–1994	Commission: DGIII; DGV Research industry: EFPIA	· Approximately 10 drafts of potential document drawn up behind the scenes – only industry is privy · Document the product of a joint Commission-industry task force · Commission seeking abolition of national price controls and convergence of prices · DGV intervenes and document has price provisions removed
	Proposal and legislative process 1994–1996	Commission: DGIII Research industry: EFPIA Member States Generics industry: EGA (Other European institutions: EP & committees; ESC)	· Generics industry catches wind of discussion, though, like consumer groups, had been intentionally kept out · (Internal Market) Council resolution reflects disparity in member state priorities; nothing really implementable emerges

Roundtables

'dialogue'	Phase	Stakeholder involvement	Issues
	Roundtable 1 (1996)	All stakeholders plus: National regulatory officials; independent experts; other interested parties	· Called for by Commissioner Bangemann · Industry-sponsored event · Parallel trade is the main discussion point, with divergent views expressed; corresponding to stakeholder priorities · 2 working groups set up to provide the industry and member state perspectives
	Roundtable 2 (1997)	All stakeholders plus: National regulatory officials; independent experts; other interested parties	· media banned · this time, meeting is financed by Commission grant · working groups report findings: WG1 suggests member states promote R&D climate while retaining control of pricing; WG2 offers 3 alternatives – price convergence, *status quo*, or increased member state-industry co-operation – but endorses none
	Roundtable 3 (1998)	All stakeholders plus: National regulatory officials; independent experts; other interested parties	· again financed by Commission grant, and again media banned · discussion hijacked by Commission's 'Communication on a Single Pharmaceutical Market' · no workable proposals on addressing the pricing issue; mainly accusation and counter-accusation regarding the industrial-orientation of the Communication

G10 (High Level Group on Innovation and the Provision of Medicines)*

Set up by DG Enterprise in 2001 and involving selected membership. Industry is again the strongest actor with EFPIA, EGA, AESGP and individual companies represented. Consumer interests are comparatively neglected with no important policy actors present, and only some member states are involved. The group has been unable to deliver any implementable policy proposals in general, and *vis-à-vis* pricing in particular. It is, however, an example of the continued pro-industry agenda pursued by DG Enterprise, along with its attempt to narrow the actors in order to try to achieve some sort of policy.

*Not a case-study, but as shown below, a policy network in its own right.

Strategy column annotations (left margin, top to bottom): 'one step at a time', 'shared interest', 'dialogue', 'competitiveness' terms. And even in this case, their interests in agreeing the legislation had more to do with wanting to keep a check on each other than in devolving authority to the Commission. As Table 8.3 reflects, the result has been the Commission trying numerous methods, culminating in the on-going 'competitiveness' approach to address the pricing and reimbursement issue.

Table 8.3 also shows that in trying to take the pricing and reimbursement issue forward, the Commission has slowly narrowed the field. The different strategies reflect an acknowledgement that securing member state agreement could only be achieved gradually, rather than imposed from Brussels. The Commission's aims have therefore evolved from an initial call for price convergence and abolition of national price controls (under the original draft of the Transparency Directive), to now indirectly promoting price competition by advancing the competitiveness of the industry (the Roundtables and G10 group). This is more or less what the industry has been pushing for in its own calls for natural market forces to be introduced. The Commission has been forced to accept that the member states must retain the authority to set their own medicine prices, as reflected in the report prepared by the second Working Group and presented to the third Bangemann Roundtable.

Despite the Commission's best efforts to galvanise support on the issue, therefore, the assertion (after the industrial policy Communication) that: 'The European Community's foray into pricing could overall be characterised as having achieved a minimum of interference in pricing and reimbursement programs run by the Member States' (Hodges 1997: 252) still rings true. Not only do the member states remain sceptical, but the industry and consumer interests remain for the most part happier with the current situation. This may in part be due to uncertainty over what harmonised prices might actually bring in practice (whether higher or lower costs, or higher or lower prices), but as the 'costs' to governments and industry could potentially be considerable, neither has much interest in following the Commission's lead. According to a report prepared on behalf of the Commission, pricing and reimbursement is ultimately 'a political issue that touches the very heart of social policy' (Deloitte-Touche 1993). The result being that all stakeholders pursue individualistic agendas, even within any policy networks which form, and such that majoritarian politics prevail.

Ad hoc development of competences and interest-group politics
In Chapter 3 the Community's history in the field of medicines policy was shown to be somewhat chequered. The incomplete regulatory framework is in large part an amalgam of competences rather than representing a concerted or integrated approach. And the Commission's numerous strategies have resulted in a host of disparate powers, most of which relate to the SEM: 'The continuing influence of Brussels on drug affairs is refracted through a variety of prisms: at one extreme, the macro-considerations of the new European Medicines Agency on the discussions of the EU on balancing research

strategies with health economics; at the other extreme, the micro-consideration of regulatory and legislative detail on medicines and their manufacture' (Albedo 1995a). The result is an ad hoc framework which fails to address some important considerations, in particular the health(care) dimensions of pharmaceutical regulation.

It has also been demonstrated that the Community's framework has in large part been shaped by struggles between the main stakeholders, with the ECJ legislating certain details. The Commission, the member states, the industry, and consumer interests have all pushed agendas within policy networks, reflecting different types of policy outcomes and contributing to the inconsistent development of competences. This relates to interest-group politicking in Wilson's framework. In involving concentrated costs and benefits, regulatory policies subject to interest-group politics are the most challenging to implement. Only a small group stands to derive the most benefit, with the majority actually losing out. Further, the high costs of the proposed policy are also to be borne by a small group. This results in a host of potentially affected actors striving to have their interests met at the same time as they seek to protect what they already have. There is, therefore, little incentive to support any policy here, especially as it may not be clear who will benefit (far less at what cost). What is clear, however, is that most will be unhappy should the policy be enacted. This is unmistakably the case over a 'completed' single pharmaceuticals market. Each stakeholder has a different vision as to what they want from a harmonised market and what it would bring in practice. At the same time, each is aware that they stand to lose a great deal if their interests are not met.

Despite the lack of clarity there are perhaps two certainties. One is that a single market will more than likely result in increased prices (Towse 1998). This benefits only the industry which has consistently called for market-based or free pricing. So long as the member states retain control over healthcare policy, it is, however, improbable. As one analyst noted at the time of the of SEM implementation: 'Total pricing freedom for pharmaceuticals throughout Europe will only come about if the national governments think it is in their best interest; no notice what so ever will be taken of the industry's views' (MARKETLETTER 1992b: 11). Full deregulation is also likely to result in a stronger European industry in output and export terms, but will come at the price of heavy streamlining. It is worth noting that although the US has considerably less employment in the sector, its output is very similar. Rationalisation will favour the larger and research-intensive firms and their 'home' countries (Rovira 1996), but ultimately means less employment in the sector generally. By extension, member states with weaker industries will bear the costs in terms of a loss of jobs and production, and are likely to pursue mitigating national measures which may impact negatively on other member states (or on the European industry's competitiveness as a whole). It will also mean the closing of many smaller innovative companies engaged in very specific research, and their closure could in turn impact on the discovery of new medicines. As stressed several times, a loss of jobs is something the member states in particular do not want to see, and it helps to explain why the industry has traditionally lent its support to national governments in opposing any Community pricing policy. The industry may favour free-pricing, but because of the uncertainties over what exactly a deregulated market would mean in practice, industry often sides with the member states, using the employment issue as a bargaining-chip when discussing prices.

Beyond these likelihoods, however, as nothing is known for certain about what a single market would bring, the stakeholders (particularly the member states) remain opposed. There would be winners and losers, but the uncertainties (who 'wins', by how much, who 'pays', etc) mean none is committed. The Commission may be convinced of the merits of a single medicines market – and there may indeed be positive public policy results in terms of equity or efficiency gains – but it is also aware of the healthcare and social policy implications. In any case, it is unable to engender support even for limited or phased price deregulation, and it lacks the authority to force the issue. Completion of the single pharmaceutical market as a Commission-driven process is thus unlikely in the short term (achieving outcomes via interest-group politics is in any event a long-term prospect). The peculiarity and sensitivity of the sector, as noted by Cecchini already in 1988, has ensured that harmonisation would not prove a straightforward process; seventeen years since publication of the report, thirteen since the inception of the SEM, and ten since the installation of the EMEA, and there is still no single pharmaceuticals market.

Insofar as the situation could be improved – although prescriptive recommendations are not the purpose here – the regulatory framework could be made more effective (and equitable), if the multiple and varied competences which comprise it were consolidated under a comprehensive agenda which incorporates at least some healthcare policy aspects as well. Entrusting pharmaceutical policy to the DG whose main duty is to promote European competitiveness, and an agency limited primarily to speeding market approval times, does not amount to an integrated, far less appropriate, regulatory mandate. Here it has been asked why the EMEA is 'located in an industrial institution of the European Commission [DG Enterprise] despite the fact that its mission is "to promote the protection of human health … and of consumers of medicinal products"' (Presc Int 2002: 9). This view is shared by nine ex-members of the CPMP who, in a 25 February 2002 open letter to MEPs regarding the ongoing review of pharmaceutical legislation, suggested that the EMEA should be placed within the responsibilities of DG Sanco (de Andres-Trelles et al. 2002). While simply passing the brief to DG Sanco would be too simplistic a solution – one that would in any event fall foul of the member states – continuing to treat medicines as simply another 'good' or 'service' subject to free movement within Europe is obviously not sufficient. Redressing the framework would, however, require a major alteration to the Treaty to

overcome the subsidiarity-free movement clash, and would also mean mitigating the costs and benefits to the stakeholders to ensure their support. In
theory, therefore, regulatory policy towards the full establishment of a single
market is achievable via interest-group politics, but in practice the requisite
widespread political support is not forthcoming.

Continuing with an industry-oriented framework

One of the underlying themes of this book has been that the current EU
regulatory framework for medicines is skewed in favour of the pharmaceutical industry and industrial policy interests. As set out in Chapter 1, the reasons for this are, primarily, because of the natural alliance between the
Commission's single market priorities and the industry's economic demands;
the institutional leaning of the Commission, where subsidiarity ensures that
it has competence only over industrial policy matters; and the fragmented
nature of the market in terms of industry being the most stable and influential actor. Accordingly, it is necessary to revisit the grounds for making this
assertion, drawing further evidence from more recent initiatives, in order to
strengthen the arguments.

Foremost of the three factors is the stability of industry within the policy-
process. This is perhaps the main finding of the case-studies. As Tables 8.1,
8.2 and 8.3 highlight, the research-based industry was present at every stage
of the policy-process in each case-study; the policy networks invariably began with the Commission and EFPIA. Moreover, the industry (including generic companies) essentially voiced the same demands in each case. Indeed,
their requirements and arguments about rising R&D costs, stricter national
controls, patent-term extension and speed of market access for new medicines have hardly changed since the original 1965 Directive. This institutional and agenda stability is in stark contrast to the situation amongst the
other stakeholders, whose involvement and positions were often fragmented
and differed according to the issue at hand.

In looking at the member states, different cost-containment priorities and
changing national administrations has meant an inconsistent approach to EU
pharmaceutical policy generally. Moreover, with regard to the case-studies,
different countries had different priorities at different times. The German
government for instance supported the SPC but opposed the Transparency
Directive and, initially, the EMEA. Inconsistency or a lack of stability in the
Commission's stance stems from, first, its constrained role, and second, the
fact that policy has to be co-ordinated amongst multiple DGs. The effect of
this was most apparent over the industrial policy Communication when the
social affairs Commissioner disagreed with his industrial affairs counterpart,
forcing a compromise position which essentially rendered the proposal little
more than a list of aspirations (COM 1993). Also important was the dissolu-
tion of the Commission in 1999 – all established lines of contact and process

were dissolved – and, in particular, the resignation of Commissioner Bangemann. His departure was a major disappointment to the industry, who praised his contribution at a farewell meeting held in the EMEA offices in April 1999 (Gopal 1999). As for consumers, their lack of stability is manifest in being at the fringes of the formal policy-process. In each of the case-studies, their interests were not actively involved by the Commission, although some groups did appeal directly to MEPs. Even then, however, when consumer interests were picked up by the Parliament or the Economic and Social Committee, the Commission was at best hesitant and at worse averse, to incorporating them in its proposals.

The second contributory factor is the complimentarity between industry's interests and the Commission's industrial policy (competitiveness) aims. This has meant that DGIII (and its successor DG Enterprise) was always a likely ally to the industry; again, EFPIA featured in all its initial consultations. The case of the SPC was perhaps the clearest example of this confluence in interests. Here DGIII uncritically adopted EPPIA's 'evidence' as a means of supporting the industry and towards serving its own single market priorities. This was again the case for the industrial policy Communication where the same arguments on the reasons for extending patent-times, why medicine registration needed to be speeded via the EMEA, how to tackle price differentials within the context of loss of market position to the US and Japan were reflected in the Commission's proposals. The industry's information 'monopoly' also contributes to its stability within the policy-process, particularly as the other stakeholders suffer from a resultant information deficit. Here it is again worth noting that the SPC, EMEA and transparency legislation were each debated by the Internal Market Council, not by the health ministers.

Finally, a Commission looking to expand its competences in a field in which it is otherwise constrained has also contributed to a pro-industry framework. For the Commission has sought to make policy where and when it could i.e. only in matters which it has been able to frame within the context of the single market. Taken together, these three factors: the Commission's constrained role, its shared interests with the industry, and its reliance on industry information, raise the question of regulatory capture hinted at in Chapter 2.

Regulatory capture and recent initiatives
The literature on economic theories of regulation suggests that one way capture can be assessed – insofar as it is measurable – is through a gradual and creeping pro-industry bias in the work of the regulator. In several countries, both in the EU and elsewhere, the patent exhaustion rights offered the industry, along with 'local content' requirements and favourable tax arrangements, do perhaps raise questions, and governments are sometimes accused of complicity. At EU level, the SPC, the EMEA's operations, and the Commission's competitiveness approach do seem potential examples. Particularly with the Commission seeking to 'meet the political objectives of a single European

market and the commercial agendas of transnational pharmaceutical companies' (Lewis & Abraham 2001: 53). It also appears that companies often collaborate over Community policy as means of bypassing (stricter) national level regulatory policies (see Chapters 5 and 6). Additionally, there has been a generally close relationship between EFPIA and the Commission since the 1970s; one which European officials were then already reluctant to discuss (Stenzl 1981). No other actor has had this sort of access. And as the case-studies have shown, this relationship has continued, bringing dividends to the companies.

For instance, we have seen how the EMEA authorisation procedures were shaped to serve the interests of industry; reflecting particularly EFPIA's demands for binding authorisations, speedier approvals and choice of *rapporteur*. Additionally, the Commission has traditionally relied on EFPIA for information – the information deficit of European policy-makers is a characteristic of the EU pharmaceutical sector which also makes it amenable to capture. This has enabled the industry to provide much of the substance on which decisions are made, and to take advantage of the Commission's interest in expanding its own influence and regulatory competences. Moreover, it allows industry to provide information in a way which underlines its own interests. We have seen this in the case of the SPC where only sympathetic voices in the European Parliament were provided with a copy of EFPIA's report. It should also be recalled that the Commission's proposal for a ten-year extension was far more generous than was available at the time in any other major market. Lobbying and the strategic dissemination of information characterise other sectors as well, but in pharmaceuticals, given the nature of the information deficit, it can have particularly egregious consequences on public health. In terms of approvals, we have for instance recently seen an entire class of drug – Cox–2 inhibitors[2] – considered for withdrawal in the US because of severe adverse reactions, with at least one company, Merck, having apparently kept certain information about its product, *Vioxx*, from the regulators. Although not withdrawn, the drugs are now required to carry so-called 'black-box' warnings regarding the risk of death. Several public health commentators have put, at least in part, the growing number of withdrawals and drugs required to carry black-box warnings post-approval down to (pressure for) accelerated approvals.

A further example of the potential for 'capture' was perhaps reflected in the Commission's original review of pharmaceutical legislation document (COM 2001). The review contained several controversial proposals which reflected industry's demands. Foremost was the introduction of a five-year pilot programme whereby companies were to be able to provide information about their drugs (for AIDS, asthma and diabetes) via the Internet or in specialised publications on request from a patient or consumer group. This met with fierce criticism from those who saw it as an endorsement of direct-to-consumer advertising of medicines; something which EFPIA generally favours, though making a distinction between the provision of 'health information' and 'advertising' (EFPIA 2004). Although the then Commissioner Liikanen stressed that 'This is not direct-to-consumer advertising ... I am against direct marketing' (Watson 2001: 184), many medical associations and independent consumer groups were (and remain) sceptical of the Commission's (and industry's) intentions.[3] On the basis of the US and New Zealand experience with DTC, they fear potential negative effects on doctors' prescribing authority, and on prices and healthcare funding as patients generally choose more expensive medicines (e.g. Spurgeon 1999, Finley 2001 and Mintzies et al. 2002). Moreover, it has been argued that DTC has not been shown to bring a health benefit (e.g. HAI 2001, CA 2001). Under the new proposals, the Commission has, however, reserved the right to make future proposals on a 'drug information policy'.

Additionally, the Commission even recommended industry representation on the EMEA management board – the regulated regulating themselves. As mentioned earlier, this was not tempered by the prospect of two Commission-nominated members from patient groups; especially not when the Commission displays a preference for working with particular consumer/patient groups which themselves are often financed by the industry (Herxheimer 2003). It also called for a strengthening of the EMEA's mandate in providing scientific advice to the manufacturers pre-application; again, advice on how to fulfil authorisation requirements is something which other medicine agencies, including the FDA, do not provide to the same degree. While these proposals were officially aimed 'to guarantee the highest possible level of health protection for European citizens via the safety, quality and efficacy criteria', they were clearly designed to speed the authorisation process and improve the industry's competitiveness. And while they did not make it through Parliament's evaluation and were dropped from the final legislation, the Commission's calls for stronger intellectual property measures did make it through, albeit in slightly watered-down format.

These relate to data and market exclusivity rights i.e. protecting branded products by denying generic manufacturers the opportunity to begin testing or to apply for generic equivalents for a given period after market authorisation. Here, the Commission had initially called for a total extended period of eleven years, but was forced to back down under pressure from MEPs and the generics industry. The result, as contained in the recent review of pharmaceutical legislation, was the so-called '8+2+1' package.[4] Although a compromise, and one endorsed by the EGA (Generics Bulletin 2004), it is noteworthy that this period of data exclusivity is once more longer than that found in either the US or Japan (five and four to six years respectively). And that the Commission had actually proposed even stronger measures.

The G10

Despite such apparently pro-industry recommendations, the Commission's initial document did also contain proposals for a fast-track registration for products of 'major therapeutic interest' (similar to that existing in the US) and for a Europe-wide system of pre-authorisation for certain medicines on grounds of 'compassionate use'. These do reflect sensibility to public health interests and were approved in the final legislation (CEC 2004). Additionally, the Commission has sought to engage the other stakeholders as well. As mentioned in Chapter 7, ex-Commissioner Liikanen followed his predecessor's lead in establishing a roundtable of sorts: the 'High Level Group on Innovation and the Provision of Medicines', or G10. The product of a 22 December 2000 meeting organised by DG Enterprise to discuss the findings of a report it had commissioned on Europe's pharmaceutical industry,[5] the G10 was launched on 26 March 2001. It is in many respects a departure for the Commission in the pharmaceutical field, as it endorses the so-called 'Lisbon Method' of open coordination.

The G10 joins DG Enterprise and DG Sanco (for the first time), and is comprised of what one assumes the ex-Commissioner saw as the sector's main interests. But its constitution is somewhat strange. Industry is again strongly represented: by the research industry's European association (EFPIA), the generics association (EGA), the Association of the European Self-Medication Industry (AESGP) and GlaxoSmithKline's European chairman. For some reason only six member states are involved. France, Germany, Portugal, Spain and the UK are represented by their health ministers, while Sweden is represented by its industry minister. Although important that ministers with a health portfolio are involved, discussions about the sector must surely involve other ministries as well, not to mention all member states. Financing is a key issue, as are pricing and reimbursement along with the competitiveness of industry, and most member states have employment concerns. Consumer interests are again under-represented, with only the Picker Institute reflecting a consumer standpoint. That said, the Institute's mission statement: 'We specialise in measuring patients' experiences of health care and using this information to improve the provision of health care', suggests it as an odd choice if DG Enterprise was truly seeking a relevant consumer perspective. Finally, the involvement of the International Association of Mutual benefit Societies (AIM), which represents European health insurance and social protection bodies, is also interesting. It has only a limited consumer focus – more a purchaser perspective – and has not been so directly involved by the Commission before. This narrowing of the field is clearly an attempt by the Commission to be seen to be doing something, but it is also aimed at convincing the stakeholders of the apparently pressing industrial policy needs facing Europe.

The G10 convened on 11 December 2001 to discuss the competitiveness report, but on the basis of the resulting consultative document of 26 February 2002, the group appears unlikely to deliver anything new (G10 2002). The document contains 14 recommendations which are given equal merit, but which are sufficiently bland as to offer no indication of a way forward. Without reviewing them here (see Hancher 2004 for a discussion), these include that the Commission develop 'a comprehensive set of indicators' to measure the industry's performance, and that these indicators be tied to data on morbidity and mortality so that the performance of individual products can be assessed. For pricing, it is simply suggested that:

> Respecting national competence, member States should examine the scope for improving time taken between the granting of a marketing authorisation and pricing and reimbursement decisions in full consistency with Community legislation.

> That the Commission and the Member States should secure the principle that a Member State's authority to regulate prices in the EU should extend only to those medicines purchased by, or reimbursed by, the State. Full competition should be allowed for medicines not reimbursed by State systems or medicines sold into private markets.

How either of these proposals address the hope expressed by Paul Weissenberg of DG Enterprise that 'In this group we need to focus on issues where there is a reasonable prospect of clear recommendations on practical steps. The way forward must avoid the impasse in the debate "price control for state health services" versus "single market free circulation of goods"' (AESGP 2001: 4) is not apparent. Nor is it obvious how the group will fulfil the Commission's hope of it agreeing 'policy approaches that do not necessarily require the Commission to take legislative action' (CEC IP 2001). Indeed the pricing recommendation reflects clearly the constraints (majoritarian politics) the issue carries. Here the G10 can also be seen as the most recent example of the Commission's continued strategy of trading with the industry, i.e. seeking to develop measures to improve international competitiveness in exchange for more latitude on proposals to free up the market and address pricing.

Admittedly, the G10 is a forum for dialogue rather than decision-making, and its somewhat prosaic recommendations reflect the stakeholders' compromise views on a host of issues. Indeed, the group's initial consultation document (CEC 2001), which led to the 2002 paper, sparked almost as many different views as there were respondents. At one pole was the BEUC, which felt that the document concentrated almost exclusively on how to promote the industry. It concluded that 'The G10's tentative suggestions need to be significantly improved in line with consumers' and citizens' needs' (BEUC 2001: 2). Speaking about his participation in the December meeting, Ueli Müller – president of AIM, and thus one of the few G10 members without a direct industrial policy interest – shared this view:

> I insisted that the proposals drafted within this group should strive to balance the interests of a truly innovative industry, the general interest of public health and fair access to medicines ... the consultative document on which all interested parties were to give their opinion seems to make little reference to the public health and consumer protection dimensions on the issue ... increasing the competitiveness of the pharmaceutical industry does not mean increasing consumption and raising prices. (Müller 2001: 1–2)

EFPIA's opinion at the other pole was that industrial policy considerations, such as intellectual property rights, were not given due priority (EFPIA 2001b). The German Association of Research-Based Pharmaceutical Companies (VFA) accused the document of concentrating on issues which impede innovation, specifically generic promotion and the potential use of cost-effectiveness as a criterion of innovation assessment (VFA 2001). Although too lengthy for analysis here, the views of other parties reveal a host of positions between these poles. The point, however, is that with such a mandate, and such a select membership, it should not come as a surprise that the policy network represented by the G10 may be able to agree a policy document, but that the recommendations contained therein show that it cannot actually agree measures which will effect policy.

Importantly, the G10 perhaps raises questions about the Commission's agenda more widely. First, despite officially announcing that the group was established to 'work on a new agenda to improve the framework for competitiveness in the pharmaceutical industry and to harness its power to deliver on Europe's health care goals' (CEC IP 2001), DG Enterprise has ensured that industry is the main participant. The involvement of the Picker Institute may reflect the Commission's wariness of more critical consumer groups such as the BEUC, but the latter has much greater experience in pharmaceutical policy matters. Second, industry's view of the G10 was that it would 'explore how Europe as a whole can become more attractive for the pharmaceutical industry' (Lawton 2001). And a spokesperson for DG Enterprise has endorsed as much, summarising it as 'a good occasion to have industry in one place ... the meeting will help to encourage innovation, and it's generally accepted that we are lagging behind [the US] in innovation' (Anon 2001). With this the case, the G10 and its recommendations have also been described as something of a 'cherry-picking' exercise for the Commission, where only those policies which the Commission feels it can pursue – or which reflect its own agenda – are taken up (Permanand & Mossialos 2005). So while the idea that member states collaborate towards the potential future use of cost-effectiveness as an authorisation criteria has been ignored, the Commission did endorse the group's data exclusivity suggestions as means of boosting research and the production of innovative therapies (a clearer definition of what might constitute such innovative medicines was not offered) (COM 2003). The Commission's apparent and continued willingness to side with the industry in such debates as on intellectual property rights, speeding market access, promoting competitiveness, and creating a group to endorse these, may indeed mean that the EU pharmaceutical sector reflects a case of (supranational) regulatory capture.

Closing observations

By way of closing, it is important to acknowledge certain limitations. The theoretical contribution involved showing the broad-based relevance of EU integration theories to the development of EU pharmaceutical competences and drawing out some important insights. These were tied into the regulatory policy-making (process-oriented) perspective to gain a more complete understanding of the constraints on the Commission's role, and how policy is made. Here Wilson's 'politics of policy' was employed as an important supplement in the use of policy networks. The objective having been to offer a more detailed understanding of the processes at work in shaping European pharmaceutical policy (a theoretical lens), as well as providing the means to test the study's hypothesis.[6]

It is nevertheless recognised that the 'macro' and 'meso' address different things, or at least, different tiers. Indeed, Hix's (1994) distinction between theories of European integration and the 'politics of the EU policy-process' was noted in Chapter 3. However, this distinction need not always be thought of so rigidly, especially not when the intent is to provide an inclusive perspective. For it is clear that with a sector as complex as medicines, outcomes (via policy networks) are not achieved in a vacuum: 'The institutional conditions of EC policy-making have been of crucial importance in defining the goals of market entry regulation for pharmaceuticals and in determining the rules under which the Commission and the national governments have been able to pursue their interests and policy strategies' (Feick 2005: 41). Policy is influenced by the macro-environment as well as by the regulatory environment; in this case the subsidiarity-free movement dissonance.

In using the politics of policy, it was acknowledged that the framework is not perfect. Not only is it something of a black and white view, and therefore quite rigid, but classifying policy outcomes as winners and losers scenarios is also perhaps slightly simplistic. Regulatory policy is admittedly more nuanced, particularly so for medicines. In addition, the typology seems a view predicated on economic gain (or cost) being actors' primary concern. Interests *vis-à-vis* pharmaceutical regulation clearly go beyond this in incorporating welfare and ethical concerns as well. These potential shortcomings do not, however, detract from the approach's wider value in establishing constraints on the regulator and the different types of politicking which result from divergent interests. It is towards this end that Wilson's typology has been applied to the EU pharmaceuticals case. This was to help understand how and where regulatory policy outcomes are possible within the free movement–subsidiarity dissonance given the stakeholders' preferences and influence.

Moreover, the framework was employed neither in isolation nor as a definitive manner of conceiving of EU pharmaceutical policy-making. Instead, as it helps to identify certain issues not captured by other theoretical approaches, it was used as one element in a wider perspective – the configurations of actors' perceived gains and losses were employed within the context of policy networks. This application helped to show where and to what extent European medicines policies have been achievable, and what took place within the networks. It seems that only over policy issues involving a clear concentrated gain or loss to one or more of the stakeholders has action been possible. And while this may be true of any industry and over any type of regulatory intervention, for pharmaceuticals it has major consequences given the public health and welfare (not to mention healthcare financing) issues at stake. Again, the case-studies demonstrated that policy outcomes have been the result of at least three of the policy-making styles, with the fourth scenario corresponding to the wider question of what an integrated medicines market might mean.

That different outcomes in the EU pharmaceutical sector fit different dimensions of the typology is itself an important observation. Regulatory policy-making in other EU sectors, where the issues at stake are likely to be less divisive both on their own merits and in terms of the way in which policy is made, would correspond to one or perhaps two scenarios. Moreover, the Commission's role in other sectors is both clearer and less constrained. Figure 8.1 thus reflected a sector in which the reaching of regulatory policy-decisions is especially complex. Indeed, when public health and healthcare concerns are coupled with the interests of a strong and profitable industry, the stakes involved are such that there are bound to be major winners and losers over each policy and within each network; the relative per capita gains or losses will also vary significantly. It is because of this, that the regulatory intervention under consideration can result in different types of politicking and, ultimately, outcomes.

By viewing policy-making through this theoretical lens, it was expected that the study would not only benefit from, but would also contribute to, the current public policy literature by demonstrating the value and applicability of the approach in a complex area. And by showing how aspects of the EU framework correspond to different cells, it underlines the politics and complexity of the sector, helping to demonstrate that industry not only can, but does dominate individual policy networks. What is especially noteworthy, therefore, is that this application of the typology reveals the multi-dimensional nature of the sector from a policy-making perspective. This goes beyond the market/industry peculiarities and economics of the industry which receive so much attention in the literature. It helps to show what the proscribed Commission role has meant in practice and what the other stakeholders have done in response. Importantly, as this establishes influences and constraints beyond subsidiarity on the Commission's role, it also helps to explain the lack of a historically consistent strategy for pharmaceuticals in the Community. This provides support for the contention that, despite different politicking styles, the regulatory framework is one which tends towards industry's interests. For it also suggests that the EU regulatory framework for medicines is moving in a client politics direction.

Finally, our elucidation of this analytical framework may run the risk of remaining context-specific. As a proponent of new-institutionalist theory,

Bulmer (1997: 1) has expressed the fear that 'We may end up with a bewilder-
ing set of policy cases explained by a further array of analytical frameworks
... taken to an extreme, this situation could atomise empirical research on the
EU, while failing to identify a common methodological strand for analysis of
the different levels of research problem.' Nevertheless, the continuing multi-
plicity of theoretical variations and illustrations suggests that European policy-
making (and ultimately integration) remains a changing and exciting field of
study. Indeed, EU governance continues to evolve such that policy-making
inter-dependencies and relationships which characterise national administrations do not feature (or at least are not yet fixed) at supranational level.
Moreover, different policy fields generate their own policy-making dynamics, particularly where complex issues are at stake; and pharmaceuticals have
here been shown to be a unique case. Given our aims then, understanding
policy-making in this sector has necessitated the specific analytical framework provided. This is not to suggest that Bulmer's fear is over-stated. The
call for a 'common methodological strand' to analyse the 'different levels of
research problem' remains a valuable one. But seeing it as a de facto case
against the pursuit of frameworks specific to individual policy cases is perhaps an unnecessary corollary.

    In Chapter 1 it was stated that the pharmaceutical sector is an inherently
political one in involving three often conflicting inputs: public health,
healthcare and industrial policy. That the outcome is a clash between governments' political and economic priorities is widely-recognised, especially as it
contributes to distinguishing pharmaceuticals as peculiar in comparison to
other industrial sectors. Yet, despite the fact that this clash is manifest in a
tension between the healthcare autonomy of the member states and the imperatives of the single market, there are few political examinations of how
decisions are taken at EU level. There has instead been an overwhelming
focus on the economic and legal issues associated with what is an economi-
cally very important industry. This represents something of an oversight. While
economic determinants are central elements in the policy-process, and ought
therefore to be given due consideration, they do not on their own decide
outcomes. 'Politics' in the sense of competition for influence, bargaining between actors, and the pursuit of compromise outcomes is, as has here been
shown, at least an equally prominent consideration; particularly given the
entrenched interests of the stakeholders. It is this gap in the literature which
this book has been aimed at.

    The study has thus considered the nature and orientation of the
Community's regulatory regime for medicines, along with the reasons for
which, despite the integrationist imperative of the Single European Market,
the market remains unharmonised. Specifically, the study has provided a political perspective on how and why certain policy outcomes have been achieved
and others not, why industrial policy measures are at the fore, and has demonstrated how the political struggle between health(care) and industrial

interests lies at the heart of the current framework for medicines. By focusing mainly on stakeholder behaviour in policy networks it has also shown the industry to have been the most stable actor throughout. More importantly, and in contrast to contemporary views on the nature of EU regulation, it reveals a Community regulatory regime which ultimately favours producer interests before those of consumers.

Notes

1   Since 2000 the AgV is under the umbrella of the Federation of German Consumer Organisations (*Verbraucherzentrale Bundesverband e.V.*).
2   A class of anti-inflammatory drugs with limited gastrointestinal effects used primarily in the treatment of arthritis.
3   Indeed, EFPIA has since argued that 'In some cases it may be appropriate to link health information with either the source and/or the registered trademark/name of the product' (EFPIA 2004), and finds it 'sensible' that the manufacturer's website be printed on the packaging. As noted earlier, the line between information and marketing is quite thin (see Jones & Garlick 2000 for a debate between the industry and consumer perspectives).
4   This means eight years data exclusivity – where generic producers cannot begin testing and manufacturing during this period – and guarantees the manufacturer of the originator product market exclusivity (no launch of a generic equivalent) for two subsequent years and one extra year for medicines with new indications.
5   The report, 'Global Competitiveness in Pharmaceuticals: A European Perspective' (Gambardella et al. 2000), found Europe to be falling behind the US and argued that a higher reliance on market-based measures was central to remedying this.
6   This also offers some insight into the forces shaping the European polity itself; something which may prove particularly useful when assessing the effects that the recent round of accessions are having on the industrial makeup of the EU.

Appendices

Appendix A Pharmaceutical expenditure in EU member states (1980–2000*)

	Total expenditure on pharmaceuticals (% GDP)					Total expenditure on pharmaceuticals (% of total health expenditure)					Public expenditure on pharmaceuticals (% of total pharmaceutical expenditure)					Total per capita expenditure on pharmaceuticals (US$ PPPs)				
	1980	1985	1990	1995	2000*	1980	1985	1990	1995	2000*	1980	1985	1990	1995	2000*	1980	1985	1990	1995	2000*
Austria*	–	–	–	–	1.1[1]	–	–	13.2	10.4	14.1[1]	–	–	46.8	43.0	65.4[1]	–	–	–	–	270[1]
Belgium	1.1	1.1	1.1	1.4	1.4[3]	17.4	15.7	15.5	16.3	16.3[3]	57.3	51.0	34.2	48.6	44.7[3]	100	139	193	309	328[3]
Denmark	0.6	0.6	0.6	0.7	0.8	6.0	6.6	7.5	9.1	9.2	49.9	45.5	47.4	45.3	46.1	50	77	109	171	223
Finland	0.7	0.7	0.7	1.1	1.0	10.7	9.7	9.4	14.0	15.5	46.7	44.5	61.9	61.4	50.1	54	82	122	199	259
France	–	–	1.4	1.7	1.9	–	–	16.8	17.5	20.1	–	–	73.1	72.3	65.1	–	–	254	346	473
Germany	1.2	1.3	1.2	1.3	1.3[2]	13.4	13.8	14.3	12.3	12.7[2]	73.7	71.9	70.3	70.0	69.2[2]	110	172	228	269	312[2]
Greece	1.2	1.1	1.1	1.5	1.5	18.8	–	14.5	17.3	18.4	60.0	–	65.0	78.3	61.6	65	83	104	195	258
Ireland	0.9	0.8	0.7	0.7	0.6	10.9	9.9	11.3	9.7	9.6	52.7	60.7	62.8	38.3	83.9	50	58	88	126	187
Italy	–	–	1.7	1.5	1.9[1]	–	–	21.2	20.9	23.7[1]	–	–	84.6	81.7	53.3[1]	–	–	280	311	459
Luxembourg	0.9	0.9	0.9	0.8	0.7[1]	14.5	14.7	14.9	12.0	11.7[1]	86.4	86.0	62.3	88.8	80.8[1]	88	132	223	255	307[1]
Netherlands	0.6	0.7	0.8	0.9	1.0	8.0	9.3	9.6	11.0	11.8	66.7	63.3	66.6	63.3	63.7	53	83	128	196	264
Portugal	1.1	1.5	1.5	1.9	2.0[2]	19.9	25.4	24.9	23.2	23.5[2]	68.6	64.7	62.3	75.8	66.1[3]	53	97	152	266	316[2]
Spain	1.1	1.1	1.2	1.4	1.4[3]	21.0	20.3	17.8	17.7	19.0[3]	64.0	62.5	71.7	71.4	78.1[3]	69	93	145	210	246[3]
Sweden	0.6	0.6	0.7	1.0	1.0[3]	6.5	7.0	8.0	12.5	12.8[3]	71.8	70.1	71.7	71.4	71.2[3]	55	82	120	202	227[3]
United Kingdom	0.7	0.8	0.8	1.1	1.1[3]	12.8	14.1	13.5	15.3	15.9[3]	67.6	64.1	66.6	63.5	64.2[3]	57	94	131	201	236[3]

Notes:

*: or latest available year

[1]: data from 1 following year

[1,2,3]: data from 1, 2, or 3 previous years

Source: Mossialos et al. (2004).

Appendix B Summary of approaches to the regulation of pharmaceutical prices in EU member states

	Market segment	Free pricing	Direct price controls	Use of international price comparisons	Profit controls	Reference pricing
Austria	in-patent		x	x		
	off-patent		x	x		
Belgium	in-patent		x	x		
	off-patent			x		x
Denmark	in-patent			x		
	off-patent			x		x
Finland	in-patent		x	x		
	off-patent		x	x		
France	in-patent		x			
	off-patent					x
Germany	in-patent	x				
	off-patent					x
Greece	in-patent		x	x		
	off-patent		x	x		
Ireland	in-patent		x	x		
	off-patent		x	x		
Italy	in-patent		x	x		
	off-patent					x
Luxembourg	in-patent		x	x		
	off-patent		x	x		
Netherlands	in-patent		x	x		x
	off-patent		x	x		x
Portugal	in-patent		x	x		
	off-patent			x		x
Spain	in-patent		x	x		
	off-patent			x		x
Sweden	in-patent		x	x		
	off-patent		x	x		
UK	in-patent				x	
	off-patent		x			

Source: Mrazek & Mossialos (2004).

Appendix C Employment in the pharmaceutical industry, 1980–2002 (EU versus US)

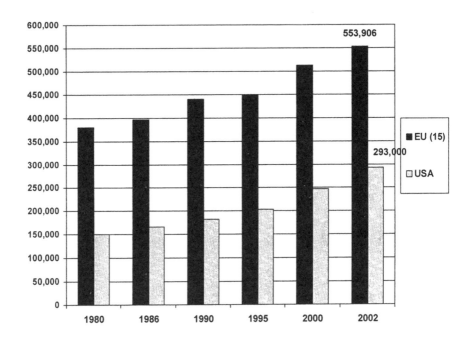

Sources: EUROSTAT (1998), EFPIA (2002, 2004), PhRMA (2002, 2003).

Appendix D European pharmaceutical legislation: medicinal products for human use, 1965–2004

Legislation in Force – Name and Type*	*OJ Reference***
Council Directive (65/65/EEC) of 26 January 1965 on the approximation of provisions laid down by law, regulation or administrative action relating to proprietary medicinal products.	L22 09.02.65 p.369
Council Directive (75/318/EEC) of 20 May 1975 on the approximation of the laws of Member States relating to analytical, pharmacotoxicological and clinical standards and protocols in respect of the testing of medicinal products.	L147 09.06.75 p1
Council Directive (75/319/EEC) of 20 May 1975 on the approximation of provisions laid down by law, regulation or administrative action relating to medicinal products.	L147 09.06.75 p.13
Council Decision (75/320/EEC) of 20 May 1975 setting up a Pharmaceutical Committee.	L147 09.06.75 p.23
Council Directive (78/25/EEC) of 12 December 1977 on the approximation of the laws of the Member States relating to the colouring matters which may be added to medicinal products.	L11 14.01.78 p.18
Council recommendation (83/571/EEC) of 26 October 1983 concerning tests relating to the placing on the market of proprietary medicinal products.	L332 28.11.83 p.11
Council recommendation (87/176/EEC) of 9 February 1987 concerning tests relating to the placing on the market of proprietary medicinal products.	L73 16.03.87 p.1
Council Directive (89/105/EEC) of 21 December 1988 relating to the transparency of measures regulating the pricing of medicinal products for human use and their inclusion within the scope of national health insurance systems.	L40 11.02.89 p.8
Council Directive (89/342/EEC) of 3 May 1989 extending the scope of Directives 65/65/EEC and 75/319/EEC and laying down additional provisions for immunological medicinal products consisting of vaccines, toxins or serums and allergens.	L142 25.05.89 p.14
Council Directive (89/343/EEC) of 3 May 1989, extending the scope of Directives 65/65/EEC and 75/319/EEC and laying down additional provisions for radiopharmaceuticals.	L142 25.05.89 p.16
Council Directive (89/381/EEC) of 14 June 1989 extending the scope of Directives 65/65/EEC and 75/319/EEC on the approximation of provisions laid down by law, regulation or administrative action relating to proprietary medicinal products and laying down special provisions for medicinal	L181 28.06.89 p.44

products derived from human blood or human plasma.

Commission Directive (91/356/EEC) of 13 June 1991 laying   L193 17.07.91 p.30
down the principles and guidelines of good manufacturing
practice for medicinal products for human use.

Council Directive (92/25/EEC) of 31 March 1992 on the   L113 30.04.92 p.1
wholesale distribution of medicinal products for human use.

Council Directive (92/26/EEC) of 31 March 1992 concerning   L113 30.04.92 p.5
the classification for the supply of medicinal products for
human use.

Council Directive (92/27/EEC) of 31 March 1992 on the   L113 30.04.92 p.8
labelling of medicinal products for human use and on
package leaflets.

Council Directive (92/28/EEC) of 31 March 1992 on the   L113 30.04.92 p.13
advertising of medicinal products for human use.

Council Regulation No (EEC) 1768/92 of 18 June 1992   L182 02.07.92 p.1
concerning the creation of a supplementary protection
certificate for medicinal products.

Council Directive (92/73/EEC) of 22 September 1992   L297 13.10.92 p.8
widening the scope of Directives 65/65/EEC and 75/319/EEC
on the approximation of provisions laid down by law,
regulation or administrative action relating to medicinal
products and laying down additional provisions on homeopathic medicinal products.

Council Regulation (EEC) No 2309/93 of 22 July 1993   L214 24.08.93 p.1
laying down Community procedures for the authorization
and supervision of medicinal products for human and
veterinary use and establishing a European Agency for the
Evaluation of Medicinal Products.

Council Regulation (EC) No 297/95 of 10 February 1995 on   L35 15.02.95 p.1
fees payable to the European Agency for the Evaluation of
Medicinal Products.

Commission Regulation (EC) No 540/95 of 10 March 1995   L55 11.03.95 p.5
laying down the arrangements for reporting suspected
unexpected adverse reactions which are not serious, whether
arising in the Community or in a third country, to medicinal
products for human or veterinary use authorized in accordance with the provisions of Council Regulation (EEC) No
2309/93.

Commission Regulation (EC) No 541/95 of 10 March 1995   L55 11.03.95 p.7
concerning the examination of variations to the terms of a
marketing authorization granted by a competent authority of
a Member State.

Commission Regulation (EC) No 542/95 of 10 March 1995   L55 11.03.95 p.15
concerning the examination of variations to the terms of a
marketing authorization falling within the scope of Council

Regulation (EEC) No 2309/93.

Commission Regulation (EC) No 1662/95 of 7 July 1995   L158 08.07.95 p.4
laying down certain detailed arrangements for implementing
the Community decision-making procedures in respect of
marketing authorizations for products for human or
veterinary use.

Council Resolution (96/C 136/04) of 23 April 1996 designed   C136 08.05.96 p.4
to implement the outlines of an industrial policy in the
pharmaceutical sector in the European Union.

Council Regulation (EC) No 1610/96 of the European   L198 08.08.96 p.30
Parliament and of the Council of 23 July 1996 concerning
the creation of a supplementary protection certificate for
plant protection products.

Commission Regulation (EC) No 2141/96 of 7 November   L286 08.11.96 p.6
1996 concerning the examination of an application for the
transfer of a marketing authorization for a medicinal
product falling within the scope of Council Regulation (EEC)
No 2309/93.

Council Directive (1999/83/EC) of 8 September 1999   L243 15.09.99
amending the Annex to Council Directive 75/318/EEC on
the approximation of the laws of the Member States relating
to analytical, pharmacotoxicological and clinical standards
and protocols in respect of the testing of medicinal products
p.9

Commission Regulation (EC) No 141/2000 of 16 December   L18 22.01.00 p.1
1999 on orphan medicinal products

Directive 2001/20/EC of the European Parliament and of the   L121 01.05.01p.34
Council of 4 April 2001 on the approximation of the laws,
regulations and administrative provisions of the Member
States relating to the implementation of good clinical practice
in the conduct of clinical trials on medicinal products for
human use.

Commission Regulation (EC) No 847/2000 of 27 April 2000   L130 28.04.00 p.5
laying down the provisions for implementation of the criteria
for designation of a medicinal product as an orphan medicinal product and definitions of the concepts 'similar medicinal
product' and 'clinical superiority'

Directive 2001/83/EC of the European Parliament and of the   L311 28.11.01 p.67
Council of 6 November 2001 on the Community code
relating to medicinal products for human use.

Regulation (EC) No 726/2004 of the European Parliament   L136 30.04.04 p.1
and of the Council of 31 March 2004 laying down Commu-
nity procedures for the authorisation and supervision of
medicinal products for human and veterinary use and
establishing a European Medicines Agency

Directive 2004/27/EC of the European Parliament and of the   L136 30.04.04 p.34
Council of 31 March 2004 amending Directive 2001/83/EC
on the Community code relating to medicinal products for
human use

Directive 2004/28/EC of the European Parliament and of the   L136 30.04.04 p.58
Council of 31 March 2004 amending Directive 2001/82/EC
on the Community code relating to veterinary medicinal
products

Directive 2004/24/EC of the European Parliament and of the   L136 30.04.04 p.85
Council of 31 March 2004 amending, as regards traditional
herbal medicinal products, Directive 2001/83/EC on the
Community code relating to medicinal products for human
use

---

*Listed under Sub-section 13.30.15 (Proprietary Medicinal products) of the Analytical Register of Community Legislation in Force. Section 13 is 'Industrial policy and Internal Market'; Section 13.30 is 'Internal Market: approximation of laws'.

**Official Journal of the European Communities.

Source: Adapted from EudraLex Collection Volume 1: Medical Products for Human Use.

Appendix E Domestic research & development spending (US$ million), 1990–2002 (EU versus US)

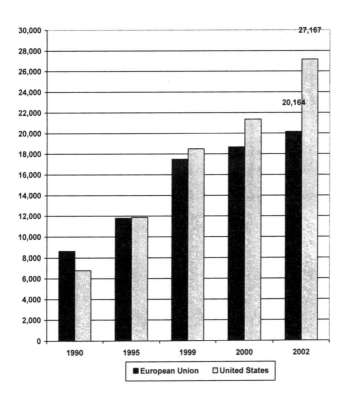

Source: PhRMA (2002), EFPIA (2004).

Appendix F Selected actors and affected interests in the EU pharmaceutical sector

Primary Stakeholder	*Actor Type*	*Example*
Consumers	Patient/Consumer groups	
	National	Consumers' Association (UK)
	EU level	BEUC (*Bureau Européen des Unions de Consommateurs*)
	Disease-specific patient organisations	
	National	*Patientförenigen* (SWE)
	EU level	European Foundation for Osteoporosis
Industry	Manufacturers	
	Proprietary medicines	Companies e.g. GlaxoSmithKline (UK)
	Generics	Companies e.g. PHC Pharmachemie (NED)
	Industry groups (national):	
	Ethical	BPI (Association of the German Pharmaceutical Industry)
	OTC	PAGB (Proprietary Association of Great Britain)
	Generics	*Aschimfarma* (Italian Association of Bulk Pharmaceutical Chemicals Producers)
	Industry Groups (EU):	
	Ethical	EFPIA (European Federation of Pharmaceutical Industry Associations)
	OTC	AESGP (Association of the European Self-Medication Industry)
	Generics	EGA (European Generic medicines Association)
Member States	National governments	Ministries of Health
	Regulatory agencies	*Läkemedelsverket* (Swedish Medical Products Agency)
		BIRA (British Institute for Regulatory Affairs)
	Medical Associations	BMA (British Medical Association)
European Union	European Commission	Working Parties
	Council of Ministers	COREPER (*Comité des Représentants Permanents*)
	(EMEA)	(CHMP (Committee on Human Medicinal Products))

Secondary Stakeholder	*Actor Type*	*Example*
European Union	European Parliament	ENVI (Committee on the Environment, Public Health and Consumer Protection)
	Committees	Regulatory Committee
		Pharmaceutical Committee
		Transparency Committee
Health Professionals	Doctor Organisations	Standing Committee of European Doctors
	Pharmacist Groups	PGEU (Pharmaceutical Group of the EU)
	Nursing Organisations	FINE (Federation of European Nurse Educators)
Other	National Pharmaceutical Associations	PhRMA (Pharmaceutical Research and Manufacturers of America)
		JPMA (Japan Pharmaceutical Manufacturers Association)
	International Pharmaceutical Associations	IFPMA (International Federation of Pharmaceutical Manufacturers Association)
		IGPA (International Generic Pharmaceutical Alliance)
	International Trade or Industry Bodies	GATT (General Agreement on Trade and Tariffs)
		TRIPS (Trade-Related Intellectual Property Rights Agreement)
		ICH (International Conference on Harmonization of Technical Requirements for Registration of Pharmaceuticals for Human Use)
	International Organisations	WTO (World Trade Organization)
		WHO (World Health Organization)

Appendix G EMEA centralised procedure

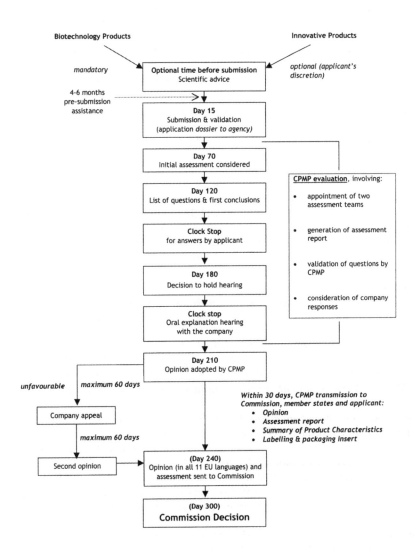

Sources: Adapted from Jeffreys (1995) & COM (2001).

Appendix H EMEA decentralised procedure

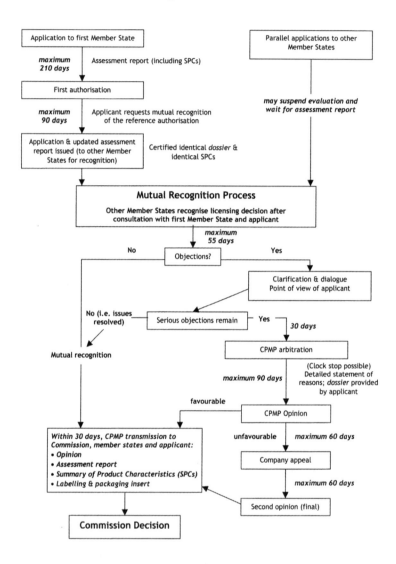

Sources: Adapted from Jeffreys (1995) & COM (2001).

References

Abbasi, K. & Herxheimer, A. (1998). 'The European Medicines Evaluation Agency: Open to Criticism. Transparency Must be Coupled with Greater Rigour', *British Medical Journal* 1998; 317 (3 October): 898–900.

ABPI (2001a). *Association of British Pharmaceutical Industry Annual Review 2000*. London: Association of British Pharmaceutical Industry.

ABPI (2001b). 'Pharmaceutical Industry Issues – Parallel Trade' (February 2001). London: Association of British Pharmaceutical Industry.

Abraham, J. & Lewis, G. (1998). 'Secrecy and Transparency of Medicines Licensing in the EU', *The Lancet* 1998; 352: 480–2.

Abraham, J. & Lewis, G. (2000). *Regulating Medicines in Europe: Competition, Expertise and Public Health*. London: Routledge.

Abraham, J. & Reed, T. (2001). 'Trading Risks for Markets: The International Harmonization of Pharmaceuticals Regulation', *Health, Risk and Society* 2001; 3(1): 113–28.

AESGP (2001). *Proceedings of the 37th Annual Meeting of the European Self-Medication Industry – Special Conference Report Part I*. Brussels: Association of the European Self-Medication Industry.

Agrawal, M., Calatone, R. & Nason, R. (1998). 'Competitiveness in the Global Pharmaceutical Industry: The Role of Innovation', *Journal of Research in Pharmaceutical Economics* 1998; 9(1): 5–32.

AgV (1994). *Communication on an Industrial Policy for the Pharmaceutical Sector COM (93) 71: Some remarks*. Bonn: Arbeitschaft der Verbraucherverbände e.V.

Albedo (1990). 'Patent Protection: Myths and Realities, Agendas and Hidden Costs', *Pharmaceutical Technology International* 1990; March: 14–17.

Albedo (1991). 'Transparency Directive II – Sequel or Remake?', *Pharmaceutical Technology Europe* 1991; September: 12–20.

Albedo (1995a). 'Brussels – Still at the Centre?', *Pharmaceutical Technology Europe* 1995; March: 10–13.

Albedo (1995b). 'At Last, A Real European Milestone', *Pharmaceutical Technology Europe* 1995; December: 8–11.

Albedo (1998). 'It's Pharma Strategy Time Again in the EU', *Pharmaceutical Technology Europe* 1998; February: 11–12.

Altenstetter C. (2001). 'EU Policies on the Regulation of Medical Goods and Equipment'. Paper presented to the 29th ECPR Joint Session of Workshops; Workshop No. 15: 'Health Governance in Europe: Europeanisation and New Challenges in Health Policies', Grenoble, France; 6–11 April 2001.

Anon (1988). 'BEUC's views on EEC pharma market', SCRIP 1988; 16–21 September (No. 1344): 5.

Anon (1990). 'Pharmaceutical Industry Perspective', *SCRIP Annual Review 1990*.

Anon (1991a). 'European Drug Regulation – Anti-Protectionism or Consumer Protection?', *Lancet* 1991; 337 (29 June): 1571–2.

Anon (1991b). Note for the Attention of Mr Perissich. May 1991.

Anon (1994). 'A Drug Tsar is Born', *The Economist* 1994: 331(7862): 74.

Anon (1995). 'European Parliament Sets its Own Agenda on Drug Industry Strategy', *Pharmaceutical Business News* 1995; 10 October 1995: 6.

Anon (2001). 'European Market Holds no Complaints for the USA', *Managed Care Europe* 2001; 11 (January).

Armstrong, K. & Bulmer, S. (1998). *The Governance of the Single European Market*. Manchester: Manchester University Press.

Atkinson, M. & Coleman, W. (1989). 'Strong States and Weak States: Sectoral Policy Networks in Advanced Capitalist Economies', *British Journal of Political Science* 1989; 14(10): 46–67.

Bahner, B. (1993). 'Generic Drugs Threatened by New European Patent Law', *Chemical Marketing Reporter* 1993; 19 July: 3–5.

Bangemann, M. (1991). 'The Pharmaceutical Sector and the 1993 Single Market', speech delivered to the European Federation of Pharmaceutical Industries and Associations meeting, Interlaken; 29 May 1991.

Bangemann, M. (1997a). 'Completing the Single Pharmaceuticals Market', *Eurohealth* 1997; 3(1): 22–3.

Bangemann, M. (1997b). 'Conclusions of Round Table' (available at: http://pharmacos.eudra.org/F2/smarket/pdf/rtconcl.pdf).

Bardelay, D. (2001). 'Information for Consumers'. Unpublished paper delivered to the Belgian Presidency International Conference on European Integration and Healthcare Systems: A Challenge for Social Policy. Ghent, Belgium; 7–8 December 2001.

Bass, R. (1998). 'EMEA Response to ISDB assessment of 9 EPARs'. Letter to Ellen 't Hoen, ISDB. EMEA (42941/98).

Belcher, P. (1994). *Analysis of Issues and Trends in the EU Pharmaceutical Sector*. European Parliament – Directorate General for Research Working Paper (Environment, Public Health and Consumer Protection Series), E–1. Luxembourg: European Parliament.

BEUC (1989). *Drug Prices and Drug Legislation in Europe: An Analysis of the Situation of the European Communities*. BEUC/112/89. Brussels: Bureau Européen des Unions de Consommateurs.

BEUC (1991). 'Longer Patent Protection Periods for Medicines: A Blank Cheque for the Pharmaceutical Industry?', BEUC press release. Brussels: Bureau Européen des Unions de Consommateurs.

BEUC (1994). *BEUC's Opinion on the Outlines of an Industrial Policy for the Pharmaceutical Sector in the EC*. Brussels: Bureau Européen des Unions de Consommateurs.

BEUC (2000). 'BEUC Answers to the Commission's Questionnaire on Advertising and E-Commerce'. BEUC/280e/2000. Brussels: Bureau Européen des Unions de Consommateurs.

BEUC (2001). 'BEUC comments on the G10 consultation paper'. Brussels: Bureau Européen des Unions de Consommateurs.

Börzel, T. (1997a). *Policy Networks: A New Paradigm for European Governance?* EUI Working Paper RSC no. 97/19. Florence: European University Institute.

Börzel, T. (1997b). 'What's So Special About Policy Networks? – An Exploration of the Concept and Its Usefulness in Studying European Governance', *European Integration online Papers* (EIoP); 1(16) (available at: http://eiop.or.at/eiop/texte/1996.016a.htm).

Bosanquet, N. (1999). 'European Pharmaceuticals 1993–1998: The New Disease of Innovation', *European Business Journal* 1999; 11(3): 130–8.

Brittan, L. (1992). 'Making a Reality of the Single Market: Pharmaceutical Pricing and the European Economic Community', speech given to the Institute of Economic Affairs Conference on Pharmaceutical Policies in Europe. London, UK; 1 December 1992.

Bulmer, S. (1997). *New Institutionalism, The Single Market and EU Governance.* ARENA Working Paper no 97/25 (available at: www.arena.uio.no/publications/wp97_25.htm).

Bulmer, S. (1998). 'New Institutionalism and the Governance of the Single European Market', *Journal of European Public Policy* 1998; 5(3): 365–86.

Burstall, M. (1992). 'The Transparency Directive – Is it Working?', *Pharmacoeconomics* 1992; 1 (supplement 1): 1–8.

Burstall, M. (1997). 'How Do They Do It Elsewhere In Europe?', in D. Green, editor, *Should Pharmaceutical Prices be Regulated? The strengths and weaknesses of the British Pharmaceutical Price Regulation Scheme.* Choices in Welfare No. 40, IEA Health and Welfare Unit. London: Institute of Economic Affairs; 72–93.

Burstall, M., Reuben, B. & Reuben, A. (1999). 'Pricing and Reimbursement Regulation in Europe: An Update on the Industry Perspective', *Drug Information Journal* 1999; 33: 669–88.

Busse, R. (2001). 'Interesting times in German health policy', *Eurohealth* 2001; 7(3): 7–8.

CA (2001). 'Consumers' Association: Response to High Level Working Group on Innovation and the Provision of Medicines'. London: Consumers' Association.

Cameron McKenna (2000). *Evaluation of the Operation of Community Procedures for the Authorisation of Medicinal Products. Report carried out on behalf of the European Commission.* European Commission: Directorate-General Enterprise (Pharmaceuticals and Cosmetics). Brussels: Commission of the European Communities.

CCC (1991). *Resolution of the Consumer's Consultative Commission Concerning the European Agency for the Evaluation of Medicinal Products,* 12 November 1991. Brussels: Consumer's Consultative Commission.

CEC (191/91). Written Question No. 191/91 by Mr Marc Gale to the Commission. Patent protection for medicines. *Official Journal of the European Communities* C161, 20/06/91: 26.

CEC (814/96). Written Question No. 814/96 by Mr Nel van Dijk to the Commission. *Official Journal of the European Communities* C280, 25/09/96: 5; and Joint Answer

to Written Questions E-0813/96 and E-0814/96 given by Mr Bangemann on behalf of the Commission. *Official Journal of the European Communities* C280, 25/
09/96: 85.

CEC (1985). *Completing the Internal Market: White Paper of the Commission to the
European Council*, COM 83(310). Brussels: Commission of the European Communities.

CEC (1987). Proposal for a 'Directive on the Transparency of Measures Regulating
the Pricing of Medicinal Products for Human Use and their Inclusion Within the
Scope of the National Health Insurance System', *Official Journal of the European
Communities* C17 1987, 23 January 1987: 6–9.

CEC (1989). 'Compilation of Comments Received on Outstanding White Paper Proposals for Completion of the Internal Market in the Pharmaceutical Sector. Memorandum III/3785/88. Brussels: European Commission.

CEC (1990a). Proposal for a Council Regulation Concerning the Creation of a Supplementary Protection Certificate for Medicinal Products. COM (90) 101 Final –
SYN 255, 11.04.1990. *Official Journal of the European Communities* C114/90:
10.

CEC (1990b). Proposal for a Council Regulation (EEC) Laying Down Community
Procedures for the Authorization and Supervision of Medicinal Products for Human and Veterinary Use and Establishing a European Agency for the Evaluation
of Medicinal Products. COM (1990) 283 Final – SYN 309, 14.11.1990. *Official
Journal of the European Communities* C330/90: 1.

CEC (1991a). 'Discussion Document: Elaboration of the proposal referred to in Article 9 of Directive 89/105/EEC'. Document III/3001/91-EN. Brussels: Commission of the European Communities.

CEC (1991b). 'Report on the Measures Taken by the Member States for the Transpo-
sition of the Directive 89/105/EEC'. Report III 3747/91. Brussels: Commission of
the European Communities.

CEC (1992a). 'Common Position Adopted by the Council in Accordance with the
Cooperation Procedure Laid Down in Article 149 (2) of the EEC Treaty: Proposal
for a Council Regulation Concerning the Creation of a Supplementary Protection
Certificate for Medicinal Products. *Official Journal of the European Communities* C65 14/03/1992: 1.

CEC (1992b). Council Regulation (EEC) No 1768/92 of 18 June 1992 concerning
the creation of a supplementary protection certificate for medicinal products. *Official Journal of the European Communities* L182, 2 July 1992: 15.

CEC (1992c). 'Comments on European Commission Paper III/3749/91 (Preliminary
Draft Measures aimed at modifying and completing Directive 89/105/EEC con-
cerning the pricing and reimbursement of medicinal products for human use).
Document III/3481/92.

CEC (1993a). Council Regulation (EEC) No 2309/93 of 22 July 1993 laying down
Community Procedures for the Authorization and Supervision of Medicinal Prod-
ucts for Human and Veterinary Use and Establishing a European Agency for the
Evaluation of Medicinal Products. *Official Journal of the European Communities*
L214 24 August 1993: 1–21.

CEC (1993b). Commission of the European Communities. *Background Report: The
European Medicines Evaluation Agency*. ISEC/B33/93. Brussels: Commission of
the European Communities.

CEC (1996). 'Council Resolution of 23 April 1996 Designed to Implement the Outlines of an Industrial Policy for the Pharmaceutical Sector in the European Community'. *Official Journal of the European Communities* C136, 8 May 1996.

CEC (2000). *Pharmaceuticals in the European Union.* Commission of the European Communities, Enterprise Directorate-General, Brussels.

CEC (2001). *G10 Medicines: High Level Group on Innovation and the Provision of Medicines*, Consultation Paper. Brussels: DG Enterprise, Commission of the European Communities.

CEC (2004). Regulation (EC) No 726/2004 of the European Parliament and of the Council of 31 March 2004 Laying Down Community Procedures for the Authorisation and Supervision of Medicinal Products for Human and Veterinary Use and Establishing a European Medicines Agency. Directive 2004/27/EC of the European Parliament and of the Council of 31 March 2004 Amending Directive 2001/83/EC on the Community Code Relating to Medicinal Products for Human Use. Directive 2004/28/EC of the European Parliament and of the Council of 31 March 2004 Amending Directive 2001/82/EC on the Community Code Relating to Veterinary Medicinal Products. Directive 2004/24/EC of the European Parliament and of the Council of 31 March 2004 Amending, as Regards Traditional Herbal Medicinal Products, Directive 2001/83/EC on the Community Code Relating to Medicinal Products for Human Use. *Official Journal of the European Communities* L131 30/04/2004: 1–90.

CEC (IP 1963). Commission of the European Communities Press Release 156, 16 September 1963.

CEC (IP 1989). 'Employment in Europe: Commission Releases its First Report on Employment', press release DN: IP/89/43, 20 July 1989. Brussels: Commission of the European Communities.

CEC (IP 1994). 'Future of the Pharmaceuticals Industry: Time to Guard Against Worrying Signs', press release DN: IP/94/167, 1994–10–03. Brussels: Commission of the European Communities.

CEC (IP 1995). 'Inauguration of the European Agency for the Evaluation of Medicinal Products', press release DN: IP/95/64, 26 January 1995. Brussels: Commission of the European Communities.

CEC (IP 2001). 'Pharmaceuticals: High Level Group Established to Look at Medicines for Europe', press release DN: IP/01/444, 26 March 2001. Brussels: Commission of the European Communities.

CEC (Memo 2004). 'Results of the Competitiveness Council of Ministers, Brussels 11 March 2004: Internal Market, Enterprise and Consumer Protection Issues'. Memo/04/58,12.03.2004. Brussels: Commission of the European Communities.

Cecchini, P. with Catinat, M. & Jacquemin, A. (1988). *The European Challenge 1992: The Benefits of a Single Market.* Aldershot: Wildwood House.

CECG (1993). *Pharmaceuticals in the Single Market.* Brussels: Consumers in the European Community Group.

Chapman, S., Durieux, P. & Walley, T. (2004). 'Good Prescribing Practice', in E. Mossialos, M. Mrazek & T. Walley, editors, *Regulating Pharmaceuticals in Europe: Striving for Efficiency, Equity and Quality*; 144–57. European Observatory on Health Systems and Policies Series. Maidenhead: Open University Press.

Checkel, J. (1998). 'Social Construction, Institutional Analysis and the Study of European Integration'. Paper presented to the 'Workshop on Institutional Analysis' of European Integration, ECPR Joint Session of Workshops, University of Warwick 23–28 March 1998.

Chitti, E. (2000). 'The Emergence of a Community Administration: The Case of European Agencies', *Common Market Law Review* 2000; 37(2): 309–43.

Christiansen, T. (1997). 'Reconstructing European Space: From Territorial Politics to Multilevel Governance', in K-E. Jorgensen, editor, *Reflective Approaches to European Governance*; 51–68. Basingstoke: Macmillan.

Church, C. (1996). 'European Integration Theory in the 1990s', *European Dossier Series* No. 33. London: University of North London.

Clive, C. (1989). 'The Single European Act: Some Potential Consequences for the Pharmaceutical Industry', *Journal of Clinical Research & Drug Development* 1989; 3: 233–45.

COM (1986a). 'Proposal for a Council Directive on the Transparency of Measures Regulating the Pricing of Medicinal Products for Human Use and their Inclusion Within the Scope of the National Health Insurance System', COM (86) 765 final of 23 December 1986.

COM (1986b). Communication for the Commission on the Compatibility of Article 30 of the EEC Treaty with Measures Taken by the Member States Relating to Price Controls and Reimbursement of Medicinal Products. COM (86) 310/08, *Official Journal of the European Communities* C310/7, 4 December 1986.

COM (1988). *Report from the Commission to the Council on the Activities of the Committee for Proprietary Medicinal Products*. COM (88) 143 final of 22 March 1988.

COM (1990). Future System for the Free Movement of Medicinal Products in the European Community. COM (90) final – SYN 309–312 of 14 November 90.

COM (1993). 'Commission Communication to the Council and Parliament on the Outlines of an Industrial Policy for the Pharmaceutical Sector in the European Community'. COM (93) 718, 2 March 1994.

COM (1998). 'Communication on the Single Market in Pharmaceuticals'. COM (98) 588 final of 25 November 1998.

COM (2001). Proposal for a Regulation of the European Parliament and of the Council Laying down Community Procedures for the Authorisation and Supervision of Medicinal Products for Human and Veterinary Use and Establishing a European Agency for the Evaluation of Medicinal Products; Proposal for a Directive of the European Parliament and of the Council Amending Directive 2001/83/EC on the Community Code Relating to Medicinal Products for Human Use; Proposal for a Directive of the European Parliament and of the Council Amending Directive 2001/82/EC on the Community Code Relating to Veterinary Medicinal Products. COM (2001) 606 final of 26 November 2001.

COM (2003). 'Communication from the Commission to the Council, European Parliament, the Economic and Social Committee, and the Committee of the Regions: A Stronger European-Based Pharmaceutical Industry for the Benefit of the Patient – A Call for Action'. 383 Final of 1 July 2003.

CP (2001). 'Comments on the Consultation Paper of the G10 Medicines Group'. Brussels: *Comité Permanent des Médecins Européens*.

CPMP (1994). *Annual Report 1993–1994*. Brussels: Committee for Proprietary Medicinal Products.

Cram, L. (1996). 'Integration Theory and the Study of the European Policy Process', in J. Richardson, editor, *European Union Power and Policy-Making*. London: Routledge; 40–58.

Currie, W. (1989). '1992. Is There the Will for There to be a Way?', *Journal of Clinical Pharmacology* 1989; 29: 770–4.

Currie, W. (1990). 'European Registration: Today, Tomorrow, and Beyond', *Journal of Clinical Pharmacology* 1990; 30: 366–89.

Danzon, P. (1997). *Pharmaceutical Price Regulation: National Policies versus Global Interests*. Washington DC: The AEI Press.

Davis, P. (1997). *Managing Medicines – Public Policy and Therapeutic Drugs*. State of Health Series. Buckingham: Open University Press.

de Andres-Trelles, F., Garattini, S., Granstad, L., et al. (2002). '25.02.2002 Open letter to Members of the European Parliament re. Proposed amendments to the European pharmaceutical legislation'. Available at: www.haiweb.org/campaign/DTCA/MariaNegristatementDTCA_files/lettertoeu.htm.

de Pastors, A. (1995). 'Supplementary Protection Certificates. Situation after Two Years of Operation of the EC1768/92 Regulation', *World Patent Information* 1995; 17(3): 189–92.

Deboyser, P. (1995). 'An Industrial Policy for the Pharmaceutical Industry', in N. Mattisen & E. Mossialos, editors, *Healthcare Reforms and the Role of the Pharmaceutical Industry*; 64–5. Basel: Pharmaceutical Partners for Better Healthcare.

Dehousse, R. (1997). 'Regulation by Networks in the European Community: The Role of European Agencies', *Journal of European Public Policy* 1997; 4(2): 246–61.

Deloitte-Touche (1993). *European Community Policy for the Pharmaceuticals Sector*. European Update series. Brussels: Deloitte-Touche.

Deutsch, K. (1966). 'Communication Theory and Political Integration', in P. Jacob & J. Toscano, editors, *The Integration of Political Communities*; 75–97. Philadelphia: J.P. Lippincott & Co.

Dowding, K. (1994) 'Policy Networks: Don't Stretch a Good Idea too Far', in P. Dunleavy & J. Stayner, editors, *Contemporary Political Studies*. Belfast: Political Studies Association; 59–78.

Dowding, K. (1995). 'Model or Metaphor? A Critical Review of the Policy Network Process', *Political Studies* 1995; 43: 136–58.

Dukes, G. (1985). *The Effects of Drug Regulation: A Survey Based on the European Studies of Drug Regulation*. Lancaster: MTP Press Limited (published on behalf of the World Health Organization Regional Office for Europe).

Dukes, G. (1996). 'Drug Regulation and the Tradition of Secrecy', *The International Journal of Risk & Safety in Medicine* 1996; 9(3): 143–9.

EAEPC (2001). 'Response to Consultation Paper by European Association of Euro-Pharmaceutical Companies (EAEPC). Brussels: European Association of Euro-Pharmaceutical Companies.

ECJ (1996). European Court of Justice: Judgment of 5 December 1996 in joint cases C-267/95 *Merck vs. Primecrown* and C-268/95 *Beecham vs. Europharm*. Luxembourg: European Court of Justice, 1996; 6285–392.

Edmonds, P., Dermot, G. & Oglialoro, C. (2000). 'Access to Important New Medicines', *European Business Journal* 2000; 13(2): 146–58.

EFPIA (1986). *EFPIA 1986 Annual Report*. Brussels: European Federation of Pharmaceutical Industries and Associations.

EFPIA (1988). *Completing the Internal Market for Pharmaceuticals.* Brussels: European Federation of Pharmaceutical Industries and Associations.

EFPIA (1992a). 'EFPIA Comments on the New Proposals Contained in Preliminary Draft Rev. 5' (25 September 1992). Brussels: European Federation of Pharmaceutical Industries and Associations.

EFPIA (1992b). *Memorandum on an Industrial Policy for the European Pharmaceutical Industry.* (EFPIA III/3485/92, 26). Brussels: European Federation of Pharmaceutical Industries and Associations.

EFPIA (1995). *The Pharmaceutical Industry in Figures (1995 Edition).* Brussels: European Federation of Pharmaceutical Industries and Associations.

EFPIA (1996). *Delivering High Quality Health Care in the European Union – Policy Concerns for the Pharmaceutical Industry.* Brussels: European Federation of Pharmaceutical Industries and Associations.

EFPIA (1997). *Delivering High Quality Health Care in the European Union – Policy Concerns for the Pharmaceutical Industry.* Brussels: European Federation of Pharmaceutical Industries and Associations.

EFPIA (1998). *The Pharmaceutical Industry in Figures (1998 Edition).* Brussels: European Federation of Pharmaceutical Industries and Associations.

EFPIA (1999). *The Pharmaceutical Industry in Figures (1999 Edition).* Brussels: European Federation of Pharmaceutical Industries and Associations.

EFPIA (2000). 'EU Enlargement and Pharmaceuticals: Key Issues', Brussels: European Federation of Pharmaceutical Industries and Associations.

EFPIA (2001a). *EFPIA Annual Review 2000–2001.* Brussels: European Federation of Pharmaceutical Industries and Associations.

EFPIA (2001b). 'G10 High Level Group on Innovation and Provision of Medicines – EFPIA comments on the Commission Consultation Paper'. Brussels: European Federation of Pharmaceutical Industries and Associations.

EFPIA (2002). *The Pharmaceutical Industry in Figures – Key Data (2002 Update).* Brussels: European Federation of Pharmaceutical Industries and Associations.

EFPIA (2003). 'EFPIA Position Paper: EU Enlargement', November 2003. Brussels: European Federation of Pharmaceutical Industries and Associations.

EFPIA (2004). 'Enhancing the Provision of Health Information to Patients in Europe: A Policy Memorandum', June 2004. Brussels: European Federation of Pharmaceutical Industries and Associations.

EGA (2000a). 'Data Exclusivity: A Major Obstacle to Innovation and Competition in the EU Pharmaceutical Sector'. EGA Position Paper. Brussels: European Generic medicines Association.

EGA (2000b). 'More Generic Competition Would Help EU Pharmaceutical Market'. European Generic medicines Association press release 13 December 2000.

EGA (2000c). 'EGA Position on "Is marketed" Problem'. Brussels: European Generics medicines Association.

EGA (2001). 'Promoting Innovation and Competition in the European Pharmaceutical Market'. EGA Position Paper. Brussels: European Generic medicines Association.

Egan, M. (1998). 'Regulatory Strategies, Delegation and European Market Integration', *Journal of European Public Policy,* 5(3): 485–506.

EMEA (1996). *First General Report on the Activities of the European Agency for the Evaluation of Medicinal Products 1995.* EMEA/MB/065/95. London: European

Agency for the Evaluation of Medicinal Products.

EMEA (2000a). *Sixth General Report 2000*. London: European Agency for the Evaluation of Medicinal Products.

EMEA (2000b). *Work Programme 2001–2002*. London: European Agency for the Evaluation of Medicinal Products.

EMEA (2001). *Position Paper on Compliance with Pharmacovigilance Regulatory Obligations (November 2001)*. Committee on Proprietary Medicinal Products. London: European Agency for the Evaluation of Medicinal Products.

EMEA (2002). *Seventh Annual Report on the Activities of the European Agency for the Evaluation of Medicinal Products 2001*. London: European Agency for the Evaluation of Medicinal Products.

EMEA (2004). *European Agency for the Evaluation of Medicinal Products – Ninth Annual Report 2003*. London: European Agency for the Evaluation of Medicinal Products.

EP (1988a). Legislative Resolution (Cooperation procedure: first reading) embodying the opinion of the European Parliament on the proposal from the Commission to the Council for a directive relating to the transparency of measures regulating the pricing of medicinal products for human use and their inclusion within the scope of the national health insurance system. *Official Journal of the European Communities* C94 11 April 1988: 62.

EP (1988b). 'Second Report Drawn up on Behalf of the Committee on Economic and Monetary Affairs and Industrial Policy on the Proposal from the Commission of the European Communities to the Council for a Directive Relating to the Transparency of Measures Regulating the Pricing of Medicinal Products for Human Use and their Inclusion Within the Scope of the National Health Insurance System'. European Parliament Document PE 119.283/fin. of 2 February 1988.

EP (1988c). 'Second Reading. Recommendation of the Committee on Economic and Monetary Affairs and Industrial Policy Concerning the Common Position of the Council on the Proposal for a Council Directive on the Transparency of Measures Regulating the Pricing of Medicinal Products for Human Use and their Inclusion Within the Scope of the National Health Insurance System'. European Parliament Document PE DOC A 2-234/88, 26 October 1988.

EP (1990a). 'Explanatory Statement: Opinion of the Committee on Economic and Monetary Affairs and Industrial Policy'. European Parliament Session Document A3-0333/90/Part B.

EP (1990b). 'Report of the Committee on Legal Affairs and Citizens' Rights on the Commission Proposal for a Council Regulation (EEC) Concerning the Creation of a Supplementary Protection Certificate for Medicinal Products (COM(90) 101 final – C3-121/90 – SYN 255). DOC_EN\RR\100265.

EP (1991a). 'Legislative Resolution (Cooperation Procedure: First Reading) Embodying the Opinion of the European Parliament on the Commission proposal for a Council Regulation Concerning the Creation of a Supplementary Protection Certificate for Medicinal Products'. *Official Journal of the European Communities* C019 28 January 1991:95.

EP (1991b). 'Minutes of Proceedings of the Sitting of Wednesday 12 June 1991, Proposal for a Council Regulation Laying Down Community Procedures for the Authorization and Supervision of Medicinal Products for Human Veterinary Use and Establishing a European Agency for the Evaluation of Medicinal Products'.

Official Journal of the European Communities C183, 3 November 1991.

EP (1994). 'Communication From the Commission to the Council and the European Parliament on the Outlines of an Industrial policy for the Pharmaceutical Sector in the European Community'. COM (1993) 718 final of 2 March 1994.

EP (1996a). 'Opinion of the Economic and Monetary Affairs and Industrial Policy Committee on the Communication From the Commission to the Council and the European Parliament on the Outlines of an Industrial policy for the Pharmaceutical Sector in the European Community'. Report PE A4-0104/1996.

EP (1996b). 'Resolution on the Communication from the Commission to the Council and the European Parliament on the Communication From the Commission to the Council and the European Parliament on the Outlines of an Industrial policy for the Pharmaceutical Sector in the European Community'. EP first reading T4-0170/1996, *Official Journal of the European Communities* C141, 13 May 1996.

EP (2001). 'European Parliament Working Document on the Proposal for a Council Regulation on the Community patent'. COM(2000) 412 – C5-0461/2000 – 2000/0177(CNS). DT\434213EN.doc. Committee on Industry, External Trade, Research and Energy: European Parliament.

ESC (1987). 'Opinion on the Proposal for a Council Directive on the Transparency of Measures Regulating the Pricing of Medicinal Products for Human Use and their Inclusion Within the Scope of the National Health Insurance System'. Report CES(87) 801.

ESC (1991a). 'Proposal for a Council Regulation (EEC) Concerning the Creation of a Supplementary Protection Certificate for Medicinal Products'. COM (1990) 101 – 1990/0255/SYN. *Official Journal of the European Communities* C069, 29 February 1991.

ESC (1991b). 'Opinion on the Proposal for a Council Regulation (EEC) Laying Down Community Procedures for the Authorization and Supervision of Medicinal Products for Human Veterinary Use and Establishing a European Agency for the Evaluation of Medicinal Products'. *Official Journal of the European Communities* C269/84, 14 October 1991.

EUROSTAT (1998). *Monthly Panorama of European Industry, Chapter 6: Pharmaceuticals Industry*. Theme 4, Series B, Issue 1/98 (January 1998). Luxembourg: EUROSTAT; 77–88.

Faus, J. (1997). 'Parallel Trade of Medicinal Products in the European Union: A Spanish perspective'. Presentation to IBC Conference 1997, available at: www.fausmoliner.com/_publica_pdf/IP04.pdf.

FDA (2003). PDUFA Financial Report Required by the Prescription Drug User Fee Act of 1992, available at: www.fda.gov/oc/pdufa/finreport2003/financialfy2003.html.

Feick, J. (2002). *Regulatory Europeanization, National Autonomy and Regulatory Effectiveness: Marketing Authorization for Pharmaceuticals*. MPIfG Discussion paper 02/06. Köln: Max-Planck-Institut für Gesellschaftsforschung.

Feick, J. (2005). *Learning and Interest Accommodation in Policy and Institutional Change: EC Risk Regulation in the Pharmaceutical Sector*. ESRC Centre for Analysis of Risk and Regulation Discussion Paper No. 25. London: London School of Economics & Political Science.

Feldstein, P. (1988). *Health Care Economics* (3rd edition). New York: Wiley.

Finley, S. (2001). 'Direct-to-Consumer Promotion of Prescription Drugs: Economic

Implications for Patients, Payers and Providers'. *Pharmacoeconomics* 2001; 19(2): 109–19.

Forte, G. & de Joncheere, K. (1999). 'Pharmaceutical Policies in Central and Eastern Europe: Current Issues and Future Challenges', *Eurohealth* 1998/1999 (Special Issue – Focus on Eastern Europe and Central Asia); 4(6): 77–9.

Friedel, E. & Freundlich, M. (1994). 'European Community Harmonisation of the Licensing and Manufacturing of Medicinal Products', *Food and Drug Legislation Journal* 1994; (49): 141–63.

Furniss, J. (1997). 'The Bangemann Round Table: A Beginning and Not an End', *Eurohealth* 1997; 3(1): 27–8.

Furniss, J. (1998). 'The Bangemann Process: Slow Progress Behind Closed Doors', *Eurohealth* 1998; 4(2): 20–2.

G10 (2002). *G10 Medicines Report of 26 February 2002.* High Level Group on Innovation and the Provision of Medicines (available at: http://dg3.eudra.org/F3/g10/docs/fr_26022002.pdf).

GAO (1996). *European Union Drug Approval: Overview of New European Medicines Evaluation Agency and Approval Processes.* Report to the Chairman, Committee on Labor and Human Resources, US Senate – USGAO/HEHS-96-71. Washington: General Accounting Office.

Gambardella, A., Orsenigo, L. & Pammolli, F. (2000). *Global Competitiveness in Pharmaceuticals: A European Perspective.* Report prepared for DG Enterprise, European Commission. Brussels: Commission of the European Communities.

Ganorkar, C. & Korth, C. (2000). 'The Case for Global Patent Protection', *Pharmaceutical Executive* 2000; May: 76–82.

Ganslandt, M. & Maskus, K. (2001). 'Parallel Imports of Pharmaceutical Products in the European Union'. *The Research Institute of Industrial Economics Working Paper* (Sweden) No. 546.

Garattini, S. & Bertele', V. (2000). 'Policing the European Pharmaceutical Market's Priorities', *European Journal of Clinical Pharmacology* 2000; 56: 441–3.

Garattini, S. & Bertele', V. (2001). 'Adjusting Europe's Drug Regulation to Public Health Needs'. *The Lancet* 2001; 358: 64–7.

Garattini, S. & Bertele', V. (2004). 'The Role of the EMEA in Regulating Pharmaceutical Products', in M. Mossialos, M. Mrazek & T. Walley, editors, *Regulating Pharmaceuticals in Europe: Striving for Efficiency, Equity and Quality*; European Observatory on Health Systems and Policies Series. Maidenhead: Open University Press.

Gardner, J. (1996). 'The European Agency for the Evaluation of Medicines and European Regulation of Pharmaceuticals', *European Law Journal* 1996; 2(1): 48–82.

Gelijns, A. & Dawkins, H., editors (1994). *Adopting New Medical Technology.* Committee on Technological Innovation in Medicine – Institute of Medicine. Washington DC: National Academy Press.

Generics Bulletin (2004) 'European Revisions Offer New Freedoms for Generics'. 16 January 2004: 18–21.

Gilmartin, R. (1997). 'Balancing Innovation, Patient Needs, and Healthcare Costs in the European Single Market for Pharmaceuticals', *Eurohealth* 1997; 3(1): 29–30.

GIRP (1998). 'Statement of GIRP. The European Pharmaceutical Wholesalers Association on the Third Roundtable 'Completing the Single Pharmaceuticals Market'. Brussels: *Groupement International de la Répartition Pharmaceutique*

Européenne.

Giuliani, G., Selke, G. & Garattini, L. (1998). 'The German Experience in Reference Pricing', *Health Policy* 1998; 44: 76–85.

Goldberg, R. (2000). 'The Development Risk Defence and the European Court of Justice: Increased Injury Costs and the Supplementary Protection Certificate', in R. Goldberg & J. Lonbay, editors, *Pharmaceutical Medicine, Biotechnology and European Law.* Cambridge: Cambridge University Press; 185–204.

Gopal, K. (1999). 'Out of Commission(ers): Dr Martin Bangemann Bids Farewell to the EMEA', *Pharmaceutical Executive* 1999; May.

Grabowski, H. & Vernon, J. (1994). 'Returns on New Drug Introductions in the 1980s', *Journal of Health Economics* 1994; 13: 383–406.

Greenwood, J. & Ronit, K. (1994). 'Interest Groups in the European Community: Newly Emerging Dynamics and Forms', *West European Politics* 1994; 17: 31–52.

Griffin, T. (1990). 'Letter: Policies on Drugs in the New Europe', *British Medical Journal* 1990; 301 (28 July): 1536–7.

Haas, E. (1968). *The Uniting of Europe* (2nd edition). Stanford: Stanford University Press.

HAI (1997). *Statement of the International Working Group on Transparency and Accountability in Drug Regulation. Report of International Working Group on Origins, Scope and Effects of Secrecy in Drug Regulation.* Amsterdam: Health Action International, joint statement HAI/Dag Hammarskjold Foundation (available at: www.haiweb.org/pubs/sec-sta.html).

HAI (1998). 'Drug Policy: ISDB Criticises EMEA Information'. *HAI-Lights* 1998; 3(1–2).

HAI (2001). 'Is the EU Edging Towards DTCA?' Examining the Consequences of Industry's Latest Lobby (by L Hyes). *HAI-Lights* 2001; August.

Haltern, U. (1995). 'Intergovernmentalism As A Way of European Governance', in J. Weiler, A. Ballmann, U. Haltern, H. Hofmann & F. Mayer, editors, *Certain Rectangular Problems of European Integration.* Project IV/95/02, Directorate-General for Research, European Parliament.

Hancher, L. (1990). 'The European Pharmaceutical Market: Problems of Partial Harmonisation', *European Law Review* 1990; 15: 9–33.

Hancher, L. (1991). 'Creating The Internal Market for Pharmaceutical Medicines – An Echternach Jumping Procession', *Common Market Law Review* 1991; 28: 821–53.

Hancher, L. (2000a). 'The Pharmaceuticals Market Competition and Free Movement – actively seeking compromises'. Unpublished paper delivered to the Belgian Presidency International Conference on European Integration and Healthcare Systems: A Challenge for Social Policy. Ghent, Belgium; 7–8 December 2001.

Hancher, L. (2000b). 'EC Competition Law, Pharmaceuticals and Intellectual Property: Recent Developments', in R. Goldberg & J. Lonbay, editors, *Pharmaceutical Medicine, Biotechnology and European Law*; 76–90. Cambridge: Cambridge University Press.

Hancher, L. (2001a). 'Pricing European Pharmaceuticals: Can the Commission Untie the Gordian Knot?', *Eurohealth* 2001; 7(2): 23–5.

Hancher, L. (2001b). 'The Pharmaceuticals Market Competition and Free Movement – Actively Seeking Compromises'. Paper delivered to the International Conference on European Integration and Healthcare Systems: A Challenge for Social

Policy. Ghent, Belgium; 7–8 December, 2001.

Hancher, L. (2004). 'The European Community Dimension: Coordinating Divergence', in M. Mossialos, M. Mrazek & T. Walley, editors, *Regulating Pharmaceuticals in Europe: Striving for Efficiency, Equity and Quality*; European Observatory on Health Systems and Policies Series; 55–79. Maidenhead: Open University Press.

Hankin, R. (1996). 'Integrating Scientific Expertise into Regulatory Decision-Making: The Cases of Food and Pharmaceuticals'. *EUI Working Papers* RSC no. 96/7. San Domenico: European University Institute.

Hansard (1991a). 'Proceedings of the House of Lords, 15 April 1991'. Hansard 1991; London: HMSO.

Hansard (1991b). 'Proceedings of the House of Commons, 1 July 1991'. Hansard 1991; London: HMSO.

Hansard (1995). 'Debate of 18 April 1995'. Hansard 1995; Vol 258. London: HMSO.

Hennings, G. (2000). 'Marketing Authorisations of Medicinal Products in the European Union', *Drug Information Journal* 2000; 34: 793–800.

Henry, D. & Lexchin, J. (2002). 'The Pharmaceutical Industry as Medicine Provider', *Lancet* 360: 1590–5.

Heppell, S. (1994). 'Pharmaceutical Pricing and Financing in the European Union', in *Healthcare Reforms and the Role of the Pharmaceutical Industry – Proceedings of a European Workshop*. London: Pharmaceutical Partners for Better Healthcare; 44–7.

Héritier, A., Knill, C. & Mingers, S. (1996). *Ringing the Changes in Europe: Regulatory Competition and the Transformation of the State – Britain, France, Germany*. Berlin: Walter de Gruyter.

Herxheimer, A. (1999). 'Towards the Single Market in Pharmaceuticals: DGIII's Hope and Suggestions', *Eurohealth* 1999; 5(1): 25–6.

Herxheimer, A. (2003). 'Relationships Between the Pharmaceutical Industry and Patients Organisations', *British Medical Journal* 326:1208–10.

Hix, S. (1994). 'The Study of the European Community: The Challenge to Comparative Politics', *West European Politics* 1994; 17(1): 1–30.

HoC (1994). House of Commons Select Committee on European Legislation – Eighteenth Report Session 1993–1994. UK House of Commons Select Committee on European Legislation: HMSO

Hodges, C. (1997). 'Pricing and Reimbursement Issues in the European Economic Area', *Drug Information Journal* 1997; 31: 251–8.

Hoffmann, S. (1966). 'Obstinate or Obsolete? The Fate of the Nation State and the Case of Western Europe', *Daedalus* 1966; 95: 892–908.

HoL (1991a). *Patent Protection for Medicinal Products (with evidence)*. UK House of Lords Select Committee on the European Communities, Session 1991–1992; 1st Report: HMSO.

HoL (1991b). *The European Medicines Agency and Future Marketing Authorisation Procedures (with evidence)*. UK House of Lords Select Committee on the European Communities, Session 1991–1992; 3rd Report: HMSO.

Holland, W., Mossialos, E. & Permanand, G. (1999). 'Public Health Policies and Priorities in Europe', in W. Holland & E. Mossialos, editors, *Public Health Policies in the European Union*; 1–48. Aldershot: Ashgate.

Hood, C. (1994). *Explaining Economic Policy Reversals*. Buckingham: Open University Press.

Hooghe, L. (1995). 'Subnational Mobilisation in the European Union'. *EUI Working Paper* RSC no. 95/6. Florence: European University Institute.

ICA (1993).'The Pricing of Medicines in the European Community'. Intergroup on consumer affairs (European Parliament, Strasbourg). III c 3; 21.04.93.

IJRSM (1996). *The International Journal of Risk & Safety in Medicine, Special Issue: Secrecy in Drug Regulation.* IJRSM 1996; 9: whole issue.

IMS Health (1996). *Roundtable: 'Completing the Single Pharmaceutical Market'.* IMS International. available at: http://dg3.eudra.org/F2/smarket/pdf/Roundt1.pdf.

IMS Health (2001). 'SPCs worth millions to Pharma Companies in Europe'. IMS Health Global insight series. (available at: www.ims-global.com/insight/news_story/news_story_000417a.htm)

IMS Health (2004). *IMS World Review 2004.* IMS Health

ISDB (1998). *ISDB Assessment of Nine European Public Assessment Reports published by the European Medicines Evaluation Agency between September 1996 and August 1997.* Paris: International Society of Drug Bulletins.

ISDB (1999). *ISDB Newsletter* 1999; 13(1).

ISDB (2000). 'The failings of the EMEA'. ISDB Position Paper. Paris: International Society of Drug Bulletins.

ISDB (2001). 'European Medicines Evaluation Agency'. *International Society of Drug Bulletins Newsletters* 2001; 15(1): 11–13.

Jackson, D. (1993). 'Bidders Line Up for New European Drugs Agency', *Chemical Week* 1993; 152(19): 15.

Jeffreys, D. (1995). 'The New Pharmaceutical Regulatory Procedures for Europe', *Trends in Pharmaceutical Sciences* 1995; 16 (July): 226–31.

Joerges, C. (1997). 'The Market without the State? The "Economic Constitution" of the European Community and the Rebirth of Regulatory Politics', *European Integration online Papers* (EIoP); 1(19) (available at: http://eiop.or.at/eiop/texte/1997.019a.htm).

Jones, T. (1989). 'Future Perspectives of Regulations – the Concept of a European Medicines Office', in S. Walker & J. Griffin, editors, *International Medicines Regulation: A Forward Look to 1992.* Proceedings of a workshop held at the CIBA Foundation, London; 20–21 September 1988: 249–60.

Jones, T. & Garlick, W. (2000). 'Head to Head: Should Drug Companies be Allowed to Talk Directly to Patients?', *British Medical Journal* 326; 14 June 2000: 1302–3.

Jordan, G. (1990). 'Sub-Governments, Policy Communities and Networks: Refilling the Old Bottles?', *Journal of Theoretical Politics* 1990; 2(3): 319–38.

Josselin, D. (1994). 'Domestic Policy Networks and the Making of EC Policy: The Case of Financial Services in France and the UK, 1987–1992'. PhD Dissertation. University of London: London School of Economics & Political Science.

Josselin, D. (1996). 'Domestic Policy Networks and European Negotiation: Evidence from British and French Financial Services', *Journal of European Public Policy* 1996; 3(3): 297–317.

Juillet, Y. (1989). 'Mutual Recognition or a Central European Office?', in S. Walker & J. Griffin, editors, *International Medicines Regulation: A Forward Look to 1992.* Proceedings of a workshop held at the CIBA Foundation, London; 20–21 September 1988: 261–4

Kaesbach, W. (2001). 'Pharmaceutical Policies in Germany and European Competition Law'. Unpublished paper delivered to the Belgian Presidency International

Conference on European Integration and Healthcare Systems: A Challenge for Social Policy. Ghent, Belgium; 7–8 December 2001.

Kanavos, P. (1998). 'The Politics of Health and the Industrial Economics of Pharmaceuticals: Is there a Single European Dimension?', in A. Dobson & J. Stanyer, editors, *Contemporary Political Studies* 1998; 1. (PSA: Proceedings of the Annual Conference held at the University of Keele, 7–9 April 1998, Keele: Political Studies Association of the United Kingdom; 72–91.

Kanavos, P. (2000). 'The Single Market for Pharmaceuticals in the European Union in Light of European Court of Justice Rulings', *Pharmacoeconomics* 2000; 18 December (6): 523–32.

Kanavos, P. & Mossialos, E. (1999). 'Outstanding Regulatory Aspects in the European Pharmaceutical Market', *Pharmacoeconomics* 1999; 15(6): 519–33.

Kassim, H. (1994). 'Policy Networks, Networks and European Union Policy Making: A Sceptical View', *West European Politics* 1994; 17(4): 15–27.

Katzenstein, P. (1978). *Between Power and Plenty: Foreign Economic Policy of Advanced Industrial States*. Madison: University of Wisconsin Press.

Kenis, P. & Schneider, V. (1991). 'Policy Networks and Policy Analysis: Scrutinizing a New Analytical Toolbox', in B. Marin & R. Mayntz, editors, *Policy Networks: Empirical Evidence and Theoretical Considerations*. Frankfurt am Main: Campus Verlag; 25–59.

Kidd, D. (1996). 'The International Conference on Harmonization of Pharmaceutical Regulations, the European Medicines Evaluation Agency and the FDA: Who's Zooming Who?', *Indiana Journal of Global Legal Studies* 1996; 4(1): 183–206.

Kingham, R., Bogaert, P. & Eddy, P. (1994). 'The New European Medicines Agency', *Food and Drug Law Journal* 1994; 49: 301–21.

Koberstein, W. (1993). 'EC: The Euro Revolution', *Pharmaceutical Executive* 1993; January: 28–30.

Koberstein, W. (1999). 'EMEA – Force for Global Development: A Conversation with Fernand Sauer', *Pharmaceutical Executive* 1999; 19(7): 64–83.

Kohler-Koch, B. (1996). 'Catching up with Change: The Transformation of Governance in the European Union', *Journal of European Public Policy* 1996; 3(3): 359–80.

Kolko, G. (1963). *The Triumph of Conservatism: A Reinterpretation of American History, 1900–1916*. New York: The Free Press of Glencoe.

Kreher, A. (1997). 'Agencies in the European Community – a Step Towards Administrative Integration in Europe', *Journal of European Public Policy* 1997; 4(2): 225–45.

Laffan, B. (1997). 'From Policy Entrepreneur to Policy Manager: The Challenge Facing the European Commission', *Journal of European Public Policy* 1997; 4(3): 422–38.

Lawton, V. (2001). 'Competitiveness, Innovation and New Market Dynamics', *Eurohealth* 2001; 7(3): 15–18.

Leibfried, S. & Pierson, P., editors (1995). *European Social Policy: Between Fragmentation and Integration*. Washington DC: Brookings Institute.

Lewis, G. & Abraham, J. (2001). 'The Creation of Neo-Liberal Corporate Bias in Transnational Medicines Control: The Industrial Shaping and Interest Dynamics of the European Regulatory State', *European Journal of Political Research* 2001, 39: 53–80.

232 References

Lowi, T. (1969). *The End of Liberalism*. New York: WW Norton & Co.

Macarthur, D. (2001). 'Parallel Trading of Medicines: The Case for a Fair Deal', *Consumer Policy Review* 2001; 11(1): 6–10.

Majone, G. (1994). 'The Rise of the Regulatory State in Europe', *West European Politics* 1994; 17(3): 77–101.

Majone, G. (1996). 'The European Commission as Regulator', in G. Majone, editor, *Regulating Europe*. London: Routledge.

Majone, G. (1997). 'The New European Agencies: Regulation by Information', *Journal of European Public Policy* 1997; 4(2): 262–75.

Mann, R. (1988). 'EEC Supranational Drug Regulation by 1992?' *The Lancet* 1988: 324–6.

Marin, B., editor (1990). *Generalized Political Exchange: Antagonistic Cooperation and Integrated Policy Circuits*. Frankfurt am Main: Campus Verlag.

MARKETLETTER (1989). 'EC Drugs Move: Recipe for Disaster', *MARKETLETTER* 1989; 2 July: 6.

MARKETLETTER (1992a). 'EC Council Approves Patent Compromise', *MARKETLETTER* 1992; 1&6 January: 17.

MARKETLETTER (1992b). 'Is Pan-European Pricing Possible', *MARKETLETTER* 1992; 19 October: 11.

Marks, G., Hooghe, L. & Blank, K. (1995). *European Integration and the State*. EUI Working Paper RSC no. 95/7, Florence: European University Institute.

Marks, G., Hooghe, L. & Blank, K. (1996). 'European Integration from the 1980's: State-Centric v. Multi-Level Governance', *Journal of Common Market Studies* 1996; 34(3): 343–78.

Marsh, D. (1995). *State Theory and the Policy Network Model*. Strathclyde Papers in Government and Politics no. 102. Glasgow: University of Strathclyde.

Marsh, P. (1989). 'Drug Industry and 1992', *British Medical Journal* 1989; 299 (14 October): 935–6.

Matthews, D. & Wilson, C. (1998). Pharmaceutical Regulation in the Single European Market', *Medicine and Law* 1998; 17: 401–27.

Mazey, S. & Richardson, J. (1993). *Lobbying in the European Union*. Oxford: Oxford University Press.

McGowan, F. & Wallace, H. (1996). 'Towards a European Regulatory State', *Journal of European Public Policy* 1996; 3(4): 560–76.

McGuire, A., Drummond, M. & Rutten, F. (2004). 'Reimbursement of pharmaceuticals in the European Union', in M. Mossialos, M. Mrazek & T. Walley, editors, *Regulating pharmaceuticals in Europe: striving for efficiency, equity and quality*; 130–43. European Observatory on Health Systems and Policies Series. Maidenhead: Open University Press.

McIntyre, A-M. (1999). *Key Issues in the Pharmaceutical Industry*. Chichester: John Wiley & Sons Ltd.

Medawar, C. (1997). Letter to Fernand Sauer, Executive-Director to the EMEA, 2 December 1997.

Merkel, B. & Hübel, M. (1999). 'Public Health Policy in the European Community', in W. Holland & E. Mossialos, editors, *Public Health Policies in the European Union*; 49–68. Aldershot: Ashgate.

Middlemas, K. (1995). *Orchestrating Europe: The Informal Politics of the European Union 1973–1995*. London: Fontana Press.

Miller, H. (1999). 'Sick Process', *Hoover Digest* 1999; No. 1.

Mills, M. & Saward, M. (1994). 'All Very Well in Practice, But What About the Theory? A Critique of the British Idea of Policy Networks', *Contemporary Political Studies* 1994; Belfast: Political Science Association: 790–802.

Mintzies, B., Barer, M., Kravitz, R., Kazanjian, A., Basset, K., Lexchin, J., Evans, G., Pan, R. and Marion, S. (2002). 'Influence of Direct to Consumer Pharmaceutical Advertising on Prescribing Decisions: Two Site Cross Sectional Survey'. *British Medical Journal* 2002; 324: 278–9.

Mitrany, D. (1966). *A Working Peace System*. Chicago: Quadrangle.

Moore, J. (1997). *Pharmaceutical Pricing 1997 Edition*. FT Management Reports; London: FT Healthcare.

Moravcsik, A. (1993). 'Preferences and Power in the European Community: A Liberal Intergovernmentalist Approach', *Journal of Common Market Studies* 1993; 31(4): 473–524.

Mossialos, E., Ranos, C. & Abel-Smith, B., editors (1994a). *Cost Containment, Pricing and Financing of Pharmaceuticals in the European Community: The Policy-Makers' View*; 357–97. London: LSE Health.

Mossialos, E., Kanavos, P. & Abel-Smith, B. (1994b). 'The Pharmaceutical Sector in the European Union: An Overview', in E. Mossialos, C. Ranos & B. Abel-Smith, editors, *Cost Containment, Pricing and Financing of Pharmaceuticals in the European Community: The Policy-Makers' View*. London: LSE Health; 17–87.

Mossialos, E. & Abel-Smith, B. (1997). 'The Regulation of the European Pharmaceutical Industry', in S. Stavridis, E. Mossialos, R. Morgan & H. Machin, editors, *New Challenges to the European Union: Policies and Policy-Making*; 357–97. Aldershot: Dartmouth.

Mossialos, E. & Le Grand, J. (1999). *Health Care and Cost Containment in the European Union*. Aldershot: Ashgate.

Mossialos, E. & McKee, M. (2001). 'Is a European Healthcare Policy Emerging? Yes, but its Nature is Far From Clear' (editorial), *British Medical Journal* 2001; 323: 248.

Mossialos, E. & Permanand, G. (2000). 'Public Health in the European Union: Making it Relevant'. LSE Health Discussion Paper No. 17. LSE Health: London School of Economics & Political Science.

Mossialos, E., Walley, T. & Mrazek, M. (2004). 'Regulating Pharmaceuticals in Europe: An Overview', in M. Mossialos, M. Mrazek & T. Walley, editors, *Regulating Pharmaceuticals in Europe: Striving for Efficiency, Equity and Quality*. European Observatory on Health Systems and Policies Series; 1–37. Maidenhead: Open University Press.

Mossinghoff, G. (1999). 'Overview of the Hatch-Waxman Act and Its Impact on the Drug Development Process', *Food and Drug Law Journal* 1999; 5(2): 187–94.

Mrazek, M. & Mossialos, E. (2004). 'Regulating Pharmaceutical Prices in the European Union', in M. Mossialos, M. Mrazek & T. Walley, editors, *Regulating Pharmaceuticals in Europe: Striving for Efficiency, Equity and Quality*. European Observatory on Health Systems and Policies Series; 114–29. Maidenhead: Open University Press.

Müller, U. (2001). 'Editorial: General Interest and Economic Interest. Striking the Right Balance', *aims (news from AIM)* 2001; 13 (December 2001): 1–2.

Murray, J. (1994). 'Submission to the Commission Hearing on the Communication from the Commission to the Council and European Parliament on the Outlines of an Industrial Policy for the Pharmaceutical Sector in the European Community', speech delivered 2 June 1994.

NCC (1993). *Balancing Acts – Conflict of Interest in the Regulation of Medicine.* London: National Consumer Council.

NCC (1994). *Secrecy and Medicines in Europe.* London: National Consumer Council.

Norris, P. (1998). 'The Impact of European Harmonisation on Norwegian Drug Policy', *Health Policy* 1998; 43: 65–81.

OECD (2001). OECD Health Data 2001. Paris: Organisation for Economic Co-operation and Development.

Orzack, L. (1996). 'Professionals, Consumers, and the European Medicines Agency: Policy-making in the European Union', *Current Research on Occupations and Professions* 1996; 9: 9–29.

Orzack, L., Kaitlin, K. & Lasagna, L. (1992). 'Pharmaceutical Regulation in the European Community: Barriers to Single Market Integration', *Journal of Health Politics, Policy and Law* 1992; 17(4): 847–68.

OTA (1981). *Patent-Term Extension and the Pharmaceutical Industry.* Washington DC: Congress of the United States Office of Technology Assessment.

Palm, W., Nickless,, N., Lewalle, H. & Coheur, A. (2000). *Implications of Recent Jurisprudence on the Co-ordination of Health Care Protection Systems.* Summary Report produced for the European Commission Directorate-General for Employment and Social Affairs. Brussels: Association Internationale de la Mutualité (AIM).

Paltnoi, M. (1998). 'Patents and Supplementary Protection Certificates', *Journal of Commercial Biotechnology* 1998; 5(1): 33–9.

Parsons, W. (1995). *Public Policy: An Introduction to the Theory and Practice of Policy Analysis.* Cheltenham: Edward Elgar Publishing.

Permanand, G. (2002). 'Regulating Under Constraint: The Case of EU Pharmaceutical Policy'. PhD Dissertation. University of London: London School of Economics & Political Science.

Permanand, G. & Mossialos, E. (2005). 'Constitutional Asymmetry and Pharmaceutical Policy-Making in the European Union', *Journal of European Public Policy* 2005; 12(4): 687–709.

Perry, G. (1993a). Letter to Seamus Carroll, Commissioner Flynn's Cabinet DGV. 20 October 1993.

Perry, G. (1993b). Letter to Dr Martin Bangemann, Vice President European Commission. 15 November 1993.

Peters, G. (1996). 'Agenda-Setting in the European Union', in J. Richardson, editor, *European Union Power and Policy-Making.* London: Routledge; 61–76.

Peterson, J. (1995). 'Decision-making in the EU: Towards a Framework for Analysis', *Journal of European Public Policy* 1995; 2(1): 69–93.

Pharma Info (1982). *An Industry like no Other: The Pharmaceutical Industry as Seen by the OECD.* Basle: Pharma Information (Information Office of the Research-based Pharmaceutical Firms CIBA-GEIGY, ROCHE and SANDOZ).

PhRMA (2002). *PhRMA Industry Profile 2002.* Washington DC: Pharmaceutical Research and Manufacturers of America.

PhRMA (2003). *PhRMA Industry Profile 2003.* Washington DC: Pharmaceutical Research and Manufacturers of America.

References 235

Pierson, P. (1996). 'The Path to European Integration: A Historical Institutionalist Perspective', *Comparative Political Studies* 1996; 29(2): 123–63.

Pirmohamed, M. & Lewis, G. (2004). The Implications of Pharmacogentics and Pharmacogenomics for Drug Development and Health Care', in M. Mossialos, M. Mrazek & T. Walley, editors, *Regulating Pharmaceuticals in Europe: Striving for Efficiency, Equity and Quality*; European Observatory on Health Systems and Policies Series; 279–96. Maidenhead: Open University Press.

Poggiolini, D. (1989). 'Future Perspectives of Regulation – National Authorities' Relationships with the EEC', in S. Walker & J. Griffin, editors, *International Medicines Regulation: A Forward Look to 1992*. Proceedings of a workshop held at the CIBA Foundation, London; 20–21 September 1988: 243–8.

Pollack, M. (1997). 'Delegation, Agency, and Agenda Setting in the European Community', *International Organization* 1997; 51(1): 99–134.

Porter, M. (1980). *Competitive Strategy: Techniques for Analyzing Industries and Competitors*. London: Collier Macmillan.

Presc Int (2002). 'European Pharmaceutical Policy is Turning its Back on Public Health', *Prescrire International* 2002; 22 (229): 464–6.

PWC (2001). 'Pharmaceutical Sector Insight – Interim Report 2001.' London: PricewaterhouseCoopers.

PWC (2003). 'Corporate Finance Insights Pharmaceutical Sector Annual Report 2003: Analysis & Opinions on Merger & Acquisition Activity'. London: PricewaterhouseCoopers.

Radaelli, C. (1998). 'Governing European Regulation: The Challenges Ahead'. *RSC Policy Paper no. 98/3*. Florence: European University Institute.

Redmond, K. (2004). 'The US and European Regulatory Systems: A Comparison. *Journal of Ambulatory Care Management* 2004; April–June 27(2): 105–41.

Redwood, H. (1992). 'Disharmony over EC Pricing and Reimbursement', *SCRIP* 1992; May 1: 20–2.

Reich, N. (1989). 'Europäischer Binnenmarkt – Auswirkungen auf Zulassung und Vertrieb von Arzneimitteln Thesen', *Pharma Recht* 1989; Heft 4A: 190–1.

REMIT (1996). *Single Market Review 1996 – Impact on Manufacturing Pharmaceutical Products*. REMIT Consultants.

Rhodes, R. (1988). *Beyond Westminster and Whitehall*. London: Unwin Hyman.

Rhodes, R. (1990). 'Policy Networks: A British Perspective', *Journal of Theoretical Politics* 1990; 2(3): 293–317.

Richardson, J. (1997). 'Series Editor's Preface', in L. Cram, *Policy-making the EU: Conceptual lenses and the integration process*. Oxford: Routledge; xi–xii.

Risse-Kappen, T., editor (1995). *Bringing Transnational Relations Back In: Non-State Actors, Domestic Structures, and International Institutions*. Cambridge, MA: Cambridge University Press.

Risse-Kappen, T. (1996). 'Exploring the Nature of the Beast: International Relations Theory and Comparative Policy Analysis Meet the European Union', *Journal of Common Market Studies* 1996; 34(10): 53–80.

Rosamond, B. (2000). *Theories of European Integration*. Houndmills: Palgrave.

Ross, W. (2000a). 'It's no FDA – Maybe it Even Works a Little Better, an Interview with Brian P. Ager, Director General of the European Federation of Pharmaceutical Industries and Associations', *Medical Marketing and Media* 2000; 35(8): 61–7.

Ross, W. (2000b). 'It's no FDA but it Works, an Interview with Fernand Sauer, EMEA

Executive Director', *Medical Marketing and Media* 2000; 35(8): 46–56.

Rovira, J. (1996). 'Are National Drug Expenditure Control Policies Compatible with a Single European Market?", *Pharmacoeconomics* 1996; 10 Suppl. 2: 4–13.

Sbragia, A., editor (1991). *Euro-politics*. Washington DC: Brookings Institution.

Scharpf, F. (1988). 'The Joint Decision Trap: Lessons from German Federalism and European Integration', *Public Administration* 1988; 66: 239–78.

Scharpf, F. (1996). 'Negative and Positive Integration in the Political Economy of European Welfare States', in G. Marks, F. Scharpf, P. Schmitter & W. Streek. *Governance in the European Union*; 15–39. London: SAGE Publications.

Scharpf, F. (1999). *Governing in Europe: Effective and Democratic?* Oxford: Oxford University Press.

Scherer, F. (1996). *Industry Structure, Strategy, and Public Policy*. New York: HarperCollins College Publishers.

Scherer, F. (1998). 'The New Structure of the Pharmaceutical Industry', in F. Lobo & G. Velàsquez, editors, *Medicines and the New Economic Environment*. Madrid: Editorial Civitas (papers presented to a conference under the auspices of the World Health Organization Action Program on Essential Drugs and the Seminar of Social Studies on Health and Medicines of the Universidad Carlos III de Madrid); 195–212.

Scherer, F. (2000). 'The Pharmaceutical Industry and World Intellectual Property Standards', *Vanderbilt Law Review* 2000; 53(6): 2245–54.

Scherer, F. & Ross, D. (1990). *Industrial Market Structure and Economic Performance (3ʳᵈ Edition)*. Boston: Houghton Mifflin Company.

Schweitzer, S. (1997). *Pharmaceutical Economics and Policy*. Oxford: Oxford University Press.

SCRIP – 1153. 'EC Price Position no Negotiable', *SCRIP* 1986; 1152; 1.

SCRIP – 1287. 'EFPIA President on Future of Pharma Europe', *SCRIP* 1988; 1287: 5.

SCRIP – 1291. 'ABPI Concern on Pharma Imports', *SCRIP* 1988; 1291: 4.

SCRIP – 1321. 'Council Oks EEC Price Directive', *SCRIP* 1988; 1321: 2.

SCRIP – 1820. 'UK Bid for Euro Medicines Agency', *SCRIP* 1993; 1820: 2–3.

SCRIP – 2106. 'Call for EU Definition of "Innovation"', *SCRIP* 1996; 2106: 3.

SCRIP (1993). *SCRIP's 1993 EC Pharmaceutical Report – A Strategic Guide to Understanding, Planning and Succeeding in the Single EC Pharmaceutical Environment in 1993 and Beyond*. Richmond: PJB Publications.

SEC (1988) 1154 Final, 22 September 1989.

Sellers, L. (2004). 'Special Report: PharmExec 50', *Pharmaceutical Executive 2004*; May: 61–70.

Sharp, M., Patel, P. & Pavitt, K. (1996). *Europe's Pharmaceutical Industry: An Innovation Profile*. European Innovation Monitoring System (EIMS) Publication No. 32, European Commission Directorate-General XIII (The Innovation Programme); study prepared by SPRU, University of Sussex. Brussels: European Commission.

Shechter, Y. (1998). 'Interests, Strategies, and Institutions: Lobbying in the Pharmaceutical Industry of the European Union'. PhD Dissertation. University of London: London School of Economics & Political Science.

Simons, J. (2003). 'The $10 Billion Pill', *Fortune Magazine*, 6 January.

Spurgeon, D. (1999). 'Doctors Feel Pressurised by Direct to Consumer Advertising', *British Medical Journal* 1999; 319: 1321.

Staples, R. (1994). 'Pierre Douaze', *Pharmaceutical Executive* 1994; February: 34–44.

Steffen, M., editor (2005). *Health Governance in Europe: Issues, Challenges and Theories*. Abingdon: Routledge/ECPR Studies in European Political Science.

Stenzl, C. (1981). 'The Role of International Organisations in Medicines Policy', in R. Blum, A. Herxheimer, C. Stenzl & J. Woodcock, editors, *Pharmaceuticals and Health Policy: International Perspectives on Provision and Control of Medicines*; 211–39. London: Croom Helm.

Stigler, G. (1971). 'The Theory of Economic Regulation', *Bell Journal of Economics and Management* 1971; 2(1): 3–21.

STOA (1993). 'New Pharmaceutical Substances – Evaluation Criteria in View of the European Internal Market'. STOA Workshop report, 22 November 1993. Scientific and Technological Options Assessment, Directorate-General for Research; Brussels: European Parliament.

Stone Sweet, A. & Caporaso, J. (1998). 'From Free Trade to Supranational Polity: The European Court and Integration', in W. Sandholtz & A. Stone Sweet, editors, *European Integration and Supranational Governance*. Oxford: Oxford University Press; 92–133.

Sykes, R. (1998). 'Being a Modern Pharmaceutical Company: Means Making Information Available on Clinical Trials Programmes', *British Medical Journal* 1998; 317 (31 October): 1172–80.

TCSDD (2000). 'User Fees Credited With 51% Drop in Average Approval Times Since 1993', *Tufts Centre for the Study of Drug Development Impact Report Series* 2000; No. 2 (October).

TCSDD (2001). 'News Release: Tufts Center for the Study of Drug Development Pegs Cost of a New Prescription Medicine at $802 Million (1/30/2001), available at: http://csdd.tufts.edu/NewsEvents/RecentNews.asp?newsid=6.

Thatcher, M. (1995). 'Les réseaux de politique publique: Bilan d'un sceptique', in P. Les Galès & M. Thatcher, editors, *Les réseaux de politique publique. Débat autour des policy networks*. Paris: L'Harmattan: 230–48.

Theofilatou, M. & Maarse, H. (1998). 'European Community Harmonization and Spillovers into Health Regulation', in R. Leidl, editor, *Healthcare and its Financing in the Single European Market*. Amsterdam: IOS Press; 13–37.

't Hoen, E. (1996). Letter to Fernand Sauer, Executive-Director of the EMEA on behalf of HAI-Europe regarding the patient package leaflet for the medicine *Fareston* (toremifene).

Towse, A. (1998). 'The Pros and Cons of a Single "Euro-Price For Drugs"', *Pharmacoeconomics* 1998; 13(3): 271–6.

Tsoukalis, L. (1998). 'The European Agenda: Issues of Globalization, Equity and Legitimacy'. Jean Monnet Chair Papers No. 98/49. Florence: European University Institute.

TVAC (2000). 'The Many Faces of Thalidomide'. Thalidomide Victims Association of Canada (available at: www.thalidomide.ca).

VFA (2001). 'VFA Comments on the European Commission's Consultation Paper "G10 Medicines"'. Berlin: Verband Forschender Arzneimittelhersteller.

Vogel, D. (1998). 'The Globalization of Pharmaceutical Regulation', *Governance: An International Journal of Policy and Administration* 1998, 11(1): 1–22.

Vos, E. (1999). *Institutional Frameworks of Community Health & Safety Regulation:*

Committees, Agencies and Private Bodies. Oxford: Hart Publishing.

Walsh, G. (1999). 'Drug Approval in Europe: The EMEA Gets Good Grades, but has Room for Improvement', *Nature Biotechnology* 1999; 17 (March): 237–40.

Warleigh, A. (2001). 'Introduction: Institutions, Institutionalism and Decision Making in the EU', in A. Warleigh, editor, *Understanding the European Union Institutions*. London: Routledge; 3–21.

Watson, R. (2001). 'News Roundup: EC Moves Towards "Direct To Consumer" Advertising'. *British Medical Journal* 2001; 323: 184.

Weiler, J. (1994). 'A Quiet Revolution: The European Court of Justice and Its Interlocutors', *Comparative Political Studies* 1994; 26: 510–34.

Wertheimer, A. & Grumer, S. (1992). 'Overview of International Pharmacy Pricing', *Pharmacoeconomics* 1992; 2(6): 449–55.

Wessels, W. (1998). 'Comitology: Fusion in Action. Politico-administrative Trends in the EU System', *Journal of European Public Policy* 1998; 5(2): 209–34.

WG I (1997). 'The European Pharmaceutical Market'. European Commission Working Party I, Report August 1997 (available at: http://dg3.eudra.org/F2/smarket/pdf/wg1en.pdf).

WG II (1997). 'The Single Market in Pharmaceuticals'. Report by Working Group II (available at: http://dg3.eudra.org/F2/smarket/pdf/wg2en.pdf).

Wilks, S. (1996). 'Regulatory Compliance and Capitalist Diversity in Europe', *Journal of European Public Policy* 1996; 3(4): 536–59.

Wilks, S. & Wright, M., editors (1987). *Comparative Government-Industry Relations: Western Europe, the United States and Japan*. Oxford: Clarendon Press.

Wilson, J. (1980). *The Politics of Regulation*. New York: Basic Books.

Wincott, D. (1996). 'The Court of Justice and the European Policy Process', in J. Richardson, editor, *European Union Power and Policy-Making*. London: Routledge; 170–84.

Windhoff-Héritier, A. (1993). 'Policy Network Analysis: A Tool for Comparative Political Research', in H. Keman, editor, *Comparative Politics: New directions in theory and method*. Amsterdam: VU University Press; 143–60.

Wood MacKenzie. (2004). 'Company Rankings by Total Ethical Drugs Sales (US$) 2003' (available at: www.p-d-r.com/ranking/PQRankings2003.pdf).

Wright, G. (1997). 'Is There a Future for Pharmaceutical Patents in the Twenty-First Century?', keynote address delivered to *Patent Protection for the Pharmaceutical and Biotechnology Industries*. EuroForum Conference; London, 20–21 November 1997.

WSJE (1994). 'Bad Medicine in Europe', *Wall Street Journal Europe*, 22/23 April 1994; 8.

Young, A.R. & Wallace, H. (2000). *Regulatory Politics in the European Union: Weighing Civic and Producer Interests*. Manchester: Manchester University Press.

Index

Note: page references for notes are followed by n.

8+2+1 package 197

Abbasi, K. 17n, 90n
Abbott 23
Abel-Smith, B. 17n, 141, 169
ABPI (Association of British Pharma-
    ceutical Industry) 35, 102, 107,
    123, 127, 131, 156n
Abraham, J. 17n, 18n, 53, 65, 91n,
    100, 127, 128, 135, 137, 139,
    149n, 150n, 196
Adalat 45n
advertising 6, 17n, 20, 44n, 196–7
Ager, Brian 121, 137
Agrawal, M. 79
AgV (Arbeitschaft der
    Verbraucherverbände) 165–6, 189,
    204n
Albedo 105, 107–8, 110, 117, 119,
    132, 163, 171, 191–2
Altenstetter, C. 54
Amsterdam Treaty
    Articles 28–30 (ex 30–36) 177
    Article 28 (ex 30) 67–8n, 154
    Article 30 (ex 36) 49, 67–8n, 154,
        156
    Article 39 (ex 34) 67–8n
    Article 152 4, 40, 43, 67n, 152, 174,
        177, 180
    see also Treaty on European Union
Anndersen, Yvone 172
Armstrong, K. 11, 58, 67n
Association of the European Self-
    Medication Industry (AESGP) 167,
    198, 199
AstraZeneca 23, 24, 156
Atkinson, M. 71
Attridge, Jim 173
Austria 153, 207
Aventis 24

Bahner, B. 107
BÄK (*Bundesausschuss der Ärtze und
    Krankenkassesn*) 153, 189n
Bangemann, Martin 33, 132, 134, 168,
    169, 176, 179n, 195
    roundtables 170–4, 176–7, 190, 191
Bass, Rolf 135
Baudrihaye, Nelly 101
Bayer 45n
Belcher, P. 21
Belgium
    EMEA 127, 130
    pricing and reimbursement 159, 207
    SPC 107
Bertele', V. 10, 45n, 53, 91n, 136, 137,
    139, 141
BEUC (*Bureau Européen des Unions de*

Consommateurs) 18n, 50, 108, 109
Bangemann roundtables 172
  'Communication on the Outlines of
    an Industrial Policy' 166, 168
  EMEA 125, 129–30, 132, 134–5,
    145
  G10 199, 200
  pricing and reimbursement 176–7
  Transparency Directive 159, 160,
    163, 190
biotechnology 25, 51, 54, 127, 148n,
    165, 174
Bolkenstein, Frederik 94
Boots 179n
Börzel, T. 11, 59, 70, 71, 90n, 182
Bosanquet, N. 141
Bottomley, Virginia 131
boundary problem 73
Bristol Meyers Squibb (BMS) 23, 24
British Pharma Group 173, 179n
Brittan, Leon 164
Bulmer, S. 11, 58, 67n, 203
Bundesgesundheitsamt (Germany) 2
Burstall, M. 34, 153, 178n, 179n
Busse, R. 178n
Butterfield, Lord 100

Cameron McKenna 141, 142, 143,
    148n, 149n
Caporaso, J. 41, 58, 62
CCC 130, 141, 148–9n
Cecchini Report 50, 52, 122, 193
Ceci, Adriana 141
centralised procedure 51, 52, 120–1,
    123, 141, 215
Chapman, S. 139
Checkel, J. 67n
Chitti, E. 118
Christiansen, T. 67n
Church, C. 55
Ciba-Geigy 27
client politics 85, 86, 183, 184
  EMEA 123–5, 146
  SPC 88, 109–14, 184, 186
Clive, C. 157
co-payments 33–4
Coleman, W. 71
Commission *see* European Commission

Committee for Medicinal Products for
    Human Use (CHMP) 18n, 120
Committee on Orphan Products
    (COMP) 120
Committee for Proprietary Medicinal
    Products 10, 49, 50, 51, 52, 143,
    148n
  appointment procedures 142
  consumer representation 134–5
  CPMP procedure 120, 122, 128, 129
  EMEA establishment 125, 127
  EPARs 134
Committee on Safety of Drugs (CSD)
    (UK) 2, 16n
'Communication on the Outlines of an
    Industrial Policy for the Pharma-
    ceutical Sector in the European
    Community' 43, 52, 164–70, 190,
    191, 194, 195
Community Patent 93–4
Concerned Member States (CMSs) 121
concertation procedure 51, 52, 120–1
consumers 76, 77–8, 195
  Bangemann roundtables 170, 171
  'Communication on the Outlines of
    an Industrial Policy' 165–6, 168
  EMEA 124, 125, 129–30, 134–5,
    144–5
  G10 190, 198, 200
  pricing and reimbursement 176–7
  SPC 108–9, 111
Consumers' Association (CA) (UK)
    176, 197
Consumers' Consultative Committee
    130, 141, 148–9n
Consumers in the European Commu-
    nity Group (CECG) 108, 109, 111,
    116n, 155, 185
cost-containment 33–4, 42, 45n, 79,
    104, 110, 143, 153, 172, 175, 207
cost-sharing 33–4
costs versus benefits 84–5, 89, 108, 184
  EMEA 123–5
  pricing and reimbursement 152–3,
    175–6
  SPC 109–12
Council of Ministers 61, 62, 67n, 90,
    116n

'Communication on the Outlines of an Industrial Policy' 167–8
EMEA 127, 129, 130–1
SPC 102–4, 106, 109, 111, 115n, 116n, 150n
Transparency Directive 161–2, 164
Cox-2 inhibitors 196
Cram, L. 67n
Currie, William 128–9

Danzon, P. 25
Davis, P. 23, 26, 44n, 76
Dawkins, H. 25
de Andres-Trelles, F. 45n, 150, 193
de Joncheere, K. 179n
de Pastors, A. 98
de Peijper case 50
Deboyser, Patrick 159, 166, 167, 170, 178n
decentralised procedure 52, 120, 121, 125, 138, 146, 188, 216
Dehousse, R. 118
Deighton, Gerald 136–7
Deloitte-Touche 191
Delors, Jacques 169
Denmark
    EMEA 126, 130
    parallel trade 156
    pricing and reimbursement 33, 207
    SPC 107
    Transparency Directive 179n
Deutsch, K. 54
DG Enterprise 4, 17n, 38, 82, 172, 190, 193, 195
    EMEA 132, 138, 145, 150n
    G10 43, 198, 199, 200
DG Sanco 38, 40, 46n, 82, 193
    EMEA 145, 150n
    G10 198
DGIII (Industrial Affairs) 38, 195
    Bangemann roundtables 171, 173–4
    'Communication on the Outlines of an Industrial Policy' 166, 168–9, 170
    EMEA 123, 125, 132, 145, 146, 147, 187, 188
    pricing and reimbursement 152, 176, 190

SPC 101–2, 164, 185, 186
DGV (Employment, Industrial Relations and Social Affairs) 38, 40, 145
    Bangemann roundtables 173
    pricing and reimbursement 166, 169, 171, 176, 190
Dijk, Nel van 134
direct-to-consumer (DTC) advertising 6, 17n, 20, 44n, 196–7, 204n
Directive 65/65/EEC 2, 48–9, 120, 149n
Directive 75/318/EEC 49
Directive 83/570/EEC 49–50
Directive 87/22/EEC 51
Directive 89/105/EEC *see* Transparency Directive
Directive 93/39/EEC 52
Directive 2309/93 38, 117, 120, 138, 142, 174–5
Directives 38, 39, 40, 47, 50, 147, 209–12
Dolder Group 116n
dossiers 31–2, 120
Douaze, Pierre 172
Dowding, K. 18n, 73, 90n
Dukes, G. 2, 36, 136
Duphar case 154–5, 158, 178n

EAEPC (European Association of Euro-Pharmaceutical Companies) 155, 178n
ECJ *see* European Court of Justice
Economic and Social Committee (ESC) 105–6, 111, 116n, 127–8, 130, 160
Edmonds, P. 10, 143, 149n
efficiency regime 65, 80
EFPIA 34, 35, 37, 115n, 194, 208, 213
    Bangemann roundtables 170, 179n
    and Commission 196–7
    'Communication on the Outlines of an Industrial Policy' 168, 179n
    direct-to-consumer advertising 204n
    EMEA 123, 129, 137, 145, 146
    G10 198, 200
    intellectual property rights 96
    pricing and reimbursement 79, 174
    R&D 25, 78, 96, 99
    SPC 100–1, 102, 103, 106, 107, 109,

110, 112–14, 186
Transparency Directive 159, 161,
    162, 163
see also pharmaceutical industry
EGA *see* European Generic medicines
    Association
Egan, M. 137
Eli Lilly 23, 24, 97–8
elusive fluidity 73, 182
EMEA *see* European Medicines Agency
entrepreneurial politics 86–7, 114, 177,
    183, 184
    EMEA 88, 117, 118, 124, 132, 144,
    146–7, 186
ethical medicines *see* prescription
    medicines
European Agency for the Evaluation of
    Medicinal Products 117
see also European Medicines Agency
European Association of Euro-Pharma-
    ceutical Companies 155, 178n
European Association of Pharmaceuti-
    cal Wholesalers *see* GIRP
European Commission 59, 194–5, 202
    Bangemann roundtables 170–4
    'Communication on the Outlines of
    an Industrial Policy' 164–70
    concertation procedure 51
    EMEA 3, 52, 53, 117, 119, 120, 144,
    146–7, 186, 188
    EMEA public health protection 141,
    143–4
    EMEA subsidy 137
    EMEA's establishment 121–3, 125,
    126, 129, 130, 131–2, 145
    G10 197–200
    generic substitution 32, 34, 109, 163,
    172
    harmonisation 193
    industrial policy 35, 37, 43, 44, 54
    interests 79–80, 81, 82
    pharmaceutical policy 4–5, 6, 36,
    180, 183
    pricing and reimbursement 13, 152,
    174, 175, 176, 177, 189, 191
    regulation 61, 62, 64, 65
    regulatory capture 195–7
    SPC 97, 98, 101, 102–3, 109, 112,

113–14, 186
    and stakeholders 77
    Transparency Directive 157–64
European Court of Justice 5, 38, 40–1,
    46n, 53–4, 59, 62–3, 64
    market harmonisation 61, 91n
    Meroni Doctrine 147–8n
    neo-functionalism 55
    parallel trade 50, 51, 156–7, 170–1
    politics of policy 89
    pricing and reimbursement 152, 154–5,
    159
    SPC 116n
European Federation of Pharmaceutical
    Industries and Associations *see*
    EFPIA
European Generic medicines Associa-
    tion 95, 179n, 197
    Bangemann roundtables 170
    G10 198
    parallel trade 156
    SPC 109, 111
    see also generics industry
European Generics Association,
    'Communication on the Outlines
    of an Industrial Policy' 166, 168–9
European Medicines Agency 2–3, 36,
    82, 117–18, 144, 179n, 181, 193,
    197
    criticism 90n, 132–8
    entrepreneurial politics 88, 146–7
    establishing 38, 121–32
    industrial policy focus 44
    market authorisations 52–3
    new licensing procedures 119–21,
    215, 216
    patients' interests 144–5
    pharmaceutical industry's interests
    145–6
    policy network 186–9
    process regulation 63
    and public health 138–44
    unique institution 119
European Parliament 59, 116n
    'Communication on the Outlines of
    an Industrial Policy' 166–7, 168
    EMEA 127–8, 130, 131, 132, 141,
    149n, 150n

patents 94
SPC 98, 103, 104–6, 111
Transparency Directive 160–1, 162
European Patent Convention (EPC) 92, 93–4, 106
European Public Assessment Reports (EPARs) 133, 134, 135, 136
EUROSTAT 35, 79, 80, 179n, 208

Fareston 134, 149n
Faus, J. 177
FDA (Food and Drug Administration) (US) 2, 38, 148n
compared to EMEA 52–3, 129, 136–7, 146, 197
public health protection 138, 140, 141, 142, 144
Feick, J. 17n, 188, 201
Feldstein, P. 45n
Fensterer, Dee 107
Finland 100, 115n, 153, 156, 207
Finley, S. 197
Fisons 179n
Flynn, Pádraig 134, 169, 171, 176
formularies 32, 34
Forte, G. 179n
France 20, 34, 60, 67n, 118, 198
EMEA 126, 127, 142, 146
G10 198
patents 100, 102
pharmaceutical regulation 135
pricing and reimbursement 152, 153, 155, 178n, 206, 207
Transparency Directive 161, 164, 179n
free movement 4, 80
EMEA 119
SPC 92
and subsidiarity 4, 6, 41, 42, 81, 180
Freundlich, M. 51
Friedel, E. 51
Furniss, J. 170, 177

G10 43, 174, 177, 190, 191, 197–200
Gambardella, A. 35, 204n
Ganorkar, C. 95
Ganslandt, M. 178n
Garattini, S. 10, 45n, 53, 91n, 136,

137, 139, 141
Gardner, J. 139
Garlick, W. 204n
GATT (General Agreement on Tariffs and Trade) 37, 53
Gelijns, A. 25
General Accounting Office (US) 137
generics industry 20, 34
'Communication on the Outlines of an Industrial Policy' 166, 168–9
G10 198
SPC 103, 104, 106, 107–9, 110, 111
see also European Generic medicines Association
German Federal Standing Committee of Physicians and Sickness Funds *see* BÄK
Germany 2, 16n, 20, 35, 65, 194
EMEA 126, 127, 139
G10 198
parallel trade 156
pharmaceutical industry 116n
pricing and reimbursement 12, 33, 152, 153, 154, 178n, 207
SPC 102, 104, 107, 110, 112, 115n
Transparency Directive 161
see also West Germany
Gimartin, R. 115n
GIRP (*Groupement International de la Répartition Pharmaceutique Européenne*) 171, 176
Giuliani, G. 178n
Glaxo 179n
Glaxo Wellcome 26, 27
GlaxoSmithKline (GSK) 23, 24, 26, 27, 198
Goldberg, R. 110
Gopal, K. 195
Grabowski, H. 45n
Greece
pricing and reimbursement 207
SPC 104, 106, 110, 115n
Transparency Directive 179n
Greenwood, J. 67n, 86
Griffin, John 107, 123, 127, 128
Griffin, T. 141
Grumer, S. 26

Haas, E. 54
Hacking, Lord 100
Halcion 125, 148n
Haltern, U. 67n
Hancher, L. 5, 17n, 40, 46n, 49, 152,
    155–6, 174, 177, 178n, 198
Hankin, Robert 51, 126, 145, 147
harmonisation 5, 13, 80, 180, 181,
    192–3
Hatch-Waxman Act 1984 (US) 103,
    107
Health Action International (HAI) 18n,
    135, 176, 197
healthcare policy 4–5, 6, 14, 53, 64, 66,
    67n, 180–1
  and cost-containment 33–4, 207
  intergovernmentalism 56–7
  neo-functionalism 56, 58
  official EU competences 38, 39
  overlapping interests 81–3
  pharmaceutical regulation 31, 32
  pricing and reimbursement 152–4,
    177
  product versus process regulation 63–4
  SPC 107–9
Hennings, G. 66n
Henry, D. 26
Heppell, Strachan 44
Héritier, A. 61, 65, 67n, 84, 182
Herxheimer, A. 17n, 90n, 173, 197
High Level Group on Innovation and
    the Provision of Medicines *see* G10
high profits–low entrants 22–5
Hix, S. 54, 66, 201
Hodges, C. 163, 169, 191
Hoffmann, S. 56
Hogg, Douglas 104
Holland, W. 81
Hood, C. 83
Hooghe, L. 59
Hübel, M. 40, 86

IMS Health 23, 27, 79, 97, 179
industrial policy 4, 6, 14, 43, 53, 54,
    62, 64, 181, 194–5
  1996 Communication 52
  EMEA 130–1
  G10 197–200

official EU competences 38, 39
overlapping interests 81–3
pharmaceutical regulation 31, 32,
    34–5
pricing and reimbursement 152–4,
    164–70, 177
product versus process regulation 63–4
regulatory capture 195–7
SPC 98–101
innovation criteria 140–1
integration theory 54–60, 181, 201
intellectual property rights 7, 13, 26,
    92–3
  European legislation 93–4
  pharmaceutical patents 20, 53, 94–7
  see also Supplementary Protection
    Certificate
interest-group politics 87–8, 89, 183,
    184, 192–4
interest-intermediation approach 70–4,
    89, 90n
intergovernmentalism 56–7, 58–9, 181
International Association of Mutual
    benefit Societies (AIM) 198, 199
International Conference on
    Harmonisation (ICH) 57, 67n, 89
*International Journal of Risk & Safety
    in Medicine* (IJRSM) 18n
International Society of Drug Bulletins
    (ISDB) 133–4, 135, 136
Ireland 126, 130, 207
Italy 20, 34, 148n
  EMEA 126, 127
  pricing and reimbursement 33, 153,
    154, 159, 178n, 207
  SPC 100, 102, 107

Jackson, D. 131
Japan 166
  patents 98, 102, 103, 105
  regulation 179n, 197
Jeffreys, D. 148n, 215, 216
Joerges, C. 61
Johnson & Johnson 23, 24
Jones, T. 148n, 204n
Jordan, G. 12, 18n, 70, 71, 74, 90–1n
Josselin, D. 11, 14, 72, 182
Juillet, Yves 126

Kaesbach, W. 178n
Kanavos, P. 17n, 32, 35, 46n, 98, 155
Kassim, H. 18n, 73, 182
Katzenstein, P. 90n
Kelsey, Frances 2
Kenis, P. 70, 72–3
Kidd, D. 143
Kingham, R. 148n
Koberstein, W. 101, 143, 164
Kohler-Koch, B. 67n
Kolko, G. 84
Korth, C. 95
Kranz, Hubertus 167
Kreher, A. 118

Laffan, B. 36, 80, 91n, 114
Lataillade, Pierre 161
Lawton, V. 45n, 79, 200
Le Grand, J. 45n
Leibfried, S. 6
Leigh, Edward 111
Lewis, G. 17n, 18n, 53, 65, 96, 100,
    127, 128, 135, 137, 139, 149n,
    150n, 196
Lexchin, J. 26
liberal intergovernmentalism 57–9
Liikanen, Erkki 174, 197, 198
Lipitor 22–3
Lisbon Method 198
lobbying 86
Locor 22–3
Losec 156
Lowi, T. 84
Luxembourg 126, 207
Luxembourg Compromise 55, 62, 66–7n
Luxembourg Convention on the
    Community Patent 94

Maarse, H. 51
Maastricht Treaty *see* Treaty on
    European Union
Macarthur, D. 50, 155
Majone, G. 6, 41, 46n, 61, 63, 67n, 83,
    85, 118
Major, John 131
majoritarian politics 85–6, 183, 184
    pricing and reimbursement 152–3,
    176–7

Mann, R. 145
Marin, B. 18n
MARKETLETTER 107, 123, 192
Marks, G. 59, 67n
Marsh, D. 70, 74, 83, 91n
Marsh, P. 153, 158
Maskus, K. 178n
Matthews, D. 45n, 148n
Mazey, S. 11, 59
McGowan, F. 6, 46n
McGuire, A. 24, 28, 153
McIntyre, A-M. 17n, 23, 28, 45n
McKee, M. 17n, 18n, 41, 174
Medawar, Charles 139
medicinal products 48
medicines *see* over-the-counter (OTC)
    medicines; prescription medicines
Medicines Act 1968 (UK) 2
Medicines Control Agency (MCA) (UK)
    145
member states 180–1, 194
    Bangemann roundtables 170, 171–3
    EMEA 124, 125, 126–7, 130–1
    G10 198
    national interests 41–3, 80–1
    pricing and reimbursement 152–7,
        175, 189, 191
    Transparency Directive 159, 161,
        163–4
Merck 22–3, 24, 170–1, 196
Merkel, B. 40, 86
Meroni Doctrine 147–8n
me-too products 20, 95, 141
Metten, Alman 161
Middlemas, K. 100
Miller, H. 137
Mills, M. 18n, 73
Mintzies, B. 197
Mitrany, D. 54, 55
Monnet, Jean 54
Moravcsik, A. 57, 58
Mossialos, E. 17n, 18n, 40, 41, 45n,
    46n, 98, 141, 154, 169, 174, 200,
    206, 207
Mossinghoff, G. 103
Mrazek, M. 154, 207
Müller, Ueli 199
multi-level governance 59–60, 64, 66,

73, 74, 75, 84, 86, 89, 182
multi-state procedure 49–50, 52
Murray, Jim 166, 168, 172, 176–7
mutual recognition procedure 49, 120,
    121, 122, 123

NAFTA (North American Free Trade
    Agreement) 37
National Consumer Council (NCC)
    18n, 108, 113, 146
national interests 41–3, 80–1
negative integration 62–3, 65
neo-functionalism 54–6, 57, 58–9, 181
Netherlands
    EMEA 126, 130, 142
    parallel trade 156
    pricing and reimbursement 153, 154–5,
        207
    Transparency Directive 179n
    networks *see* policy networks
New Drug Applications (NDA) 31–2
new institutionalism 57, 59, 67n, 202–3
New Zealand 197
Noonan, Michael 172
Norris, P. 149n
Norway 100, 115n, 149n
Novartis 24, 27, 172

OECD (Organisation for Economic
    Cooperation and Development) 79,
    99
orphan drugs 120, 141, 148n
Orzack, L. 31, 91n, 128, 129, 135
over-the-counter (OTC) medicines 20,
    44–5n

Palm, W. 18n, 155
Paltnoi, M. 96
parallel trade 6, 17n, 50, 155–7, 177,
    178n
    Bangemann roundtables 170–1
    single market 51
Paris Convention for the Protection of
    Industrial Property 93
Parliament *see* European Parliament,
    patents; intellectual property rights
path-dependency theory 72, 73, 89
patients, pricing and reimbursement 176

PDUFA *see* Prescription Drug User Fee
    Act (US)
Perissich, Ricardo 130
Permanand, G. 24, 40, 200
Perry, Doug 166, 168–9
Peters, G. 59
Peterson, J. 58, 67n, 70
Pfizer 22–3, 24, 26, 27, 35
Pharma Information 17n, 19
pharmaceutical industry 8–11, 18n, 19
    atypical demand and supply 21–2
    Bangemann roundtables 170
    'Communication on the Outlines of
        an Industrial Policy' 164–70
    EMEA 123, 124, 128–9, 136–8,
        145–6, 186, 188
    employment 179n, 208
    expenditure 206
    G10 198, 200
    interests 78–9, 81
    international dimension 37
    market deregulation 192–3
    market structure 22–5
    oligopoly or quasi-monopoly 27–8
    patents 93, 94–7
    pricing and reimbursement 175–6,
        189
    R&D 25–7, 213
    regulatory capture 28–9
    SPC 184, 186
    Transparency Directive 159–60, 163
    unique product 20
    see also EFPIA
Pharmaceutical Inspections Convention
    (PIC) 57, 67n
Pharmaceutical Manufacturers of
    America (Pharmaceutical Research
    and Manufacturers of America)
    (PhRMA) 112, 208, 213
Pharmaceutical Partners for Better
    Healthcare 170, 179n
Pharmaceutical Price Regulation
    Scheme 45n, 152, 153, 159, 164,
    177n, 178n
pharmaceutical regulation 1–2, 30–1,
    200–4
    ad hoc development of competences
        and interest-group politics 191–4

constituent interests 75–83, 214
development of EU regulation 47–54
diversity 36
empirical questions and case-studies
  13–15
EU competences 60–6
EU framework 36–44, 209–12
EU policy-making 7–11
healthcare policy and cost-
  containment 33–4, 207
industrial policy 34–5
industry-oriented framework 194–
  200
and integration theory 54–60
in practice 31
product and market 31–2
supranational context 2–7
theoretical approach 11–15, 180–3
see also European Medicines Agency;
  pricing and reimbursement;
  Supplementary Protection Certificate
Pharmacia Corporation 26, 27
Picker Institute 198, 200
Pierson, P. 6, 59, 62
Pirmohamed, M. 96
Poggiolini, Dulio 129, 148n
policy networks 11–13, 69–70, 90–1n,
  182–3, 194
  empirical questions and case-studies
    13–15
  European Medicines Agency 186–9
  interest-intermediation 71–3
  pricing and reimbursement 189–91
  scepticism 73–4
  SPC 184–6
  structure, model or theory 70–1
  wider frameworks 74–5
  see also politics of policy
politics 7–9
politics of policy 12, 16, 69, 74, 83–4,
  88–90, 183, 184, 201
  costs versus benefits 84–5
  see also client politics; entrepreneurial
    politics; interest-group politics;
    majoritarian politics
Pollack, M. 57
Porter, M. 24, 45n

Portugal
  G10 198
  parallel trade 170–1
  pricing and reimbursement 33, 153,
    207
  SPC 104, 106, 110, 115n
positive integration 62–3, 65
PPBH (Pharmaceutical Partners for
  Better Healthcare) 170, 179n
PPRS (Pharmaceutical Price Regulation
  Scheme) (UK) 45n, 152, 153, 159,
  164, 177n, 178n
Prescription Drug User Fee Act 1992
  (US) 137, 149n
prescription medicines 20
  atypical demand and supply 21–2
  lists 34
  market structure 22–3
Prescrire International 18n, 193
pricing and reimbursement 13, 62, 88,
  151–2, 174–5, 180, 181, 207
  Bangemann roundtables 170–4
  'Communication on the Outlines of
    an Industrial Policy' 164–70
  cost-containment 33–4
  costs versus benefits 175–6
  defence of national competence 152–7
  EMEA 142–3
  G10 197–200
  liberal intergovernmentalism 58
  majoritarian politics 176–7
  pharmaceutical industry 78–9
  policy network 189–91
  process regulation 63–4
  SPC trade-off 101
  spill-over 56
  Transparency Directive 7, 51–2, 157–
    64
  UK 45n
Primecrown cases 170–1
process regulation 63–4
product regulation 63–4
proprietary medicines 20, 48
Prozac 97–8, 110
public health 4, 14, 50–1, 53, 137–8,
  196
  development of EU regulation 47,
    48–9

EMEA 127–8, 131–3, 138–44, 188–9
national and Community interests 42
overlapping interests 81–3
and pharmaceutical regulation 31–2
see also Amsterdam Treaty, Article
    152
PWC (PricewaterhouseCoopers) 26

Radaelli, C. 61, 65
rational use package 147
Redmond, K. 17n, 66n
Redwood, H. 108, 153
Reed, T. 91n
Références Médicales Opposables
    (RMOs) 153
Reference Member States (RMSs) 121,
    138, 146
Regulations 38, 39, 40, 114, 209–12
Regulation 1768/92 51, 98
Regulation 2309/93 117, 125, 138,
    142–3
Regulation 297/95 131
regulatory capture 28–9, 195–7
regulatory state model 43, 61–2, 64–5,
    68n
Reich, N. 161
reimbursement *see* pricing and reim-
    bursement
REMIT Consultants 95
research and development (R&D) 25–7,
    37, 78, 96, 99, 213
Rhodes, R. 70–1, 182–3
Richardson, J. 11, 59, 67n
Risse-Kappen, T. 67n
Ronit, K. 67n, 86
Rosamond, B. 64, 67n, 90, 91n, 183
Ross, D. 24, 31, 45n
Ross, W. 121, 136, 137, 138
roundtables 170–4, 176–7, 190, 191
Roussel case 154, 158
Rovira, J. 192

Sandoz 27
Sauer, Fernand 101, 115–16n, 138,
    139, 161, 162, 164, 186
Saward, M. 18n, 73
Sbragia, A. 67n
Scharpf, F. 63, 67n, 90n

Scherer, F. 17n, 19, 21, 24, 28, 31, 45n,
    96
Schneider, V. 70, 72–3
Schwab, Berthold 101, 105
Schweitzer, S. 17n, 37, 45n
SCRIP 100, 102, 106, 109, 131, 141,
    162
Sellers, L. 24
Sharp, M. 96
Shechter, Y. 7, 17n, 67n, 101, 103, 113,
    116n, 186
Simons, J. 23
Single European Act (SEA) 1986 50, 55
Single European Market (SEM) 28, 50–2,
    53, 64, 114, 181, 192–3
neo-functionalism 55–6
subsidiarity and free movement 4, 6,
    41, 42
SmithKline Beecham 26, 27, 95, 179n
Spain 34, 104
EMEA 126, 127, 130
G10 198
parallel trade 156, 170–1
pricing and reimbursement 33, 153,
    154, 207
SPC 106, 110, 115n, 116n
Transparency Directive 179n
spill-over 55–6, 57, 58, 63, 181
Spurgeon, D. 78, 197
Standing Committee of European
    Doctors 176
Staples, R. 145
Steffen, M. 18n
Stenzl, C. 196
Stephar case 51, 171
Stigler, G. 29, 84
Stone Sweet, A. 41, 58, 62
subsidiarity 5, 17n
EMEA 126
and free movement 4, 6, 41, 42, 81,
    180
versus Community interests 41–3
Summary of Product Characteristics
    (SPCs) 120, 133, 134, 136, 148n,
    149n, 179n
Supplementary Protection Certificate
    (SPC) 16, 51, 88, 92–3, 97–8, 109,
    114–15, 146, 179n, 181, 195

adopting the proposals 103–9
collective action and capture 112–14
costs versus benefits 109–12
initial dialogue 98–103
policy network 184–6
Sweden 20, 65, 78, 100, 115n
  EMEA 139, 142
  G10 198
  pricing and reimbursement 207
Sykes, R. 79

't Hoen, Ellen 149n
Tagamet 95, 96
Thalidomide 1, 2, 5, 9, 16n, 47, 53, 138
Thatcher, M. 73
Theofilatou, M. 51
time-to-market (TTM) 47, 132–3, 143
Towse, A. 178n, 192
transparency, EMEA 132, 133–6
Transparency Directive 51–2, 53, 63, 101, 152, 157–64, 169, 176, 177, 179n, 189, 190, 191
Treaty on European Union 59, 116n
  Article 3(b) 17n, 41, 42
  Articles 28–30 (ex 30–36) 177
  Article 28 (ex 30) 67–8n
  Article 30 (ex 36) 49, 67–8n, 154, 156
  Article 39 (ex 34) 67–8n
  Article 100 42, 80, 92
  Article 100(a) 41, 104, 105, 126, 127, 148n
  Article 129 40, 67n
  Article 130 43
  Article 152 4, 38, 40, 43, 67n, 143, 152, 154, 174, 177, 180
  Article 235 126, 127, 130, 148n
Treaty of Rome 62
Tsoukalis, L. 61
Tufts Center for the Study of Drug Development (TCSDD) 45n, 137

United Kingdom 20, 60, 65, 78, 108, 125
  Committee on Safety of Drugs 2
  EMEA 126–7, 130–1, 142, 145, 146
  G10 198

  Medicines Control Agency 145
  parallel trade 156
  pharmaceutical industry 34, 35, 146
  pricing and reimbursement 33, 45n, 152, 153, 154, 177n, 179n
  SPC 100, 102, 104, 110, 111, 112
  Transparency Directive 159, 163–4, 179n
United States 29, 60, 65, 78, 108, 125
  advertising 197
  General Accounting Office 137
  patents 26, 97, 98, 102, 103, 105, 107, 115n, 197
  pharmaceutical industry 79, 178n, 208, 213
  pharmaceutical policy 1–2
  policy-making 84, 88, 91n
  R&D expenditure 37, 99, 213
  regulation 60, 61, 118, 179n, 197
  regulatory capture 28–9
  see also FDA

Venables, Tony 157
Vernon, J. 45n
VFA (Verband Forschender Arzneimittelhersteller) 199
Viagra 35
Vioxx 196
Vogel, D. 51, 96, 121, 148n
Vos, E. 145, 150n

Wallace, H. 6, 8, 46n, 67n
Walsh, G. 66n
Warleigh, A. 67n
Warner-Lambert 27
Watson, R. 197
Weiler, J. 67n
Weissenberg, Paul 199
Wellcome 179
Wertheimer, A. 26
Wessels, W. 59
West Germany
  pharmaceutical policy 1, 2, 16n
  pricing and reimbursement 159
  see also Germany
Wilks, S. 62, 71, 72
Wilson, C. 45n, 148n
Wilson, J. 12, 16, 69, 74, 83, 84, 85,

86, 88, 89–90, 109, 113, 114, 132, 183, 192, 201

Wincott, D. 41, 59, 152

Windhoff-Héritier, A. 74

Wood MacKenzie 22

Working Time Directive 85

World Trade Organisation (WTO) 37, 57, 66n, 89

Wright, G. 95

Wright, M. 71, 72

Wyeth 24

Young, A.R. 8, 67n

Zeneca 179n